BEAUFIGHTERS
OVER SEA, SAND AND STEAMING JUNGLES

BEAUFIGHTERS
OVER SEA, SAND AND STEAMING JUNGLES

JACK COLMAN AND RICHARD COLMAN

To Mary for her patience, perseverance and common sense when reviewing the copy.

Fonthill Media Language Policy

Fonthill Media publishes in the international English language market. One language edition is published worldwide. As there are minor differences in spelling and presentation, especially with regard to American English and British English, a policy is necessary to define which form of English to use. The Fonthill Policy is to use the form of English native to the author. Jack and Richard Colman were born and educated in the United Kingdom; therefore, British English has been adopted in this publication.

Fonthill Media Limited
Fonthill Media LLC
www.fonthillmedia.com
office@fonthillmedia.com

First published in the United Kingdom and the United States of America 2020

British Library Cataloguing in Publication Data:
A catalogue record for this book is available from the British Library

Copyright © Jack Colman/Richard Colman 2020

ISBN 978-1-78155-746-4

The right of Jack Colman/Richard Colman to be identified as the author of this work has been asserted by him in accordance with the Copyright, Designs and Patents Act 1988.

All rights reserved. No part of this publication may be reproduced, stored in a retrieval system or transmitted in any form or by any means, electronic, mechanical, photocopying, recording or otherwise, without prior permission in writing from Fonthill Media Limited

Typeset in 11pt on 13pt Sabon
Printed and bound in England

Dedication

In writing these pages, it has been a personal pleasure to remember the splendid chaps I was privileged to meet, particularly those who were prepared to train, mix, and fly with me.

If, however, I was to dedicate these pages to anybody, it would be to a group of men with whom it was an honour to co-operate, but none of whom I knew personally: the British, Indian, and African soldiers of Slim's Forgotten 14th Army, who achieved the impossible in clearing the Japanese out of Burma, even though, with hindsight, the taking of Rangoon had little effect on the outcome of the war.

CONTENTS

Abbreviations   9
Introduction   11

1. The Beautiful Beau   13
2. The Road to Morocco   26
3. Training for Torbeaus   42
4. Morocco Again   53
5. North Sea Capers   59
6. The Full Wing in Action   67
7. East Coast Torbeau Squadrons: The Context   79
8. 'Snakecharmer' Goes East   80
9. Holiday in Cairo   98
10. East of Suez   108
11. The Train to Bombay   122
12. Getting the 'Gen' at Poona   133
13. Preparations for Burma   141
14. The Wettest Place on Earth   153
15. Bill Briefs Us for Battle   163
16. The Fright of My Life   171
17. The Rains Ease Up   183
18. Two Important Visitors   188
19. The Beau Bows Out in Style   195
20. The Mozzie: Wood, Glue, and a Silly Stick   199
21. Mozzie Out: Stinson Back   209
22. We Leave the War Behind   225

23	The Good Life, Even in Hospital	228
24	David and I Go on Holiday	241
25	We Hear of VE Day	252
26	Training for What?	259
27	The Wedding Season	265
28	I Send Peter to the Cocos, Then the War is Over	269
29	Getting the Folks Home	276
30	Our Time at Bhopal	279
31	Dinner with the Nawab	285
32	Flying Again	293
33	The Best Job in the RAF	300
34	I Come Home, Twice	309

Epilogue	315
Appendix I: Henry Everest Colman	317
Appendix II: List of Significant Events	319

Abbreviations

ACSEA:	Air Command Southeast Asia.
AC2:	aircraftman second class.
AOC:	air officer commanding.
ASV:	air-to-surface vessel, a form of airborne radar that could identify ships or coast lines.
ATS:	Auxiliary Territorial Service.
BAFSEA:	British Air Forces Southeast Asia.
BABS:	blind approach beacon system.
Dak:	Dakota, a transport plane.
EFTS:	Elementary Flying Training School.
Erk:	RAF slang for ground crew Aircraftman (from cockney 'erkraft').
FALTs:	formation camera attacks against moving target.
FARTs:	formation attack with runner torpedo.
FTU:	ferry training unit.
GCAs:	ground-controlled approaches.
Gee fixes:	a form of radio navigation. It measured the time delay between two radio signals to produce a fix, with accuracy in the order of a few hundred metres at ranges up to about 350 miles (560 km).
GR trained:	general-reconnaissance maritime and naval-cooperation trained navigator.
HEs:	high explosives.
IFF aerial:	identification friend or foe.
IO:	intelligence officer.

IORs:	Indian other ranks.
JACSEA:	Joint Air Command Southeast Asia.
KG:	Khumbirgram, an operational unit base in Assam.
LAC:	leading aircraftman.
Mainly D/F on W/T:	direction finding on wireless telegraphy.
MF D/F:	medium frequency direction finding.
MO:	medical officer.
MU:	maintenance unit.
NAAFI:	Navy, Army, and Air Force Institute.
NCO:	non-commissioned officer.
PO:	pilot officer.
PSP:	perforated steel planking.
QDMs:	magnetic bearings to an airfield.
R/T:	radio telephony communications.
RAF PR squadron:	photographic reconnaissance squadron.
RP:	rocket projectile.
RTO:	railway transport officer.
SHQ:	southern headquarters.
TAT:	torpedo attack trainer.
VLR Lib:	very long-range Liberator.
W/op:	wireless operator.
W/T:	wireless telegraphy.
WRNS:	Women's Royal Navy Service.
Zig:	a Czech pilot in Ferry Command who gave Jack lots of good advice.

Introduction

Shortly after retiring from being a branch manager for the General Accident Insurance Company (now Aviva), Jack put together his memories of his war years as an RAF pilot. The book *Liberators over the Atlantic* documents his ambition to fly, pilot selection, training in Canada, and his time spent ferrying Hudsons across the Atlantic and with Coastal Command based in Iceland.

When his twelve-month 'tour' in Iceland came to an end, he was given a choice of what to do for a 'rest'. The option to train new pilots did not appeal, but the chance to fly Beaufighters did. Selected to train as a Torbeau pilot (Beaufighters capable of carrying a torpedo), he would be trained to operate over the North Sea to attack German convoys. Operating closer to home, he expected to see more of Peggy, his new wife.

This book covers the start of that training till the end of the war, but circumstances meant that he would be sent to the Far East shortly after the Allied Invasion of Normandy to support the Forgotten Army in Burma. He was away for nearly two years.

The detail recalled in these pages shows how alive and receptive this builder's son (who was encouraged to leave school at sixteen and get a 'respectable' job) was to these new experiences lived between the ages of twenty-one and twenty-six. His writing style, at times in the present tense, is in keeping with someone reliving his memories and excited by his time flying. In India, he is exposed to and appreciates a whole new world, geographically, climatically, culturally, and socially. He experiences the privileges shown to commissioned officers on the subcontinent yet his heart is with the people with whom he shares his day to day living.

Flying twin-engined fighter-bomber Beaufighters and later Mosquitoes was very different from flying the Very Long-Range Liberators (Libs) over the Atlantic. Action was more intense and concentrated with loss in action accepted as a real possibility. He protects Peggy from concerns about what he may be doing, by not telling her, and is aware that 'missing in action' would be a terrible message for her to receive.

Aside from this introduction, Chapter 7, the epilogue, and the appendices, this book is entirely the work of my father, Jack Colman.

Richard Colman

1

The Beautiful Beau

There she was—two big Bristol Hercules engines protruding beyond her stubby little pug nose, a strong little smooth body, and two very strong shortish legs. She looked as strong as an ox and through those canvas covered cannon ports right under her nose, she seemed to be smiling at me and saying, 'Come on. Try me.' I bet she was a fast one. She must have been with those two big Bristols. I wanted to have a look inside.

'Not a lot of room. I won't be able to walk around as you could in a Lib. Once in that seat you stay put until you get back. By Jove, what a view: sitting up here, right in the middle, you don't even notice that little pug nose in front of you and everything seems to be within easy reach. Will have to get used to the throttles being on the left-hand side. What are these other levers just outboard of the throttles? They must be the pitch levers in which case where are the mixture controls? There don't seem to be any. Those must be the supercharger controls, 2 speed, "M" and "S". These things just behind are for the cooling gills. Just outboard of the supercharger controls are another two levers, oh, yes, they are the carburettor intakes, forward for cold and back for hot. The main fuel cocks are just by my left elbow with fuel gauges on either side. The flap lever is just outboard of the undercarriage lever. Everything seems to be very handy and I like the "spectacle" shape of the wheel with the brake lever handy for your right-hand thumb so your differential braking must be by using the rudder pedals like in the Hudson. The cannon button is handy for your left-hand thumb but I still can't see any mixture controls or primer pump or switch. Still, the view ahead is fantastic and those two big Bristols are really something. Bit of a change from the Lib but I think I'm going to enjoy this and they won't be such long trips'.

In the mess at our base at East Fortune, Scotland, I learnt that the usual course was about four months, the first month being on Beauforts, which seemed a bit of a letdown. The next morning, however, I found that the four-month course was for lads who had not had previous operational training and that there was a dozen or so of us who had already done a tour of Ops who were together on a shorter course. As you could not have dual control on the Beaufighter, we were to have a few days on Beauforts to check out on instrument flying, blind approaches, and the like, then we would go on the Beaufighters and the course would be mainly flying, a little ground training, but mostly in the air. That seemed more like it.

The Beaufort was a diabolical contraption and I immediately had great respect for my instructor who had done a tour dropping torpedoes from these death traps. He was a flying officer, who was well over 6 feet tall. He also knew my uncle, who was chairman of York rugby league football club and before joining the Air Force, my instructor, Bill, had been secretary of the Rugby League. I found it bad enough even getting into a Beaufort, climbing up the wing and dumping your parachute through the roof light onto the seat and then clambering in yourself but at 6 feet plus, he had a hell of a job; we could never have got out of the thing in a hurry.

These were old retired Mark I Beauforts, some with Bristol Taurus Mark II engines of only 1,010 hp and others with Taurus Mark IV of 1,130 hp, but even those with the bigger engines seemed terribly underpowered. They took an eternity to get off the ground so they must have been absolute devils to get off if carrying a 1,605-lb torpedo, especially as the torpedo would not go fully into the bomb bay; it was hanging half out with the bomb doors still partly open. At night, as you lumbered down the runway, the exhausts glowed red hot, with bits of red-hot metal scaling off like sparks. The props were not variable pitch or 'constant speed' but 'two speed', operated by buttons, with a piece of jagged metal, like a tobacco tin lid, hinged over them to prevent them being knocked by mistake; this piece of metal cut the back of your gloves.

We did circuits and landings in these blessed Beauforts, as well as instrument flying and blind approaches using the blind approach beacon system (BABS), but Bill seemed to be taken up with showing me how, with a reasonable wind blowing down the runway, you could come over the end of the runway at 1,000 feet, then put the nose straight down, until you were looking at the runway through the cockpit roof and, at the last minute, pull the stick back and do a three-point landing, stopping in a matter of yards. Each time, he would say, 'But don't try to do that in a Beaufighter', so I could never work out why he kept doing it; he obviously enjoyed it but he frightened me to death and would keep insisting I 'had a go'.

I had found out why there were no mixture controls on a Beaufighter. The mixture was controlled automatically by the setting of the throttle. There were two 'gates' on the throttle—you could feel these as you moved the throttle lever. When the throttle was at, or behind, the 'cruising gate', the mixture was set to the most economical; when forward of the 'rated gate', the mixture was full rich for take-off or combat. The throttle should not be left between the two 'gates' for very long as the mixture in this range was unsuitable. I also found out that the fuel priming pumps were operated externally by the ground crew. I had always found it difficult to get hold of a copy of the Pilots' Notes and this was no exception, but eventually, I managed to borrow a copy, also a copy of the ground engineer's manual on the Bristol Hercules Mark VI engine. I studied these books in my room and made up my own little notebook. The instructors' attitude seemed to be that they would tell you all you needed to know and there was nothing you could do about the engines anyway but I remembered O. P.'s advice—the more you know about them, the more likely you are to do the right thing if things go wrong (O. P. was an experienced civil pilot whom Jack met while training in Canada who gave him lots of valuable advice; an Irish man with a Welsh name, he asked to be called O. P.).

After ten days, I had passed the written examinations on the Beaufighter and the cockpit drills, and had been taken for two demonstration Beaufighter flights, standing in the 'well' behind the instructor who explained some characteristics such as 'Watch for the swing'; 'Make sure both throttles go through the rated gate together, otherwise she'll swing like hell'; 'Get your tail up early'; 'If you used flap leave them down till 300 feet'; 'Nose comes up as the wheels come up'; 'Nose goes down as the flaps come up'; 'Nose goes down as the gills open'; 'We're coming in now, reduce to 150 knots, gills closed, Supercharger—low gear, Carburettor intake—cold. Hydraulic power—on. Undercarriage—down. Pitch—2,400 rpm. Fuel—check on fullest tanks. Flaps—20 Degrees'; 'Turning in now, flaps are fully down. Speed 115 knots. Reduce to 100 knots. Ease her back. Now be ready for swing. Cold throttles back. Use coarse rudder if necessary as tail settles. We can brake now'. There seemed to be so little to do compared with a Lib but I had got this blessed swing to watch out for like I had in the Hudson, and wondered why we did not have nose-wheel undercarriages like the Yanks did; they made even bad landings seem good.

'You can have 822. Take her up for an hour and a half to get the feel of her. Just sign this to say that you understand the fuel, oil, hydraulic, brake and emergency undercarriage systems and the Form 700.' As I walked out to 822, parachute over my shoulder, I noticed the letter on her side: 'P'—good old 'P for Peggy' but I better not call her Peggy here, like I did in Iceland; better use the official 'Peter'. I settled in my seat to go through the preliminary checks then signalled the ground crew and started the starting procedure:

> Fuel cocks: Inner tanks ON
> Suction balance: OFF
> Drop tank cock: OFF
> Throttles: Three-quarters of an inch open
> Pitch: Fully forward
> Superchargers: 'M' (low gear)
> Carb. Intake: COLD
> Gills: OPEN
> Signal to ground crew to turn props two revs by hand
> Signal to ground crew to operate priming pumps till suction and delivery pipes are full. Then prime four strokes. Plug starter battery in.
> Ignition: ON
> Press STARTER and BOOSTER COIL Buttons

Hey presto, with a puff of black smoke, she fired, so, we repeated this for the other engine. The ground crew signalled that the priming pumps had been screwed down and the ground battery removed so, I gradually opened up to 1,000 revs to warm up, checked the temperatures, pressures, and the mags, opened up a bit more, exercised the pitch, opened throttles fully, checked boost and rpm, throttled back, checked the mags again, signalled ground crew to remove locking pins from the undercarriage and hold them up for me to see, and indicated hatches closed; after a check on the brake pressure, I was ready for off.

Following taxi out and pre-take-off check, the watch office gave me the OK so we moved on to the runway and opened up against the brakes. They were responding evenly, so we throttled back with the brakes off and then off we went.

As I eased the throttles right forward through the rated gate, I felt a real kick in my back as the full power was unleashed. In seconds, I seemed to be at 150 feet, selected 'undercarriage up', and throttled back to climb at a gentle 150 knots, leaving me sitting there like a king on a throne. At 5,000 feet, I set the throttles at the cruising gate and played about with revs between 1,600 and 2,400 rpm, noting the speeds this was giving. I felt so free up here, sitting right in the nose, she responded beautifully. I threw her into a few steep turns, put her in a bit of a dive, and watched the airspeed indicator reach 320 knots. Then, I came back to cruising and let this speed drop back to 150 knots and selected 'undercarriage down' to get the feel of the change of trim. I flew around at 130 knots with the undercarriage down, then put down 20 degrees of flap noting the change of trim and how she felt, then dropped down to 115 knots and put the flaps fully down.

I whipped the wheels up, brought the flaps up by stages, and did a few turns, then went through the procedure again, altering the trim. With wheels and flaps up, I banged the throttles right open to see how they responded; she was absolutely magnificent. Time was nearly up. I had been swanning about over the Firth of Forth for over an hour so it was time to go home. She sat down like a dream and tried to shoot off as the tail came down, but it was no worse than a Hudson. As I was taxiing in, the watch officer told me I could have another hour if I wanted, so I checked my fuel and set off again. I had been told that she might feel heavy on the controls but, after a Lib, she handled like a dream and with a bit of careful trimming; she would fly 'hands off' as steady as a rock. She tightened up a bit in a really steep turn; you had to really push the wheel forward to bring her out of it, but in the coldish air of a November afternoon, I noticed a white 'vapour trail' form at the wing tip in a really tight turn so I kept trying to see if I could make it appear again. There was no danger of this baby's tail coming off—she was built like a battleship; this was really flying. That hour was up all too quickly and I came in just before dusk.

For the next few days, it was lots and lots of short trips, take-offs, and landings; single-engine flying and landings with one engine throttled back; the take-offs were speeded up, doing the cockpit checks as we were rolling so it was a turn on to the runway and straight off; the landings were speeded up too, keeping the tail up, and taxiing fast to clear the runway; ground-controlled approaches (GCAs) and talk downs; and night 'circuits and bumps'—I reckoned I had now done more take-offs and landings in a Beau than I had done in a Lib over the last twelve months.

It was now time to get 'crewed up'. I had become 'pally' with a lad from Lancashire—a flight sergeant who had done a tour on Blenheims. He came from St Helens and worked in the accounts department at Callender Cables. He seemed to be well clued up and, most important of all, he was good company—cheerful and with a nice sense of humour. We automatically seemed to find ourselves together in the mess and we both just seemed to take it for granted that we would be flying together. Using a typical Lancashire expression, he remarked one night, 'Happen, I'll be your observer, if you'll have me.' My reply was, 'Happen I will, what are you drinking?' Douggie was particular that he was an 'observer', wearing the 'Flying O' brevet, not just a navigator like some of the newer lads.

Whenever we could, Douggie and I went out to a Beau together. I would sit in my seat, familiarising myself with the positions of the levers, switches, cocks, and buttons so that I could go straight to them without looking. Douggie would call out various controls and I would touch them without looking. He would test me on the dials and the warning lights (which seemed relatively few after a Lib), especially as there was no autopilot and no de-icers; the poor ground crew had to spread a horrible thick paste over the wings' leading edges if there was likely to be any ice about. We would crawl around tracing the run of cables, pipes, and wires, then study the emergency systems. We particularly liked the escape hatches; we had one each so you could drop straight through the bottom. They were used for normal getting in and out on the ground but if the release lever was pulled during flight, they were supposed to be whipped open by the slipstream and hang down in front of the opening to protect you as you dropped clear, but how they did this took a while to figure out as you would think the slipstream would keep them shut; we were, however, assured that they did work OK. The pilot pulled one lever to collapse the back of the seat, another lever to open the hatch, then grabbed hold of two bars up near the roof, dragged himself backwards out of the seat, hung over the hatch, and then just let go; yet we hoped we would not have need to do so. We genned up on the four channel

VHF R/T and on the W/T set in Douggie's position and were looking forward to our first trip together. We moved into the same billet—a nice little room for two—for a couple of evenings; Douggie had my Pilots' Notes and tested me on the pressures, temperatures, fuel, hydraulic and pneumatic systems, what services ran off each engine, engine limits, and anything else he thought of.

We were soon off on a few 'cross-countries' but they were mainly over the sea; they were not very long, lasting about a couple of hours, and the most important thing seemed to be to avoid 'restricted' areas and firing ranges. The night ones were the most interesting as the runway lights were only switched on when we were on the approach; on certain runways, we had to do a right-hand circuit to keep us away from Drem airfield, which was only a few miles to the west of us, from where an operational squadron of Beaufighter night fighters were operating. At least we had electric runway lights and also approach 'funnels' as well as the 'glide path indicator', which showed red, yellow, or green to tell you whether you were coming in at the correct angle of descent. This system of lighting was actually originally tried out at Drem airfield and subsequently became known, throughout the RAF, as the 'Drem lighting system'. On one night, with a part moon, we were instructed to 'hold' at 5,000 feet over May Island because there were enemy aircraft approaching Edinburgh. While in our 'holding pattern' I saw, very clearly, the outlines of a Junkers Ju 88 drift across just below us. Instinctively, I swung around to try and find it again but saw no more sign of it. Calling the airfield, I was told, in no uncertain terms to turn 360 degrees and return to May Island as I was heading for a balloon barrage. What the hell I would have done if I had spotted the Junkers Ju 88 again, I do not know as I had no ammunition.

Towards the end of November, we were told that, as we could all fly Beaufighters now, we could have a long weekend leave next weekend, after which we would get down to the real operational training. I phoned Peg and we arranged that she would come up on the Friday and I would book us in a hotel in North Berwick. There was nothing at East Fortune itself; it was just a 'halt' on the main line from York to Edinburgh, although there was a little monument on the roadside showing an airship, reading:

> To commemorate the first crossing from east to west and the first double crossing of the Atlantic by air accomplished by the British

Airship R34 which left East Fortune, Scotland on June 2, 1919 landed Mineola, Long Island on July 6 and returned to Fulham, England arriving July 13, 1919.

I thought those trips I did in Libs were long but that westbound flight of four weeks must have been really something. I never could figure out why they set off from East Fortune of all places. This little monument made me think of the chaps I met in York at Airspeed who had been working on the airship at Howden; Airspeed were now making hundreds of Oxfords that were taking over from the faithful old Anson as a twin-engined trainer. By all accounts, it was a better trainer than the docile Anson as it had a few mild vices, making it a bit more like a real aeroplane. That Atlantic crossing by the R34 was the year I was born, twenty-four years earlier.

I arranged to meet Peg at Drem, some 2 miles further along the line, from where we could get a bus to North Berwick. Both Drem and East Fortune were really only halts for slow trains, but, even though this was the main line from London to Edinburgh, all the trains now seem to be slow ones, stopping at every little station along the way. Gone were the days of the fast expresses, stopping only at York or Newcastle along the way. The *Flying Scotsman* in its green LNER livery and the streamlined *Silver Jubilee* were things of the past. The carriages were grubby, the engines dirty and rusty, some engines were odd looking things we had either borrowed or bought from the Americans, and timetables meant nothing. Engines broke down through lack of maintenance, trains were delayed to fit in military or ammunition trains, and there were detours due to track repairs. However, on a dark, cold winter's evening, I met a smiling Peg off the train and eventually we found our way in the blackout to the hotel where we soon forgot about the world outside.

The Saturday night was a very lively affair. We went to a local dance, dancing Reels and Gay Gordons like lunatics. They did not seem to mind a couple of Sassenachs but when I told a laddie that I was entitled to wear the Buchanan tartan because my family were a sect of Clan Buchanan and I happened to know that the Buchanans came from the east shore of Loch Lomond and their badge was either a Bilberry or a Darag (an Oak), then things really got moving. Peg and I had been drinking a rather rough beer but we got involved with whisky chasers, then, to make matters worse, I told our friends that my mother was a Grant (a Highland clan from Strathspey), so with the Clan Grant war cry of 'Stand fast, Craigellachie', another round of whiskies appeared, doubles this time. Returning to this mad dancing, jigging around at a ridiculous rate, mainly in the hope of getting a rest from drinking, the room was going around and around, everyone letting out whoops and shouts; the trouble was, the room kept going around and around after we stopped dancing.

Eventually, we decided we had better be on our way while we were capable of doing so, but as soon as we got out into the cold night air, I felt terrible, though Peggy seemed reasonably OK. Fortunately, there seemed to be a bit of a moon and I did not dare go back to the hotel like that, so we had a weave up to the harbour where, leaning over the harbour wall, most of that good whisky and rough beer went back into the Firth of Forth. We felt better now, so, with our arms around each other, we made our way to the hotel. I pulled myself together as we asked for the key and made straight for bed. We spent a nice quiet Sunday with a walk around the golf course and along the beach, but Monday came all too soon and I was seeing Peg disappear in a grimy train, back to York. I thought, 'this was better than being in Iceland.'

Back to work, we now started to use some different Beaus, they were still the Mark VIs but had cannons and machine guns fitted and, to my surprise, radio altimeters that would read down to 10 feet. I thought what a godsend these would have been on the Libs and here I found them on training planes and wondered if the lads in Iceland had got them yet. We were teamed up in threes for formation flying, did cannon firing singly on a floating target and a target further down the coast, air-to-air firing on a towed target with the machine guns, and low-flying mainly over the sea. At first, the formation flying seemed very strange to me. I had not done any since early training days and for the past eighteen months or more, I had not been used to having another aircraft within several hundred miles of me. Flying Number Two seemed the worst, having another aircraft close by at each side. Eventually, I got the hang of it, setting the boost and gently controlling the airspeed with the pitch levers.

After a week, I got to quite like tucking in close, making hand signals to each other. One beauty of the Beau was that, with sitting bang in the middle and with that wonderful forward view, it was equally easy to formate on either side. Soon, however, we had to start tight formation flying, making sure that no one got lower than the leader; this was preparing for the next phase when we would be formation flying at really low levels and if you got below the leader, you would be taking an early bath. Sometimes, if not careful, you could lose the leader under your wing or engine and when really tight, you could not allow this to happen, especially if you were the one in the middle.

Running along with the formation flying, we were individually doing low-flying, which I really enjoyed; I was used to this but the sensation sitting right in the nose was really something and the radio altimeter read the height so accurately that it even measured the height of the waves, although the waves were nothing like the size they were over the Atlantic—just a dull grey sea with what seemed to me to be a slight swell. The air-to-air firing was great fun, peppering the target towed by a little Martinet; although I would not have fancied flying the Martinet, most exciting of all was the cannon firing. They seemed much more concentrated than they were in the old Lib Is and with the Beau being smaller, they made a hell of a noise and you felt the aircraft shudder as you pressed the tit (cannon firing button); the sea around the target was ripped apart into a seething mass of foam with splashes rising into the air and with them being belt-fed, there was no need for some poor soul to keep changing magazines. The poor observer, however, got the full benefit of the cordite fumes, which were choking enough, even upfront.

We had a cine-camera installed in the nose that went into action when the cannon tit was depressed so the next day, these were analysed to assess results. Sometimes, we used the camera on its own as we were getting through too much ammunition, or we would use the camera with the wing machine guns. The days were short, getting well into December, but the weather did not cause us much bother. As Christmas approached, it became clear that we were not likely to get any Christmas leave—so much for this 'leisurely' course our late Wingco had talked about.

I scrounged a couple of trips sitting in the back to get an idea of what it was like for the observer, checking on what he could see and, more important, what he could not see. Sitting there with your head in the plastic cupola, about halfway down the fuselage and more or less in line with the trailing edge of the wing, the visual all around and above was excellent but not very good below leaving large blind areas if we should be attacked from below and I did not think he had a very good view for low-level navigation.

It was all coming together now. Three or maybe four times a day if the weather permitted and the daylight lasted, our 'flight' of three would do a quick scramble, quickly form up, drop down to 10 or 15 feet over the water, fly for maybe forty-five minutes or so around two or three turning points, then head for a target (which was sometimes a rock), pull up to about 300 feet a couple of miles away, open up into a wider line abreast formation, dive onto the target with cannons blazing (or sometimes just the cine-camera), make off on a straight course at low level, close back into tight formation for the flight back, then make a quick landing with Number One just turning off the runway as Number Two had touched down and Number Three on final approach.

We always made sure that Douggie kept his eyes on the other two aircraft when going in to the target as, like the other two pilots, I would be concentrating on the gunsight and we did not fancy bumping into each other. The CO was very keen on these quick landings, telling us that when we were operating as a squadron, or as a complete wing, there would be no time for messing about with maybe thirty or forty aircraft to get down, some of which may be getting low on fuel. Occasionally, we would be allowed to stay at low level for a pass over the airfield, weaving round the little hillocks that dotted the ground between the coast and the airfield. This was when you really felt to be 'motoring', sitting right up in the nose with your feet almost sticking out of the nose and the ground immediately in front whipping under in a blur. It was even more impressive to be on the grounds when a flight of three, tucked close together came over because, even though there would be six Hercules at almost full power, you did not hear a thing as they approached, then a big roar and whoosh as they passed over. It was a wonderful thing as far as the Beau was concerned; at low level, you would not hear it coming until it was too late (no wonder it had been christened 'whispering death'—the beautiful, pugnacious, tough baby with the lethal 'caress').

She was a tough nut, too. Roaring into the target on one exercise, in the middle of the line of three, the cannons fired for a second or so, then, there was the biggest, almighty bang I had ever heard in my life, accompanied by one hell of a thump. Immediately, I released the cannon button and pulled up, thinking one of the other lads must have shot me, but she responded OK and Douggie came on the intercom, 'Are you all right? Happen there's a bloody great hole under your seat—can see the bloody sea.' Even with my helmet on, I could hear the noise of rushing air. I told the other lads what had happened and Douggie came forward to have a look; he told me that one of the cannons must have 'blown up' as there were bits of metal all over the place, the breech of one cannon was nowhere to be seen, and there was a great hole with jagged edges in the bottom of the fuselage.

All the controls seemed to be working OK and the instruments did not indicate anything wrong; I had climbed up to about 1,000 feet and one of the other lads—a great guy, a flying officer from Devon—came up close right under me, while I flew straight and level, to have a good look. I lowered and raised the undercarriage (which worked OK), so we returned to base. It seemed that this was not the first time this had happened; one of the armourers remarked, 'it's that bloody American ammunition again, it's all supposed to have been checked after they found some of the rounds were not within the accepted tolerances.' It seemed that one empty case had failed to be injected and the next round, which happened to be a high explosive, had been rammed up behind it with the result that it exploded and blew everything apart. When I saw the jagged bits of shrapnel embedded in the underside and back of my seat, I felt sick at the thought of what would have happened to my private parts but for that armour plate. On the other hand, thank goodness it was an explosive round that blew up and not an incendiary as we had a mixture of tracer, high explosive, and incendiary. Yet the good old Beau, strong as an ox, stayed in one piece and although I had landed her a bit faster to be on the safe side, it did not affect her handling—just needed a bit of different trim.

Christmas Day was spent on the airfield. We were all off duty for the usual voluntary church service in the morning then over to the airmen's mess to serve them with their dinner and free drinks. Douggie and I spent most of the evening with the airmen in the NAAFI; it was all very jovial, but it was the one day of the year when you really wanted to be at home. I did not seem to feel this as much when miles away—in Canada or Iceland—but knowing Peg was only a couple of hundred miles down the road made me feel it more.

It was back to work on Boxing Day when the CO announced that we had just over a week to go and this would be spent mainly on sorting us out for torpedo training. We would not have any torpedoes at this station and we had no torpedo-dropping sights but the drill was to be that we would approach the target (a particular little rock out in the Firth) at high speed, flying right on the deck, then pull the throttle back and pull up to 150 feet, knocking off the speed so that at 1,000 yards, we were at 150 feet, between 190 and 200 knots with everything straight and level. At this point, we would press the camera tit, which would give a picture that would enable them to check our range and attitude; another camera in the cockpit would 'take' the instrument panel and show the airspeed and height shown on the radio altimeter. It was an absolute bugger to get this right—either miles too far away or else too near before you could get the airspeed down—but each day, we studied the previous day's pictures to see where we went wrong. After a few days, six of us were made up into two flights to try it in formation; this was a real bugger, having to make sure we opened up enough to not hit each other while concentrating on other things and one of the lads in the flight flew so low when leading that you could see the water being fluffed up by his props, but he reckoned he could see the same when I (or the other one) was leading. Never fly lower than the leader was certainly the golden rule.

I was surprised when the CO informed me that I was one of those who were to go on to torpedo training because I felt I had made a real hash of these exercises but he seemed to think I was good enough to improve with practice. However, as I had three months or so to go before returning to Ops, I was not going straight on to the torpedo course; I was to go to an FTU at Melton Mowbray for six weeks or so, delivering new Beaufighters to Africa. I asked about a bit of leave and was told I could have a couple of days and report to Melton Mowbray on 3 January 1944, but transport being what it was in Scotland over the New Year, I did not get home till late on New Year's Day.

2

The Road to Morocco

Here, on the outskirts of Melton Mowbray (a delightful little market town in Leicestershire, famous for its pork pies and surrounded by pleasant rolling hunting country, which even looked nice in January), Douggie and I met our new colleagues, or at least those of them who were not away on a delivery. Douggie and I seemed to be about the only ones who were not in the officers' mess but they were a cheerful, friendly bunch, especially one relatively old Polish officer.

The drill was that we would be allocated a new Beau that would be delivered here from the factory at Filton. Firstly, we would take it up on an air test, checking the controls (elevators, rudder and ailerons), the setting of the trimming tabs and general feel, then the engines for correct settings, temperatures, pressures, and the like, and the correct functioning of the hydraulics, pneumatics, and electrics, filling in a great long form for the engineering officer and the riggers. Any necessary adjustments would be made and then we would take her up again. When these were OK, she would be 'tropicalised', which mainly involved fitting sand filters to the carburettor intakes and coolers, bits of 'operational equipment' would be fitted (including the cannons), then we would do at least a couple of 'consumption tests' of about four and a half hours each until a satisfactory fuel consumption figure was achieved, to ensure that we could reach Rabat/Salé in Morocco. This may have meant making carburettor and other adjustments between tests.

The first thing however, was to get our vaccinations and inoculations up to date, plus some tropical ones, especially yellow fever. We were issued with 'goolie chits', which were cards written in both English and Arabic telling an Arab that the holder of this card was a British officer and if they provided him, as a friend of all Arab peoples, with food and water and returned him safely to the nearest British or American forces, he would be handsomely rewarded. We also had passport-type photographs taken—one for some papers we would be carrying as civilians in case we came back through Portugal and other copies that could be used on forged papers if we landed up in occupied territory; however, as we all wore the same sports shirts and spotted tie for these photographs, the enemy would probably know immediately that we were British aircrew.

There seemed to be all sorts of variations of the Mark VI Beaufighter. They all had four cannons but some had six machine guns in the wings (two on the port and four on the starboard) while others had extra fuel tanks in place of the wing guns; some had a Perspex cupola on top of the fuselage, just aft of the pilot, housing the loop aerial for a radio compass, whereas others did not; some had provision for a single rear-firing machine gun to be fitted in the observer's cupola; and some had external bomb racks and some had aerials for 'special equipment'. They were fitted out for the particular role that they would be carrying out. Soon, some appeared fitted with four rocket rails under each wing.

The observer in a Beau had to be a real 'all-rounder'—a navigator, a wireless operator, an air gunner, and able to sort out any snags with the cannons—and I felt I had been jolly lucky to have teamed up with Douggie. He seemed competent as a navigator and a wireless operator but perhaps most important of all, he was a jolly, cheerful lad, who was keen to take an interest in my side of the job as well. I felt it a pity that I could not let him have a go in my seat, at least just to get the feel of the controls, which may be useful in case of an emergency, but there was no way you could change places in the air in a Beau. Sometimes, he would crawl upfront and stand behind me, his legs straddling the 'well' over the hatch, to see what was going on. With all the jobs Douggie had to do, in the relatively confined space and restricted downward view, it made you realise what an easy time a pure navigator had on the Libs, with much more room, a better view, and only the navigation to think about.

Douggie and I soon got a job—to flight test a Beau that had just had a new 'stern frame' fitted. It seemed that on its previous test, it could not be trimmed to fly straight; it kept yawing from the side to side, which would certainly be no use as a 'gun platform'. I felt a bit apprehensive about what she may want to do on take-off—probably want to go off in a wild swing—but she behaved perfectly and could be trimmed to fly 'hands off' as steady as a rock. I ticked off all the prescribed manoeuvres on the test sheet, which I had clipped to a board strapped round my right leg, and that was that, our first job done. The main thing that struck me, on the prescribed route over Lincolnshire and out to the North Sea, was the vast number of aerodromes; it seemed as if the whole country was one big aircraft carrier.

It came as a big surprise when I was promoted to warrant officer. Promotion to warrant officer did not seem to be automatic, like promotion to flight sergeant. I could now claim to have held every non-commissioned rank other than corporal. I had to get fitted out with new gear—best blue in officer material with the warrant officer badge on the lower sleeve, new hat and shoes, Van Heusen shirts and collars, but all provided for free. I hung on to my old, well-worn 'battle-dress' as I did not want to part with that. Warrant officer seemed to be the best rank in the Air Force—as much pay as a pilot officer with only a fraction of the mess bills and a reserved table in the mess if you wished to use it (which I rarely did as I usually ate with Douggie). It took a little time, however, to get used to the NCOs and other ranks calling me 'sir' and the officers calling me 'mister'; it was a very nice and cosy rank, particularly as aircrew.

We were soon allocated an aircraft and took her up on a two-hour 'acceptance test', out over the North Sea. We put her through her paces, filling in the forms as we went along. She handled perfectly; the engines were like silk as those Bristol Hercules were so responsive and smooth, and everything worked just fine, except the R/T, which packed up halfway through and there was no padding on the back of the seat, so I felt a bit further away from the controls than I had been used to. This was soon put right as a nice WAAF in the parachute section made me a cushion of thick blue canvas stuffed almost solid with kapok, which became a standard part of my equipment; it seemed that some of the other chaps had had the same trouble.

The aircrew were a really grand lot. We all seemed to be doing this job as a rest between Ops. We often congregated at The Bell in Melton Mowbray; some had their wives or girlfriends staying there and many pleasant evenings were passed. New chaps kept appearing after having made a delivery; a bit of 'line shooting' went on about things that had happened on air tests, or experiences in Rabat or Casablanca. One flight lieutenant who had just returned told us graphically about being 'jumped' by a couple of Focke-Wulfs (German fighters) while crossing the Bay of Biscay, so he took her right down to the deck to avoid attack from below and then, as his observer gave him a running commentary, he put her into a skid every time they came in, so their fire passed at the side of him. I took him up on this. It transpired that he had done his Ops on Beaus and the trick was to apply hard rudder in one direction and hard aileron in the opposite direction with all the strength you could muster; this kept the aircraft level but skidding, so though you were crabbing along, pointing several degrees off the track, you were actually making good. He said the Beau was perfectly strong enough to take the strain—the worst strain was on your legs, back, and arms—but when the fighter (or ground gun for that matter) allowed for deflection, he would offset ahead of the nose, but that was not where you were going to be; the only danger of being hit was if the fighter was bloody bad at his job and did not lay off the deflection correctly. I remembered that the first job I had was testing an aircraft that had had a new stern frame fitted and asked whether he thought this could have been caused by somebody 'skidding it'. He pooh-poohed the idea, saying that 'the Beau was so bloody strong that it would break your leg before it hurt the Beau'; in any case, every Beau in his old squadron would have needed a new stern frame if that were the case.

It was funny how, like on the previous ferry job (across the Atlantic), you seemed to pick up useful information, possibly life-saving information, in a bar or a pub. As dear old O.P. told me in Montréal, 'you are always learning on this job'. Other tips I picked up in The Bell were 'not to open the throttles too fast on an overshoot as you have so much power for an aircraft of this size that she may flip over upside down; always carry a knife in your flying boot to puncture the dinghy if it inflates by accident as there had been cases of this happening and jamming the pilot up against the roof; in an emergency at low altitude, cut both engines and go straight ahead, regardless of what is ahead—just make sure that a tree is not going to come between the engines, let the engines bash down any obstructions, the cannons will act as skis, and to put a hand in front of your forehead to keep it off the windscreen'.

In a couple of days, our aircraft was ready for the first 'consumption test'. They tackled the consumption business differently here from the way it was done at North Atlantic Ferry Command. Instead of carrying sheets and sheets of paper showing weight–power ratios, boost and revs combinations, adjustments for height, temperature, and God knows what, here the whole business was reduced to a simple 'air miles per gallon in still air'. After all the calculations (which Freddie and I used to have to do on the Libs) I was, at first, rather sceptical about relying on just 'air miles per gallon' as surely this must alter as the aircraft gets lighter. Then, it dawned on me that on a VLR Lib, almost 40 per cent of our take-off weight was made up of fuel so there was a hell of a difference in weight as the flight progressed but in the Beau, the fuel would only account for about 20 per cent of our take-off weight so the alteration in weight would not be anything like as much.

We would be taking off at about 21,000 lb and 550 gallons of fuel. Our Beau had machine guns in the wings so did not have the auxiliary wing tanks; we also had four cannons but we would not carry any ammunition. This is when I really realised what a hell of a 'war load' the Beau could carry because the maximum take-off weight would go up to 25,500 lb, thus she could carry 4,450 lb of ammunition and 'external stores', such as a 2,127-lb torpedo, two 500-lb bombs, or nearly 800 lb of rockets; it was over twice the 'war load' of a fully loaded Lib, but, of course, the Lib had a much longer endurance.

We had two approved routes for the consumption tests—one around several turning points and a run up the Irish Sea, the other out over the North Sea near Cromer, then north, and back over the land. Which route we took was usually governed by 'Operational Requirements', but the main thing was to cross the coast each time at specific points and to avoid firing ranges and restricted areas. We would stay up for four and a half hours, which meant going around the course two and a bit times. To start with, we would fly at 175 knots, which was supposed to be the best cruising speed for maximum range; after take-off, I would set the throttles to the 'cruising gate' and keep the speed dead on 175 knots by adjusting the revs, keeping a note of the boost and revs every fifteen minutes. On the first test, we would be given just a few rounds for the cannons and machine guns and fire them off, just to check that they were working OK; the shudder and racket when the cannons went off brought bits of 'putty' down from around the cockpit canopy, though only loose bits that had not been cleaned off. My cushion was really comfortable; I thought, 'must tell that WAAF, when we get back'.

This first trip was over the North Sea route. It seemed a long time just sitting there, hand flying, keeping the air speed dead on 175 knots. The third time around, we could cut it short and crossed the coast near Scarborough. I pointed out to Douggie where I had had my first flight (from Oliver's Mount). We passed by York; the Minster and the gasworks were visible for miles. Our aim was to get 2.18 air miles (nautical miles) per gallon, but after the tanks had been dipped to check the gauges and all the calculations done, we had only achieved 2.15. So, we had to do the job again in a couple of days; this time, we were told to 'try 170 knots' and it worked, so we got 2.18 exactly. It seemed a bit funny to me that in the calculations they seemed to ignore the fuel used on take-off because at +10 lb of boost and 2,900 revs, you were gobbling up fuel at the rate of 400 gallons per hour albeit only for a short time; on the other hand, by working on the average over 4.5 hours, they should be on the safe side as the trip to Africa was going to take about six hours and the aircraft was getting slightly lighter all the time.

So we were now ready to set off for Africa. There was always a bit of a kick to be got out of going somewhere completely new. We collected the 'ships papers', our own 'civvy papers' in case we needed them, as well as maps and charts, packed our things (including civvy clothes) in our grips, and set off on the trip to Portreath in Cornwall, which lasted one hour and thirty-five minutes. That evening, Douggie and I worked on our provisional flight plan. There were 46 miles to the Scilly Isles; 294 miles to 46 00N, 10 30W, which would put about 100 miles between us and the German fighters near Brest; 180 miles due south to 43 00N, 10 30W, about 50 miles off Cape Finisterre; 257 miles to 38 50N, 09 50W, about 18 miles off Cape Roca, near Lisbon; 113 miles to 37 00N, 09 10W, some 8 miles off Cape St Vincent; then 200 miles to the coast of Africa at 34 30N, 06 30W, which was a deliberate error to make sure of hitting the coast north of Rabat and thus being sure which way to turn; and finally 32 miles along the coast to Rabat at 34 01N, 06 48W, making a total of 1,122 nautical miles.

At 2.18 nautical miles per gallon, we would need 515 gallons for the 1,122 miles but that would be in perfectly still air; there would be no margin for evasive action if we encountered fighters and precious little scope for errors in navigation. We decided that we wanted a wind component of at least plus 3 knots, better still plus 10, with a bit of cloud cover over the Bay. It was now up to the Met boys, so we strolled over to the Met before going to bed; on the Met officer's scribbled chart, he had a 'low' pencilled in, the centre of which he estimated to be roughly over Bordeaux and he estimated it was moving towards Paris. This seemed to be just what we wanted; it could give a following wind almost all the way, perhaps well over 10 knots, but there would be no cloud cover. We decided that it looked all set for the morning so arranged a call for 6 a.m. so that if the picture developed as it looked like doing, we could be away soon after dawn. I would have preferred to have gone in the dark but for some reason these flights were always done by day. As we turned in, I could sense that Douggie was a bit 'on edge'; it would be the longest flight he had made. I told him that he could forget all about navigation until we got past Cape Finisterre; all I wanted him to do was to 'keep his eyes peeled' for any little black dots in the sky, all the way around and that every so often, I would do a quick steep turn in both directions to give him a view below in case anything was creeping up on us.

It was still dark as we went to the mess for breakfast. It was a nippy January morning with a bit of frost on the ground and hundreds of stars, the chilly wind on our cheeks was coming from the north-east—just the job—but I would have liked a bit of cloud.

The Met man had updated his chart on the latest available information and drew in a nice 'low' over France, which showed we should be following an isobar practically the whole way and should have a following wind varying between 5 and 15 knots; however, there seemed little chance of any cloud cover—perhaps a bit of 'fair weather cumulus' over northern Spain, but that would not be any use to us. It was just getting light as we phoned the 'flight' and asked them to have the aircraft ready in half an hour. There was not a cloud in the sky as the winter sun burst into a new day, and the sea beyond the cliff took on a deep blue.

I had cut strips from two Mercator Charts (navigation charts used to take account of the curvature of the earth so that any straight line on a Mercator projection map is a line of constant true bearing that enables a navigator to plot a straight-line course) and stuck them together to cover the route, marked in the track, and folded them so that they would fit on a board I would have strapped to my left leg, so that with the Dalton 'Computer' (early equipment used as navigational aids, though not a computer in the modern sense) strapped to my right leg and a couple of pencils hanging round my neck on pieces of string (so that I would not drop one), I could do the navigation for the first half of the trip while Douggie just looked out for trouble. I worked out the course for the first two legs using the forecast wind; I had to get used to these new Mercator Charts though as they were a new series printed in red instead of black and the spot heights over land were shown in metres instead of feet, which could be bloody dangerous if misread.

We were soon aboard and settled down, the Hercules engines came to life, a quick run-up not to use too much fuel, and we were away down the runway, with a quick turn on to course, a little correction to make up for the fact that I did not set course from dead over the airfield, and a slow climb to 3,000 feet. We flew almost parallel with the Cornish coast, looking down at the waves gently splashing against the cliffs. I told Douggie I was flying the course we had calculated and would hold it to the Scillies. If it brought us slap over the most southerly of the islands in fifteen minutes, it would show that the forecast wind was dead on. It did, so, we turned on to the 294-nautical mile leg out to 46 00N, 10 30W, and I told Douggie to keep his eyes outside, especially remembering that anything coming out from France will be coming out of the sun and that, in these conditions, we would stand out like a glittering star on a dark night. We would then be at our nearest point to France.

It was such a vast open space of sea and sky, which felt lonelier than being miles up into the Arctic in a Lib; I suppose it was because I was all alone up here in the front and even on the Hudson, Tug would keep buzzing around and come for a sit by me. The direction of lazy 'white caps' on the sea below told me that, allowing for the veer between sea level and 3,000 feet, the wind was still roughly as forecast—about the same speed too by the size of the 'white caps'.

Douggie and I kept having a little chat. He could see my back, but I could not see him, so it was nice to know he was still there. I kept making sure he was looking out. The sea surface began to look as if the wind was freshening. I would select a 'white cap' some way ahead and try to watch it approach—if it stayed long enough—to estimate the amount of drift and tack a little on the estimated wind speed. After a few such drifts, I was confident enough to alter course and told Douggie I reckoned we had a better ground speed than expected. As there was not a ruddy cloud in the big blue sky, we had nowhere to hide if we were jumped, so it would have to be down to the deck and try the skidding business. Yet there was not a sign of anything. I at least expected to see some of the dozens of anti-U-boat patrols that they say we have over 'The Bay'; maybe they were nearer in. There was not a boat or an aircraft to be seen—just blue sea and clear blue sky.

After ninety-five minutes on this leg, I reckoned we were at our turning point so turned due south for the next leg of 180 nautical miles, which I reckoned would take us exactly one hour. So we had done 340 miles, leaving us 782 miles to go. I told Douggie that I would keep up the short steep turn routine until the end of this leg as we were not 'out of the woods' yet. It seemed a long hour. I estimated the drift of surface wind again; the change of course enabled me to fiddle with the Dalton Computer and work out an approximate wind, which came pretty near to the forecast, but I altered course a couple of degrees more. It was a bit boring hand-flying, keeping the course and airspeed dead on, but the Beau trimmed beautifully 'hands off' and I was glad to have the bit of navigation to do.

Nearing the end of this leg and miles away to port, I could just see the top of a cumulus cloud. Douggie thought I was mad when I asked him to take a bearing on that very distant cloud. I said, 'just take a bearing and note the time, then I'll tell you why.' That bearing taken, I told him that 'I'd bet my bottom dollar that that cloud is sitting right over that 1,036-metre mountain in northern Spain, it's marked on your chart, about 43 28N, 07 36W. We'll take another bearing at the end of this leg, if we can still see it. Reckon our ground speed is 182 knots, so you will know how far we have travelled between bearings on a track of 180 degrees true, so you've got your triangle, get working on the old trig and you've got us a fix, if the cloud is where I think it is'. Douggie replied, 'Bloody hell, never heard of taking fixes on clouds before.' To this, I responded, 'Now's your chance to show you are a navigator, as well as an observer.'

At the turning point, Douggie got his bearings and that kept him quiet for a good quarter of an hour. Then he came on the intercom to announce that, if I had been flying the correct airspeed and if my ground speed was right and if I was where I bloody well thought I was in the first place, when we turned onto the present leg, we were at 42 55N, 10 40W; that seemed good enough to me—only about 10 miles out—so I told him he could do the navigation now. We were now about halfway and should be flying parallel to the coast of Portugal, about 60 nautical miles out. This was another long leg of 257 miles. Eventually, perhaps some 35 miles on the port side was a black smear—a definite coastline with two lumps of high ground beyond. We gradually closed to within about 20 miles of a headland that then fell quickly away; that must be Cape Roca, off Lisbon, ten minutes early on the original flight plan time. We only had another 345 miles to go as we altered course for Cape St Vincent. The land receded, so there was no problem about making it now as I found I could ease the revs back a bit more, but I was dying for a pee and undid the harness to try and direct it into the 'pee tube'—what a bloody business—ending up half in the pee tube and half God knows where. The engines were purring away like a dream. Bristols certainly made beautiful engines and they were the only company who made both engines and aeroplanes and they had a couple of winners here.

It was time to open the flask of coffee and have a sandwich, but, in no time, we were converging with land again and this time heading just to the west of a prominent headland—Cape St Vincent. Our track should have taken us 8 miles out to sea, passing this cape, but it looked deserted, so I altered course to pass within 1 mile so we could have a good look. I told Douggie it was just as well to see what it looked like in case we found ourselves down here sometime in bad weather. It looked very black and barren, but the big Atlantic rollers were crashing against the rocks and we spotted a lighthouse. Now for the 200-mile leg across the Gulf of Cadiz to Africa; there were 890 miles already behind us, but by Jove, I wished I could get up and stretch my legs.

It was getting noticeably warmer as we headed south-east and there was still not a cloud in the sky. Douggie was speculating about seeing belly dancers in Casablanca when ahead, and slightly to port, I spotted a long, low, flat yellow line. Soon this flat yellow line extended all the way across in front of us, and then a thin white line as rollers lazily ran up the long, flat, sandy beach. A long ribbon of a lagoon ran away to port as far as the eye could see, just separated from the sea by a narrow strip of sand. We turned smartly to starboard just after crossing the coast and followed the coastline. In 15 miles or so, we flew over Port Lyautey, which looked far from romantic and identified ourselves on the R/T. I congratulated Douggie on his navigation, which had been spot on, and following another 15 miles, we were over the impressive big white buildings of bustling Rabat/Salé.

The nearby airfield was easy to pick out, the PSP (perforated steel planking) runways standing out clearly on the flat sand, and lots of aircraft on the ground. I did not think to warn Douggie of the noise and rattle when you land on PSP; he wondered what the hell was happening but at least we did not get hit by flying stones as often happens on some airfields. We had made good time—six hours and five minutes. It was a perfect trip and gosh, it was warm. It was like a midsummer day; I could not believe it was January.

After handing over the ship's papers, we went for a meal in the mess, where we were served by Arabs wearing red fezes and long white nightshirts. Following a quick wash to freshen up, we decided to have a look at the town before it got dark. This was a new scene for both of us, with jostling Arabs and youths trying to sell 'genuine' Parker Pens that they produced from their shirt pockets. The youths telling you they had 'very nice sister—very clean'. There were camels in the streets pulling carts; big, ornate, and impressive white buildings; vividly coloured flowers; crowded bazaars; everybody talking loudly; and old men trying to force carvings, leatherwork, or silver jewellery into your hands—'only one pound, very cheap'. Douggie and I lost each other several times. It was just like a summer's evening as we made our way back in the dark; so this was Africa.

The next morning, we made our first 'boob'. We inquired the position as regards getting back to the UK; we learned later that you do not make such inquiries so soon. We were told that there may be a Dakota going that night and were asked to report back about 5 p.m. We went for a further look round Rabat, particularly the magnificent wide, tree-lined streets and big, impressive buildings; I bought a big bunch of ripe bananas to bring back as they had not seen bananas in England for years.

Sure enough, we were on that night's Dakota and true to form, the worst part about any ferry trip was the journey back as a helpless passenger. At least we had seats in this Dakota, but all the windows were blacked out and twenty-two others were encapsulated in this blacked-out tunnel for eight and three-quarter hours, not having a bloody clue where we were or even whether it was day or night. The thing seemed to have a struggle to get off; it vibrated and wallowed. The passengers were a mixed lot; some were obviously not flyers—serious looking civilians in dark suits and carrying official-looking briefcases; some were in Army uniform; others looked like spies.

I had a word with the skipper as he came aft to use the Elsan. He said we were going to Whitchurch, near Bristol. After an eternity, the note of the engines and feel of the aircraft indicated we were coming down. Someone shouted, 'Fasten seat belts. Pass it on.' Soon, there was a little squeal as the wheels touched, the tail came down, and you could tell we were taxiing. It had got bloody cold and when the door was opened, it seemed even colder and still dark. We were escorted to a custom shed, feeling hungry, cold, and tired. As we filed past some trestle tables, a young customs officer in his elegant uniform asked me what I had to declare: 'Just this bunch of bananas', I replied. 'What's that?' he inquired, pointing to my cushion. 'Just my cushion, I take that whenever I go flying', whereupon the cheeky devil took out a knife, slit open the stitching, and a mountain of kapok exploded all over the table. He rummaged about in it, then said, 'OK pass along'. I saw stars, saying, 'What the hell do you mean, pass along? I can't carry that lot all loose in my arms, you'd better get it all put back and sewn up again'.

With that, he disappeared without saying another word and I just sat on the table. Soon, everyone else had passed through; only Douggie and I remained, and even the customs officers had vanished. We sat on a couple of chairs and just waited; 'what the hell,' we thought, 'it doesn't matter if we wait all day!' We ate a banana each. Eventually, another customs officer appeared and asked what we were waiting for. I told him and he disappeared, without comment. It was light now. Douggie went outside to investigate and came back shortly with a couple of mugs of tea.

Next to appear was a female cleaner who seemed to be going to sweep up all my kapok so I told her to leave it until someone came to put it back and sew up my cushion. Douggie took the mugs back and came back with a couple of newspapers, so we just settled down, had another banana, and read the papers. Then an elderly customs officer appeared and obviously wanted to lock up the hut as presumably, no more flights were expected. I told him what had happened and he said he would send one of the girls with a needle and thread. Sure enough, the girl appeared with a little needle and cotton and started putting the kapok back, so we went to help her and the three of us had a hell of a job getting it all stuffed back. We had to keep stoving it down with our feet and the cotton was far too weak, so she found a bigger needle and some twine and eventually we had it all put back. I gave her a couple of bananas and we set off to find somewhere for breakfast.

By lunchtime, we were on a train on the first leg of the journey back to Melton Mowbray. I had nothing in which to wrap the bananas so they were loose on the luggage rack. A little lad opposite kept looking up at them and asking his mum what they were, so after a while, I gave him one and one for his mum and then gave him another when we changed trains. The same thing happened in the next train till there were only about four left, so we ate them ourselves and we never did get them home.

On returning to Melton Mowbray, surprise was expressed that we were back so soon and, although the CO did not say so in so many words, we got the message that most chaps took a few days in Rabat or nipped home for a day or two before reporting back.

We had a few days of leisure with evenings in The Bell and then we were given another Beau. Someone had already done one acceptance test in her; a few minor adjustments had been made and the cannons had been fitted. It was decided that we should do another acceptance test on her before starting the consumption tests as we could test the cannons at the same time, before they were aligned in the butts. This was a good idea because firing the cannon often buggered up the compass, unless for some unaccountable reason, you were heading due north. This would mean that the compass could be re-swung before we did the consumption tests instead of having to fly over half the consumption test with a dodgy compass.

Fate must have been smiling on us because I decided to check the cannons when we were at 8,000 feet over the North Sea, whereas, on a consumption test, we would only have been at 3,000. What exactly happened when I pressed the cannon tit, I am not 100 per cent sure. I remember warning Douggie that I was going to fire, braced for the anticipated shudder, racket, and smell of cordite, then pressed the tit; I think there was a shudder and a crack but I took my finger straight off the tit because the nose fell and everything went quiet—the bloody engines had stopped; they just faded out. I put the wheel forward and was opening the throttles as Douggie came through, 'There's clouds of white stuff coming out of the engines.' I put her into fine pitch and told Douggie, 'The bloody fire extinguishers have gone off—I'll try to blow it out—if we get down to 3,000 feet, open your hatch and get out at 2,000'.

The glide angle on the Beau was a bit steep, so I let the speed drop to 100 knots then put full flap down and held the nose up letting the speed drop to 80 knots. I knew she would stall at 75 knots. It seemed as if those engines were never going to start again; we were at 4,000 feet, with the sea getting nearer, then one engine began to splutter and burst into life, the wings rose, and we seemed to be going to roll over. I quickly throttled back, with a lot of rudder, then trim. 'OK, Douggie, stay put, let the flaps up a bit', then the other began to splutter and instantly roared into full power. For a few seconds, I was juggling with revs, boost, rudder, ailerons, and trim, while we rocked about in the sky; then, all was under control again, the altimeter reading 2,300 feet.

Douggie came on the intercom, 'Don't do that again. Happen that's not funny.' I replied, 'Neither do I. I'm taking this little bitch straight back.' I did not tell him my heart was pumping away twenty to the dozen. On the way back, we chatted, trying to figure out what had happened. There was no possible connection between the cannon button and the extinguishers; they were not even both remotely connected. In any case, if you use the extinguisher, you select one engine, not both; if the fire extinguishers went off when I pressed the cannon tit, what else is wrong—are the cannons likely to go off when I move something else? Douggie came up front and made the cannons 'safe' but even then, we were a bit worried in case something else happened when he did that. Anyway, the engines were running perfectly now and we landed quite normally but I warned the ground crew not to touch anything.

We could check that the cannons had actually briefly fired by the spent cases and the fact that the canvas had been shot off the 'ports' under the nose. It seemed to be taking ages to get to the bottom of the trouble. In The Bell, some of the lads speculated that it must be one of the Beaus made at one of the two 'shadow' factories now turning out Beaus (one not far from Bristol and the other somewhere in Lancashire or Cheshire) as all those from Filton seemed pretty trouble-free. The aircraft remained grounded and we were given another one; from then on, I vowed that all my cannon testing would be done at 8,000 feet at least. Much later, we heard a theory suggesting that particular Beau had an automatic device so that the fire extinguishers would be set off in the event of a crash and it must have been set so critically that it was set off by the judder of the cannons.

Everything went fine with our next aircraft. Consumption tests were OK at 175 knots but even so we took ten minutes longer to get to Rabat than on the first trip at 170 knots. This time, however, we did not rush to get back and spent three days in Rabat. Douggie and I wondered around the Medina (the Old Walled City) down near the mouth of the river, mingled with the Arabs in the smelly Kasbah, watched rats running around bags of cereal, and dismissed the youths selling 'Parker pens' and offering us their sister, as if we were hardened travellers. We strolled along the fine, wide roads outside the old town. Apart from Arabic, French was the main language, which was not surprising as we were in a French colony. We walked around the magnificent open spaces and buildings around the Royal Palace and on our last day ventured across the river to the smaller place called Salé, which was almost entirely an Arab-walled Old City. We never fancied buying anything to eat or drink. There were plenty of dates, grapes, and tomatoes on sale, but we would only risk fruit that could be peeled, so we stuck to smaller oranges. We could not find any bananas this time; we gathered they were imported. We did all our eating in the Nissen hut mess on the airfield where I briefly met some lads from Ferry Command based in Montréal; it seemed they were running regularly through here now and very rarely went to Montréal.

I thought it a bit funny when we were told our plane would be leaving in the early afternoon, thinking this would mean we would be in 'The Bay' before dark. Then we were told to pack our service kit and have our papers ready. The Dakota had civilian markings and the crew were wearing uniforms that I presumed were BOAC. The seats were a little better than in the previous Dak (not much, but at least they had a bit of padding) as before all the windows were blacked out. There were only about twelve of us on board when we left Rabat. After nearly two hours, we were told we were going in to Lisbon; we could go in the passenger building but we must all stick together and we should leave our kit on the plane.

As we walked from the aircraft, it was funny to see a couple of German Junkers; with three engines, they looked to be made of corrugated iron. Some officials looked at our 'papers', then looked up at us, nodded and handed the papers back; we trooped through into a restaurant-cum-waiting room. It was a funny feeling, looking around, wondering who everybody was, and speculating as to which were the Germans. We did not even know who the others in our party were. An English fellow joined us and took us to a table where we had a very nice meal—lots of little fish with sauce, along with white wine, finishing with fresh fruit and very black coffee. The whole atmosphere was one of mystery and intrigue. You had the feeling that all sorts of plots were being hatched, wondering who everybody was and what they were up to. I thought that this seemed a bloody silly place for us to be, the moment we left somebody here was going to tip someone off that we had left for the UK and they would be waiting for us over the Bay.

Shortly after the meal, the chap who had bought us the meal brought four men and two youngish women to join us, telling us that they were joining us for the flight to England. We got the impression that he was from the consulate. We had a little longer hanging around and some idle chat when no one was listening, then the captain appeared and asked us to follow him to the aircraft. It was dark now. The officials only took a quick glance at our papers this time and we were soon shut up again in our tin tunnel. It still took us nearly seven hours to get to Whitchurch, so presumably we went a long way out to the west to cross the Bay. We had no trouble with the customs this time and as we had been in Rabat for over three days, we thought we had better go straight to Melton Mowbray.

I was greeted with the news that Douggie and I were to go on the Torpedo course on 15 February, but before that, I was to appear before a commissioning board in Edinburgh next week so, we could both go on leave and I would meet up with Douggie at Turnberry on the 15th. So, I was on the phone to Peggy: 'I'm coming home tomorrow, love, get some time off starting next Monday, I'm taking you to Edinburgh for a few days, we're booked in at the North British'.

3
Training for Torbeaus

I only spent the one night in York, and then Peg and I boarded the train for Edinburgh, as we may as well spend a few days of quiet luxury at the North British, even though I would have to pay for the extra days myself; as a warrant officer, I was really quite well off. Although it was only February, we enjoyed a few days' early spring weather and did not mind in the least, it getting dark rather early. We met another couple in the hotel who were there for the same purpose; our interviews were on the same day.

The interview was an odd affair—five officers sitting at a long table covered with green baize. I was not really bothered whether they granted me a commission or not as I was enjoying being a warrant officer. One of them asked me why I had not been commissioned on gaining my wings; I could have offered one or two suggestions but thought it wisest to say I did not know. I thought they must have decided to grant me one now or they would not have said that. Then the senior officer in the middle asked me about the Wingco in Iceland, saying he knew him and his father well and that Dick would have gone a long way in the service if he had survived. He told me that he had recommended me for a commission but he had not finalised his report when he failed to return from that operation, so he did not know what else he was going to say, but he gathered that the Wingco and I had flown together several times. He then talked about the Wingco at some length. I told him how everyone on the squadron, aircrew, and ground crew alike, liked and respected the Wingco, what an encouragement he was, how he flew regularly with all the twenty aircrews on the squadron, and how he seemed to have the knack of attracting U-boats. We had no doubt that he got his U-boat on his last Op. The old boy remarked that, 'from his report, as far as it goes, he seemed to have quite a regard for you too'. He asked how I was getting on now. I told him I liked the Beau, although it was a bit of a change from a Lib, that I had taken two to Rabat, and was now about to start on a torpedo course. He wished me well and that was that. On the way out, I remembered that the Wingco had said that he would be making a couple of recommendations and would let me know what they were when he said, 'Goodbye.'

So, I had a nice meal and one more night with Peggy, then she boarded the train to York and I went the other way—to Glasgow and out to the Clyde coast.

The torpedo school was in a delightful setting. The runways had been laid on a golf course; I bet that made a few golfers turn in their graves. It was right by the seashore, overlooking Arran some 15 miles across the water and dear old Ailsa Craig some 8 or 9 miles away to the south-west. Ailsa Craig seemed to be playing quite a part in my life; it had been the first sight of land on my first Hudson crossing. I wondered where Tug was these days. Part of the magnificent club house was the officers' mess, but I was not in there yet.

The next morning, it became obvious that we were in for a very hectic course. The course consisted of twelve crews and we immediately started with a lecture on the torpedo. We were shown drawings and cutaway diagrams showing the system of propulsion; the gyros and linkages; the warheads and detonators; and the depth control arrangement. Usually, there would be a 'contact pistol' in the nose for exploding against the side of the ship but 'magnetic heads' could be used for exploding under armoured ships. Then there were 'practice heads'—the sort we would be using here. Torpedoes would be set to pass under the target ship; then, at the end of their run, the head would blow and the torp float vertically in the water, its head just above the water level, so that it could be fished out, serviced and used again.

Time and time again, the cost of a torpedo was stressed. We were being entrusted with the most expensive single piece of ammunition in the services. A figure of £2,000 was mentioned and woe betide anyone who 'lost one'—either 1,650 lb or 2,127 lb of warhead and sophisticated machinery. For dropping from the air, a wooden 'air-tail' was fitted to steady and guide its drop down to the sea, where the tail would snap off; this seemed to be made of plywood, about 4 feet wide with a fin at each end. It was explained what happened when the torpedo left the aircraft: wires uncaged the gyros and activated the motor, which had a delay system so that the props did not start turning until in the water.

As for the inside of a Torbeau, the instructor explained:

> First there is the 'Torpedo Selector switch', that's on the right-hand window sill. A red light comes on when switched to 'Selected' and goes off when the torp is dropped. Always set this selector to 'On' for take-off so that, in an emergency, the torp can be immediately released but switch to 'Off' on reaching 1,000 feet so that it won't be dropped by mistake and leave at 'Off' until preparing for the attack. The Torpedo Release is the 'tit' in the end of that horizontal extension, like a cotton-reel, sticking out on the right at the top of the right-hand throttle. It's just right for pressing with your left-hand thumb as the two throttles nestle in the palm of your left hand. Pressing this release also operates two cameras, one in the nose and the other over your left shoulder, this takes a photo of the instrument panel at the time of the release, in particular the reading of the radio altimeter, the airspeed and the turn and bank indicator. The Torpedo Sight is that glass-like tube running horizontally across the bottom of the windscreen. A little light moves in this tube as you set the sight, this light should then be placed on the bow of the ship. The Sight Control is there, on the left side of the instrument panel, it jots the position of the light to take into account the direction the ship is going, its speed, length and angle of attack. The Torpedo 'Depth Indicator and Control' are on the floor, just in front of the Observer's seat. Finally, remember that if landing with a torp on, add 5 knots to your normal approach and landing speeds and, if you still have the torp on you will have to get out the same way as you got in, through the canopy above the pilot's seat, as you cannot use the bottom hatches with the torp in position.

What a belly-full for one day, trying to remember all that, no wonder we all got stuck into a few beers in the mess that night while we chewed over the day's events.

Day two was even more of a belly-full as we covered 'The Drop'. We were shown diagrams showing the correct angle at which the torpedo must enter the water, its oscillations in the vertical plane after it enters the water, large at first, progressively reducing, until it is running level at the pre-set depth. Then, we studied charts showing heights and airspeeds to achieve this correct entry angle. For the Beau, we were to work on an optimum height of 150 feet and airspeed between 190 and 200 knots. At the point of drop, however, not only had the height and speed to be right but the aircraft had to be perfectly level fore and aft and laterally and completely steady. There could be no skidding or slipping, otherwise the torpedo could dive straight down to the bottom; belly flop and break its back; cartwheel and go off the wrong way; or veer off in the wrong direction—in fact, do anything except what it should do.

> If you get all that lot right it is still vital to drop at the correct range; too near and it may not have settled at the correct depth and pass under the ship; too far and it could 'run out of steam' before it reaches the ship or give the ship time to take effective avoiding action. You will have to judge to drop at 1,000 yards. If you know the size and length of the ship you will have to be able to judge the distance, if you don't know this beforehand you will have to be able to estimate the range quickly—it may sound daft but the Queen Mary at over a mile could be mistaken for a cross channel ferry at 700 yards unless you know the outline of your target—we will give you some practice and tests on estimating distances by using slides.

It got even more confusing when the following was explained:

> You do not want to be at right angles to the ship but at right angles to its course some way ahead so that when the ship and torpedo meet it should strike at right angles and amidships, so, not only the angle but the speed of the ship must be estimated.

The use of the sight was explained and how to set it but it sounded as if you would have precious little time to do all this. By now, we were all getting a bit overwhelmed with data, especially when the instructor started talking about 'director angle intended', 'director angle used', 'hitting director angle', 'calculation error', 'sighting error', 'target turning towards', 'target turning away', 'hit −200', and 'miss +50'. I began to wish I had stuck to dropping depth charges or ferrying.

Anyway, we were not to be entrusted with proper torpedoes yet. Our first air work would be just using cameras, which would take pictures when we pressed the tit, these would be analysed and discussed with us. Firstly, they would be using a target ship maintaining a straight course, so as we progressed we would get used to coming in low at speed, pulling up and losing airspeed to make the 'drop' then getting away fast straight over the ship, then the ship will take evasive action and give us practice in 'sector positioning' and 'timing'; from there, we would move on to formation work, first in threes, then sixes and nines, and finally drop at least twelve actual torpedoes but the next stage was introduction to the TAT (torpedo attack trainer).

The TAT must have been the most advanced synthetic trainer of its day; it was a huge sphere with a Link Trainer stuck up on a stalk right in the middle of this great ball. Projected on the 'walls' of this sphere, by some ingenious system of lenses, was a life-like moving sea, a horizon all around, above which the most realistic sky, complete with clouds that could change from a murky, misty day to a clear sky with little tufts of white cumulus cloud. Projected on the sea were models of ships that increased in size as you 'approached' them; they could take avoiding action, and everything was to perfect scale. The Link had a torpedo sight and control; when you pressed the tit, a line of light moved along the sea to show the path of the torpedo, the ship continued to move, and you watched to see whether the line of light hit the ship. At this point, everything 'froze' and over the headphones you held a '*post-mortem*' with the instructor. The star instructor on this affair was said to be a WAAF officer whose avoiding action was legitimately 'spot on'.

Day three started with an hour on an ordinary Link Trainer doing beam landings, followed by sessions watching cine films of torpedo dropping, studying pictures taken by the nose camera at the time of dropping, as well as looking at slides of ships to estimate their approximate size, speed, range, and angle of approach. Then, by early evening, it was time for my first 'go' on the TAT; this was most absorbing, but at this stage, the 'ship' did not take any avoiding action and we just came in at a steady 150 feet.

Day four saw us take to the air for five short flights of between thirty and forty-five minutes. A Naval minesweeper was cooperating with us in the Firth—HMS *Heliopolis*. Two flights were standing behind an instructor, who demonstrated firstly 'height and range' and, later in the day, 'sector' (which meant getting in the correct sector to make the drop). Between these demonstrations, Douggie and I did a couple of camera runs just for 'height and range' and finally a camera run for 'height, range, and sector'. Straight after tea, it was an hour and a half on the TAT and, before going to bed, an hour with the instructor studying the photographs from the nose and cockpit cameras of my airborne efforts. They certainly did not waste any time on this course. The first effort was 1,600 yards range, 60 feet too low, nose 1 degree up but wings dead level; the second was 1,700 yards range, 40 feet too high, nose still 1 degree up and this time the left wing half a degree down. These were all plotted carefully on our personal chart. The instructor did not seem to think they were too bad. He said we had another ship—HMS *Malahne*—laid on for tomorrow, so we all ought to get in four or five exercises; my first would be at 9.30 a.m.

The weather around the Firth of Clyde was wonderful as we made our camera attacks on the *Malahne*. She did not take any avoiding action but varied her speed between 10 and 20 knots and we crept low round Ailsa Craig, trying to take her by surprise and get into the right 'sector'. We only managed three trips but the time between was taken up either on the Link or in the TAT where the instructor started taking avoiding action. After the evening meal, it was 'back to school' to study the day's photographs in conjunction with reports from the ship, plotting the results on our chart, finally arriving at whether the 'drop' would have been a hit or a miss and the hitting angle. One miss was 15 feet in front of the bow, one miss 35 feet in front of the bow, and one hit 150 feet aft of the bow. The following day, we had the *Heliopolis* again, and she would be doing runs up to 28 knots.

So, another day of camera attacks on the *Heliopolis* was followed by a day attacking HMS *Cardiff*, but now we were not coming all the way at 150 feet but right down on the water, pulling up to 150 feet, hoping to get everything settled at 1,000 yards, then right down to the water again and straight for the ship, showing as small a profile as possible and hopefully too low for the ship to depress its guns. Beforehand, we had to decide whether to pass below the stem (the most forward part of a boat or ship's bow), below the stern, or pull up over the funnel. All the time the ship would have its cine on us as practice for its gunners and on one trip, I gave myself a hell of a fright; passing under the stem, I thought we were going to ram each other as she was bearing down at 30 knots and if I had banked away and exposed my belly, the ship would have surely scored a 'hit'. Between flights, we had more sessions in the TAT, where, at last, I encountered this 'WAAF Wizard'.

She assured me that she was not making the ship do anything that a real ship could not do. You would spot this little ship on the horizon, perhaps nip up a bit to have a quick look to determine its direction, then hare off to get in the right sector, then she would 'see' you and commence a turn—maybe only a slow turn, but she would get you on the outside of the turn. You would realise that you were never going to get into a dropping position if you kept going that way so would try to sneak round to take her by surprise. The two of you could keep that up all day so you would hold off, reckoning that eventually the ship would resume course and try to be holding off in a suitable sector to catch her. Having played 'cat and mouse' for a while, you would feel confident you had 'got her' and drop the torp. Just as you did so, you could see the stern of the ship starting to slide and as the line of light moved along the 'sea' to show the track of the torpedo, the helm would start taking full effect and she would 'comb' the line of light, so that the torpedo would be washed to one side by the bow wave.

The photos showed that on the last two days of camera attacks, we had just over 50 per cent hits and had only been shot down twice. We did not know whether that was good or bad.

Now the ships were taking proper 'avoiding action', but we were still only using the cameras. You could bugger around all day trying to get into the ideal position, so you just had to make your mind up and go in, using any trick you could to avoid being spotted until the last minute—come out of the sun (if any), sneak around Ailsa Craig, or get a bit of land behind you so you might not be noticed. By now, it was getting rather an exciting game, but we knew that one day the target would not only be using cine guns on us, though we did not want to think about that.

We thought the CO was coming over to tell as we could have a day off but no such luck. He was coming to tell us that tomorrow we would start flying in formation—first in pairs, then threes and nines. We were paired up with another crew, reminded of the golden rule ('Never get lower than the leader'), and told that in the morning, we would each fly, standing behind an instructor, for an hour of 'formation attack demonstration', then we would take turns in being the leader. 'Now let's get along and check on today's photos'.

Then followed a couple of hectic days of 'FALTs' (formation camera attacks against moving targets), mainly against the *Heliopolis*, which seemed very manoeuvrable, and one against HMS *Ramillies* out in the Irish Sea. Being the leader was an easy job, except you took the blame if the attack was not made from the correct sector, but following the leader was bloody hard work—keeping an eye on him all the time, making sure you did not get below or lose him on a turn, then opening out enough as you went in for the drop so that, while you were concentrating on the height, speed, setting the sight, steadying and dropping, you did not bump into each other; then as you dived down again, at full power, heading for the ship, you did not touch each other or get him in your cannon sight (because in the real thing, you would then both be letting the cannons off). Maybe most important of all, you had decided at which point you would pass the ship because although there was only two of us now, eventually, in a full squadron attack, there may be nine Beaufighters converging on the ship from three different directions and if the timing was spot on, you would all arrive at the same time so; if you had not worked out who went stem, who went stern, and who went over the top, there could be a collision. When not flying it was still analysing photos and films, the Link Trainer or in the TAT.

The formations were now in threes, but we could only raise two lots of three plus one pair because four crews had quietly left the course (posted to a Beaufighter anti-flak Squadron, the ones who went in first with cannons to silence the 'flak ships'). The 'threes' were a bit more difficult to handle as when you slipped into 'line abreast', you had to remember that the chap on the inside of a turn had to slow up while the chap on the outside had to put on quite a bit more speed; you must also be a little above the leader and it could be fatal if someone lost sight of the next aircraft, so the leader had to appreciate the other chaps' problems. On some days, we had quite a bit of rain and low cloud, which helped as far as the element of surprise was concerned but made formation flying that more tiring. Most trips were only thirty to forty-five minutes.

At last, we had a day off. It was a lovely, cool, clear, sunny day too. I did not bother to go off the station. It was a most beautiful setting, right on the water's edge with lush green grass of the golf course between the runways and around the dispersals. Douggie and I spent the whole day on the beach, first writing letters, then throwing stones in the sea, walking along the beach, and clambering on rocks. It did not look far across the water to Arran and just to the left stood Ailsa Craig, a solid, immovable lump of rock. I told Douggie about the first trip Tug and I had across the Atlantic and how we made our landfall on that rock. There was a little movement of shipping in the Clyde—nothing very big and I thought of those convoys out in the Atlantic, heading for this river and wondered how things were going out in the Atlantic. I had heard that my old squadron were back in Northern Ireland now and that another Lib squadron had replaced them in Iceland. I hoped the Lib boys all had radio altimeters now, like the ones we had—what a godsend they would have been to us. I supposed they would have got the Mark III ASV by now. After our meal, we had three or four beers and turned in early—what a lot we seem to have crammed into the last couple of weeks.

It was back to work with a vengeance with some demonstrations on a blackboard about 'positioning and timing' for a squadron attack—three flights of three coming in on different sectors so that if the ship saw the flight coming in dead ahead and stayed on course in order to 'comb' those three torpedoes, both of the other two flights should score hits, even though they would not be at the optimum hitting angle. If the ship spotted one of the flights coming in on the bow and turned to 'comb' their torpedoes, this should present one of the other flights with hits at a good angle and the other with hits, although not at the best of angles. Provided the operation is properly coordinated and timed, at least three torpedoes out of the nine should score hits.

This business of 'positioning and timing' was to engross us for the rest of the course. The responsibility fell on the three leaders (the leader of the 'squadron' and the leaders of the other two 'flights'); the rest just had to follow, and we all took turns in the various positions. The leader of the squadron had to get the whole lot of us to a suitable position when he had spotted the target and observed which way it was moving; he would then send the other two flights off on headings, one flight maybe going nearly flat out and the other maybe doing an orbit at slow speed to take up time. This way, after a given number of seconds, all three flights were approaching the target on different sectors and, if all was perfect, all torps were dropped at the same time and the target was faced with Beaus converging on it from three different directions. We had four or five flights a day for the next eight days plus a daily session on the TAT, and we were beginning to get something like … This is where I found the TAT a great help—not particularly while I was 'in it' but sitting with the 'WAAF Wizard' watching her at work. Her plot showed the movement of the aircraft and she moved her little model ship which was projected on the 'wall'. By watching this you could picture where you should be sending the Flights – how far they would have to go in relation to each other, therefore who would have to travel like hell and who would have to 'lose' time and roughly how long was needed.

Now the 'FALTs' gave way to 'FARTs'—very appropriate but it meant 'formation attack with runner torpedo.' We had proper torpedoes but with practice heads, of course—the ones that blew off and floated at the end of their run. It was quite a thrill to see a torpedo with its big air-tail, slung under the Beau. It did not feel any different on take-off although lift off speed was about 5 knots higher. The main difference was that you had to climb in through the roof. We did everything just the same as when using the cameras only and I did not even feel the torp go; I was not sure whether it had actually gone until, when we were almost up to the ship, Douggie called to tell me he could see it running a long way behind us.

All our flights were in formation now, usually two a day using actual torps and another three with just the cameras. All the actual torps were dropped against the poor old *Heliopolis* or *Malahne* who had to scurry around fishing them out so that they could be refurbished for further use. A couple of 'special' attacks were laid on against HMS *Dido* and HMS *Royalist*, steaming up the Irish Sea, on joint exercises for us and their gunners. On the way, I thought, 'I hope to goodness they have been told this is only an exercise'. There were still plenty of *post-mortems* studying the photos, completing our individual charts and discussing the results of the attack as a whole, when, even your individual 'misses' or 'combed' may be regarded as satisfactory if they did their job by enabling one of the other flights to score hits. There was still more work in the Link and the TAT to make sure we were kept busy. We were also cutting down the seconds between aircraft taking off and landing so that we were formed up and away in the minimum of time; on return, we were following each other in very closely.

A couple of days before the full month was up, the CO announced that the following day, there would be two full-scale attacks, with torps; he would be flying himself to make up the nine. We would draw lots to decide which position we flew and that would be the end of the course. I drew to be No. 3 in one of the flights for the first exercise and to be a flight leader in the second.

It was a nice crisp March morning. We were all airborne in very quick time, three aircraft on the runway at a time, making a circuit at about

1,000 feet and we were all formed up. I was on the extreme starboard position. We went down to sea level and were belting across towards the Mull of Kintyre, keeping one eye on the aircraft on my left, with the other eye noticing the little island of Sanda coming up on my starboard and the tip of the Mull very rapidly approaching almost dead ahead. The leader called for a turn to port. I thought, 'Hope he throttles back a bit or I'll never get around here on the outside', but it was a very slow turn, taking us just over the coast of Antrim and with increased revs, plus a bit of throttle, I was able to keep position. Another turn then my flight was sent off 45 degrees to starboard, so, now being on the inside, I had to throttle right back. Now we were off again, like the clappers, for thirty-five seconds; we turned almost 90 degrees to port. I just managed to keep up and switch torp to 'select'. 'Right boys, open out, pull up'.

I swung out to starboard, 'There she is'. I pulled the throttle back and adjusted the sight. 'Looks about 15 knots—director angle about 15 degrees—come on, drop-down you bloody airspeed—height is OK—195 knots—that will do—a bit of throttle—range—that's it—away you go'. Now on full throttle, we were down to the sea again, going behind the stern, knowing we must leave room for Rod and Bertie. I glanced to port; there they were, so we could see each other; in a flash, we were past the ship. Three Beaus had cut across in front of us, but where were the other three? Anyway, we were clear now. We stayed low for a while, then pulled up to 1,000 feet and throttled back to cruising. We closed up, joining up with another flight; shortly after, the third flight joined us and we headed back over the airfield, peeling off and coming in in a continuous stream. We had only been up fifty minutes. The afternoon trip was very similar. At the *post-mortem*, reports from the ship showed that on the morning run, our flight all scored hits but, in the afternoon, all our three torps were combed. Anyway, the eight of us had passed out as Torbeau pilots, so that night, for the first time, we were able to have a thrash in the mess. Whether becoming a Torbeau crew was something to celebrate is a matter of some doubt, but anything was a good excuse for a booze up. We would not know what next until the morning.

Six crews were to go to Torbeau squadrons but neither myself nor one other pilot had yet quite completed our 'rest' period between Ops, so I was to go back to Melton Mowbray for a few weeks prior to joining a squadron. I had to smile at the idea of East Fortune and the torpedo school as being a 'rest'. I had never worked so hard in all my previous time in the services. Anyway, Douggie was to stay with me.

4
Morocco Again

Back at Melton Mowbray was almost like being on holiday—a rest from the concentration of formation flying, plenty of free time, leisurely chats with the ground crews, pleasant air checks and consumption tests (as long as we avoided firing ranges and other prohibited areas), and jovial nights in The Bell. There were some new faces and some of the other chaps we had got to know had moved on, but the most talked about 'new face' was the Beaufighter Mark X.

I did not think there were any production aircraft between the Mark VI and the Mark X, but the Mark X was a beauty. It had a new Bristol Hercules engine (a Mark XVII) producing 1,770 horsepower (340 more than in the previous Beaus), thus giving us 3,540 altogether, but the great thing was that it produced its maximum horsepower at low level, somewhere between 1,000 and 2,000 feet. This reduced the maximum ceiling considerably—from around 26,000 feet to 15,000 feet—but this did not matter to us as we were never likely to go above 3,000 feet anyway. She was about 1,000 lb heavier than the Mark VI, and the permissible loaded weight was increased from 21,600 lb to 25,200 lb.

She seemed to be the ultimate attacking weapon for low-level work, capable of being opened up to 300 knots straight and level at 1,300 feet and 345 knots in a shallow dive. She was a wonderful aeroplane, one which felt so much a 'part of you' when you took to the air. Settling in the seat of a Beaufighter felt somehow like slipping into a comfy, well-worn, tweed sports jacket—you felt to be 'putting it on'. You and the aircraft seemed to become one. Perhaps it was because you were sitting right up in the nose, in the middle, with everything arranged around you.

I never quite got this feeling in any other aircraft. We had confidence in each other; I would find myself talking to her and giving her a pat on the bottom when I got out, even though sometimes I had to pee against her tailwheel. This Mark X baby really gave you a kick in the backside when you eased the throttles through the 'gate' on take-off and the fin area had been increased a bit to help counter the increased torque, but I was always ready to bring one throttle back on take-off if the other engine failed; otherwise, she would have probably flipped over on her back but those Hercules engines were lovely, smooth movers.

After about ten days, Douggie and I handed over our Mark X in Rabat and even though we cut a fair few miles off the trip by not going so far out crossing the Bay (as there was some very convenient cloud cover), we still did not better the time of our first trip. We spent a couple of days enjoying the sunshine, then another direct flight back to Whitchurch in a blacked-out Dak. Gosh, those things sounded so underpowered and you did not have a clue where you were.

Peggy came down for a weekend at The Bell. I was free practically all the time and spring had arrived; the daffodils were out, hedges showing signs of green, and the evenings were light. Peggy met some of the lads and we had a nice room, making it a lovely weekend. Little did I know that I would be at home in a matter of a few days.

Douggie and I were given a new Mark X. On the first test, we were back on the ground within ten minutes. The port engine would not give anything like full power, so I called the tower to tell them I was coming in but the R/T box went up in a puff of smoke. With no intercom either, I made a steep approach and came in. Douggie told me his W/T had packed-up as well, although it was OK when he did a ground check before take-off. The mechanics and electricians worked on her for a couple of days. Everything seemed OK on the ground, so we had another go. The engine was perfect, with all dials where they should be, so off we set for the spot where we could cross the coast, then headed north, working my way down the checklist, checking this and that.

I told Douggie that we would head for a spot on the coast just north of Scarborough, and he gave me a course. We were nicely converging with the coast and could see Scarborough Castle on the port, then Douggie popped up on the intercom. 'What's that smoke behind you?' I looked outside to port and starboard but could not see anything. 'What smoke?' I asked. 'That smoke behind your seat on the starboard side.' As I turned to look around, I not only saw it, but I smelt its choking fumes.

Switching the generator off and swinging her around to port, I told Douggie, 'Right we are off to York.' Maybe Driffield or Leconfield would have been fractionally nearer, but there was not time to bugger about with maps. I knew my way to York and I knew where the airfield was; they flew Halifaxes off there so it would be OK for a Beau. Although I had switched the generator off, these acrid fumes and the smoke seemed to increase. The normal draught in the aircraft was carrying the worst of the fumes back to poor old Douggie, so I told him to come forward and stand behind me 'but don't touch that electrical stuff'.

I called York on the radio frequency 116.1, telling them I was making an emergency straight-in approach but I hardly expected a reply, as only being a maintenance unit, the chap in the tower would probably be away having a cup of tea. I repeated the message twice and then left it but, to my surprise, after about a minute, an Australian accent came on the air with a string of 'Rogers' and even gave me the runway heading—no altimeter setting or anything like that, but it did not matter in the circumstances. By now, I had opened the motors to damn near flat out, figuring that as I had switched the generator off, I would not be pushing any more current into the circuits and the sooner we got to York the better. Douggie was now standing behind me with his chin resting on my shoulder, so I opened one of the 'clear vision' panels, which let a hell of a jet of fresh air in, though with our masks on we now had no bother in breathing but what a relief it was to get some fresh air. The only problem was that my eyes were all bleary; the fumes and now the wind were making them water and tickle. Twelve minutes after we first noticed the fumes, we were rolling down the York runway; before we came to rest, I reached up and released the top hatch and Douggie (almost knocking my head off) pushed it open.

I pulled off the runway onto the hard grass, cut both engines (wasn't going to wait for them to cool down), and in a flash we were both out through the top hatch and slithering down the wing. An officer and some erks (RAF name for aircraft men in the lower ranks) arrived in a truck at about the same time as the fire tender; I told them that the electric wiring was on fire, or at least melting, and I thought the battery had burst. I showed them how to open the bottom hatch from the outside and they drenched the inside with carbon dioxide. We were still both coughing a bit and my eyes were very sore and watery, so we were taken to the MO room to have our eyes washed out. Then, I got on the phone to Melton and explained to the engineering officer what had happened. He said he would get a 'lift up' and see me later. As it happened, he could not get up that day but would be up the next day. An officer started to apologise about the accommodation; he seemed relieved when I told him there was no need to worry as I only lived in Clifton and my observer could come with me. Peggy was a bit surprised when she came in from work to find the two of us waiting for her.

The next morning, Douggie and I walked up to the airfield; I wished my father had been there as I am sure he would have been interested to see my Beaufighter. My first call was at the control tower (or watch office, as they were called in those days) and to my surprise, there was the Australian 'voice' we heard on our R/T, who turned out to be a New Zealander, not an Australian. There, sitting on his knee, was the wife of one of the chaps I worked with before the war. They were having a real lovely-dovey session at 10 a.m. Anyway, when we got this chap's attention, he informed us that the aircraft bringing the engineering officer from Melton would arrive in about ten minutes.

We spent the day with our engineering officer and a flight sergeant he had brought with him along with an officer from the local unit. The local lads had done what they could to neutralise the spillage from the accumulators, which had spread over quite an area and they had got down to sorting out the trouble. Yards and yards of burnt wiring were ripped out; there seemed to be bloody miles of it and towards teatime, they seemed to have traced the seat of the trouble. It seemed that in addition to the normal generator on the starboard engine (which supplied the whole of the 24-volt system), there was also an 80-volt alternator on the port engine for supplying 'special equipment', such as various forms of radar. I do not think they knew that that alternator was there—I certainly did not—and as far as I could gather, the wires from this alternator had, somehow, been connected, somewhere or other, into the normal wiring circuit. By the end of the day, the three of them seemed to have decided on rewiring and the officer from the local MU said they had all the gear for doing it so. My little Beaufighter was taken into a hangar next to a Halifax, which was being assembled, and they got to work. Our engineering officer and flight sergeant were to supervise the work and the engineering officer said that I may as well push off home and come back the day after tomorrow to see how things were going.

So it was to be another couple of nights at home, at least. Peggy was working, so during the day Douggie and I took my dog for walks by the river and in the evenings, we visited local hostelries, meeting Peggy's friends, along with her uncle Tommy and auntie Muriel. We wore 'civvies' as we only had our scruffy flying gear with us. I found Douggie a jacket and pair of flannels that more or less fitted. There was the odd comment in one place about us not being in the forces from some RAF types and when Peggy told them we were in Coastal Command, it brought a sarcastic remark about Coastal, which we ignored. I thought, at least we did not blab our mouths off like some of them did, and if Peggy believed that Coastal was a 'cushy job', so much the better. However, I wondered what they would have thought on the torpedo course.

The engineering officer seemed pleased with progress, telling us that she should be OK to fly the next day, but back at Melton, they would probably fit a new fuselage and a stern frame before she was cleared for Ops. He said he would fly back with us, so I thought that was a good sign; he would not do that unless he felt she was safe.

Four days after we arrived, we took off to return to Melton. There was not much point in doing an air test as the flight would only take about forty minutes; in any case, there was nothing wrong with the engines. So, with the engineering officer and flight sergeant standing behind me and Douggie in the back, I flew down to Melton, not doing any drastic manoeuvres; it took just forty-five minutes.

On arrival, I was told to report immediately to the CO. After a few remarks about me having had a few days at home, he held out his hand and said, 'I'll see you in the officers' mess for dinner, your Commission has just come through, congratulations.' I was a bit nonplussed. This meant I could not eat with Douggie. We were to be separated, so we could not eat or drink in the same mess and would only see each other 'on duty' or when off the station. We would travel in different 'classes' on trains and would have to salute each other. I had always 'lived' with my crew—whether we were two, three, or seven—and now I was to be detached. I was quite happy as a warrant officer. If I had been commissioned straight from getting my wings, it would have been different, but now, after all this time, from being a respected warrant officer, king in the sergeants' mess, I was to be a mere pilot officer, the lowest rank in the officers' mess, the same rank as 'wet-ears' straight from training school; in fact, I did not think there was anyone as low as pilot officer on the station. I was not at all excited.

However, the chaps in the officers' mess were all very friendly; I knew them all anyway. The meal was certainly a cut above that in the sergeants' mess and the CO made a little speech welcoming me, saying that they did not often have the privilege of welcoming an ex-warrant officer and some joke about me still having the warrant officers' coat of arms on my sleeve, so they had better watch out.

Over the next couple of days, it was a matter of sorting out the payment of my pay into the bank; memorising a new number (no longer 1064014 but 173638); visiting a bespoke tailor for a hat and odds and ends, but I only needed the WO's badge replacing by a thin pilot officer's band on my uniform and did not bother with a greatcoat at this stage as summer was coming on (my battledress only needed the rank changing) and I was keen to keep the unfaded marks of my sergeant's stripes and the slightly less unfaded marks of the WO's badge on the sleeve. The lads soon poured beer in my new hat, so I soon knocked it around a bit by taking out the stiffening ring and walked under the oily underside of a Beau's wing to make it look as if it had seen a bit of service and I had to buy another one for 'best'.

I had just been given another Mark X Beau and had done the initial air test and one consumption test when I was posted to the Torbeau squadron of the East Coast strike wing. Douggie and I had a farewell night with the lads in The Bell, and then it was off to the Lincolnshire coast on a right roundabout train journey, ending in a bloody long wait for someone to collect us from the nearest station.

5

North Sea Capers

What a diabolical place; it seemed like the end of the earth—what a contrast to the beautiful Clyde coast. The surrounding countryside as flat as a pancake—not a tree in sight, just deep ditches and beyond an embankment, at the edge of the airfield, was supposed to be the sea. At the foot of the embankment were coils and coils of barbed wire. The tide was so far out that you could not see any water, just miles and miles of mucky-looking sand and silt with lots of stakes sticking up, which were presumably driven in to prevent enemy gliders from landing; it was probably also mined. Nearer in, this mucky-looking stuff was pockmarked with tufts of brown grass or weeds, making it more like a marsh than a beach. Even the grass on the embankment looked scruffy. Here and there were concrete pillboxes. To the north side of the runway were a collection of buildings, dominated by a water tower, while all round the perimeter were 'dispersals' full of Beaufighters and nearby, grass humps over ammunition stores. The only good thing I could see about the place was the fact that there were virtually no obstructions around but I thought this must be a place that will be pretty high on Jerry's list of 'military targets' and it should be fairly easy for him to come in low to avoid detection, drop his load, and be off, so let us hope they have better defences than we had when York was bombed.

However, in spite of the awful surroundings they seemed to be a good, cheerful, and friendly bunch of lads and, in spite of my lowly rank of pilot officer, they made me very welcome in the mess, although I was sorry that Douggie could not be in there too.

I still had not become used to suddenly becoming 'an officer and a temporary gentleman'.

The next morning, I officially met the CO of the squadron, a wing commander who had his own observer and actually flew regularly himself, always leading the squadron if it was to be a full squadron operation. He looked at my chart (showing the results of all my practice camera and running torpedo attacks), grunted, and nodded, then thumbed through my logbook, asking a few questions about the Ferry Command job and about my Liberator trips, especially in the Arctic, then asked why I had decided to come on Torbeaus; the only answer I could think of was that I did not fancy becoming an instructor.

He then took me next door to see another wing commander; this one was, according to the notice on his door, 'wing commander—flying'. It transpired that his job was to relieve the station commander of all matters related to 'flying'. It was technically a ground job. He was not actually on any of the three squadrons but he had his own observer; they flew regularly and it seemed that when there was a full turnout, he led the wing. He seemed a good, down-to-earth bloke with bags of torpedo-dropping experience, starting with 'Swordfish' before the war.

After a brief explanation of the set-up (the wing comprised three Beau squadrons, the 'anti–flak' squadrons equipped with cannons and rockets, and my squadron, the Torbeaus), he told me that we always drop at 100 feet and 180 knots and that most drops will be off the Dutch coast, pointing out Borkum, Ameland, Terschelling, Vlieland, Texel, and Den Helder on the wall map, which also showed the known Ack-Ack positions on these islands. The object of the other two squadrons was to engage the 'Flak ships' or AA guns while we went in to make our drops. Then, remarking that he saw that I had already flown a Mark X, said that after lunch, we would spend an hour in the air together, do a bit of work on the range, and be allocated an aircraft.

Each cannon had its full belt of 240 shells, and with the camera loaded, I took off almost alongside him as he pointedly pulled right onto one side of the runway. For twenty minutes or so, I stuck close by him, very slightly above, as we flew very low over the sea and implemented numerous turns. I had no idea where we were as I was watching him all the time, then he pulled up, told me to open out, and pointed out the firing range. I could see we were south of the airfield. He pointed out the targets, then told me to take the lead and do some short runs, so I went down and around, up a bit, making a shallow dive and in to the target. Douggie told me he was right beside me. Those juddering cannons really ripped the water and mud apart, then after four runs, he told me to do a camera drop on one of the targets; it was not moving of course, so it made setting the sight easy. I pulled up a bit too early, so had to be a 'sitting duck' at 100 feet for a second or two too longer than ideal, but I got it a bit better the second time. 'OK, let's go home at 1,000 feet. Have a look round to familiarise yourself with the area'. I saw a lake a couple of miles or so south of the airfield, then two ugly looking brick forts just to the north, one barely surrounded by water; the lighthouse of Spurn Head to the north-east. Then, he took the lead and we made a rapid approach; I landed as close behind him as I could. He did not say much, except that I went up too soon on the first drop and he ran over the signals we should give each other when about to make a turn.

That night, I wrote to Peggy but I did not tell her where I was. I did not want her to worry; someone may tell her what we did here. I wrote as if I were still at Melton Mowbray. I knew the letters would be forwarded on. I could never understand chaps wanting their wives with them on an operational station.

The next day, we did couple of two-hour practice flights with two other crews, the three of us were to be one of the squadron 'flights'. One was a flight lieutenant on his second tour, the first having been on torpedo Beauforts; the other was a flying officer who had been on this squadron about a month—both grand chaps and bloody good flyers, Tony and Dick. We flew damned low, in Vic formation, in echelon and line abreast, then did some firing on the targets using the cine gun and a few practice drops. Tony and Dick took turns at leading but I was always No. 3.

Then, I was given an air test to do, which gave me chance to have a look around and memorise some landmarks instead of just having to keep my eyes on another Beau. The atmosphere in the crew room was first-class but such a contrast to the Lib squadron; there seemed to be so many crews around, but I felt very much the 'new boy' (especially as a pilot officer). If I had still been a warrant officer, at least the other lads would have known that I had 'seen a bit of service'. I discovered that the wing had been formed about eighteen months ago, and its first success against shipping was about a year ago. They had had considerable success but not without losses; officially, one of the squadrons carried bombs but for quite a while, they had been using rockets instead.

I was beginning to feel a bit apprehensive; had I done the right thing? I could possibly be starting my second tour on Libs right now. I was socially segregated from Douggie. The lads seemed nice enough but it was a bloody awful place. I phoned Douggie at the mess and we decided to go for a walk and find the pub. Walking up the lane from the airfield, Douggie and I talked about an armoured door we had noticed in these Beaufighters behind the pilot. Although they would give the pilot some protection in the event of an attack from the rear, I did not fancy cutting myself off from Douggie by a thick metal door; it would mean that, if the intercom packed up, I would be unable to make any signals to him and if he went quiet, I would not be able to crane my neck round to see what had happened to him. It transpired that Douggie had similar feelings about the door; he did not fancy not being able to see me and I appreciated that it would be worse for the poor observer if he could not see the pilot's head and shoulders and at least know you were still there and in control.

I had nothing but admiration for observers in Beaufighters—putting themselves at risk with a pilot they knew nothing about and having to stick with him however he turned out, but above all, there was not a damn thing they could do if the pilot got knocked out and on our job, we were too low to bail out. Yet, I never heard an observer complain about his pilot; they all maintained that they had the best pilot on the squadron—a Beau crew really knew the meaning of comradeship. By the time we got to the end of this rather uninteresting lane, we had mutually agreed that we would leave the armoured door fastened back in the open position and that we always did. The lane merged into a narrow public road in a couple of hundred yards, and just around a slight bend, there, on the left-hand side surrounded by green fields, was the pub The Fleece. The first door led to a bar seething with RAF chaps so we tried the second door; this was a little less crowded and, eventually, we managed to get a couple of pints.

Douggie and I were soon joined up with several other crews—a lively, friendly lot—and, as new boys, they would not let us buy the beer, telling us that they would make sure they got it back after our first Op. Douggie made sure they knew that I had been a warrant officer and when one of them asked about my first 'tour', he reckoned he 'would have been bloody scared taking a U-boat on in the middle of the Atlantic as there would be no one to pick you up out there, whereas here you at least have a chance of pranging on one of the islands or getting picked up'. I think he was just trying to be cheerful. After a considerable number of beers, it was back down the lane—some on bikes, some walking, but nearly all singing. I felt a lot better after that night out, but I wished we could get on an Op pretty soon, then we would know what it was all about.

We did not have long to wait. It was not a full strike—merely Tony, Dick, and I on a reconnaissance/patrol along the Frisian Islands. Tony talked about these islands as if they were his own 'backyard'; he seemed to know where every gun was and exactly where ships may be, although, at briefing, we were told there was no intelligence about any movements. He told me briefly:

> 1,000 feet in echelon to start with, dropping to 10 or 15 feet as we get within radar range; no need to formate very close to start with; no R/T unless I break it for an attack or we are jumped; Observer is to keep an Air Plot in case you have to come home on your own but his main job is to look out for 'bogeys'; do a one-second burst with the cannons to check them.

I knew this was just a routine patrol—the sort of thing that lads from all three squadrons did almost every day—but it would be the first time I had had a proper explosive warhead on my torp and a full load of cannon shells. As the six of us were driven to dispersal, Tony, Dick, and their observers were speculating as to whether The Fleece would have any beer tonight, as it seemed they ran short two or three times a week. I felt as if I was going to the dentist; it would be nice when it was over. In quick time, we had the engines going, ran up, and followed each other out. Tony carried on a little way inland before commencing his turn so that Dick and I could slip into place as he came around and, in no time, we were the three black dots disappearing into the East. We had watched those dots for several days and wondered when it would be our turn.

What funny weather—it was influenced by a 'high'. There was not a breath of wind and the sea was flat calm, so I spaced myself from Dick at about the same distance as he was from Tony. We were not very close, so I was able to look around a bit. Douggie had loaded the cannons and set them to fire so I let off a short burst. We were now getting quite low and it was very hazy. The haze seemed to get thicker; however, for brief moments, the sun seemed to be trying to break through, yet there was no horizon and the sea was so smooth that I kept hoping that Tony did not fly into it. I made sure to keep a fraction higher than Dick. It was a funny feeling, belting along in this haze, with visibility less than 1,000 yards. There would be no chance of dropping a torp in this. Dick waggled his wings and we commenced a slow turn; I had no idea where we were and this slow turn continued a long time till we were heading almost south-west.

Then, suddenly, I realised we were going up a fraction and some flat land flashed under us in the haze. A weak sun broke through the haze and I could not see a bloody thing, except Dick. Good job I could still see him as we turned gently to starboard, then to port, and I got the impression we were flying a zig-zag course.

Twice more we flashed over low, flat land, but it was still very hazy and Douggie told me that we were now averaging a course that was almost due south and he reckoned we were south of Den Helder. After a while, we did a gradual turn to starboard through more than 180 degrees, along with a few little turns, then Dick signalled that we were going up and indicated 'cannons'. I adjusted the intensity of the cannon sight, slipped my thumb under the spring-loaded safety flap on the firing button, and waited.

Through the haze, some land loomed up, we did a rapid turn which made my heart miss a beat, then bore down on what seemed to be a square compound. I yanked the stick to bring the sight just short of the square and pressed the firing button with all my might. I saw turmoil in and around this square and edged away from where I knew Dick would be as we levelled out at ground level. I then saw him and tried like hell to close with him as he was turning away to port. I followed him around; we were over the sea again. I adjusted the revs so as not to overtake him, got settled down, and Douggie told me we were heading west—we were on our way home. I told Douggie to keep his eyes peeled aft, as they would know we are around now. Soon, the haze had almost cleared and the sun had broken through; I reminded Douggie to still keep looking out, then the low outline of Spurn Head came into view and in no time we were closing up a bit to fly over the airfield (just to show off) and following each other down the runway. We had been away about four and a half hours—only four and a half hours, but I felt knackered—hand-flying all the time, keeping an eye glued on Dick's aircraft and looking into that funny haze. With still having the torp on, we had to climb out through the roof and I was as stiff as 'old Harry' and bursting for a pee.

On the drive over to debriefing, Tony seemed satisfied with our performance but was cursing the weather, saying we couldn't do anything in that visibility and the only reason why we let off a few rounds at that gun position was that it would 'keep them on edge' knowing we were around, as they would not hear us coming and soon lose us in the haze. I asked how the hell he found it as the bits of land we passed over were absolutely featureless. He obviously knew the area very well. It was the oddest Op I had been on—not knowing exactly where we were, just following another aircraft all the time and making sure I did not lose them; I was not worried about finding the way home but I would have hated to have lost them on my first trip and arrived back on my own.

Next came a couple of days hanging around the crew room, an air test, a session on the firing range, plus supervising a compass swing and helping with a cannon alignment so that the shells and the gunsight met in a 'cone' 300 yards ahead, then it was time for another recce/patrol.

This time, the weather was more normal, with plenty of cloud at 2,000–3,000 feet, patches of rain but the visibility was quite good so keeping position was much less of a strain. Yet, the sea looked drab and miserable, either a mucky grey or brown, so different from the big rollers of the Atlantic or the deep blue of the Arctic, just a lumpy, dismal, grey. Then it was the same routine as before, up and down off the Frisian Islands at about 15 feet, but we did not go over any land this time, although sometimes it was not far away. We did not see a thing. Dick took over the lead on the way home as we switched to Vic formation, but Tony slid into the lead as we approached the airfield to lead us over in echelon before peeling off for the landing. What amazed me most was that we could be so near the coast for so long without them sending any fighters after us; perhaps, if they knew there was no shipping about, they did not bother. That night in The Fleece, Douggie and I had to buy the drinks; we were very pleased to do so. The place was beginning to seem a bit better but we would be glad when we had a proper 'strike' behind us.

It was to be third time lucky on another recce/patrol with a very early take-off, almost before first light. A chilly morning with a bit of a mist on the ground, we had to keep our navigational lights on for the first few minutes so that we could see each other. It only seemed to be getting properly light an hour later as we neared the coast, the R/T sprung to life, Tony had pulled up a bit and announced, 'Cannon attack on an E-boat'. We wheeled round, still climbing, levelled out and there ahead was this little boat going like the clappers, presumably hoping to make Den Helder after a night sortie. With the gunsight already in position, and thumb under the safety flap, we started our dive. She was starting a fast turn, so I had to bank and press the tit. The water leapt up in white columns and frothed as our twelve cannons ripped the sea apart. I eased back on the wheel to try and make my splashes bisect the boat but could hardly see the boat for white spray.

She flashed underneath as I levelled out and eased to starboard, away from Dick, who I knew would be almost rubbing shoulders with me on the port side. As we scurried away at 15 feet or thereabouts, I saw Dick, then Tony came on the R/T telling Dick and I to turn starboard for another attack while he went around the other way. So around we went, up to about 600 feet and there she was, still floating but she seemed to have stopped. Opening up at about 800 yards in a 20-degree dive, the line of splashes crept up to the boat. Some tracer was coming the other way, then there was a blinding flash and I heaved her away to starboard, in case the boat blew up underneath me; as I did so, Tony flashed across just above me. Which one of us actually caused the damage I had no idea, but as Tony said on the R/T, 'We must have hit one of his torpedoes—either of you any damage?' When we both reported OK, he asked how much ammo we had left; Douggie checked and reckoned we only had enough for a couple of seconds of burst and Dick had none at all, so Tony decided we would, 'Go for an early breakfast'. I pondered that if that is what happened when cannon shells hit a torpedo, I was sitting on top of one.

6

The Full Wing in Action

'All personnel are to stand by until further notice', so spoke the Tannoy, repeating the message for good measure. A ripple of excitement ran around the crew room and Dick remarked, 'It looks as if there's a Strike in the offering, so it's no ale tonight'. In the mess anteroom, word got around that 'Intelligence had some 'gen' on a convoy, expected to be off Terschelling shortly after dawn, the Wingcos are down at Intelligence now'. We took dinner early as we could not spend the usual half hour having pre-dinner drinks, even though the two Wingcos were not there. I thought of the words of that guy who checked me out on Libs at Dorval, 'You know what to do, now let's see if you can put it all together'. I should soon know whether I can hit a ship with a proper torpedo. The Wingcos appeared; among ourselves, we referred to the Wingco Flying as Tony (same as the flight lieutenant who led my flight) and the one who was CO of my squadron as Paddy. Tony confirmed that a strike was on—a full turnout with nine Torbeaus. The weather was OK, so briefing would be at 3 a.m. with breakfast laid on for 2.30 a.m. I chatted to Tony (not the Wingco) and Dick for a while, then we pushed off to our rooms for a bit of sleep but I only dozed a bit. Fortunately, I was 100 per cent happy with the Beaufighter, and the one I had was a cracker, so the actual flying was more or less automatic but I kept going over the dropping routine as I must not let the squadron—or more importantly, Tony and Dick—down on my first drop. I wondered if Douggie was OK; I wished he were in the same mess.

The briefing was such a contrast to a Lib briefing. Not just one crew getting the undivided attention of the briefing and Met officers but a room chock-a-block with pilots and observers, about sixty of us. Some had grabbed a chair, others found a form, and the rest had to stand. With the aid of a map and a blackboard, the Wingco Flying showed us the anticipated track of the convoy (I wondered where it had come from and where it was going, as to me it seemed bloody silly to send stuff by sea as it looked as if it would be safer to send things between Denmark and Holland overland) and told us its composition (I wondered how we knew this, was it from photographic reconnaissance (PR), the 'underground', or from interception of signals).

It was only a small convoy by comparison with an Atlantic convoy, but there were three 'flak ships' that would look like trawlers with platforms fore and aft mounting rapid fire anti-aircraft (AA) guns, a tanker that would probably be in the middle, three other vessels, and two minesweepers. He ran over the routine: all squadrons would form up over the airfield, then formate as a wing at 1,500 feet. He would be leading and descend gradually to 15 feet with R/T silence all the way in. Two squadrons to lead with cannon attacks on 'Flak ship' gun platforms, followed by rocket attacks. The speed of the convoy was believed to be about 12 knots. Then, our squadron Wingco took over. He did not expect the convoy to be able to take violent avoiding action, so each flight would take one ship. We were allocated the largest merchant ship, and the Wingco's flight would take the tanker. The names of the flight leaders and flight codenames were read out. We synchronised our watches and take-off time was given. A few questions were asked, mainly about direction of attack in view of the sun, if any, being almost due east.

With the briefing over, we piled into the trucks, which dropped us off at our aircraft. On the way, I checked that I had my sheath knife tucked down my flying boot (in case the dinghy inflated by mistake) and Peggy's St Christopher in my breast pocket. It was just getting light, with quite a nip in the air. Our three Beaus were parked together; just over half an hour to take-off, we were to be the last flight off so that meant I will be the very last, but if all went smoothly, we would all be off within five or six minutes.

Tony, Dick, and I had a little chat; I then had a walk around the aircraft, had a look at the torp, made sure the air-tail looked OK, that the wires had all been connected, and that it was firmly in place; that stranded wire holding it up never looked very strong considering the weight it is supporting but it must have been. The ground crew told me the engines were run-up about an hour ago and the tanks topped up. Douggie was OK and the ground crew had put my parachute in my seat, so I tied up the tapes on my Mae West while Douggie went up the ladder onto the wing and dropped in through the roof hatch. I followed him and we checked up on the ammo and the torp depth setting before he went to the back. I checked that the armoured door was fastened open then settled myself in my seat. It was a bit early to start the engines yet; we had to remember not to let them idle below 1,000 revs or the plugs might oil up and that would be a real 'black'. It was getting lighter now and we could see clearly across the airfield. I looked at my watch. I reckoned it would be about five minutes before we started the engines; I would keep an eye on Tony and start up when he did. Sitting there waiting in this silent aircraft, except for checking the intercom with Douggie, I reckoned that, instead of my heart pumping all the blood around my body in one minute, it was doing a full circuit in about thirty seconds. I was partly scared but mainly I did not want to let the squadron down. I remembered that guy who said 'Let's put it all together'.

Tony was signalling to his ground crew, so I did the same. The trolley acc. was already plugged in. His prop was starting to turn (as we had already had them turned around by hand) so I went into the starting routine. Soon, they were both going and as the Beau had come to life instead of being just an inanimate lump of metal, I felt a lot better. The Beau's heart had started to beat; I had something to do now. Those engines sounded beautiful and when they had warmed up for the run-up, it was like bringing a full symphony orchestra into action. Everything was running fine. I checked the mags for a third time to keep myself busy while the ground crew held up the undercarriage locking pins to show me that they had been removed. I looked at my watch—three minutes before the first one takes off. Tony waved his chocks away so I did the same. In a few seconds, Tony began to roll; Dick followed him and I tagged along behind. We had a fair way to taxi from the dispersal on the south side of the field. As we slowly moved along the perimeter, the first aircraft were taking off and I automatically went through the pre-take-off checks:

Hydraulic power line: ON
Trim: Elevator at 'take-off'
Rudder at 'neutral'
Aileron at 'neutral'

Pitch: fully forward
Throttle: tension nut OK
Fuel: Cocks to 'Inner'
Suction balance: OFF
Flaps: 15 degrees
Gills: third open
Supercharger: low gear
Carb. Intake: 'Cold'
Torp: Selector ON

Aircraft were taking off in a continuous stream. We stopped just before the runway so I opened the engines up against the brakes to check they were responding OK and evenly, set the gyro to the runway heading, and caged it. We were rolling again; Tony followed another Beau onto the runway, with Dick and I following. We uncaged the gyro and were on our way. The reassuring kick in the back as the throttles went through the 'cruising gate' came, and after a bit of rudder to keep her straight, in no time, I was raising the flaps at 300 feet, keeping the power on a bit longer to take up position on Tony as he was turning away from me.

The three of us were soon in Vic formation, with Tony in the lead, Dick on his port, and myself on the starboard. Torp selector switched 'off', I just followed Tony, with no eyes for anything else. We seemed to be doing a very gentle long turn to port; following a hand signal from Tony, there was a short turn to starboard and we straightened out. I was overshooting a bit so cut back the revs and realised we were on our way. Settled down at a reasonable distance from Tony, I had the chance to take a quick look around—the other two squadrons were just ahead of us, making for a most impressive sight, with all those lovely Beaufighters in little groups of three going ahead so that in theory at any rate, we could drop our torps unmolested. Somebody was in for a surprise with all those cannons and rockets, plus some machine guns. I was on the extreme starboard side of our squadron—the Wingco with his other two were in the middle, our flight was on his starboard, and the other flight was on his port, like a big 'V' composed of three little 'V's.

I thought of the violent manoeuvres we got ourselves into at Turnberry in order to get ourselves into the correct dropping position, especially if the ship was taking avoiding action. There were only three of us then, except on the last two exercises, and I thought that these Wingcos must be bloody good if they could position all this lot of aircraft without bumping into each other. Douggie had loaded the cannons and set them to fire; it must have been a bit boring for him as he had no navigation to do, just try to keep an 'air plot' going when there were not enough 'white caps' on the sea for him to get any drifts on the drift recorder so he was just keeping a lookout.

We were down to about 250 feet now. I checked my fuel as I had gone on to the outer tanks shortly after take-off (three small coupled tanks on each side holding 140 gallons on the port side and 161 on the starboard), as I liked to empty these tanks first and get the weight nearer the middle as I reckoned it handled slightly better then, but other chaps had different ideas and liked to get the fuel further away from them. I would swap over to the main inner tanks before the attack to make sure I was not going to have a tank run dry if we had to run at full power for any length of time. I switched the radio altimeter on; it was just beginning to register. I could not do much with the torpedo sight yet as I did not know from which side of the convoy we would be making the attack and consequently which way the ship would be travelling, nor did I know the angle of attack until the last minute. Anyway, I set the ship speed at 12 knots provisionally and checked that the light was working. Now we had got really low, with the mucky, grey sea flashing underneath in a blur. Douggie told me he reckoned another fifteen minutes should see us there. I went over to the inner tanks and made damned sure I did not get below Tony.

I was just telling Douggie, 'This seems a bloody long fifteen minutes' when Tony signalled a starboard turn; I hated these starboard turns at sea level when you were on the starboard side as it was so easy to lose the leader under your wing. I brought the revs back and just managed to keep him in sight, then we straightened out after about 90 degrees and I had to catch up. I noticed the other chaps were still ahead of us. We seemed to stay on this course for several minutes, then turned to port when we three had to open up like hell; being on the starboard side with Joe Muggins on the extreme starboard, I was almost at full boost and revs. We then had to throttle right back as we straightened out. I could not see any others in front of us; I thought, 'where the hell have they gone?'

It dawned on me that we were about to make the run-in. Tony gave me the signal to open out, so I switched the Torp selector on and glanced at the red light, then took a quick look to port. I was about 75 yards off Tony; that would do, giving us a bit of room. Then ahead, just sitting on the horizon, were some ships with barrage balloons flying. We were on the starboard so ours must have been the right-hand one of the three biggest ones. We set sight on the ship travelling left to right; the sector angle looked perfect, say 8 degrees, leaving speed at 12 knots.

We were approaching bloody fast—where the hell were the others? I pulled the throttles right back and gradually went into fine pitch to slow us down and at the precise instant that I pulled back to bring us up to 100 feet, I saw black spots swarm around the ships and all hell broke loose—splashes in the water, white rocket trails, red flashes, and black smoke. I almost forgot what I was doing but placed the light on the bow of the ship, with my hand on the throttles, then opened them a bit. She was all level, with speed and height OK. I pressed my left thumb on the torp release, opened the throttles, and dived for the sea.

There was all hell going on ahead, with Beaufighters wheeling around white rocket trails, bloody great columns of water, and what seemed like a great ball of steam. I shot across in front of the bow, leaving plenty of room in case Tony was coming along my side as well in view of the barrage balloon amidships; a column of water from somebody's cannon or rockets splashed us. I fired the cannons as we went by, but they did not do any good. I could not get the sight to beam on anything but sea. Our torps would be following us. I felt sure mine would hit but I was not going to hang around; it was too bloody dangerous with all these Beaufighters letting off cannons and rockets, so I carried on a good distance at sea level, then nipped up a bit and spotted Tony. I slowly closed with him and we did a slow port turn up at about 100 feet.

We looked to port and could see the tanker was enveloped in a huge pall of black smoke; our ship was on fire and giving off lots of smoke, while the third ship looked as if it was already sinking by the stern. We stayed at 100 feet and started to head for home. We saw a Beau, pouring black smoke, heading the other way, presumably heading to either bale out, or crash-land, on one of the islands—if he could make it. With all the organised chaos around us, I had not really realised that R/T silence had been broken for brief messages between flight leaders; someone was reporting a duff engine, then a voice that sounded to be American broke in—our top cover had arrived.

We were on our way home when Douggie said there were several columns of smoke receding on the horizon; we had a little relieved chat on the intercom. 'What did you think to that?' I asked. 'Happen

I wouldn't like to have been on those ships, bloody hell, it was scary enough up here,' he replied. 'I was a bit surprised to see those balloons, dead giveaway those were, could see them before I saw a ship'. To this, Douggie replied, 'Happen they are to stop the ships sinking'. 'Don't un-cock the cannons yet, in case we need them'. Douggie then said he could see some fighters way up above and thought they looked like Mustangs; I told him they probably were but to keep an eye on them, just in case. I mused at what a fantastic job those two Wingcos had done; the positioning and sectoring was perfect and the timing of the cannon and rocket attacks were uncanny—absolute precision.

Those two chaps certainly knew their jobs and made it easy for us. Our two Hercules were purring away as happy as sandboys. We were up at about 500 feet, the sun was behind us, and even the mucky North Sea looked almost blue in patches between the shadows of the clouds. We had gradually climbed to about 1,500 feet in fairly loose formation, so I was able to keep looking around; the low coastline was in sight. I asked Douggie to make the cannons safe; he then told me that one seemed to have jammed and another had not fired at all. We joined the circuit and were soon safely down, quickly taxiing to get off the runway and back to our dispersal on the south side of the field. We could get out by the bottom hatches for a change as we had dropped our torpedo and so the six of us stood in a group watching other Beaufighters coming in. One of the ground crew produced a lighter so we could light our fags. I looked at my watch; it was still only something after nine and I thought Peggy will just be settling down at the office for the day's work. Tony seemed to think we had done a good job. I felt relieved that we had managed to 'put it all together' but the credit must surely go to our Wingco for bringing us in at exactly the right angle and the other Wingco for swamping the 'flak ships' with cannon and rockets at exactly the right moment—a masterpiece of timing.

We were quite happy sitting on the grass, chatting to the ground lads and having another fag, while watching the last few coming in. One sounded to have an engine that kept cutting and banging but he got down OK; we reckoned two of the cannon and rocket crews had run into trouble but one of them may have got away with it and made land. Back in the debriefing room, there was a lot of chatter and as we sunk our mugs of tea, someone shouted out 'don't drink the tea lads, it's full of bromide'. Then we ran through the debriefing and it was only then that I got a proper picture of what had actually happened.

As soon as the convoy was spotted, the Wingco (Tony) had taken the other two squadrons up to just over 2,000 feet, where he was just skimming the bottom of some broken cloud; he took them behind the convoy and around to the east so that he would have the sun behind him. That manoeuvre we did was to give him time to get around, as well as bringing us into the correct sector. As soon as the Wingco upstairs saw us commencing our run-in, they commenced their dive on the 'flak ships' with cannons closely followed by rockets and, by Jove, they could not have timed it better; the first lot opened up just as we pulled up to 100 feet for dropping. It seemed to me that these cannon and rocket boys had a much more hazardous job than we had had, although the talk was always of 'giving protection to the vulnerable Torbeaus'. It seemed to be agreed that all three ships had been hit and damaged to such an extent that they would sink. 'Intelligence' (that mysterious word) would no doubt confirm the results by tomorrow, 'when we will also have your photographs'.

We were in the mess for a few drinks and lunch, then, as nothing else seemed to be happening, I went to the bed for a nice kip. A flight from each of the other squadrons was detailed for patrols the next day but the rest of us, almost to a man, finished up in The Fleece that night. It was packed out and we were certainly letting our hair down but what impressed me was that there was no 'careless talk' or chattering about the job; it was such a contrast to what you heard in Betty's Bar in York.

At the *post-mortem* the next day, it was confirmed that our ship had been hit by two torpedoes and had sunk, but whose torpedo? We never found out because the photos from the nose cameras were taken directly into the sun; one edge was OK, showing the beginning of a level horizon, but the rest of each of the three pictures was fuzzy white light. The cockpit pictures each showed speed, height, etc. 'OK,' Tony said, 'What the hell does it matter anyway, it was a team effort and we sunk the ruddy ship and whatever they say I reckon they all hit'. I remarked to Tony that I did not have a clue what was going on until I realised we were going in for the attack and saw the ships in front of us. He said it was always like that when flying Nos 2 or 3, but the flight leader was able to look out most of the time and the wing and squadron leaders were looking out all the time; it was a lot different from having to concentrate on keeping formation all the time.

It was back to routine patrols in two or three day intervals, with some dodging around the Helgoland Bight to catch anything entering or leaving Hamburg, but there was nothing to be seen. One trip aborted early as the weather was hopeless, but it gave Douggie a chance to get some Gee fixes as the Gee navigator was new equipment as far as we were concerned. In between these trips there was always some practice to be done on the range, compass swings, or an air test.

Then we were warned to stand-by for another strike. This followed the same build up as before; the target was a small convoy of a troopship, two smaller vessels but two 'flak-ships', plus two other escorts, all behind a couple of minesweepers. All our nine torps were for the troopship, with each flight coming in from a different direction. The same apprehension crept in before take-off, especially when we were standing around at dispersal, waiting to get started. I felt several times to make sure St Christopher was still in my breast pocket. Once away, it was OK. We had a bit further to go this time. The Met was right; the weather was OK (about 7/10ths cloud at about 3,000 feet) and visibility was OK. We seemed to do a lot more turning about as we neared the target, including one complete 360-degree turn, then I knew we were on the run in. The other Beaus were not to be seen, but I did not worry about that this time as I knew what they would be doing. Then I saw the ships—they all seemed to be very close together; I edged away from Tony then we pulled up, throttled back, pitched forward, a quick turn on the sight knob to set direction and angle, left hand back on throttle, brought the light in line with the bow, held everything steady, and applied a bit of throttle to hold air speed. My left thumb squeezed the button, with the throttle wide open down to the deck. I had not noticed the other Beaus with concentrating on lining that light up with the bow but there they were and all pandemonium let loose—splashes, foaming water, rocket trails, black smoke, and (from the angle that we were so rapidly approaching at) all the ships seemed to be touching each other, so with no gap for us to go through, we had to pass in front of the stem.

As this turmoil of boiling sea, ships' masts, funnels surrounded by black smoke bore down on us at an alarming rate, the white rings flashing in the water flashing underneath in a blur, there seemed nowhere to go; so keeping my thumb hard on the cannon button, I had to pull up and do a hell of a turn to miss a mast as a black sheet of something like a house door flew through the air right in front of the nose and we flashed through a cloud of black smoke. Once through that lot, I hugged the sea and got out of there with the throttles hard forward. How the hell we did not hit anything, God only knows. 'You OK? Douggie,' I called, though the first time I tried to say it, my mouth was so dry nothing came out. 'Yes, are you?' From seeing the ships and pulling up, it could only have been about twenty seconds, but what a twenty seconds. I throttled back, pulled up a trifle, and looked around. Douggie said there was a hell of a lot of smoke over the ships. I started a gentle turn for home and after a few minutes, Douggie said there was someone moving in to formate on us.

In another five or six minutes, I had loosely joined up with another four, and I saw that one of them was Tony; all the others were rocket Beaus. The six of us came home together in loose formation. After maybe forty-five minutes, Douggie said the Mustangs were up there but some of them looked like Hurries, so it should be all over now, bar the shouting, but I could not see Dick in our lot. After landing and getting out at dispersal, the four of us were anxiously looking for Dick's aircraft. We had each smoked about four fags before the truck came to pick us up, yet there was still no sign of Dick. We never knew for sure what happened to him; we reckoned he either hit one of the ships or caught a stray shell. The strike was regarded as a success as the troopship blew up, believed hit by four torpedoes and an escort blew up under rocket fire but, in addition to Dick, two of the other lads did not make it and several Beaus suffered damage. Tony insisted that the four of us go to The Fleece that night.

There was a bit of a reorganisation of flights as two crews had completed a tour (but how the devil anyone got through 200 hours of operational flying on this game, I was beginning to wonder) and then we had lost Dick. Some new crews had arrived and, to my surprise, I was 'given' two crews, one of them new arrivals, and told to take them up and get some practice as the leader; however, the Wingco stressed that this was only for practice and did not necessarily mean I would become a proper flight leader. So, we got cracking, range-firing with cine and cannons, doing some practice run-ins and camera drops, as well as formation flying and turns at 1,000 feet and down on the deck. This was much less tiring than just following; I could look around and Douggie had something to do too.

We had a few days of this and then we were given a patrol. This was just what Douggie had been waiting for—a chance to do some proper navigation instead of just following somebody else. I enjoyed it too, being able to look out all the time, take stock of the weather, particularly the cloud, and make my own mind up about what to do if we spotted anything. At one stage, we were in and out of cloud, almost touching the deck but that radio altimeter was a godsend and it was not thick enough to put the other chaps in any danger. The time passed very quickly, Douggie brought me straight over the airfield and I got the lads to come in pretty tight as we flew over, to show them (on the ground) we could do it.

One more patrol that we had to call off early because the weather was making it impossible—nothing violent or icing or anything really nasty, but just North Sea muck—seemed like about four fronts all rolled into one with very low dark grey cloud, bags of rain, and very little visibility. It was just a waste of time.

Then the Wingco sent for me. He was grunting and chuntering as I entered the office and saluted as I wished him, 'Good morning, sir', and I wondered what the hell I had done wrong. 'Bloody Air Ministry', he said, 'got a signal from group that you and Eric are to be posted to Southeast Asia Command where they are going to form a Torbeau squadron. I've been on to Chatham to see what I can do about it, it's a damn cheek, but they say Air Ministry want you and Eric because you are both GR trained and we are all moving to the south-east coast tomorrow'. I did not know what to make of this, it was such a surprise. I did not know whether to be pleased or sorry. At first, I thought that this station was the last place on God's Earth, but now I had settled in and was at home with the chaps in the mess, it was not so bad after all. What did Southeast Asia mean? How would I get there? Was Douggie to come with me? The Wingco told me to come back in the afternoon and see the adjutant who would have more gen by then. I went to the crew room to tell Douggie all I knew and had a chat with Eric in the mess. I had not had much to do with Eric previously. He was a bit of a smooth character, been an officer a long time and seemed to fluctuate between flying officer and acting flight lieutenant as he kept putting up 'black marks'. He was a handsome-looking chap, with longish hair (for those days), who was always the life and soul of a party and undoubtedly a 'ladies' man'. A real 'happy go lucky' chap, he was reputed to be a good pilot, but we were so different in many ways. Everybody liked Eric 'as long as you did not let him near your wife or girlfriend'.

The adjutant had all the 'gen'. We were to take our observers with us, go (of all places) to Melton Mowbray, where we would each pick up a new Torbeau and fly it to Karachi, where we would receive further instructions from Southeast Asia Command in Delhi. We were to take our 'personal documents' with us in sealed envelopes, but before we left the country we were to arrange for 'yellow fever' and other tropical inoculations. Now this all began to sound rather exciting. Our rail warrants were being prepared and we would be leaving tomorrow. All the other lads would be taking the Beaus to Manston.

We had a farewell thrash in The Fleece. Some of the chaps called us 'lucky buggers' and 'trust Eric to fix a trip to the Orient'; others joked that 'the water will be warmer down there but watch out for the sharks'.

We paid our mess bills, picked up our 'clearances', and boarded the truck to take us to the station and picked up the little two-car train on the first leg of the journey. Already knowing Melton Mowbray, I was able to show Eric the ropes and introduced him to The Bell, where he soon left me to chat up a likely looking bird. No one here seemed to regard our trip to India with any urgency; they did not have our aircraft yet and the CO, who remembered me from before, told us we may as well push off for a few days as he had just received instructions that as from the next day, there was to be no non-operational flying until further notice. He remembered the York episode and said that if I wanted to go to York, I could have a lift up with one of the chaps going to Edinburgh, then to ring up in four days' time to see if he wanted me back. That sounded great, so Eric took the train to London and I had a ride in the back seat of a Beaufighter up to York. I nipped out through the bottom hatch, waved to the pilot who took straight off again while I went to the tower to book him in and out again, and then got a lift home to arrive five minutes before Peggy came in to find I had messed up her tennis plans for the evening. She told me I took a long time to answer some of her letters; I had let her think I had been at Melton all the time but told her, 'it will take longer shortly as I have a Ferry job out to India, but, come here love, we'll talk about that later, I am home for at least four days.'

7
East Coast Torbeau Squadrons: The Context

Germany needed the premium-quality iron ore mined in Sweden. To get this to the industrial heartland of the Ruhr, the ore was sent from Norway by sea to Rotterdam and then up the Rhine. The ore and other materials were shipped in convoys, heavily defended by mine sweepers, flak-ships, and fighter air cover. Between 1940 and 1942, Coastal Command was not very effective at attacking these convoys, it being costly in lost crews and aircraft. In fact, mine-laying from aircraft was more effective in terms of tons sunk per airman lost.

Coastal Command needed a more effective anti-flak aircraft and a better torpedo bomber. The Beaufighter (a development of the underpowered Beaufort) was further adapted with these requirements in mind. A strike wing was based at North Coates on the Lincolnshire coast, where three squadrons combined different capabilities to be a more effective strike force against the convoys. These were 254 Squadron (of Beaufighters armed with cannon and a torpedo (Torbeaus) to sink the ships) and 236 and 143 Squadrons (of Beaufighters armed with cannon, rockets, and machine guns, acting as a diversion and attacking the flak-ships).

The three strike wing squadrons were co-ordinated to attack together with the added protection of single-engined fighters above (Spitfires and Mustangs). After April 1943, having developed and refined the tactics described by Jack, there was a significant degree of success. The Coastal Command RAF North Coates strike wing operated as the largest anti-shipping force of the Second World War, accounting for over 150,000 tons of shipping and 117 vessels for the loss of 120 Beaufighters and 241 aircrew, killed or missing. Attacks by these Beaus were classed as some of the most dangerous and ferocious encounters of the war.

8

'Snakecharmer' Goes East

It was 6 June 1944, the second day of my leave. I was still in bed; Peggy had left to go to work. Mother had brought me *The Daily Telegraph* and another cup of tea. I told her that I would take Jeff for a walk shortly and started reading about the Allies having entered Rome. A few minutes later, I heard Mother rushing up the stairs—'They have just said on the wireless that Allied Forces have landed in force on the coast of Normandy and established several beachheads'. She went downstairs to listen for any more news. I glanced over at the 'wings' on my tunic, which was hung over the back of a chair, then sank back and gazed up at the ceiling. 'So this is what we have all been waiting for—the Invasion has started—and here I am in bed. I ought to be bloody well up there—that's why there was no non-operational flying for a few days—the buggers must have wanted me out the way so I did not cock it up; what a thing to have to tell my kids—I was at home in bed on Invasion morning. All those hundreds of ships must have got enough stuff over the Atlantic OK—in my mind's eye, I saw those convoys battling their way across the ocean, and bloody grand chaps they were'.

I pulled myself together and went downstairs. Mother was listening for further news, so we had a cigarette together, then I had breakfast, a wash and shave, and took Jeff for a walk. I met Peggy at lunchtime and, naturally, all the talk was about the invasion; I felt like such an impostor being on leave, especially when anyone asked what I was doing and I told them I was waiting to fly out to India.

I saw my uncle, who was delighted to tell me that Henry had just got his pilot's wings in the Canadian Air Force. It was hard to imagine

Henry as a pilot as he looked such a youngster when I saw him in Toronto. Cousin Mary was still at the Bomber Group Headquarters; he showed me photos of her looking very glamorous in her WAAF officer's uniform. One night, we met Peg's uncle Tommy in the 'Burton Stone' and happened to bump into the chap who had been in the tower when I flew into York; he told me that the ban on non-Op flying had been lifted and that, as they often got an aircraft going south, if I gave him a ring when I wanted to go, he may be able to fix me up with a lift, so I made a note of the phone number. When I phoned Melton, they gave me another day so I phoned this bloke at York and he told me I was 'in luck'; there was a Beau on its way to Filton the next day, 'See you about 10.30'.

I duly got the bus up to Rawcliffe Lane on that lovely June morning, feeling a bit sad as I had no idea how long it would be until I saw Peggy again. I walked up to the airfield and up into the tower, where my friend offered me a cup of tea. From the tower, I could see a horrible-looking Beaufighter, looking as if it had been painted with soot, with two tiny-looking Merlin engines, a flat tailplane, and a very small fin. I pointed it out and said, 'That's not it, is it?' He told me it was, so I asked him, 'What mark is that then?' He told me he thought it was a Mark II Nightfighter. 'Bloody hell,' I say, 'I don't like the look of that, where's the pilot?' Then he told me:

> There is no pilot, he was taking it down from Charter Hall back to Filton, probably to be broken up, but a red warning light came on so he thought he was losing fuel pressure and he dropped in here and went back by train but, you fly Beaufighters and the Warrant Officer fitter says it's just a fault in the light and he wants to get to Nottingham so he will go with you, you can leave it at Melton and someone will pick it up from Filton.

I looked at my watch, it was too late to catch the train, so as I was going to be late anyway if I took the train, I might as well have a chat with this warrant officer as warrant officers usually know what they were talking about. My 'friend' picked up the phone and told this warrant officer that, 'Your pilot's here'. Soon, a cheerful, middle-aged chap bounded into the tower and so he did not think I was a green pilot officer, I told him that I was a WO before getting 'this' (pointing to my PO's ring). Told him I had never flown with a Merlin, only

Beaus VIs and X's with Hercules. 'In any case, what's all this about a red fuel light?' He told me that he had worked on both Merlins and Hercules, had checked the fuel system and run both engines up several times, and was absolutely sure it was purely an instrument fault as the red light stayed on all the time, but there was no point changing it as she was going back to be scrapped anyway. Without the fact that he was prepared to come with me, I would have turned the trip down there and then. He told me that Merlins are only 1,280 hp that go around the opposite way from the Hercules, so she would swing the other way. Yet, 1,280 did not sound much after the 1,770 I was used to. I asked him about boost and critical revs (the revs you should avoid due to excessive vibration) and decided that we would, at least, go and give it a run-up and see what it was like.

Settled inside, I checked over the fuel cocks; there were gaps in the instrument panel where night-fighting equipment has obviously been removed, quite a few instruments were different, and the whole cockpit looked 'tatty'. Those two Merlins looked so small after being used to sitting between those two great big Bristols. I thought to myself, 'Which of us is the biggest idiot if we fly in this heap of crap?' However, Mr Stead (as I now knew him) seemed perfectly happy, so, with him sitting astride the well behind me, and looking over my shoulder, I asked him if he knew which VHF channels were set up on the four buttons and we started the engines. They started OK but it made such a funny sound. 'Steady' put his thumb up, so they must have sounded OK to him. The props were going around the 'wrong' way.

We let her warm up and checked the mags. I pointed to the rev. counter and he stuck a hand in front of my face with a thumb stuck up, but that ruddy red light was shining, steady as a rock. I went through the run-up and pre-take-off checks, pointing to the temperature gauge (as I did not know what it should be on a Merlin). The thumb went around in front of my face so I pointed upwards to indicate that we would have a go. I called the tower and started to taxi. I had no gills to control the cylinder head temperature on these engines, so, just before take-off, I pointed to the gauge again; the thumb came around to indicate they were OK, so off we went. I thought the bloody thing was never going to get airborne; with no kick in the back, the engines seemed as sluggish as hell, whining away, but the speed only crept up like a snail. Eventually, she lifted off, vibrating like buggery. At 500 feet, I throttled back and played around with the pitch but could not get rid of the vibration. After twenty-five minutes of map-reading and constant vibration and throbbing, I was relieved to see Melton Mowbray and, in thirty minutes, we were down. Mr Stead thought it was a great trip; I thought it was terrible, especially when the engines started popping as I throttled back on the approach. The ground crew looked at it and said, 'Where the hell did you find that thing? EL649. It's out of the Ark'. I was not very popular, having lumbered them with that heap of scrap; it was still there when I eventually left and probably still is. 'Steady' was delighted and dashed off to get his bus to Nottingham.

The aircraft that we were to take to India had arrived at Melton. The CO suggested that I should do an air test in the morning and then have some more inoculations in the afternoon, as there were some extra ones required for the Far East. Some made some chaps feel a bit groggy, so I could then have a couple of days on the deck while the aircraft was being tropicalised. Eric appeared in the mess about 11.30 p.m. after a hectic few days in London; he had been to a show and several clubs and met some 'popsies'. I really knew very little about Eric. He never spoke of his private life. I did not know whether he was single or married, but he was certainly not short of cash and he knew his way around. His philosophy seemed to be that our stay on this Earth was only temporary, so he was going to make sure he enjoyed his stay, however long that may be, to the full. He was a cheery fella to have around; he seemed to know his stuff when it came to flying and I was looking forward to being with him on this Torbeau squadron, wherever it turned out to be. We both agreed that we were going to make the best of the trip out to see as much as we could.

The next morning, we had a look at our respective aircraft. Mine was KW334 and underneath the number was stencilled 'SNAKE'. I smiled at this thinking, 'That's not very secretive, Snake for India is just about as subtle as Cress was for Canada'. As I walked around her, I remarked to the ground flight sergeant, 'She looks a real charmer compared with that black thing I brought you yesterday'. Douggie and I had a good look over her; she was going to take us to some interesting places and we hoped she would remain ours when we arrived at the squadron so we had better get to know her intimately. So, we got set to take her on her first test; we were back on the ground in twenty-five minutes with an oil leak. They had this fixed in an hour or so, so we had another go, checking everything off, filling in the test report forms. She flew nicely, just needed a bit of adjustment on the rudder trim, then back for a late lunch and off for our inoculations. Eric had not become airborne yet as, with him not having been on the delivery job before, they had to run over the test procedures with him and explain what was required on the subsequent consumption tests. However, as he had his inoculations at the same time as I did, we had a couple of days off flying together. One of these we spent obtaining our 'tropical kit', although Eric already had some as he had already been to the Middle East. I bought 'KD' (khaki drill) tunics, shorts and slacks, shirts, socks, mosquito boots, shoes, and a mosquito net, but I resisted the tailor's efforts to sell me a 'Bombay bowler'.

Eric and I were rather enjoying our second day of leisure (fortunately for Douggie, he had befriended Eric's observer), when we met this frightfully keen chap who was also supposed to be going to this new Torbeau squadron in south-east Asia. He had called at some RAF medical place to have his inoculations before arriving at Melton and was panicking about how badly they wanted us out there. 'It must be important because they pulled me off Ops', so we let him carry on a bit before telling him that we had all been taken off Ops too; it seemed he had been on a Torbeau squadron with the Scottish wing. He had not taken-up the CO's offer to 'push off for a few days' but had hung around, grabbing one of the three Torbeaus as soon as they arrived and was going to do his consumption test the following day. He was on about the route he had worked out and seemed a bit surprised when we told him we were just going to take it 'one leg at a time' because we had no idea of approved routes or restrictions after Rabat (although I had had a look at a school atlas to get a rough idea of where we were likely to go); when I offered a bit of advice for the first leg to Rabat, he interrupted, saying he knew something that was quite different from what I was going to say, so Eric phoned for a taxi and we went down to The Bell for a quiet drink.

I arranged with the flight that I would take my steed on another air test, now that she had been fitted out, before doing a consumption test. As I walked out to her, I saw that someone had very tastefully painted on one side of her little nose 'SNAKECHARMER' in yellow letters shaped like a snake poised to strike. I got quite a 'kick' out of this and told the flight sergeant I thought it looked great; he told me he had mentioned to one of the lads that I had said she looked a 'charmer' and that gave him the idea. I asked who it was so that I could show him my appreciation. She really was a beauty. We went over the North Sea, carefully avoiding the ranges and restricted areas around the Wash, up to 12,000 feet; she would have gone higher, but we had no oxygen, so I felt sure she would have reached her 'ceiling' of 15,000 feet if need be (the Mark X having a much lower ceiling than the Mark VI but a better performance at low levels, which was the most important to us). At 10,000 feet, I tested the cannons bearing in mind what happened when we tested the new cannons once before, then threw her around, feathering each engine in turn as we approached the coast on the way back. Douggie had tested all his W/T channels; he had no Gee box to play with as there was no point in putting that in for going out east. We were both happy with her and decided, 'She was a good 'un'.

Now on with the consumption test. We put in a little ballast to approximate the full kit which we would both be taking and had to flog round the Irish Sea route this time as operational flying was taking place over the North Sea. That accounted for an entirely uneventful four and a half hours. Eric had now done his air tests and, not to be outdone, his aircraft had been christened 'Orient Express'. I liked my name better. Our frightfully keen fellow had left for Portreath.

The next day, I took up the offer of a trip in Mosquito MM579 (a Mark XIII), which a flying officer was taking up for an air test. I did not like it at all; it looked lovely and sleek, but after the Beau, it seemed so fragile. It was a bugger to get in—through a little door and sitting beside the pilot, just a few inches behind him. The windscreen seemed even further away that in a Lib; there was no elbow room and the pilot had a funny little bent stick instead of a decent wheel. There was no kick in the back as we took off and to see out to the rear, I had to undo my harness and squirm round to kneel on the seat. It certainly seemed to handle easily and when we did a low pass, we were certainly shifting. It seemed to fly easily with one engine feathered, too. With the short air test completed, we started doing aerobatics; I could not see any point in that and was quite ready to get down when we landed after ninety minutes. I much preferred my 'Snakecharmer'.

In the afternoon, I had a nice little trip in a Beau, taking a pilot and his observer over to Gransden Lodge, travelling twenty-five minutes each way. I heard that evening that the figures on my first consumption test were OK, so there would be no point in doing another one so it looked as if I would soon be on my way. According to the news on the wireless, the beachheads in Normandy had all been secured and troops were pressing on through France; a Japanese thrust at Imphal had been defeated, although the latter did not mean much to us at the time. We also learned that some 'rocket bombs' had landed in southeast England, although this was not mentioned on the wireless (they were later called V-1s).

Sure enough, the following morning, I learned officially that the consumption was OK, so we had a few final preparations left and then I could push off to Portreath the following morning. I collected another 'Goolie chit'; Eric asked why I wanted another when I had one already, so I told him, 'I may as well have one for each Goolie'. I collected a sealed envelope, about 18 inches × 12 inches, that I was told contained my 'records', which was to be handed over when I arrived in Southeast Asia Command; I made sure I had the little sealed envelopes containing my inoculation certificates, packed my kit, gave Peggy a ring, and then had a drink or two with Eric, telling him that I would try and wait for him somewhere to catch up.

The next morning, I paid my mess bill and stowed our gear. I then slipped in to see the CO, who told me that the chap who was in such a hurry left Portreath three days previously, but there had been no news of him since; the CO therefore asked me if I could find anything out when I got to Rabat. So, with that, it was out to the 'Snakecharmer' to wind her up and off we went, only to be back on the deck in ten minutes because the bottom hatch had not been shut properly and it blew open. However, we were soon off again and one hour and forty minutes later touched down at Portreath.

There was an operational Beau squadron at Portreath. They were all sporting the wide black and white stripes painted on top, under the wings, and around the fuselage (invasion markings, but that was no longer our war). We were being sent to another one—the Forgotten War—somewhere out in the east. I hope some silly bugger did not shoot us down over the Bay because we were not showing those black and white markings. The Met chap thought the weather would be OK for us in the morning; in fact, there should be some nice cloud at around 3,000 feet to give us a bit of cover and the wind looked good. After dinner, I met Douggie; we risked a couple of halves of scrumpy at the nearby pub, then turned in for an early night, still almost light, on 21 June.

Sure enough, on the morning of 22 June, the Met forecast was as expected so we got away to an early start only to be back on the ground at Portreath again in seventy minutes, as, almost twenty-five minutes out, I noticed a slow stream of oil coming from the starboard engine. It was not a lot and we did not lose any oil pressure. The ground crew soon traced it, fixed it, and topped up the oil; they also replaced the W/T aerial, which, for some unaccountable reason, had decided to break off.

At about lunchtime, we got away again and waved goodbye to the Scilly Isles for the second time. Douggie then kept his usual constant watch all around. We had just remarked that there should be no fighters around as they would all be busy with the invasion job when he thought he saw a couple of black specks which may be 'bogeys'. I told him to keep his eye on them but not concentrate on them so much that he missed spotting any others. After a few minutes he said they were getting a bit nearer but the nice cloud the Met man had talked about was not far ahead, I altered course a little and soon we were out of the sunshine and enveloped in lovely cloud so I came back on to course. If this cloud held, as the Met chap had seemed to think it would, we would be in it for a good long time and it was getting darker inside so I decided that we need not keep on this course as far as 46 00N, 10 30W but we could 'cut a corner' and make straight for 43 00N, 10 30W.

Douggie had no need to look out now so gave me a new course and for two hours, we were in continuous cloud. When we emerged, we were just about 50 miles west of Cape Finisterre. The rest was just a pleasant ride; the sun was belting down on a glorious blue sea and snow-white breakers as we passed close to Cape St Vincent. We felt it getting hotter and hotter inside the aircraft and when we came to rest at the end of the rattling plank runway, it felt as if we had landed in an oven.

As we strolled very slowly along the marshalling apron, I saw a Ferry Command Lib; walking out to it were three fellows carrying briefcases. As we passed them, I thought, 'No. It can't be'. Yet it was—it was dear old 'Zig'. I broke into a trot and called, 'Hello, Zig. Remember me? Gander. June '42. On the Hudsons'. He beamed, dropped his brief case, embraced me in continental fashion and said, 'Sure it's Jacko, how you doing?' I could hardly speak but came out with, 'OK thanks to you. I wouldn't be here now if I hadn't met you'. He told the others to carry on and he would be with them in a minute. He asked where I had been; I told him, 'After Ferry Command, a year on Libs mainly from Iceland, then Beaus, a bit on Torbeaus and now I'm taking that one to India, what are you doing?'

'Mainly on the South Atlantic routes now, we are on our way to the Azores. Wish we were stopping the night and then we could talk again.

Must be away, look after yourself Jacko', he said. I replied, 'You too Zig, and thanks again'. With that, he gave me another hug, then picked up his briefcase and made off to his Lib. Douggie wondered what all that was about. I told him I would tell him about Zig one day. We went to book in, then making the excuse that I wanted to find someone with a truck to go and fetch our kit, I went outside and stood in the shade under an aircraft wing until I had watched Zig take off.

It was early evening but still very warm. As it was rather late, the movements chap suggested we 'call it a day' for today, call, and get genned up on the next leg sometime tomorrow and press on the following day. This sounded a very civilised arrangement, so we went to our billets and I immediately got out my new tropical kit and had a shower. After sundown, it was a beautiful, warm, balmy, and moonlit night. I reckoned I was going to enjoy this.

The next morning, at the briefing for the next leg, I was amazed to learn the height of the Atlas Mountains over which we would have to fly. I had always thought of North Africa as being a flat, sandy desert but here, from north of Rabat and running right across our route, was this range of mountains with peaks of 13,352 feet, 13,665 feet, and 7,636 feet; the highest in the range actually reaches 14,500 feet, but, thankfully, that was not near our route. The idea was to get to Tripoli in Tripolitania (now Libya) in one day; however, as this was well over 1,000 nautical miles and we would be flying at well above the Beau X's economical cruising height for the first 700 nautical miles, we would refuel and have lunch (very civilised, these chaps) at a little desert landing strip called Biskra, nestling against the southern foothills of the mountains. We went over the route:

> Meknes to Fez, then up the Taza Pass to Oujda, on towards Oran—when we see the sea and Oran appearing, call RAF Oran for onward clearance, then turn starboard over the 'high plateau' for Biskra, drop down the mountains at the south side of the plateau and there it should be—a few crumbling white buildings and a rolled strip of sand marked by a black 'oil line'. After that, you can't miss Tripoli, just another 400 miles or so over the flat desert until you pick up the coast and follow it to Tripoli, the airfield, Castel Benito, is just south of the town.

We asked advice on safe heights, useful pin-points, things to watch out for, places to avoid, radio frequencies, and any navigation aids, then collected some maps and charts and Douggie got down to plotting the route. I was then asked if I would like to do an air test on another Beau and have a little look around; Douggie nodded in assent. We decided to go straight away before it got any hotter, then had a forty-five-minute trip down the coast to have a look at Casablanca and then inland to see the beginning of the Atlas Mountains. Casablanca did not look very special, as it was a big fort; Rabat looked much nicer, but those mountains looked pretty big and wild.

We decided to get away as early as possible, before it got too hot as it was 24 June and the hottest place in the world is supposed to be somewhere in that desert, with a recorded temperature of 136.4 degrees F. We made sure we had plenty of water bottles with us and at 6 a.m., we clattered off the steel plate runway and turned into a dazzling, low sun. We climbed towards Meknes with the mountains beginning to rise on our starboard side; they looked as barren as hell. From 8,000 feet, we looked down at the collection of dirty white square buildings of Meknes and picked out a track heading into the mountains towards Fez. Some rising dust indicated that something was travelling along this track and the mountains were now beginning to rise on both sides. In no time, we picked out the next collection of buildings; this must be Fez. It was even bigger than Meknes and that seemed pretty big to be stuck out in these mountains. We could see some very big buildings, one of which was clearly a mosque. There seemed to be a lot of movement around Fez—a line of camels and, judging by the clouds of dust, some lorries or trucks; it looked to be a really busy place and was much bigger than I expected.

Still following the road, we came to a much smaller place: Taza. We were now entering the Taza Pass, with steep-sided mountains closing in on the road—ruddy barren, craggy, bare, sand-coloured rock. If the ruddy engines packed up here, we would just have to bail out and smash every bone in our bodies when we hit that lot, but, thank goodness, the Bristols were purring nicely and what a fantastic view you got from the front seat of a Beaufighter. This pass seemed to be going on for ages, with another line of camels on the road (going our way) and a very small collection of buildings. It was nice and smooth up there in spite of the rugged earth below, but I suspected it could get a bit bumpy later in the day when the heat started rising. I could now tell Douggie that 'Oujda is coming up'. It only looked about half the size of Fez, maybe less, but there was a fair bit of movement on the road, judging from the rising dust. Then there was another little place, which looked quite busy; it must have been Tlemcen, which meant we had passed from Morocco into Algeria. We were coming out of the mountains now; there even seemed to be some cultivation and it was not long before we saw the Mediterranean Coast and Oran in the distance. I told Douggie, 'Right, I followed the roads as far as here, now you get us across the high plateau to Biskra'. Oran confirmed that we could proceed to Biskra, so we headed a bit south of due west over the high ground. There was nothing to follow here—not a track, bugger all, but at least there were some bumps and shadows on the ground on which Douggie could get a drift reading; there were just about 375 nautical miles to go.

It was not a very flat plateau, with lots of bumps and little ranges of hills but not distinctive enough in shape to identify on the map. We spotted a little group of three camels being led in a straight line; I wondered if they knew where they were going. After another ten minutes or so, we spotted a green patch that became a clump of palm trees—quite a big oasis; there was one shown on the map and it looked as if we were OK. We had been nearly two hours over this featureless high plateau when—in the distance and a bit to port—we saw a mountain peak about as high as we were at 8,000 feet; that must have been the 7,636-foot job about 70 miles north-east of Biskra. Douggie seemed delighted at this and confidently gave me an ETA for Biskra. Five minutes before ETA, we were still over the high plateau with some slightly higher ground coming up ahead; as we flew over this ridge, the whole mountain range seemed to fall away at the other side with a desert of rolling sand beyond stretching away to the horizon.

Suddenly, the land had just dropped away from us and there, some 8,000 feet below, was a collection of dirty white buildings; it looked too big for Biskra by what the chap had said, there must have been quite a few thousand folk down there by the look of it. I started letting down, circling this collection of buildings; I saw a black line on the sand, then an aircraft that looked like a Hurricane. 'Good lad, Douggie, that's Biskra, all right'. I could feel it getting hotter and hotter as we came down. No one answered on the R/T, so I looked at the windsock and landed on this sand strip. We had been three hours and twenty-five minutes.

If landing at Rabat had felt like entering an oven, this place felt as if we had landed in front of a blowtorch. I flung open the top hatch, opened the 'clear vision panels', and taxied towards a 15-hundredweight truck, which was leaving a ribbon of dust as it came out to meet us. I followed it back towards the buildings, keeping to one side to keep out of the clouds of sand. Douggie said he could not see a thing out the back for the clouds of sand we were blowing up. After about 1 mile, the truck stopped. Out popped a chap wearing 'regulation' shorts, coming almost below his knees, socks rolled down over his big black boots, shirt hanging outside his shorts, and crowned with a big floppy hat; he waved his arms across his body so I cut the engines, looked around at piles of old drums and jerry cans, draped the back of my parachute harness over the seat, and put my cushion on top, hoping that this would prevent the seat from becoming too hot and descended through the hatch.

Although I was still wearing my flying boots (mainly so that I had somewhere handy to keep my sheath-knife), the heat from the sand soon started coming through the soles, even though I had nipped under the wing for a bit of shade. The erk put a couple of chocks under the wheels. I gave him the locking pins to put in the undercarriage and nipped in the front of the truck. The driver told me to 'Watch the metal—it's a bit hot'. Douggie nipped in the back under the canvas cover. We headed for the mess, which was in the 'town'. I asked what the temperature was, to be informed that it was just over 120 almost half an hour ago. By Rabat time, it ought to be only about 9. 25 a.m., but local time here was 11.30 a.m. and it was just getting nicely hot. I was asked how much fuel I required and as the next leg was only about 400 nautical miles, I asked for just the inners to be filled—it was suggested that I should leave take-off till 3.30 or 4 p.m. as it should have cooled off a bit by then—to be about like it was now. We drove past a few gnarled, twisted olive trees and a few date palms, heading into this quite sizeable town. Yet it seemed deserted, dirty white buildings that all seemed to be cracking and crumbling away in the intense heat, hardly a sign of life—just the odd group of three or four youngsters sitting in the shade and the odd dog, all the older people must be inside. We pulled up outside a hotel, the outside of which was probably once smartly painted in white but now was just as crummy-looking as the rest of the buildings. I was told that this is the officers' mess but it will be OK for the flight sergeant to go with me and that we would be collected when we phone.

In its peacetime heyday, this had probably been quite a posh hotel with its elegantly tiled floor and Moorish design, yet now it looked drab and tatty, but at least it was a bit cooler inside and its fans were just struggling around fast enough to cause a slight waft. Soon, a smiling cross between an Arab and a Frenchman appeared and very politely directed us to the washroom. We were ready for a good wash in lukewarm water; we were dying for a drink but did not risk drinking the water. On returning to the main area, we found a couple of officers had turned up; they seemed delighted to see us and we soon had a cool drink. I did not know what it was; they had gin but Douggie and I refused alcohol as it tasted a bit like fizzy lemonade. What a bloody place to be stationed—it seemed it was a 'staging post' for the shorter range aircraft like ours. They assured us that Rabat had been informed of our arrival, and they seemed glad to see someone. At one time, it was an outpost for the French Foreign Legion; before the war, it was a winter resort, but 'No one with any sense comes here in the summer'.

On the foothills side of the town, they grew some dates and olives. Rain here was unheard of, although they did get a bit of light seasonal rain up in the mountains. During a quite presentable meal, which included some kind of meat, and with which our two hosts consumed a bottle of wine, they tried to persuade us to stay the night, but we insisted we must press on (at least it should be cooler than this near the sea at Tripoli). At 3 p.m., I used the 'wind-up' phone to ask for transport and some twenty minutes later the truck arrived. Driving out, with the mountains behind us, it looked as if we were heading out into the never-ending Sahara, there was supposed to be a track and an old railway running south, but I saw no sign of it.

On arrival at the aircraft, my first thought was to get in and get away from this heat, but I was soon out on the deck again, rubbing my bottom and doing a 'war dance' (much to the amusement of the two erks). One of the bits of metal on my parachute harness had not been covered and it was so bloody hot that it burnt my backside and I had to leap out in agony. I soaked my slacks with water from a water bottle, then wetted the metal and wrapped a bit of sacking around it and tried again. Those poor erks—the one who worked the primer pulled the chocks away and passed the locking pins up before closing the hatch must have got sandblasted by all the sand we were swirling up. However, they led us out to the black oil line that indicated the runway of rolled sand, and we left them in a shower of dust.

The next leg was nice and easy—no high ground to bother about, all very flat with bags of sand but some very big oases, and here and there a string of camels kicking up dusty sand. My bum was a bit sore from the burn but the sun was not in our eyes now—it was almost behind us—and we knew that within an hour and a half, we would see the blue water of the Mediterranean on our port as the coast of Tunisia came sweeping down into the Gulf of Gabès. If we did not see it, all we would have to do is nudge a bit to port to converge with it as it curved around towards the east. Sure enough, the coastline appeared on cue—what a pretty sight.

I told Douggie that he could 'pack his bags' and enjoy the view as we roughly followed the coast to the big, white sprawling port of Tripoli and there, just south of the town, was the big airfield of Castel Benito (C. B.) with its most efficient Air Traffic Control and big concrete runways. We were down after a mere two and a quarter hours and cutting engines in front of some big hangars with green metal doors, which were absolutely riddled with bullet holes.

After the usual formalities, a wash, and a meal, I met Douggie and we got a lift into town. That was a really beautiful evening—hot but beautiful after the unbearable heat at Biskra. On the way, we passed camels pulling flat carts with rubber tyres loaded with produce, palm trees, and scrubby little trees and shrubs. There were lots and lots of people here. We wandered through the bazaar area where, jostling in the narrow streets, there were more little lads trying to flog 'Parker' pens, then we headed along to the seafront. This town had been the showpiece of Mussolini's African empire, where Italians flooded for their holidays and it certainly looked like it. There was a magnificent promenade, lined with palm trees, big spectacular buildings, and a big harbour, inside which were two sunken ships—one a big white one with a green band along the side; I did not know whether they had been sunk by us or scuttled by the other side to prevent us using the harbour, though by the position of one, I think probably the latter. As it got dark, we were still strolling on the prom, then decided we had better get back as these chaps at Castel Benito seemed pretty well organised and expected us to shove off in the morning. We promised ourselves that we would wangle a free day when we got to Cairo.

The briefing officer suggested that our next leg should be a fairly short one, only as far as a staging post known as 'Marble Arch' on the border between Tripolitania and Cyrenaica, a matter of 300 or so nautical miles. He said Met conditions indicated a possible sandstorm further east and we should get the latest information at Marble Arch before pressing on; we would have no problem in finding Marble Arch as it was just at the side of the coastal road and there was a bloody big arch across the road right by the airstrip. We collected another set of maps and charts; it looked as if, for well over the last half of the trip, we would merely have to follow the coast.

This was a nice easy ride for one hour and three quarters. The first bit was over generally low scrubland, mostly sand, with the sea out of sight (about 50 miles away to port), then we converged with the coast at the Gulf of Sirte and just followed the coast to the south end of the gulf where I started looking for this Arch. By Jove, there it was—a great big arch, just like the one near Hyde Park or the Arc de Triomphe, stuck right out in the wilds of the desert and, not far away, a collection of tents and markings to indicate a runway. So, we gave them a call and put down in the desert. It was hot, but nothing like Biskra. The Mediterranean was only a few yards away at one side and the road with this great arch over it at the other. We had a snack in the mess tent—tea with sandwiches of corned beef in sour bread gritted with sand—while the Met-cum-briefing officer checked on the weather. It transpired that Cairo was OK, but there was a sandstorm around about the border between Cyrenaica and Egypt; moving west, top reported as about 7,000 feet and was expected here later in the day. I had no idea that sandstorms could reach 7,000 feet, but I was told this was only a little one; some reached twice that height. I had no desire to be caught here in a ruddy sandstorm as I had seen them on the pictures, and this officer agreed that if he were me, he would get away as soon as possible. He said we should clear the top but if we could not, we could fly north to the coast, where one of the other staging posts (at El Adem or Mersa) should be clear. So, we had another cup of tea and a pee, then off we went to the Snakecharmer.

Now the Snakecharmer was a bit naughty at Marble Arch. Lined up with the runway, all checks done, I opened the throttles; she responded beautifully, with the kick in the back as we went through the gate and full power came on. I had just lifted her off and selected undercarriage up when all power seemed to go in the port engine, the starboard wing rose up, and we were slewing violently to port. The port throttle was still wide open, so I brought the starboard back to get her under control, slapped a bit of flap down, and tore along just clear of the ground till I got 150 knots and then climbed gently. Thank God I did not have a full war-load on. Douggie came through on the R/T. 'What's up? Happen I thought you were going by road'. I got up to 1,000 feet, then came back over the airfield to take stock. Everything seemed OK when I had both throttles at the cruising gate; boost, revs, temperatures, and pressures were all OK. The power just seemed to fade out shortly after we went through to full-rated power. I figured that Marble Arch was not much of a place for them to do a full engine inspection; in any case, she was OK at cruising, so I told them we were OK and set course for Cairo. After a while, Douggie came on the intercom saying, 'It was interesting about that Arch. One of the chaps told me that Mussolini had it built over the road so that he could make a triumphant entry into Tripolitania'. 'Yes,' I replied, 'if we had slewed the other way, I reckoned we'd have been making a triumphant exit'.

Soon, the sky in the far distance took on a strange brown tint. I started to climb early at a gentle rate as I did not want to leave it until late and have to call for a lot of power. At 5,000 feet, the entire desert below was blotted out by a dark brown sea, we were still in the clear but the sky ahead looked yellow; at 7,500 feet, I could see straight ahead across the top of this yellowish-brown mass, which had the appearance of being something solid. I called Douggie. 'There must be one hell of a wind down there to blow up all these tons of sand. I'd try to get a few bearings from El Adem or Cairo, otherwise we may be ruddy miles off course'. 'Happen that's a good idea,' came his reply. I looked at my map and reckoned we were well and truly over the desert, about 100 miles south of Tobruk and over 400 miles to go to Cairo.

For a whole hour, we flew just above this blowing sand and I could not help thinking about those poor buggers in the Army (the Desert Rats) who had to fight and exist down there in sandstorms. It must have been like being rubbed with sandpaper and it would get everywhere—in your throat, your hair, your clothes, your food, your eyes, and your nose (Christ, it must have been bloody) for days and days on end, with no returning to a cosy billet after an hour or two. I felt almost ashamed to be enjoying the luxuries of being in the RAF. The folks back home have little idea of what lads go through in these far away, almost unheard-of wars; if they have not seen the country and felt the heat, they cannot imagine it. I thought to myself that I had not known any hardship during this war, and I felt a bit guilty.

Now and again, I did think about that engine; subconsciously, I was worried about it, but even more, I was baffled as to what the trouble was and how to explain it to the engineers at Cairo, but for sure I was not going any further until it is properly sorted out. The blister on my backside was beginning to itch. Douggie had got a fix and gave me an alteration in course, as well as a revised ETA—about another hour and three quarters.

Soon after this the sky started to clear, gradually, we could see the ground; it was just rolling, featureless sand. I started to lose height gradually, relieved to know that now, even if that port engine did do something daft, we could make it on one, as there was no high ground to cross and we must hit the Nile somewhere if we carried on going east. As we came lower, I could identify marks in the sand as being abandoned vehicles and tanks; in one place, there seemed to be hundreds of them, some almost covered by drifting sand. Once again, I thought of those Desert Rats—the poor sods.

We closed with the coast near El Alamein, where the desert was absolutely littered with the wrecks of war, then altered course for our landing field, which, at one time, was only known by a number but was now known as Cairo West. The green strip of the Nile Valley came into view. We saw the sprawling city of Cairo and there, this side of the city, was the airfield, on which there were dozens of aircraft. We had been three hours and twenty-five minutes. It was pretty hot here—well in the 90s—and having been directed to a parking place over the R/T, we waited in the shade under the wing for damn nearly half an hour for someone to pick us up, but I was not going to walk in this heat; in any case, we wanted all our kit out. Eventually, we booked in at the tower and I told them I had no idea when we would be leaving as I had a duff engine; in due course, I got to see the engineering officer. I tried to explain the trouble; I suggested it may be something to do with the automatic mixture control, the supercharger slipping, or maybe the inlet control flapping about and giving me hot air. He promised that they would have it checked in the morning and that I should call in about the same time tomorrow to see what was what. So, we were OK for at least two nights in Cairo.

We therefore needed somewhere to sleep; I called on the movements officer, who regretted that all the accommodation on the airfield was taken up, so he would have to send me to 'Mena House'. I asked if Douggie could come with me. The officer looked a bit hesitant, muttered something, and then said, 'Well, OK then. I'll get you some transport'. I told Douggie that we were going off to some place called Mena House; it sounded like an Arab boarding house. I changed my money and cashed a cheque for some piasters by which time a car had arrived; we were driven through the town and left by a road going south, looked as if we were going back into the desert when, in just over thirty minutes, we pulled up at the most fantastic white building, surrounded by gardens of the most colourful flowers I have ever seen. As we drew up, the driver said, 'This is it, sir, very popular with the officers'. With that, two Egyptians opened the doors, so we got out and admired the building while they picked up our kit and carried it up the steps. I thanked the driver and we followed them up the steps where we were met by a bowing Egyptian, who said we were expected and said something to the two porters, which must have been to tell them to take us to a room; he beckoned us to follow and we followed them to a luxurious room, containing two single beds, fans from the ceiling going full belt, and a view of the Pyramids. When the two had deposited our kit, we looked at each other, shouted 'Yippee', and flopped on the beds.

9
Holiday in Cairo

Mena House at Giza was the most fantastic place I had ever seen. I thought such places only existed on film sets and had to pinch Douggie to make sure we were both actually alive, that we had not written ourselves off at Marble Arch and this was a sight of the world beyond. From our window, we had watched the sun setting behind the three Great Pyramids, soaked in a big pink bath, changed into fresh clean kit, and enjoyed the tastiest dinner (my first introduction to kebabs—chunks of lamb grilled on a skewer—followed by pomegranates, coffee, and local brandy). It was only then we realised how tired we were but before turning in, we decided that we would have a look at the Pyramids in the morning as we might not get another chance and they were the number one Wonder of the World.

It was in the morning that we could really take in the glory of Mena House. Originally built as a Royal Hunting Lodge, it was set in extensive and beautiful gardens full of colourful exotic flowers, with its brilliant white walls dazzling in the sunlight. Inside were spectacular Arabesque decorations, tiled floors, and intricate woodwork in the lattice windows (harem screens); also, everywhere, servants were in spotless white, crowned with a red Fez, waiting to leap into action at the clap of a hand. We learned at the hotel that we could ride to the Pyramids by camel, so two camels were laid on to meet us at the gate.

Now this was a peculiarly odd experience. The handlers got the camels to sit down. We mounted our respective camels, sitting astride a piece of tatty old carpet, and were told to hold on to a couple of leather-covered handles sticking up in front. At first, my camel did not seem inclined to shift, then it started to get up one corner at a time and seemed to do this in two stages. I was pitched all over the place—backwards, forwards, sideways, even two ways at the same time—and eventually, hanging on like grim death, I realised we were up and on an even keel.

Then, the awkward thing did not want to move and after a lot of Arabic swear words, it reluctantly began to walk but still tried to chuck me off with every step. It was not a very long way, but mostly up quite a steep slope. I was beginning to get the hang of its funny movement and risked looking behind me to see where Douggie was; then, nearly at the top of the slope, the damn thing broke into a funny trot and I was relieved to see that the minder could almost keep up with us. We were now nearing a flat area right by the base of the big pyramid; there were lots of folks and camels up here. My ruddy camel seemed to take a fancy to another one and felt like a bit of courting because it went right up to this other one—very close, face-to-face. I could not see what mine was doing, but the other one was turning it lips up and showing some brown teeth, then it belched straight at my face and the stink was like everything you could imagine—all rotting at once. By now, the minder was pulling and shouting at it, and, in its own time, it agreed to sit down, but I could not remember the order we got up in, so I just clung on for dear life and eventually was able to slide off. There was a little haggling over the number of piasters and although I gave him half what he asked for, he must have been happy as he promised to look out for me to take me back.

For some considerable time, we just stood in amazement at the gigantic size of the Pyramid at the base of which we were standing. It was Big Cheops, which was 480 feet high; the stones looked worn and had crumbled a bit in places, but you could still see the huge size of each block and right up to the top, like a snow-cap on a pointed mountain, the summit was capped with alabaster. Originally, the whole Pyramid was covered with alabaster, but over the years, most of it had been pinched to make little Pyramids and Sphinx souvenirs to sell to tourists. Behind us, and all around, were the ruins of tombs of princesses and ancient nobles. We linked up with a guide, who spoke quite good English, for a tour inside the big pyramid. Before going inside, he told us it was built a bit before 2,500 BC by Pharaoh Khufu, who was better known as 'Cheops', to be his tomb. It took twenty years to build and the other two Pyramids, somewhat smaller and built almost in a line, were built by Cheops' successor and his son—hence, Big Cheops and Little Cheops. He produced a cigarette paper and showed us how the stones fitted so well that it was impossible to poke the paper between, even though no mortar was used. Each stone was huge.

Before going inside, there was a bit of bargaining over the price; he explained that he would have to use so many candles and so, counting that there were ten of us in the party, divided the cost of the candles by ten and wanted this on top of the fee. All paid-up, we entered the small opening and immediately the temperature dropped from something in the 90s to be pleasantly cool. We followed the flickering candle along a narrow corridor. We felt to be walking uphill and soon it became decidedly colder and my sweaty shirt felt clammy and wet on my back.

We stopped while the guide transferred the flame to a fresh candle and pressed on. Goodness knows how far we had gone, or where we were, but there was quite a breeze passing down that corridor. Shortly, the guide stopped and we gathered round; he told us that there were two ventilation shafts incorporated in the structure and the air in all the corridors and chambers was kept fresh. As we talked, the flame on the candle was almost horizontal, hanging on to the wick by its toenails. He told us we were now about to enter a corridor 153 feet long and 28 feet high, leading to the funeral chamber. It was so cold that I rolled my sleeves down to cover the 'goose pimples'. Gathered in a little group in the funeral chamber, he lit another candle and told us how big it was, but the light did not reach as far as the walls and roof, so we had to take his word for it. The tomb and body were apparently no longer there.

We now had a conference; he told us that, above this chamber (the King's Chamber), there were five other compartments, supported by the huge granite blocks above our heads. The guide would take us up there if we wished, but you could not stand up after a while, which made some people frightened; also, we would have to pay more piasters as he would use more candles. We conferred and decided to have a go, so the guide moved round us with his candle, checking on our money then off we went. Now this bit was a bit scary, first of all walking with one hand above your head so that you could feel the roof getting lower, then walking double up following the glow upfront, then, I think on purpose, he let the candle go out and kept us in suspense while he found a match. I then realised what it must be like to be a coal miner and thought that if we lost contact with the others, we would never find our way out. It seemed an eternity before we reached these compartments and we could not see anything special when we did. I was relieved to know that we were on the way back and when we could stand erect, it was sheer delight. Two more candles were required on the way down from the main chamber; we passed a couple of other parties on the way up and then, we were out into the brilliant sunshine and the heat. I have never before been to such effort to see so little, but it was worth it to think we had been inside one of the Wonders of the World and stood in the chamber where a pharaoh was laid to rest over 4,500 years ago.

A short stroll from the base of the Big Pyramid took us to the Sphinx, 190 feet long and 66 feet tall, carved in rock with a human head for intelligence and the body of a lion for strength, facing the east to watch for the rising sun, with the Pyramids in line behind it. The lower part of the face had collapsed on the right-hand side and a big pile of sandbags supported the chin.

It would be about 2 p.m. by now and was jolly hot. We mounted our camels for the ride downhill to Mena House. It was just as uncomfortable as the ride up, and that blister on my bum was getting very sore. After a good wash and a light meal on the terrace, we decided we had better think about getting a taxi to Cairo West and see how our aeroplane was coming along. The taxi took us into the outskirts of Cairo and then to the airfield. We found the engineering officer, who said they had been over all the usual things on the engine, the mags. and plugs were perfectly OK, and she behaved perfectly when they had run her up several times. We talked a while and he did not exactly say that he thought I was imagining it but wanted to go over again as to what actually happened. I repeated that 'it was perfectly OK at 'C. B.'

We took a bit longer to get off at Biskra, which would be due to the terrific heat, but at Marble Arch, the port engine had just faded away as I selected wheels-up, but this was definitely not due to the throttle having slipped back'. We decided that the only thing to do was for me to try a take-off; he would come with me and we would see what happened. I must say that I had every respect for these ground chaps who would fly with a pilot they knew nothing about in an aircraft that may be suspect; some of the non-commissioned ones maybe did it just to pick up a day's extra 'flying pay', but I do not know whether officers got this perk. I tried to put him at ease by mentioning that I had been a warrant officer before I became a mere PO.

However, we left Douggie on the ground and this engineering chap stood up behind me. It was getting a bit cooler now. There was a good long runway, so I went right to the very end. He was going to keep his eyes on the instruments, especially the port boost and revs. She was OK on the run-up, so I opened up as much as I dared before letting the brakes off and away we went. Everything was fine as we went through the gate and speed was building up nicely. I held her down a bit longer than usual then she started to whip off to port, so I snatched the starboard throttle back; we were off the runway and dashing over flat sand, but with bags of rudder and some short jabs of brake, I managed to straighten her up, both throttles hard and back, and we came to rest. We stayed where we were, and the engineer chap said, 'Christ. I see what you mean. She fell right back from +10 to +5 or 6. Better see if she will shift on this sand and take her back'.

Back outside the servicing hangar, he told me they would have to give her a thorough going over. It might have been the automatic mixture control, but they would have her in for two or three days. He suggested I could contact him in a couple of days to see how they were getting on. That was great; I got to spend a few more days in Cairo, but I was a bit concerned about the money situation. It must be costing a bomb to keep us at Mena House and I did not want to be faced with a mess bill that I could not pay, so I wandered around the offices and found the movements officer who had sent us there. I asked him what sort of bill I was likely to be faced with. To my relief, he told me not to worry as the RAF would settle with Mena House for the accommodation and food, but I would have to pay them for extras (such as drinks and laundry) and on obtaining my clearance to leave, I might get a 'very reasonable' mess bill. That sounded to be just the job, so we could enjoy the rest of our 'holiday'.

Douggie and I decided to get a taxi back to Mena House, then have a bath and another good meal, especially now we knew we were not going to have to pay for it. We had at least another couple of days to have a look around Cairo, so there was no need to rush about like mad things, like we had done today. It seemed to get dark much earlier than it did in England at the end of June and we finished the day sitting on the terrace drinking the local brandy. It was still almost like a dream. I thought of Peggy, back in austere wartime England; if only she could be here with me, it would be like heaven. She would look rather nice in those see-through baggy trousers and veil like those dancers were wearing while we had dinner. As we were two hours ahead of GMT, with their double British Summer Time, it would only be about 6.30 p.m. at home, so I wondered what she was doing.

The next day, after visiting a very impressive museum and learning a lot about the history of Egypt, right up to the modern day, by mid-afternoon, we felt like some food and a sit, so we took a taxi to find a club we had been told about—the Gezira Sporting Club. This gave us our first sight of the Nile—a great, wide, blue river with some boats on it with a big, single sail. We crossed a long bridge over the river and arrived at this posh-looking place in the midst of colourful flower beds and plenty of greenery. Then the formalities began. As an officer, I could become a temporary member, but Douggie could not. In that case, I said I would not bother, telling this cocky receptionist that Douggie was my observer and that if he could not go in, neither would I. I fumbled with some piaster notes and he started to think, 'Well, sir, you could sign him in as your guest, if he wasn't wearing those stripes and the crown'. The stripes were only held on by press studs and the crown by a pin, so I motioned to Douggie to take them off.

This Egyptian receptionist then smiled and I slid over a couple of notes before he passed me the membership form for completion. Formalities completed and the fee paid, I was given a temporary membership card for one week. I signed Douggie in and, bowing and scraping, this receptionist directed us through to a luxurious lounge with big windows opening on to a terrace. We nonchalantly strolled through, out on to the terrace, settled on a couple of loungers in the shade and clapped our hands for a waiter to bring us lemon tea (the milk tasted funny here) and tea cakes. Douggie and I smiled at each other and he remarked, 'Happen, not a bad life, this'. Then, he got his eyes firmly stuck on some bronzed girls in the nearby swimming pool. We were quite happy just to sit here and did so for at least a couple of hours.

We eventually decided we had better drag ourselves to our feet and have a wander around. It covered a hell of an area—many beds of brilliant geraniums; not only a swimming pool but a golf course, tennis courts, and a polo field; and then we came across the river again on the other side. So we were not on the east bank as we thought; we were on a big island—all green and lush. It was surprising what a bit of water could do when you thought of that desert only a few miles away. We wandered round the club buildings, reading notices about all sorts of events; by now, we had realised that the place was for Europeans only (and only some Europeans at that). We flopped on some seats on the terrace, ordered a couple of long gin fizzes, and stayed till about 7 p.m., when we ordered a taxi and returned to Mena House to see what was on for dinner. We knew where to go the next day, bringing our swimming gear too, and Douggie would wear a sports shirt to avoid any bother. Fortunately, I was able to cash a cheque when we got back to Mena.

For our third full day in Cairo, we decided to have a look at the town and then go to the Gezira Club. We wandered down the narrow, winding alleys, full of funny smells, spices, and incense, looking at food shops and shops hanging with fancy cotton clothes. We smiled and nodded at folks trying to sell us leather goods, jewellery, and ornaments; we looked up at mosques and towering minarets and everywhere there were crowds of people. On a wider road, there were clanging tram cars full to overflowing. Outside a large mosque, a chap tried to convert us to the Islamic faith. We thanked him for the information, telling him, 'it sounds very good'. He bowed and smiled, saying, 'Allah be with you,' Douggie replied, 'And with you to,' and we pressed on.

The terrace round the swimming pool seemed very attractive so we hailed a taxi and crossed the big bridge to the Gezira Club, where, this time, we were greeted by the smiling receptionist. I signed Douggie in, wearing his checked sports shirt, and we were soon settled on the terrace with a drink. This would do for the rest of the day. We had a dip in the pool. Douggie was keener on swimming than I was; I had a couple of swims, keeping my head above water, but Douggie was in and out, diving and going down the chute and chattering to some girls. I did not know where they came from, but I was quite happy to watch from the shade of the terrace and when Douggie kept nipping back, I told him to watch out that he did not get sunburnt. It was a delightful afternoon. I decided to try and phone the airfield from here. The receptionist got them for me with no trouble at all. I was told that they were still working on her and that they had been held up but it would be ready for an air test the day after tomorrow. I also asked if Eric had turned up yet, but he had not. Douggie was delighted when I told him we had another couple of days for sure. We returned to Mena House in good time for dinner.

The main course for dinner was a very tasty dish, very spicy but mainly pigeon—a great delicacy in Egypt—followed by the usual fruit. As we sat out on the terrace with our brandy, looking towards the Pyramids, which were still faintly visible in the fading light, I remarked to Douggie how there was something very mysterious about those Pyramids—the sheer bloody engineering involved, not so much the fact that they got those damn great stones, especially that huge piece of granite over the funeral chamber into place, but if they had no drawings, how did they know where to start at the bottom so that all sides met in a perfect point at the top? How did they work it out to leave those passages, which had a perfectly even slope on the floor and perfectly smooth sides and get them to go where they wanted them to go?

Moreover, that ventilation shaft (or two shafts) to keep fresh air flowing through the corridors, yet nowhere did we see any light coming in. It was bloody marvellous, almost impossible. Also, what tools would they have? It does not sound as if they had any metal tools, and yet every stone is perfectly rectangular and a perfect fit. All this happened nearly 5,000 years ago, 1,000 years before the Bronze Age began in Britain. There must have been some super civilisation then, which knew a lot more than we think they did, and, for some reason wrote themselves off. What we had seen in the six days since we left Cornwall was almost too much to take in, especially on this trip of over 2,000 miles across North Africa (about the same distance as across the Atlantic).

We made 29 June an easy day. We went down to the Gezira Club at about noon. Swimming and lazing about till 6 p.m., although Douggie was much more active swimming than I was, then back to Mena House for a quiet drink before dinner when one of the boys came around paging me. I was wanted on the phone. I expected it would be the airfield but no, it was Eric: 'Just got in, old boy. They told me you were at Mena House'. 'Great to hear you Eric, where are you?' 'Only one place to stop in Cairo, Jacko that's Shepheards. Have you had dinner yet?' When I told him we were going to eat soon, he said, 'Get a cab down, soon as you have finished and we will have a look at the town'. I gave Douggie the news; we went straight in for dinner and took a taxi down to the famous Shepheards Hotel; Douggie was wearing a sports shirt, in case it was one of those officer-only places. When, at long last, I got my commission, I was not particularly bothered, but now I was beginning to appreciate the advantages of being an officer and was getting the feel of it quite well; it looked as if overseas, it makes a lot of difference.

We arrived at this big, old fashioned Arabesque hotel with its lofty hall, archways, harem screens, and ornate floors. Looking as if he had lived here all his life was Eric; he was a bit of a mystery man, our Eric. He clapped his hands, said something to one of the boys, and, in double quick time, there were whiskies in front of us plus a soda siphon. He had arrived early afternoon, having had a straight run through since he left Portreath. We related our experiences to him. His observer was not here; Eric was paying to stop here himself and his observer had been put up on the airfield. We decided that from then on, we would go together; he would wait for Snakecharmer to be fixed, which suited him fine as he wanted a day or two in Cairo.

After our drinks, Eric said we would go to a little place 'just down the road' where they put on a bit of music, so he ordered a taxi even though the trip took less than five minutes. Here, we entered a funny little place; we heard funny wailing music and entered a room so full of smoke that you could hardly see across it—blue smoke turning to purple as it drifted in front of dim red lights and a strangely sweet smell of incense. It seemed to be full of men, about half service chaps and the other half wearing red Fezzes. Eric seemed to be arguing with one of the boys as we sat at a table; he told us he had ordered a bottle as they charged too much for individual drinks. We tried to talk above all the hubbub and wailing music, occasionally coughing as a bloke smoking a thing like a water jug blew sweet smelling smoke right across us; it was probably opium. The whisky was OK; it tasted like the real stuff. After a while some announcement was made, which we probably would not have understood even if we could have heard it, but it was obvious from the change of noise that something was about to happen.

Sure enough, a girl appeared dressed as if she had come out of a harem. The service lads cheered and she started to gyrate. Now, this was quite interesting and clever too; she must have had wonderful muscles, as well as other things. The service lads started shouting and cheering. She had a fair enough figure and was a good mover but she was not Egyptian; she was not even from the Middle East, in all probability she was from Barnsley, but she put on a good act and at the end a fair number of piasters were thrown on the stage. Eric seemed to be settled for the night but Douggie and I thought better of it and, leaving Eric with about a quarter of his bottle of whisky, we decided to push off, arranging to meet him at the Gezira Club about midday tomorrow. We were glad to get in the fresh air and soon managed to get a taxi home. We had now seen a bit more of life in Cairo but were pleased to be going back to our beautiful Mena House.

The next morning, we sat in the shade around the swimming pool at the Gezira Club, Douggie being in and out of the pool like a yo-yo, but I kept off the booze in case Snakecharmer would be ready for an air test later in the day. We all took a taxi to Cairo West in mid-afternoon just as the temperature passed the 100 mark and found that Snakecharmer was supposed to be OK now. We decided to put off the air test until it cooled off a bit and went to the briefing room to get genned up for the next leg. It looked as if it would be an interesting trip—cross the canal at Ismailia (making sure to get clearance on the R/T before doing so), then to the northern tip of the Dead Sea, then to pick up the oil pipeline across the Syrian Desert following this to Habbaniya in Iraq, about 50 miles this side of Baghdad. We studied the charts; there seemed to be some pretty high ground in Palestine and Jordan, then 400 miles or so of desert. We then passed by some interesting place names, such as places referred to in the Bible.

By six o'clock, it had cooled down a bit so I went to see the engineering officer to fix up the air test. A flight sergeant who had been in charge of the work said he would come with me. They seemed confident that they had found the trouble; they thought it was something to do with the fuel supply and the automatic mixture arrangement. It seemed that when the throttle went through the gate, we initially got the extra fuel through to give maximum power, but in a matter of twenty seconds or so, the supply dropped right back to give a cruising mixture. This sounded to tie up with the symptoms, so the flight sergeant and I went off for the air test with reasonable confidence.

She behaved perfectly. For forty-five minutes, we flew around, pushing the boost up to +10 and 2,900 revs, leaving them there for four or five minutes, then back to cruising and opening up again when she had cooled down; to maintain full power for over five minutes was not advised as it could weld the plugs into the cylinders. The sun was beginning to throw long shadows. We avoided flying over the sprawling mass of Cairo but the green strip along the Nile stretched north and south as far as the eye could see, changing abruptly to arid, sandy desert at both sides—what a difference a river can make to a desert. Happy that everything was now OK we arranged to depart about 9 a.m., before it got too hot; we had an early night with no booze, packed our kit, and prepared to go 'East of Suez'.

10
East of Suez

At 9 a.m. local time, we lifted off from the desert at Cairo West, skipped the town to avoid disturbing Muslims at prayer, and headed just north of east, into the brilliant sun, heading for Ismailia. Eric had formated with me, loosely on the starboard side; it was nice to be in the air again, heading towards more strange lands. The Beaufighter is the perfect 'sightseeing' machine (for the pilot), sitting there with a panoramic view and such a short nose that you can almost see directly under your feet. In twenty minutes, we saw the canal coming up, identified Ismailia, and called the RAF station on the R/T to get permission for the two of us to cross.

It all looked pretty wild and barren over here—generally flat but the land rose a bit to the south. Soon, we saw the blue Mediterranean sweeping in, in a big curve ahead and to port; we flew a tangent to this coastline, passing over a little settlement (Rafah) and as the coast swept away from us to the north, we saw another settlement on the coast (Gaza). We could now see the high ground some way ahead, so we gently climbed to 5,000 feet. The temperature up here was very pleasant; Eric and I were using one of the spare R/T frequencies so that we could talk to each other. The ground below was now becoming very rugged, with big outcrops of rock, a few small trees (probably olives), and bits of scrub. It was a miracle anything at all could grow here; it looked to be all bare brown rock and dust.

We were now over what used to be called Judaea, looking down at wild and rugged country, scorched by the heat of the sun. To the south, there were rugged mountains with which we were slowly converging;

some 10 miles or so to starboard was the 3,040 feet summit of Mount Hebron. After another five minutes, we were almost slap over Bethlehem, which seemed to be clinging to a mountainside. Almost immediately, 7 or 8 miles to port was Jerusalem. Then there was little Bethany, just 1 mile or so east of Jerusalem, nestling in the hills. Too busy looking at all these Biblical place names, I had hardly noticed that we were coming to the edge of these mountains; they had suddenly fallen away and instead of us being only about 2,500 feet above the ground we were about 6,000 and right below was the northern tip of the Dead Sea.

The shores of the Dead Sea are the lowest point on the surface of the earth and for a while, Eric and I debated over the R/T whether we should nip down there as there was plenty of space, just to say we had actually flown at 1,200 feet below sea level; it was a bit of one-upmanship. However, we decided that we had better not as the RAF at Amman may be equipped with radar and if they saw us disappear off their screens, we could be in bother. Reluctantly, we set off for Amman where we altered course to head out over the Syrian Desert to pick up the pipeline.

Soon, we saw a black ribbon, stretching like a ruler, across the barren desert, straight as a die right up to the horizon. It was the pipeline, carrying the lifeblood of the twentieth century—oil—from the wells in Iraq to the Mediterranean port of Haifa. All we had to do was follow this pipeline to Habbaniya, on the banks of the Euphrates, where there was a big lake near the airfield, so we should not miss it.

We were nearly halfway now. A couple of hours of following this pipeline would see us there. There were pumping stations along the pipeline, each with a rolled sand strip nearby so that light aircraft could land. They were numbered 'H5' etc., and we checked them off as we went along. The sun had moved round a bit now, so it was no longer straight in our eyes. We were flying in very loose formation; in fact, you could hardly call it formation, more like merely 'being in company'. From time to time, Eric moved in a bit closer and waltzed from one side to the other to relieve the monotony. The desert was absolutely featureless and seemed to go on forever. After about an hour, the pipeline began to sneak about a bit, presumably to keep as level as possible as the desert looked to be slightly undulating, but there was still nothing but rolling, drifting sand. More or less on cue, a mark on the horizon turned out to be some trees and a lake, on which there was an old biplane flying-boat. We called Habbaniya on the R/T and at the same time saw the airfield that had lots of very permanent-looking buildings, all set out like a UK peacetime aerodrome with a big tented camp nearby; it looked like a town stuck in the middle of the desert.

They gave us clearance to land, telling us there was no other traffic about and Eric moved in, almost on my wing tip. We had stayed at 5,000 feet as it was reasonably cool up there. Eric said we would go in together; he would follow me. So, as they said there was no other traffic about, Eric said, 'We'll give them a bit of a show'. So, I came down in a diving turn from 5,000 feet to just under 1,000 feet. We did a relatively tight circuit, on the crosswind leg. Eric called me: 'Keep well over to port. I'll be beside you'; in we went. When I saw him out the corner of my eye, I thought, 'By, Jove, he's close'. Eric and I had never formated on each other when on the squadron and as we taxied in, I thought he was pretty good, but he must have had confidence in me, too, or he would never have landed that close to me; he was almost alongside. Meanwhile, I kept talking to Douggie, but there was no answer; I could not get a peep out of him, although he had been talking OK before we came down. As soon as I stopped the engines and undid my harness so that I could look round, I could see him slumped over his table.

I got to the back as quickly as possible. He looked as white as a sheet and had passed out. We got him out the aircraft; it was absolutely boiling hot, so we carried him to the shade under the wing. A truck soon arrived and we took him straight to the station hospital. This was a big, modern, and fully equipped hospital, tolerably cool compared with outside. The MO soon saw him and he began to come around but had a terrible pain in his head and a very high temperature. They soon had him in bed, and I left to sort out the formalities with the aircraft.

By Jove, it was hot here; it seemed as hot as it had been at Biskra. It was a matter of dodging from shade to shade. It was 1 July and just after midday. We had spent three hours and forty minutes on the journey. I could not get over the buildings here, permanent solid buildings to typical RAF peacetime specifications. With proper roads bearing names like 'Cheapside', I had never been on a station like this before. When a batman showed me to my nicely furnished room, I remarked about a big radiator on the wall just under the window, saying, 'I don't suppose you ever need that?' To this, he replied, 'Oh, you do, sir, gets very cold at night, gets below freezing'.

So, the next three days were spent mainly with Douggie in his hospital room; at least it was about the coolest place on the station. One day, I did think of having a trip to Baghdad on a truck going to fetch provisions, but it was so bloody hot and I knew the road would be so dusty that I decided it would be far more comfortable with Douggie. He did not seem to be making a lot of progress; he was white, still had a temperature, and had a pain in his ear, but he kept insisting he was feeling better and the pills were doing the trick.

The mess was quite a revelation with bags of silverware and trophies. The pre-dinner drinks in the anteroom and the food were out of this world. There were pictures on the wall of the local hunt all dressed up in their Hunting pink—all service officers, of course. I only had Eric's company for one night as the station commander would not hear of him waiting for me, so now he was ahead of me. The second night in the mess was a full-scale peacetime 'dining in night'. All very proper and correct, they seemed to be able to produce any drink you could imagine—English gin, Scotch whisky (malt and blended), wines, the port to pass around, and a very smooth brandy. You could have imagined yourself in Cranwell instead of out in the middle of the desert in Iraq. The Groupie seemed a pleasant enough fellow but obviously wanted everything done correctly which I think was great to see; after dinner one of the chaps remarked:

> The Old Man is OK, but he's got eyes in the back of his head. If he notices any one at table, holding a knife like a spoon, or using the wrong cutlery, he has a quiet word with them in the nicest possible way—telling them that they would be letting him down if they did it somewhere else when they left here.

The few pilots seemed interested to ask questions about the Beaufighter, moaning that, the only thing they seemed to do was to fly patrols along the pipeline, flying slow, obsolete aircraft and get a few days' detachment to one of the staging posts at the head of the gulf. The engineering officer was joking about another Stirling he had stuck here, making two, both of which were likely to stay here for good; it seemed the Stirling had a complicated system of operating the control surfaces, not simple cables like most other aircraft but a system of servos and relays that kept packing up and they could not get spares. He said there were US Stirlings all over the Middle East; it cheered him up even more when I told him I had noticed one at Cairo West.

On 5 July, I had some bad news. Douggie seemed a lot more cheerful when I called at the hospital, but the MO told me that he thought he would have to give up flying and that he would be making arrangements for him to be sent back to the UK. This was a real blow as Douggie and I had got to know each other very well; we understood each other as we had been through a bit of flak together and we seemed to have mutual faith in each other. Douggie insisted he was feeling a lot better and would soon be OK, but the MO seemed to have made up his mind. Later in the day, I saw the officer in charge of the transit flight; he wanted me to get away as soon as possible, 'Before the aircraft went U/S with standing in this heat', saying I should formate with the next Beaufighter to come through. I hoped this would be in a few days and that the MO may change his mind, but drat it, a Beau arrived that afternoon and it was arranged that I would go with him in the morning. I took Douggie's kit to the sergeants' mess, along with his sealed envelope of documents, and had it locked up in the mess office. I went to the shops in Cheapside and bought some fruit and after dinner, sadly went to the hospital to say 'Cheerio'.

The next leg was to be down to the head of the Persian Gulf, then down the western shore to Muhurraq on Bahrain Island. I got myself a set of maps and charts, made a note of R/T frequencies, and met this rather cocky fellow on whom I was supposed to formate. As we taxied out, I could not make out where he was going and he was blowing up so much sand that I could hardly see. I asked him which side he wanted me but he did not answer; then he pulled slap bang in the middle of the runway and blew up such a cloud of sand that I never saw him again. I waited for the sand to drift away before I could see to pull onto the runway, he was nowhere in sight so, after take-off, I just throttled back to cruising and set off on my own.

Navigation was no problem. I had hardly seen a cloud since we passed the Bay of Biscay, just little puffy white cumulus here and there. All I had to do was to keep the Euphrates on my right and make sure I did not cross the Tigris on my left and I was bound to get to Basra. In twenty minutes, just to starboard, I saw some buildings on both sides of the Euphrates; a reference to the map told me it was Babylon. It looked to be mostly ruins covering quite a large area, but there were signs of life down there, as well as quite a bit of movement, so it looked as if it was still active as a small town. The map showed 'Babel' a little further on; I supposed that was where the tower was, but I could not see any signs of it. Some areas seemed to be reasonably well-cultivated down here; there were a number of little rivers, meandering across this flat plain, some of which seemed to be dried up. I had no one to talk to—no Douggie in the back to tell me when something interesting was coming up—so I talked to myself. I was not used to being all by myself in an aircraft; I felt like a sultan, sitting all alone on a magic carpet. I maintained course and let the Euphrates slide away on the starboard side, knowing it should come back to me soon. Sure enough, a big lake was coming up, which looked most extraordinary; it was either studded with little islands or there were hundreds of rafts on it. It was a bit difficult to tell exactly from up there, but they looked to be floating rafts of reeds with little reed houses on them. There was Basra, which looked a big busy place. The two rivers had met by this point—one big wide one carrying on, there also seemed to be other smaller ones, like a delta. There were about 60 miles to go to the head of the gulf, so it was nearly time to give Shaibah a call to tell them I was carrying on to Bahrain.

When the Persian Gulf came into view, it was just like coming to the open sea, being so wide that I could not see either side of it. I altered 40 degrees to starboard to pick up the western shore. There was no joy from Shaibah on the R/T. I was picking up the coast of Kuwait and could see a small forest of oil-drilling rigs. Ahead, it was beginning to look all hazy and very soon, I seemed to be in a thin, hazy cloud. I decided that the R/T had packed up as I could not hear anything from anybody and as there was no chance of me using the W/T (which was in the back), I decided that the wisest thing to do was to go back to Shaibah and get the R/T fixed before going down the Gulf.

I turned around and set course across the water for Shaibah; it was quite clear back there, and as the airfield was easy to find, down I went. It was only a staging post with tents, but the lads fixed the R/T while I had a snack in a tent with a card saying 'officers' mess' nailed to a pole by the entrance. I gathered that the haze over the gulf was a 'sand haze', which was quite a normal thing due to the high humidity. With the R/T working, I set off, knowing that, if necessary, I could get the VHF bearings from Bahrain. Following the coast of Arabia, trying to identify little off-shore islands, bumps, and inlets, some one hour and forty-five minutes after take-off, I picked up the large island of Bahrain and the two smaller islands, on the second of which was the airfield.

However, it all looked fuzzy and indistinct. I called control but circled around to try and sum-up what I was seeing—the surface of the sea did not seem to be there. It was so dashed calm and clear that you could not see the surface; you seemed to look straight through to the bottom, which was like white rock (maybe coral). The threshold of the runway was right at the edge of the water, but I did not have a clue how high I was above the water by just looking out. Then, I remembered that I had a radio altimeter; thank goodness it still worked. So, I set about the landing procedure. Approaching over the water felt most peculiar, looking straight down through the water to the bottom yet everything around was hazy. The radio altimeter was a godsend. Then as I got nearer to touch down, the whole land in front of me started violently shimmering. The runway looked to be covered with huge pools of water; I had no idea really where the surface of the runway was until the wheels touched and I gave the wheel a nudge forward to keep her down as I cut the engines. Then, as we rolled down this shimmering, wet-looking runway, a bloody great ship seemed to appear right across the runway. It was weird; my heart came into my mouth as it looked as if I was going to shoot over the edge of the harbour wall when, just as quickly as it had appeared, this ship disappeared. When I pulled up at the end of the runway, I could see it, far enough away, in the harbour. It must have been a mirage. It was funny; we saw one in the Arctic where it was very cold and now I had seen one where it was bloody hot. What a funny place; everything you looked at was shimmering and I was perspiring like hell. In the office, I noticed that everyone was sweating; if you put your bare arm on the desk, all the loose papers stuck to it. It was not actually as hot as at Habb, but everybody was wet and looked 'buggered'. The humidity was over 95 per cent.

Before dinner, I thought I would cool off by having a shower. This was not a very good idea at all. Out of the shower, I realised that I was getting wetter instead of drier; the exertion of drying myself was making me sweat faster than I could dry it up, so I tried just dabbing myself with the towel but finally gave up and just put my clothes on over the wet. I pitied the poor blokes who were here for any length of time; they must have lost pounds in weight and had to stuff themselves with salt tablets to avoid getting cramp. After dinner, I sat in the station's open-air cinema; at least you could sit quietly there and look up at the stars. I had seen the film before—Deanna Durbin in *Three Smart Girls*—and although the sound was awful, there were some funny remarks made by the audience.

I was glad to get away the next morning and headed just south of due east—once again into that dazzling sun—across the big bay at the south of the gulf, getting on for 300 miles to Sharjah. I incorporated a 'deliberate error' into my course so that I would hit the coast south-west of Sharjah; I would then be sure which way to turn on arriving at the coast, as the briefing officer had told me at Bahrain that the coastline along there was absolutely bare except for this little airstrip and a clump of palm trees just to the south-west. After an hour and a half, I was flying up the coastline. By Jove, he was right; there was no place in sight. Then, there was a clump of palm trees and a bit further along a few tents, a bit of a jetty, and a few buildings, then just beyond the tents were the markings of an airstrip on the sand.

I had not intended to stop here for longer than it took to pick up some fuel and get briefed for the final leg to Karachi. However, one of the erks noticed a hydraulic leak and the officer who seemed to be in charge of everything told me that he would not advise me carrying on that day, especially without a navigator, as by late afternoon, they were beginning to get some build-up of cloud over the Baluchistan Mountains and it could drift over Karachi. The night there was interesting—still hot and humid but not as bad as at Bahrain. I stayed in a little tented mess, which seemed to be shared by three officers and a couple of senior NCOs. It was all a bit balmy but good fun.

Bright and early in the morning, I left Sharjah on the last leg of my journey to India—the land of diamonds, rubies, and other priceless gems. First of all, it was a matter of following the coast, north-east to the tip of the Oman Peninsular, then turning south-east across the Strait of Hormuz for 90 miles or so to a point off the coast opposite Jask. It was either that or going over some rugged looking mountains going up nearly 7,000 feet. I thought I had better navigate properly along this bit, not just follow the coast, in case these clouds they told me about did materialise, so I tried to estimate the wind speed and direction from the state of the surface of the sea below. I reckoned there was no wind or if there was, it was very slight. I set courses from the chart, which should have kept me parallel to the coast, so if I drifted one way or the other, it would give me a reasonable idea of the wind and I could check my ground speed as we passed any point I could identify. From a couple of miles out, the mountains seemed to rise almost directly from the sea—some pretty high, too—and they all looked rugged and unfriendly.

I could pick out a pointed peninsular near Jiwani, a rounded knob sticking out near Gwadar, a smooth rounded headland at Pasni, then a big peninsular shaped like a 'T' at Ormara. From here, I altered course to starboard, left the coast, and headed across the water for 140 miles to Karachi. The clouds were building up ahead and over to port. An uninteresting coastline appeared looking very drab under grey clouds. I picked out the town, then the big, black, corrugated iron hangar that was built especially for the R101 (but she never made it) and then the airfield. It had taken me three hours and fifty minutes. It was 8 July—seventeen days since I left Cornwall—but I had only flown (apart from the air tests) on seven of those days, the total time in the air being thirty hours and twenty-five minutes. It was not exactly a speed record, but I had seen a lot of interesting places on the way.

First of all, I had to report to the medical officer and this was where my troubles continued, as if it was not bad enough having had to leave Douggie behind. The MO was an Indian flying officer. He asked for my Yellow Fever inoculation card, which I had in my pocket as I had been warned that they would want to see it. The card was in a little sealed envelope, marked 'Only be opened by Medical Staff'. I handed it over; he opened it and then started doing his little nut—waving his head about and throwing his arms in the air and chattering at great speed something about it not being any good. When I calmed him down, he showed me the card and there was nothing written on it, only a rubber stamp on the back showing the name of the medical centre where it was done. He rushed out and told me not to move; I think he thought I had Yellow Fever. He returned with another MO (an English squadron leader) and the Indian chap started blaming me for not having the card completed. I was beginning to get a bit fed up and pointed out that it was not up to me to fill it in; also, how the hell was I to know that the MO had not filled it in when I was given it in a sealed envelope that I was not allowed to open? The squadron leader seem to understand this and after me telling him the date when it was done and that the chap who did it told me it was against Yellow Fever, he seemed to accept the position, filled in the date and the words 'Yellow Fever', put the card back in another envelope, and handed it back.

The next call was to 'book in' and here I got a rollicking for having flown solo from Sharjah, especially at this time of the year, when the clouds were building up, and there was a standing order that 'All aircraft not carrying a competent navigator must only fly between

Karachi and the gulf if in formation with an aircraft which is carrying a fully qualified navigator and fully equipped with radio navigation aids'. I argued that no one had told me about any such order; in any case, I was going to formate but the silly bugger pissed off without me. Even so, I could not see what all the fuss was about because although I was wearing pilot wings, I was a fully competent GR navigator (general-reconnaissance maritime and naval co-operation trained navigator) and a wireless operator, if it came to that. This bloke reckoned that did not make any difference and that I should not have flown solo. I thought he was going to 'put me on a court martial' so I said I wanted to see the station commander; he then dried up and told me to remember that standing order in future. I was beginning to get fed up with this place.

The third call was to the movements officer to find out where I was to go next. I cheerfully knocked on the door and went in saying, 'Good afternoon. I've brought a Torbeau from the UK for a Torbeau squadron which I understand is being formed somewhere out here. I was told to report to you for instructions as to where I am to go next'.

'Not another one,' was his reply, 'had another fellow in four days ago and said exactly the same thing. We knew nothing about it so I checked with ACSEA, JACSEA, and BAFSEA, even with the Navy chaps at Kandy and after a couple of days I'd heard from all of them and none of them knew anything about using Torbeaus out here'.

'Who are these Ack-sea, Baf-sea and Jack-sea you talk about and where is Kandy?' I inquired.

'ACSEA is Air Command Southeast Asia, the others are Joint Air Command Southeast Asia and British Air Forces Southeast Asia and Kandy is in Ceylon—the Headquarters of the Supreme Commander—between them they cover everything which is going on from here eastwards'.

'What has happened to the Flying Officer who came in the other day?' I asked.

'We sent him to a Reception Centre at Worli, in Bombay as there was no point in him staying here – he went by train yesterday'.

'What happened to his aircraft, because it would be fitted with all the torpedo gear like mine is?'

'Oh, that will have gone to the MU and they will probably whip the torpedo gear out and fit it out for rockets. So, if you let me have your documents and your observer's, I'll get things fixed up and you can go down to Worli in a few days—there isn't a suitable train for a day or two'.

'I'm afraid', I replied, 'I haven't got an observer. I had to leave him at Habb with a bit of ear trouble, but please don't start on about me coming solo, I've already been through all that. I'd like to think that he will be following me but I have a feeling they are going to send him back to the UK'.

'That's a pity', he said, 'Worli won't to be very pleased to get only half a crew; anyway, you'll be wanting to get over to the mess and they will fix you up with a room. Drop in and see us in a couple of days and we will see what we can fix up'. Well, what a cock-up. Old Paddy on the squadron would really say, 'Bloody Air Ministry', if he knew about this balls-up. There I was stuck in the worst place I had seen since leaving England with no observer, no aeroplane and no one wanted me.

The officers' 'transit' mess was little better than a UK NAAFI, except it had some 'easy' chairs and plenty of surly servants hanging around. My room was like a little prison cell—cream white-washed walls, with splashes of blood as decorations, presumably where previous occupants had swatted cockroaches, and a rope charpoy. A *'coolie'* deposited my kit and waited for his *'baksheesh'*; I soon twigged that you do not carry anything yourself out here. Then a 'bearer' appeared, his hands together as if saying a prayer and nodding his head from side to side, *'Salaam, sahib'*. By the use of pidgin English, signs, and antics, I gathered that he would be looking after me and several other *sahibs* in this block. He shook his head in disgust at the sight of the charpoy and indicated that for *baksheesh*, he would get me a better one, then seemed horrified that I had no bedding; he would borrow some for me and also a mug for when the *'chai wallah'* came around.

He nodded and smiled when I showed him that I had a mosquito net. He soon returned with another *wallah*. With a lot of shouting and gesticulations, they removed the rope charpoy and replaced it with one with canvas webbing; I bet they would swap them back after I left so that they could get *baksheesh* from the next chap to move in. In a while, he returned again, this time with a roll of bedding; he fixed my mosquito net on to some poles tied to the legs of the charpoy to make my bed. Then he wanted to unpack my kit, but I was a bit particular here and only let him have my clothes. He whipped away some that had been worn and I gathered he was going to send these to the *'dhobi wallah*'; then, he started spreading out those that he had decided I was going to wear for dinner.

Dinner was actually very enjoyable, but it seemed to get dark very early for the time of year; it was getting dark by about 7.30 p.m., and then we were infested with flying insects of all shapes and sizes. I knew it was long slacks and sleeves rolled down by sundown because of mosquitoes, but mosquitoes were in the minority. There were buzzing little things, big flying beetles and moths, then a blister came up on the back of my hand and another on my neck. The fellow I was with said they were called something or other and they pissed on you as they flew over, which brings up these blisters full of liquid. 'Don't touch them,' he said, 'otherwise other blisters will come up where the liquid runs. They will have gone by morning. By the way, you did take your mepacrine tablets at dinner, didn't you? They were the yellow ones; the white ones in the other bowl were salt tablets. All these bloody insects are about because we are beginning to get the rains'.

To cap it all, a damn big blue insect, with wings like a dragonfly, perched itself on the rim of my glass. It seemed to be sitting on its big rear legs, its two little front legs hanging down like a miniature kangaroo; two little eyes on its pea-sized head seemed to be looking straight at me, and two little antenna sticking out the top of its head moved around as the whole creature swayed from side to side. 'What the hell is that?' I asked. 'Oh, for Christ's sake don't touch that, it's holy to these folk. It's a Praying Mantis. If you shoo it off, all the bloody mess staff will walk out. You will just have to wait till it decides to go. It's supposed to bring good luck'. The blessed thing stayed there for ages, staring me in the eyes and swaying from side to side; in fact, I soon began to admire it as it was such an amazing creature.

Back at my room, I found that was also full of insects; three or four were big, black beetles, flying around very slowly, crashing into the plaster wall with a crunch, followed by another crunch as they fell to the floor. I put my foot on a couple but decided this was going to be a losing battle, as more were coming in, so I dived under the mosquito net as fast as I could and got undressed inside. Then I realised that I had left the light on, so, after making sure the net was tucked well in all-round and there did not seem to be anything in with me, I called to the bearer, who was in the corridor outside, to come in and put the light out. Until I got to sleep, all I could hear was the high-pitched buzz of mosquitoes and the low-pitched noise of flying beetles followed by a crunch as they hit the wall, sometimes followed by another as they hit the floor. I was not at all sure that I was going to enjoy India.

I realised that I would have to get myself a decent bedroll as you needed one wherever you were and for sleeping on trains. I had also been advised to get a trunk with a good airtight seal in order to keep out ants and termites, so I ventured into town, got some cash from Cox & Kings, and did a bit of shopping. I was not very impressed with Karachi—there were not any particularly nice buildings, as well as lots of folks on bikes, old cars, and bullock carts. Walking around sacred cows sitting in the middle of the footpath and circumnavigating piles of sacred shit, I strolled around lots of children asking for *baksheesh*; then it started to rain so I got a *gharry* (a four-wheeled horse-drawn vehicle with a pram-type hood) back to the station. I examined my money to get used to the coinage—the round rupee and the half rupee, the square two anna and half-anna pieces with rounded corners and the round one anna with its wavy edge. A rupee was worth 1/6*d*, and as there were sixteen annas to the rupee, an anna was about a penny. There were also some pice or pies, but they were too small to bother about, except for *baksheesh*.

There seemed to be absolutely nothing to do in this place. There was an English paper in the mess that I read from cover to cover to see what progress there was with the invasion. I studied a map of India and tried to learn a few more Indian words. The weather was lousy, warm, and raining on and off. The movements officer was evasive when I asked him what was going on and, in spite of the insects, I was glad when it was sundown and we could have a few drinks.

This went on for five depressing days and then I could not believe my eyes as walking on the station, I saw Douggie coming down towards the mess. I shouted out 'Douggie'. He came running up, saying, 'Thank God I found you'. For a while, we were both talking together and when we got over the excitement, it transpired that they let him out of hospital two days after I left and told him to go back for a check-up in a couple of days to see whether he should go back to the UK. Then he got talking to some Yanks who were night-stopping on their way to Karachi and persuaded them to give him a lift, so he just left with them the following morning without telling anybody, and he was relieved when a chap in the movements office told him I was still here. I took him to my room, called the *chai wallah*, and we had a long chat. I was overjoyed to see him and not a little touched by the fact that he had got himself here just to be back with me, but I was worried in case he was going to do himself any harm if there was still something wrong with his ear. Anyhow, as he had his documents with him, still in the sealed envelopes (no one had asked for them in Habb). I decided that we would get ourselves along to the movements officer and I would tell him that, 'Here is my observer. He is OK now and here are his documents'.

The movements officer seemed a bit surprised but at the same time very pleased and said he may be able to get us away to Bombay in the morning as there was a train. Things were looking up. Not only was I going to get away from this dump, but Douggie and I were together again.

11
The Train to Bombay

The train was due to leave at 4 a.m. It did not sound as if this was going to be an 'express' journey to Bombay. There was no direct line from Karachi to Bombay. It meant three different railway companies and three changes of train. The way we were going was a little less than 1,000 miles and looked like taking about thirty-seven hours, but we were excited to be on the move as we had had enough of hanging around in Karachi. As the train would be in the station, we went down at about 1 a.m., threaded our way through bodies sleeping on the platform, found the RTO who directed us to our reserved compartment, gave the *coolies* their *baksheesh* for loading our kit, and sat down to take stock of the situation. Douggie and I were to be together on the first three trains but on the final train, his warrant was for second class only, which seemed unfair to me. It seemed that on the first three trains, there only were two classes so they allowed NCOs to travel first class, but on the final train, there would be three classes, so they only allowed officers to travel first class.

The first thing that struck us was that there was no corridor, but we were relieved to find the door in the corner of the compartment led into a little toilet and washroom. The main compartment had long bench seats, which were reasonably soft and covered with dark green leather; one side would seat five or six people and the one on the side where the little toilet door was, about four. Above each was a let-down bunk, supported by two chains. The RTO said there would be another couple of chaps in with us, so Douggie and I felt the seats and the bunks and decided that we would grab the bunks. So, we unrolled our bedrolls and were just clambering up at about 2 a.m. when the other chaps arrived. We really could not get to sleep as there was so much shouting outside—everyone sounded very excited—and at about 4 a.m., with a big jerk, we started to move. We were on our way and I went hard asleep for a couple of hours.

The first change of train was to be at about 7 a.m. at Hyderabad; it was called Hyderabad (Sind) to distinguish it from the other Hyderabad in Central India. We left the North Western Railway and got on the Jodhpur railway. Shortly after getting up, having a wash and shave, and rolling up our bedrolls, we came to a little place where there seemed to be hundreds of folk around; we ran parallel to a road, doing at least 30 mph, then crossed the River Indus and entered the large town of Hyderabad. The platform was an absolute bedlam. *Coolies* buzzed around to carry our kit and hundreds of folks seem to be trying to get on our train to go north towards Lahore or Rawalpindi. They were fighting to get into the second-class carriages, which were just covered wagons with slatted wooden seats, and those already inside seemed to be pushing newcomers off.

The RTO told us that our train would leave in about two hours, but it would be in the station in another hour or so. He would see to our kit being put on it and we might as well go for breakfast. After a jolly good breakfast in the station restaurant, we walked around the station but could not get much of a view of the town, folks tried to sell us silk scarves and bits of jewellery—'Genuine silver, *sahib*, very good, very cheap'—then we got settled in our train. This leg was to be about 300 miles across the Sind Desert; it was already getting hot, although only nine o'clock. We should be off this train after nine or ten hours, so sleeping arrangements did not matter and there were six of us in the compartment, which was the same arrangement as in the previous train. The extra two were Army types, who appeared to be quite experienced at travelling in India.

About 9 a.m., we set off with the usual jerk and fiddled around with the windows; there was a choice of closed windows of dark blue glass or lowering the glass and pulling up a wooden slatted screen; the latter was best for getting some ventilation but you could not see anything. Alternatively, you could just have the whole lot open but smoke from the engine and dust blew in then, so it was a matter of compromise. For ninety minutes, we seemed to run right by the side of a dusty road, overtaking bullock carts, even a camel cart, as we were doing at least

35 mph on this straight stretch. Groups of folks waved to us; women were trudging along with brass or clay pots on their heads and near a small river, some poor-looking crops were trying to grow. We seemed to have got away from the clouds and rain of Karachi and at a small place, we came to a halt. Immediately, the side of the track appeared to be swarming with folks who had jumped off the train; everyone seemed to be waving their arms about and talking excitedly. I hung out the window; the engine was taking on water and also some fuel, which looked to me to be wood. Then, with a lot of shouting, some *coolies* opened our door and, with big iron tongs, dragged in a huge piece of ice, about 3 feet × 2 feet × 2 feet, which they dumped in the middle of the floor of the compartment. Shortly after, the whistle blew, folks climbed back on board, and we moved off.

From here, we seemed to leave the road and strike out across the desert. There was nothing to see but scrub and dust. The ice was melting and water was flowing all over the floor and running out under the door, so we had to keep our feet off the ground. Dust was blowing in, so we settled on having both the glass and the wooden shutters up; two chaps got on the top bunks, so we all had room to stretch out with our feet off the floor. After another stop for no obvious reason, then another where we seemed to be taking on water from a big metal tank, then, at about 2.30 p.m., we stopped at a small spot called Barmer for lunch in the station restaurant. We seemed to be in the middle of nowhere; there was a track from here going up north. Folks were milling around making a lot of noise, boxes were being unloaded and put on old lorries, and there was even a clapped-out bus. The arrival of the train seemed to be a big event; as we walked to the restaurant, we passed cans of petrol being unloaded from our train.

The food was OK but it was hot in that restaurant in spite of a '*punkah wallah*' busy working his *punkah* with a piece of string tied to his big toe, while he sat on the platform outside slowly moving his foot. This long *punkah* (a bamboo pole about ten feet long with a strip of canvas about three feet deep dangling from it) kept slowly waving to and fro, but one of the Army chaps who was with us complained that he was not 'punking' fast enough; it had little effect. He also told us that there was no need to rush our meal as the train would not go without us.

Another hour or so of absolutely nothing, then we reached a bit of poor looking cultivation and soon got glimpses of a river on our right;

there was a bit more life around now and it was getting pleasantly cool. Just as it was getting dark—it seemed to get dark very quickly here—we steamed into Jodhpur. This seemed to be a big place too. Once again, it was a matter of keeping our eyes on the *coolies* with our kit while we found the RTO. We had nearly two hours to wait, so, as before, the RTO looked after our kit and we made for the restaurant and a leisurely dinner. So far, we had been travelling east all the time; we were no nearer Bombay than when we set off, even though we had done about 400 miles.

The next leg was just a short one, 60 miles or so, on another line of the Jodhpur railway (although for the first 20 miles or so, we were retracing our tracks) to Todgarh, where we would pick up our last train—the Delhi to Bombay train on the Bombay, Baroda and Central India Railway. Being dark, we saw nothing to speak of, but we stopped a lot and there seemed to be plenty of life around.

At about 11 p.m., we pulled into Todgarh and then the fun began. The Bombay train was already in. The RTO took us to our reserved compartments, only to find them already occupied. After a lot of shouting with Indian officials, he got the occupants turned out; a big crowd had gathered by now and were pushed away by the military police, and people were waving bits of paper at each other. I was keeping a watchful eye on our kit; in due course, all was sorted out. Four of us got our first-class compartment and I hung on to make sure that Douggie and another NCO were fixed up OK. Just before midnight, we moved off and in next to no time, we had our bedrolls spread out and went out like a light. It had been a long day, but these beds were grand. The next thing I knew was being shaken and being told, 'It's half past seven. We are in Ahmedabad for an hour. Are you coming for breakfast?'

They did jolly good meals in the station restaurants and very cheap too. Leaving Ahmedabad at about 8.30 a.m., we then took it in turns to use the washroom, have a good shave and so, after a good sleep, a good breakfast, and a good wash, we were ready to settle down and enjoy the rest of the day. We seemed to stop about every half hour, sometimes at little stations, sometimes just where a track crossed the line, sometimes for no apparent reason at all. At the little stations, a *chai wallah* would appear with his brass urn and tin of '*doodh*' (milk); one thing I had discovered about India was that you could always obtain a good cup of tea.

It was beginning to get jolly hot when, after a couple of hours, we pulled into Baroda. This was a most superior station—spotlessly clean, tubs of brightly coloured flowers, a big wide platform, with a row of tall, ornate lights running down the middle, the station building looking more like a palace, a tall elegant tower in the middle, flanked on either side by long, lofty, single-storey wings, in front of each wing being a covered walk behind carved stone archways. There were plenty of people around but not the rabble we had seen at other stations. Everyone looked prosperous—some in their European style white cotton suits; some in loose white 'skirts' right down to their ankles, plus a long white shirt and white turban; some wearing the white *dhoti*; others had white slacks and loose jacket with their shirt tails hanging out below the jacket and all sorts of colours and shapes of turban. Everybody looked clean; there were no beggars about here. The town seemed very big; we could see the tops of many splendid-looking buildings, temples, and palaces, and there were green trees about—by far the nicest looking place I had seen in India so far. A huge slab of ice was put in our compartment and after a bit of jogging backwards and forwards as we were coupled to a different engine (a big rugged affair with four men on the footplate), we were on our way, passing fields of corn and colourful fields of poppies. It was getting very hot and humid too; our clothes were wet with sweat, in spite of the thawing ice block in the middle of the floor.

The next 45 miles to Broach must have been done at record speed, with no stops, and the big long train arrived in the hour. We were glad to see the *chai wallah* but did not fancy the highly coloured sticky cakes his pal was offering from a tray covered with a piece of muslin, weighed down with beads to keep the flies off. A railway official came around the first-class compartments taking orders for 'tiffin', which we would be taking in Surat, 40 miles further on, where there would be an hour's stop. Our orders, he said, would be passed to Surat by telegraph and if we told him what curried dish we would like, it would be waiting for us. I was quite impressed by this efficiency and it worked, too. On arrival, we found a piece of paper by each place setting on the table, a name was written at the top; below was some script I could not understand but it presumably said what we wanted and, in no time at all, a boy was putting the dish in front of us. The *chapattis* here were really good (flat wheat cakes served hot). I was already getting to like the Indian *chapattis* and poppadoms (thin crisp pancakes), which scattered crumbs all over the table as you broke them. Strolling back to the train after tiffin, I noticed that there were no shadows, although the sun was beating down; the sun was absolutely dead above us, so even a tall pole did not throw a shadow. We were now inside the Tropics.

Shortly after leaving Surat, the hills started rising on the left and it began to get stickier and stickier. We crossed some fair-sized rivers, and the land looked better cultivated. We kept stopping, bought a few cups of 'char', and after an hour or so, we had a glimpse of the sea out on the right. We could see clouds building up over mountains on the left. After another hour, the sun was obscured, but it was still very warm and sticky. Then it started to rain—really heavy rain—as we crossed a couple of wide estuaries and in ten minutes or so, we were running by a lot of buildings of all shapes and sizes. After another fifteen minutes, we were pulling up at Victoria Terminus, Bombay. It had just turned 6 p.m.; it was still light but raining, very warm and sticky.

The platform at Victoria Terminus was reasonably clear of people, except for crowds of *coolies* wearing official armbands, but once off the platform, we were engulfed in a hoard of beggars—some with the stump of an arm, or leg, wrapped in a dirty piece of cloth; some using a stick as a crutch; some with eyes which could not see; and even some with no legs, squatting on a trolley made out of an old box with casters on the corners, propelling themselves with their hands. There was an absolute babble of languages but audible above all this the constant *'baksheesh, sahib baksheesh'*. They all seemed to have very red lips and red teeth from chewing betel nut and, where it was possible to see the ground, it was so splattered with red that you would have thought the whole population of Bombay were dying of consumption, had you not known it was the betel-nut spittle. We managed to keep an eye on our *coolies* through this crowd and to find the RTO, who soon had us on our way by car to the RAF Reception Centre.

With lots of horn blowing, we eventually got away from the crowds and just as it was getting dark, we arrived at a place that looked more like the promenade of an English seaside resort than anything you would expect to find in India—a long sweep of modern five-storey apartment blocks, built of concrete, with flat roofs and balconies overlooking the sea. In front of the buildings was a road, then a hedge, beyond which were two very wide pedestrian promenades, then a concrete wall and steps down to the beach. It was called, appropriately, Marine Drive.

The RAF had taken over a number of these apartment blocks and after booking in, we were taken to our quarters. I had a whole apartment to myself, complete with a balcony overlooking the sea, a proper bed instead of a charpoy, and a magnificent bathroom. Having decided that the first job was to have a bath, I opened the bathroom door, to find that a solid stream of ants, about 2 feet wide, were rushing in from one corner, running like hell across the smooth marble floor and disappearing underneath the bath. I called the bearer who had been sent to look after me and pointed them out to him; he nodded his head from side to side and then, firmly scraped his bare heel on the floor, at right angles across their path. He did this three or four times then stood back to watch. When the ants approached this invisible line that he had drawn on the floor with his heel, they did not know what to do; they ran sideways, in circles, backwards, and forwards in utter panic, but they never crossed the line. Then there was a big pile up as they met oncoming ants as they tried to run back. In a matter of maybe five minutes, all the ants that had already crossed the line had carried on and were out of sight; the others had returned whence they came. I tried this myself many, many times elsewhere, but it never seemed to work.

After my bath, I found that the bearer had decided what I was to wear for dinner and had laid the clothes out on the bed for me. He had also decided what was to go to the *dhobi*. You could not keep any secrets from the bearers.

The next day, we tried to sort out what was going to happen to us. One chap thought there was a Torbeau squadron in Southeast Asia Command. His papers showed 22 Squadron on Torbeaus in 222 Group. It transpired that this group with headquarters in Colombo covered the whole of the Indian Ocean from Madagascar to the Andaman Islands, with units dotted about on little islands or atolls; it was one hell of an area, some 4,000 miles, and no one seemed to know where 22 Squadron was. I told them about Eric, who, it transpired, was now at Poona, so this chap I was talking to conferred with his colleague, who remembered Eric, as he had tried to locate 22 Squadron when Eric arrived, but 222 Group had told him that there was no such squadron.

However, they decided to contact 222 Group again and if they got the same answer, I was to follow Eric to Poona where there was a 'refresher' unit for Beau pilots returning to Ops. I began to think that if they did locate this Torbeau squadron, they would be a bit peeved that I had 'lost' my Torbeau in Karachi. However, it looked as if we would have a day or two free in Bombay. They gave me a rubber stamp and a pile of outgoing mail, asking me if I would 'censor' it and let them have it back when it was done. In the meantime, Douggie and I went off to have a look at Bombay.

We were not to see Bombay at its best. The monsoon season along this coast started in late May or early June and went through to the middle of September. July was the height of the monsoon season with between 24 and 25 inches of rain in the month and temperatures up in the nineties. It did not seem to matter much about trying to keep out of the rain because you were just as wet from sweat if you kept undercover, and at least the rain was slightly refreshing. We took a *gharry*; as we approached the town from our relatively quiet area, the traffic began to build up. Traffic police, known as 'Buttercups' because of their yellow caps, stood under an umbrella on a raised box at the crossroads, continuously whistling and pointing (somehow, they seem to know what they were doing) surrounded by a chaos of every conceivable form of traffic—cars, taxis, grossly overloaded lorries, bicycles, hand-carts, rickshaws, crowded buses, slow moving bullock-carts, camel-carts, two-wheeled *tongas*, little Ekkas carrying just one person, *gharries*, and heavily laden donkeys. Everyone seemed to be blowing a horn, shouting at their animal, or just shouting abuse at someone else.

Here and there was extra chaos as a shaft broke or a wheel came off, with produce being scattered all over the road; a horse, bullock, donkey, or camel refused to shift; cyclists skidded and fell off; or a sacred cow took up station in the middle of the road like a traffic island. It was great fun watching all this all around us. Our driver seemed to be cursing everyone within earshot and how the devil the police coped at the main crossroads, God alone knows because the speed of the vehicles varied so much that it could take a bullock cart ages to get across, especially if it lost its load halfway.

We were blessed by the rain stopping for a while when we looked at the spectacular museum building with its big central dome and two little domes at each end, fronted by a garden of colourful bedding plants and palm trees; the Hindu temple in Hornby Road of brilliant white stone, very ornate, lots of pinnacles and a tall, slim tower; the tall municipal building, a mixture of typical English and Victorian architecture and Oriental domes; the Church of England with its tall square tower and fancy pinnacled top, surrounded by a garden of English trees plus a few palms; then down to the harbour area to see the Gateway of India (like an ornate Marble Arch) surrounded by a big open area on the quayside and across a big wide road to the Taj Mahal Hotel—a huge six storey hotel, very fancy with gilded domes on each corner and a big gilded dome rising in the middle. We decided to take tea and toasted teacakes there—what a place; it was a bit like a cross between a cathedral and the museum, with dozens and dozens of servants around, electric fans whirling everywhere, and a boy to lift the silver cover off the plate of teacakes when you indicated you were ready for another. Everybody who is anybody has stayed at the Taj Mahal, so they said. No beggars were allowed to hang around outside the Taj.

By the next day, we had the layout of the place more or less sorted out. Bombay was on the end of a tongue of land with the open sea to the west and a big natural harbour to the east, which was why we seemed to have water all round us. This time, we left our quiet Marine Drive area on the south-west tip of the peninsula and took a *gharry* along the coast northwards to Malabar Hill. This was an area of very superior Indian residences, some almost like small palaces, posh cars around, and women dressed in colourful silk saris, decorated with gold patterns. It occurred to us that this was about the first time we had noticed any women (except those working in the fields, who we saw from the train). There was a good view from up on this hill but big black clouds were building up. From here, we rode to the busy Indian quarter, spent a little time around the narrow alleys, jostling through the crowds, goats, and donkeys, and then made for the business area. Here, we made a big mistake by ordering 'Bombay Duck' for tiffin. It was not duck at all, but some tiny dried fishes served with curry and they stank to high heaven; we never had that again. Everywhere we went in Bombay, we came across 'Quit India' daubed on walls with white paint; after a while, you got the impression that they were not too pleased about us being here but they did not seem to show it in any other ways.

In the commercial area, I spotted the offices of the Yorkshire Insurance Company. I remembered that my uncle had spoken of Charlie Agar, who came out to Bombay ten years or so ago to be the company's manager for India, so I decided to call in and see if he was still there. With due dignity, I was led through the main office, where thirty or so Indians suddenly began to look busy, and shown into his office. There, he was in an immaculate white suit, behind a huge desk, in a big, wood-panelled office. He ordered tea, then we talked about various people in York, and he seemed pleased to see me. He explained that this was the worst time of the year in Bombay; his wife was up in Poona for the rainy season and he went there at the weekends. I remarked about his staff appearing to be all Indians and he explained that most of them were Anglo-Indians, the result of Indian women having children to English men, maybe many generations ago.

The poor 'Anglos' were in an invidious position, looked down on by the English because they were coloured, not recognised by English society, and rejected by the Indians. It seemed OK for an Indian prince to marry, or have a child with, a white woman, but not the other way around. Over the generations, some were almost as white as we were, others darker, but the Anglos were in a sort of 'no man's land'. They tended to stick together for moral support and some of them got jobs as clerks in European offices, but the vast majority of them worked on the railways; the Indian railway companies were almost exclusively staffed by Anglos from the top to the bottom. On the whole, they were very capable and good workers but unfortunately always felt they had a stigma hanging over them. Charlie then suggested that we should have lunch at his club one day; I told him I did not know how I would be fixed from day to day, so it was left that I would phone him when I could make it and then meet him at the office at about noon.

Back on the street, we were interested to watch a *munshi* (a professional letter-writer) at work. Squatting on the pavement under a covered archway, with his box of paper beside him, he was writing with an ivory-handled pen that he frequently dipped into a pot of ink, as the customer, squatting beside him, dictated what he wanted to say; then he would write the envelope and collect his fee. There were lots of *munshis* around this area; all seemed to be doing a good trade. They performed a necessary service in a country where so few could read or write, but they would be unable to check whether the *munshi* had actually written what they had asked him to do. Another lucrative job must be selling *chuttas* (umbrellas) as everybody seemed to carry one. There was probably also a good trade in fancy sock suspenders as, in the business area, most of the chaps wearing a *dhoti* had short socks supported by gaily coloured suspenders.

On our return, we learned that the folks in Colombo knew nothing about this elusive 22 Squadron, so it was decided that we may as well move on to Poona the next day. The postings officer seemed to wish he could come too, saying it was very pleasant up there compared with all this heat and wet down here. Also, a troopship was expected to arrive any day and then this unit would be packed out for a while.

It was raining like I had never seen before, bouncing inches off the road, as we drove to Victoria Terminus to board the 10 a.m. Great Indian Peninsular Railway Express for Poona, hauled by a big electric locomotive. This was a corridor train with a restaurant car and did not appear to be fitted out for sleeping; after a little persuasion, the movements officer had given Douggie a first-class warrant, so that was nice. Shortly after leaving the station, we realised that there was no 'clickety-click' coming from the train wheels – we were just gliding silently along. I mentioned this to another fellow in the compartment who informed us that this was the first stretch of continuous line anywhere in the world, but it did not extend all the way to Poona. We had to start off by going north to get off the peninsular, and then we gradually curved towards the East and entered the mountains. The rain was coming down even heavier than before and it seemed to get even darker. We stopped at Kalyan Junction, where one line set off right across country to Allahabad while we bent around to the south, right into the middle of the Western Ghats—the range of high mountains that run all down the west side of India. If only we could have seen it, it would have been most spectacular; all we could see was rain and mist as the big train kept climbing, stopping, and climbing. While we were in the restaurant car, we kept hearing water thundering on the roof as waterfalls cascaded off the steep sides of cuttings, pouring streams right into the track. There seemed to be water and mist everywhere.

After some three hours, we realised we were no longer twisting and climbing but were actually going slightly downhill. After another half an hour, it had stopped raining. We were going at quite a speed now, then, as if by magic, the sun came out. Shortly, the only clouds in the sky were little, isolated tufts of white cumulus. We now no longer felt sticky, just pleasantly warm and the sun was beating down from a blue sky. Twenty minutes later, we arrived at Poona. We had been four and a half hours.

12

Getting the 'Gen' at Poona

'Where the devil have you been?' queried Eric when I located him in his room at Poona. After telling him about Douggie being kept at Habb, and then my solo trip from Habb to Karachi, the hold-up in Karachi and my relief when I saw Douggie coming looking for me, I inquired what went on here. Eric had started doing a bit of flying and rocket firing, mostly low-level stuff, which he said was much more exciting overland than overwater. He said it looked as if we could say 'Goodbye to Coastal Command' and that we were bound for low-level intruder work in Burma. 'You'll be in "D" Flight, same as me,' he continued, 'that's the Beau Flight for ex-Ops chaps. The Sqn Ldr is called Gandy, not the Gandhi who walks around in a loin-cloth; he's OK. I've got a form somewhere for you to fill in for the Poona Club, I'll find it before dinner, then we'll pop down.'

The quarters were quite good, being little blocks of three or four rooms. Each room was a good size with a smaller toilet room at the back containing a table, a wash basin, a big jug, and a 'thunder box' (the commode holding a tin Jerry). There were back and front doors, each opening on to a wider veranda, brick walls painted white inside, and a couple of paraffin pressure lanterns. I got myself organised with a bearer, asked him to find me a webbing charpoy instead of the string one (which I bet he had purposely put in the empty room), and to get me a tin bath (as I had noticed that Eric had one). I supervised him unpack my kit, put Peggy's photo on the dressing table, asked him to be getting some warm water for the bath, and then I was all set.

I was not very thrilled with my first visit to the Poona Club. Certainly, it was a nice building in lovely gardens illuminated with spotlights and had big comfortable leather chairs, but the folks were a bit of a bore. Half seemed to be the posh types (those who could afford to travel port out and starboard home—the expensive cabins on the shady side of the ship—and wanted you to know it) and the other half were service officers who were trying to impress, although, to be fair, there did seem to be one or two genuine types.

The next morning, I met my 'instructor', a grand lad called Brian (a warrant officer who had completed a tour on low-level Beaus in Burma). I casually remarked that I had been a WO as I did not want him to think I was a green PO; nevertheless, he came up with me for an hour's local flying, including a couple of landings and a dummy air-to-ground cannon attack to see whether I was fit to go on my own. Then, I took Douggie for an hour to show him the surrounding country. The programme was to be that we would do a couple of cross-countries of about two hours at 2,000 feet, then we would do the same routes again at 30 feet and finally as low as we possibly could. Some parts of the routes would be in the Ghats, where it would be raining like hell, and other parts would be over the flat plain. Brian said the squadron leader was also keen on formation flying, but they had found in Burma that formation flying was not practical; they usually went singularly or maybe in a pair. In a day or two, we were to start firing practice rockets, which called for a slightly different technique from cannon firing as you wanted to come in flatter, about 13 degrees, launch at 600 yards, and then make sure you got out of the way of flying debris.

The weather around Poona was perfect. Every day, there was a blue sky with just little white cumulus clouds and the occasional light 'fair weather' showers but always big black clouds over the Ghats to the west. Two rivers, the Mutha and the Mula, flowed swiftly through the town, taking the rains from the eastern side of the Ghats right across to the east coast, some 600 miles away. With being some 2,000 feet above sea level, it was pleasantly hot. The low-level flying was exhilarating and you could not have a better aircraft for it. With the unobstructed forward view, the ground seemed to pass just under your feet, you could gently weave between trees and could appreciate why the Beau got its name of 'The Whispering Death', as peasants in the field never even looked up as you approached and Douggie would say they were flat on the ground behind us; I felt a bit mean about this as I certainly did not set out to scare them. However, birds were a bloody nuisance. Big, scruffy looking 'shitehawks' would suddenly flash past. We hit one or two, but they only put a little dent in the wing, which no one seemed to bother about but they made you 'duck' sometimes and I soon made a point of avoiding anything like a building, or a village, as there would be a host of them hovering overhead. The only thing that was tricky was that Douggie could not see ahead to pick out any pin points. I had to do the map reading ahead while he looked aft to check whether we were OK. Thankfully, his ear was not giving him any bother and we were both enjoying it.

We had a couple of days of light relief when Eric and I and four other chaps moved into a palatial building in the Poona Cantonment, possibly the Sandhurst for the Indian Army, for some talks arranged for 'Officers recently arrived in India'. The first was basically about the religions of India so that we would not do anything which could spark off a mutiny.

We were introduced to Hinduism: their various Orders or Castes; associated sanctions for flouting the caste system and various rituals and customs; the Jains, an off-shoot of Hinduism beginning about 600 BC; the Sikhs, the fighting men of India, all these gentlemen having Singh (which means lion) as part of their names and finally the Buddhists, Parsees, and the Religion of Islam.

> You must know a little about them to deal with any Indians under your command or to mix with civilians you may meet. At the end of the course, obtain a list of the various religious feast days and festivals and be aware of them; do respect the Hindu's sacred cow; don't offend a Hindu with beef; don't expect a Muslim to touch a pig or pork; be aware of the Hindu caste system and for goodness sake don't expect him to do anything to break caste; do respect the Hindu Temples and the Muslim mosques and never, never lift a hand to an Indian, shout at the servants if you must, some of them expect it, and respect you for it but, never lay a hand on them. I hope none of you are politicians as, this afternoon I am going to try to compress the political events in India over the last 100 years, into about 40 minutes, so that you will appreciate the situation we are in today. Then a few words about your dealings with your servants, and that will be it for today. Right, gentlemen, let's see what for tiffin.

That afternoon, we heard about the political history of India from the days of the East India Company—how they skilfully negotiated with the native rulers, playing one off against the other and then making treaties with them, and the Mutiny of 1857 that lasted four very bloody months with atrocities committed by both sides, as a direct result of which Queen Victoria had to take the heat out of the situation by dissolving the East India Company and taking over the Government of India herself. Her proclamation disclaimed any right to interfere with religious belief, all subjects were to enjoy equal protection under the law, all existing treaties with the princes were accepted, and we promised that we had no further territorial ambitions. Thus began 'The Golden Age' for those native princes who still had their own states. We had set up a first-class judicial system; an excellent civil service in which more and more Indians progressively became employed; and set up representative councils' assemblies and other institutions until a country of 350 million was virtually governing itself under the supervision of a few thousand Englishmen. Having done all this, the British politicians now seemed to be hell-bent on trying to get rid of India. Out of this, a new sort of Indian 'middle class' had evolved. Some of this group began to think that they could run the country perfectly well without the British and started agitating for nationalism. The Indian National Congress came into being, which said it represented the interests of all Indian peoples, and the British Government now saw the writing on the wall and independence as inevitable but not without difficulties.

The lecturer continued:

I will finish for today, with a few tips to help you deal with the multitude of servants.
\#   Some acknowledge that the servant structure has arisen out of the caste system; others think it is merely a very strong Trade Union to create jobs as a result of strict job demarcation; there are some who think it was devised by the English as an excuse for surrounding themselves with a lot of servants as a status symbol. As long as you stick to the rules, it works very well for all concerned. All servants who are permitted to work on Army or Air force establishments will be in possession of an Identity Pass carrying a photograph and a thumb-print, it will show a name (which they have probably made up anyway), their religion and age (which is probably also made up as they have no birth certificate). Always examine this Pass before engaging the servant and see that it is registered at the Orderly Room, or guardroom, or wherever your records are kept.

To you, as an individual, the most important servant is your Bearer. You may share the bearer, or have one to yourself. You will pay him yourself, at the rate suggested at your particular unit but you may reward him with *baksheesh* as you think appropriate. You will have to provide him with rupees with which to pay for the *dhobis* or any other jobs, like repairs to your kit which he gets done for you. Your bearer is the only servant that you will have any direct dealings with. He will deal with all the other servants and keep them on their toes. If you get a good bearer, he will look after you as if he were your mother. He will see that the clothes you want are put out ready for you; your dirty washing is sent to the *dhobi* and checked when it comes back; he will see that there is hot water for you in the morning and again in the evening for your bath; he will call the sweeper when you have been to the 'thunder box'; check that your mosquito net is down before sundown; see that the *bhisti* keeps your *chatti* full of cold water and will sit on the veranda outside your room while you are away and light your lantern when you return at night. These bearers go in and out of your drawers or trunks where clothes are kept, as if they were their own so, if you have things you do not want the bearer to see, or touch, tell him where they are. Most of them will do as you say but, if you find one who does not, you should report him. Most of them are extremely loyal and take a great pride in looking after 'their *sahib*'; the older ones are proud to call themselves British and will dress up in the evening by wearing a band across their turban—like one of those belts we wore at school with a clasp like an 'S' shaped snake—in the appropriate Army or Air Force colours. Some have even provided themselves with wide belts in the same colours to wear round their waist. Look after your bearer and he will look after you.

The other servants, descending down the scale, are:

The *bhisti*, or water carrier. He is of lower caste than the bearer. He will bring water from the Station supply, probably carrying it in a goatskin or canvas '*chargul*'.

The dry sweeper, an untouchable, who flicks around with a twig broom sweeping the floor but all he's really doing is scattering the dust from one spot to another. He will also sweep the path, or road outside.

The wet sweeper, an even lower untouchable than the dry sweeper. His job is to empty the 'thunder box', taking its contents to a tank on a bullock cart which is then emptied in some approved place. He then charges the thunder box with a little creosote oil. A little tip here, drop a sheet of paper in the box before sitting down because, if that creosote splashes up, it can make your eyes water. The wet sweeper also gets rid of your washing water.

The *bhisti* and the sweepers will work for three or four bearers.

The *dhobi* may be an outside contractor. He will take the washing down to a nearby river, wet it, bash it on a smooth rock; rub it with a big bar of green soap; bashing again, and again and again, until it is rinsed; laid out on a rock to dry; if necessary starch it with rice-starch; then iron it with a bit flat iron heated over charcoal. If you find that there are pink marks on anything, get your bearer to complain to the *dhobi*—these chaps have a knack of spraying a mouthful of water, like a fine mist, over a garment as they iron it. The pink means he has been chewing betel-nut and it will never come out.

Another chap you may come across is the *chowkidar*, or night watchman. He is usually an ex-army type and probably being chosen because he is a bit of a rogue, who wouldn't hesitate to belt the daylights out of anyone with his *lathi* and it has been made abundantly clear to him that, if anything is missing, he is the person who is going to suffer for it.

In the mess you will come across the major-domo, he is in charge of all the mess servants. You will also come across the *abdar*—he is the Wine Waiter. The young boys doing odd jobs are called *chokras*. Incidentally, in the mess, or in any of the European Clubs, we do not pay cash for drinks. It is all done on the 'chitty' system. Sign the chitty for everything you have and it will come on your mess bill.

Finally as regards language, there are fourteen major languages spoken over India, plus, it seems, about 500 lesser used languages and hundreds of different dialects. It is not uncommon therefore, to find Indians making themselves understood to each other by using bits of English, as they cannot understand each other's language. Therefore you are in no worse position than the Indians themselves. However there are a number of words, mainly in Hindustani or Urdu, which have found their way into a sort of Indian English. It is useful for you to know these so, I have some sheets here for you, showing you the words it is useful to know to help you get around.

Lectures were over for the day and it only being about 4.30 p.m., Eric and I decided to pop along the road to the Poona Club for a spot of afternoon tea before we had to get changed and ready for dinner. It was during our tea that I nearly frightened myself to death and learned a practical lesson about India. We had ordered char and teacakes while we sat at a table by the side of the swimming pool. The char arrived in a silver-plated teapot and the teacakes under a silver-plated cover. Casually talking about the day's lectures, I took a piece of teacake and did not think to replace the cover. The next moment, something bit me on the side of the face, tea cups and plates went crashing to the ground, and a bloody big shite hawk disappeared up into the sky with my teacake. It scared me rigid—the whoosh as the thing flashed by and the horrible feel of its feathers on my face. I turned as white as a sheet. Two or three waiters rushed up, picked up the broken crockery, smiled as they nodded their heads from side to side, and said *'Thik hai sahib'*. Another waiter was waiting to replace everything. Some Army chaps were laughing their heads off. I hated those bloody big, scruffy-looking birds, but at least, as Eric pointed out, they do help to keep the country tidy. This was not my day at all.

Back at the Army place, I went for a shower prior to dinner. It was a very elegant wash place with a fine marble floor, a row of washbasins with brilliantly polished taps, and several shower cubicles. A Sikh officer was at one of the washbasins, combing his extraordinary long hair (which seemed to come down to his waist), then coiling it up into a net on the top of his head. There was a lot of coughing and spluttering coming from one of the showers, then another Sikh came out with a lot of very polite *'Namaste'*, so I went in, only to put my bare heel right on some spittle he had left on the floor. I went arse over tit, finishing up on the floor with my back against the door. Sitting there, I had to smile; I thought, 'is this some diabolical way the Sikhs have thought up to bring down the British Raj?'

The mess at this place was quite something, being an interesting mixture of British and Indian Army types and six from the Air Force. It was a very enjoyable evening, in spite of a scratch on my face from that bloody bird and a bruise on my bottom from sitting down in the shower. The Sikhs I met in the wash place were actually very pleasant chaps who went out of their way to be ultra polite. Still, I preferred the more relaxed atmosphere of an Air Force mess.

The next day we had a thorough introduction to 'The Indian Princes', their status, their wealth, the 'good', and the 'not so good'. Our lecturer concluded:

Well, gentlemen, I hope that has given you an insight into the Indian Princes and some of their States. If you find yourself posted to a Native State at least ascertain the name of the Ruler, his Religion, the number of guns, his special interests and any particular accomplishments of his State. It may even result in you getting invited to dinner, or at worst stop you being slung into jail.

It was nice to get back to my own room on the airfield that night; it was funny how anywhere seems like home when you have your own things around and a few photos on show, but the blessed jackals and hyenas were making a noise all night; at least one hyena sounded to be just outside the back door.

13

Preparations for Burma

It was now time to get cracking with the rockets. They looked such simple weapons, but they were very effective—just a long steel tube with a venturi and four little fins at one end, the other end threaded to take the warhead. An 11-lb stick of cordite was poked down the tube before the warhead was fitted and, just before take-off, when the rocket was mounted on the rail under the aircraft wing, the 'tails' were plugged in; these were connections for the electric ignition system. That was your rocket projectile (RP). The warheads were 60-lb high explosive (HE) or 25-lb armour piercing (AP), but for practice, we used concrete heads. The Beau carried four rockets under each wing and they could be fired in pairs (one from each side) or the whole lot together. The firing was quite straightforward—a master switch on the port side of the cockpit, just below the VHF radio control box; a selector switch below the left corner of the windscreen to select 'pairs' or 'salvo'; a firing button on the control wheel, next to the gun button (the one without the spring-loaded safety flap); and finally, the same sight as used for the cannons.

The eight rockets under the wings made the Beau look even more deadly as I climbed in behind Brian, who was going to demonstrate a few launchings. We pulled up to about 1,000 feet, then came down fairly flat; Brian commented, 'this is the angle you want, supposed to be about 13 degrees, line up the target in the cannon sight, open the throttles, wait till about 600 yards, right, let 'em go …. Dive down; pull to one side, right on the deck and away'. As he pressed the tit, there was a slight 'whoosh' and a cloud of smoke momentarily seemed to envelop the wings. There was a slight smell of cordite and two streams of smoke shot ahead of us heading for the ground, almost as straight as if they had been running on tram lines. A shower of sand and dust flew into the air and we were away, scurrying over the scrub. As we flew around before making the next 'attack', Brian pointed out that there would be a much bigger explosion than that if he were using HEs, especially if it was something like a fuel dump, so it was important to get well away. He also reckoned we would be far too vulnerable if we went in as high as 1,000 feet, but he had done that to give me a better idea of the angle, so on the next three runs, he progressively reduced the height.

On the last run, he nipped up a bit, immediately started his dive, fired, and was away. He said, 'you'll have to do it quickly like that, if you want to stay alive'. We landed, had a cup of char while they loaded eight more rockets, and, this time, I was in the driving seat with Brian standing behind me. My first two pairs, starting off from a fair height, went within the target area, but when I came in low, I could not find the target, so I had to go around again and then spotted it too late to do anything about it; therefore, I had to go round about six times before getting it right. Brian had a good laugh, saying I would have been shot down about ten times by now, but all I needed was practice.

Over the next few days, I was getting rid of sixteen rockets every morning and another sixteen in the afternoon; it was a good job they were only cheap things and not torpedoes. I asked Brian, 'how the hell do you find your targets when you are belting along at very near 315 feet? You're so busy watching for trees and obstructions, that even when you know where the target is, you're over the damn thing before you realise it and you say that if you don't keep low until the last moment, you are going to cop it?' Brian explained that what he did was to get right down when he reckoned he was where the Japanese might be, then when he got to the area where he hoped to find something, he started flying like a porpoise, up and down for quick looks and a bit of cork-screwing, or skidding, at the same time. Brian was a grand chap, most unassuming, but a bloody good flyer and had completed nearly thirty operations on Beaus in Burma, so he knew what he was talking about. Although I reckoned that warrant officer was the best rank to have, I already realised that, in India, it made a lot of difference to be commissioned, and I reckoned Brian should have been; maybe it is true that if you are sent out here, you are forgotten.

So we carried on for a few more days, sometimes scurrying in the rain through valleys in the Ghats before coming down on to the flatland and launching our rockets; sometimes, Brian would come along to see how I was making out. I would practice porpoising, cork screwing, and skidding till Douggie asked me what the hell I was playing at and I told him I was doing it so that he got a better view. A couple of times, I let all the rockets go in one 'salvo' (the bigger cloud of smoke that engulfed the amidships brought some apt remarks from Douggie), remarks that probably stopped me from being so mesmerised by those eight lines of smoke that I followed them all the way to the deck.

They were happy days at Poona. There was no need to check with the Met people before every trip; in fact, I never saw a Met officer. There was a faded 'weather forecast' pinned on the crew room wall, headed 'Weather forecast until the 15th September'. It read something like the following:

The wet Monsoon will strike the coast from the SSW giving rise to heavy formations of nimbus and cumulo-nimbus cloud cover, and to the west of the Ghats, bringing continuous rain, heavy at times, with thunderstorms in isolated cyclones. Possible icing above 10,000 feet. The Deccan Plateau will have varying amounts of well-broken cumulus and occasional light showers.

Weather forecasting here seemed to be done by the calendar. It was very pleasant on the Deccan Plateau.

Eric spent most evenings at the Poona Club; I went with him sometimes but, frankly, found it a bit of a bore. One evening, I donned a sports shirt and went with Douggie to the 'Anglo' Club in Poona, which was only supposed to be for NCOs, and this was much more interesting. Very austere compared with the Poona Club but much more lively; a band, reinforced by one lad from the Army and another from the RAF, played things like 'In the Quartermaster's Stores', 'The Hut Sut Song', 'Run Rabbit Run', 'Praise the Lord and Pass the Ammunition', 'A Pair of Silver Wings', and 'Paper Doll'. The latter reminded me of Ferry Command days. The Anglos were all excessively friendly, fussy chaps in smart white shirts, and the women were absolute stunners—all with jet black hair and complexions varying from a nice bronze tan to almost black—but everyone had the features of a film star. All wore earrings and shining necklaces, and some had a diamond stuck on the side of their nose—either Western style or a colourful sari; thank goodness none of these were in *purdah*. What a waste it would have been. Yet it was all really rather pathetic; there were rows of beautiful girls, like wallflowers, all hoping to get a British chap. They were a charming and intelligent crowd of people who were neither Indian or European and no one seemed to want them. One girl I danced with immediately told me she was Spanish and came to live in India some years ago. Another told me that she had lived in London and when I asked where, she told me 'Just beside the railway station'; I did not have the heart to ask her which one, just remarked that it was nice there but she would be finding it much more warmer here. It seemed terrible that people should feel that they had to live a lie because none of us could help what our parents or earlier generations got up to and, after all, what was wrong with a young English trader, living out here, marrying an Indian girl? However, I thought it wise, as a young married man, not to go to the Anglo Club again.

It dawned on Eric and I that we could soon be bound for Burma—there was nowhere else to go from here—and that although we had kept following the war in Europe, we really knew very little about Burma. We had heard that the Japanese were right on the Indian border near Imphal and Kohima, that some glider landings have been made well behind the Japanese lines, that Wingate had been killed in an air crash, and that Burma was a hell of a place for disease; however, that was about it. So, we decided to find out as much as we could from Brian, as he had been there less than six months ago.

With Brian, we studied a map. He pointed out a long range of mountains, shaped like a banana, starting in the south near the coast, sweeping northwards and curving towards the east to meet some huge mountains on the border with China. To the east of this long banana were two main rivers—the Chindwin and the Irrawaddy—on their way to the sea near Rangoon, then more mountains were on the other side of the plain. The trouble was, Brian told us that the maps were not all that good. There were no accurate maps when the war started, but the RAF PR squadrons had covered the whole country with 'vertical line overlaps', and from these, new maps had been produced; they were first class as far as rivers, roads, and railways were concerned, but you could not get accurate heights from vertical photographs, so the heights shown want to be taken with a dose of salt. Seeing the Japanese occupy the whole of the plain, except for the groups of chaps we sent

Preparations for Burma

in by glider and had to supply by airdrops, our airfields were now all on the wrong side of those mountains, so you had to cross them both ways.

We looked at the odd 'spot height' shown on the map: 9,890 feet, 2,619 feet, and 7,100 feet—'Christ, some of those are high', I remarked, to which Brian replied, 'too true, I've been up to 18,000 trying to avoid cu-nims [a particularly dangerous cloud formation] and you will often have to go well over ten, especially in the dark, so you carry oxygen and it can get bloody cold up there. We had the Beau VI and at 18,000 in a high blower, you needed the throttles damn nearly wide open and were guzzling fuel like no one's business; if you have a Mark X, that will be even worse at altitude but you couldn't have anything better down in the plain where most of the Ops will be'.

Brian pointed out airfields at Agartala, Chittagong, Fenny, Cox's Bazar, Akyab, and Ramree, but the Japanese held the last two by that point. Then, he showed us airfields near Silchar, Imphal, and Kohima, some of which he thought may be in Japanese hands, and strips in Assam, mostly quickly made on parts of tea plantations. Most of the strips were of steel planking. 'What are the 'nav' facilities like?' we inquired. He replied:

> Mainly D/F on W/T or VHF but this is not any use when you are down in the plain, it's all map reading then. A few light beacons on airfields switched on 'on request' and that's about it. The Yanks have some beacons for their transport aircraft on the China run—'over the hump' but we couldn't get much gen on those.

'What are the main targets?'

> The close support for the Army seemed to be mainly done by Vengeance dive bombers and Hurri-bombers (Hurricanes fitted to carry bombs), the Beaus mainly go out in pairs attacking airfields; looking for any form of transport—trains, lorry convoys or river traffic, bridges or special targets like army stores or depots. They are all small targets – there are no big targets – so it's all low level stuff, and when I say low, I mean low, as the Jap light Ack-Ack is red-hot at 500 feet or more, even snipers sitting in a tree are crack shots so you want to be right down on the deck where the Beau is an absolute smasher, as they do not hear you coming but, do not hang around

too long after they know you are there. If you get there before the end of October you will find it raining like hell – their rain makes the Bombay Monsoon looks like a shower—and watch out for cu-nims.

'Thanks, Brian'.

Next came yet more flying, usually morning and afternoon, except on a Sunday, combining low-level cross-countries, usually partly in the clouds and rain over the Ghats, then over the plateau with an attack on a target sometimes with camera alone, sometimes plus cannons or rockets. The CO was also keen on us doing some trips in formation (but I realised what Brian meant when he said formation was not very practical in this job) and 'emergency handling for the observer', which was a bit of a farce—Douggie trying to reach over me to get at the wheel and throttles. We were issued with revolvers and spent several hours firing these, and .303 rifles, on the range. I was not a particularly good shot. I also got myself a 'jungle suit'—a one-piece affair like a mechanic's overalls, in green with brown marks all over it and plenty of good big pockets.

One Sunday morning, Eric caused a bit of a commotion. The CO sent for me, telling me that he had had a call from town that someone, believed to be an RAF officer, was on a yacht, stuck up against the weir on the river; it sounded like that pal of mine, so I had better take a 15-hundredweight truck and go down to see if I could sort him out without causing any trouble. It was a lovely, sunny, and warm morning with little tufts of cumulus, snow white against the deep blue sky. Passing the slow-moving bullock carts, cyclists, and *gharries* on the way to town, I arrived at the bridge over the river and stopped to look upstream.

A couple of hundred yards upstream was the weir, with water coming over the 10-foot drop pretty rapidly. There were some yachts and motor boats above the weir, but I could not see a boat against it. I hoped he had not been washed over. Below the weir, there were rocks on both sides and some sticking up in the middle. The rocks on the side were quite a sight, covered with whitewashing spread out to dry and dozens of *dhobi wallahs* bashing washing on the rocks, singing, and shouting (although the Indian singing is more like wailing). However, there was no sign of Eric, so I knew I had better get to the Yacht Club, which I could see a little further upstream and see what I could make out. I got a few funny looks as I drove in, parked the 15-cwt truck, and went down to the moorings. There, I found Eric, talking to a group of Europeans (all in splendid yachting gear), and there was a girl in a long evening dress. As I moved in, the girl was busy trying to explain to these chaps that 'Daddy said it would be all right for us to take the boat out'. Eric saw me and in his usual smooth way called over, 'Hello, Jacko, thanks for coming to pick us up, the 'old man' said he'd let you know where we were'. They must have thought it was the girl's old man he was talking about as everyone then seemed OK, so I said, 'Come on then, let's be getting back to the house. Sorry I'm a bit late'.

With that, I led Eric and the girl to the 15 cwt and we shot off. He introduced the girl as 'Lucinda' and I asked what the hell had been going on, and where we were to take her to. It seemed he had met the girl at the Poona Club dance and she had said it would be OK to go down to Daddy's yacht. They had decided to slip moorings and drift a bit downstream into a wooded part of the bank, as there was a motor they could use for getting back. They tied the boat to a tree, or so they thought, but, after skipping what happened during the next few hours, they woke up with a bump; they could hear rushing water and found themselves up against the weir. It was fully daylight, folks were honking at them as they passed over the bridge, and then they discovered that the ignition needed a key, which they did not have.

Eric eventually managed to bypass the key with some wire and they got the motor started, but Lucinda was scared they were going to get washed over the weir; when they got back to the jetty, this group of chaps were accusing them of having stolen the boat. Anyway, we seemed to have got over that; it was then a matter of getting Lucinda back and then Eric. I told Eric that I was not going to the house and pulled up some yards away, telling Eric to be no more than five minutes or I would be off. He duly deposited her—whether he went in the house, I do not know—and we set off back to the airfield. 'What the hell were you doing?' I asked him. 'Trying to be an Indian prince? I expect your arse will be covered with mosquito bites and next thing you will have malaria. The old man knows about it, it was he who asked me to come and rescue you—no wonder you keep getting demoted—you'll be joining me as a PO if you're not careful'. 'Thanks, Jacko. I'll sign for your drinks for the next week. It was worth it'.

Back at the airfield, Eric had a shave, then went to make his peace with the CO, who gave him a rollicking but nothing more was heard about it, although the CO did ask me what the folks at the club seemed like and whether the folks at the Yacht Club sounded as if they were going to do anything about it. By some coincidence, Eric did find himself duty officer twice during the following four days, which meant he was in the mess to buy our drinks.

We were now given a pile of leaflets about how to live in the jungle: how to bivouac and thatch a roof, move quietly and watch the ground, catching monkeys to eat and to suck roots of creeping vines, young ferns or shoots of bamboo for moisture; how to recognise snakes and what to do about snake bites; to watch out for tiny ticks, or mites, carrying the deadly 'scrub typhus', and huge hornets with a fatal sting; warnings about water-borne spirochaetes carrying a fatal disease like jaundice, the anopheles mosquito carrying malaria and rabies picked up even from a lick; cholera, dysentery and bubonic plague; warnings of leeches, lice, fleas and scorpions and what to do about prickly heat.

Also included were warnings about an 'Indian National Army', which we may come across in Burma; it seemed that a chap called Subhas Chandra Bose, a Bengali who had studied at Cambridge, joined the Indian Civil Service, and was at one time Mayor of Calcutta. He was also a strong nationalist and a member of the Congress party. Like Gandhi, he preached that if the Japanese drove us out of India, they would immediately clear off and give them their independence; he also expounded Nazi ideas. We had imprisoned him for his agitation, but he had escaped and was then heard broadcasting from Germany to India calling for volunteers to form an 'Indian Legion' against us.

Early the previous year, he was reported to be in Tokyo trying to organise a 'Free India' movement from Indians in various parts of Southeast Asia; the previous October, he publicly announced the setting up of a government of Free India, under the Japanese in Singapore, and formed the Indian National Army, mainly from Indians who had been taken prisoner by the Japanese when they overran Burma and were given the option of either joining the INA or being tortured to death. It was not known how many of these chaps there were, or where they were, but it was expected some of them would be used along with Japanese troops to try and trap us, so we needed to be on our guard. Then there was another 'army'—the 'Burma Independence Army', organised by the Japanese; it was not known where we stood with this lot either. We knew that some Burmese would be pleased to see us chucked out, but some of our intelligence seemed to indicate that the BIA was now getting fed up with the Japanese as they had made no effort to hand any power back to the Burmese where they had pushed us out, and the BIA might be doing a good job for us behind Japanese lines. No one should be trusted just because they did not look like a Japanese until it was known for certain that he was OK. We would find all sorts of folks in Burma: Burmese, Chinese, African, and Indian, as well as British and American with blackened faces, so we needed to lie low until we were certain who they were.

It was pretty obvious that Eric and I (along with another crew) would be moving on very soon and as I had a day off coming up, I decided to phone Charlie Agar at the 'Yorkshire' in Bombay to see whether it would be convenient for me to take up his offer of having tiffin with him. It was.

The Deccan Queen must be the premier train of all the Indian railways. It was a non-stop business-man's express from Poona to Bombay in the early morning, returning in the late afternoon, made up of first-class, magnificent Pullman cars and an elegant lounge car, with free-standing, leather-covered easy chairs and ivory inlaid tables. The snow-white linen tablecloths and napkins were so starched that they could hardly bend; there was also silver cutlery, crested crockery, silver table lamps with silk shades, comfortable armed dining chairs, a rich blue deep-pile carpet, and velvet curtains. A copy of *The Times of India* rested on each seat. I asked one of the waiters, in his smart white uniform, to show me to a table as I did not want to cause a disturbance by taking a seat usually occupied by one of the 'regulars' as the passengers seemed to know each other and had obviously formed their own groups. I started reading my *Times of India* as the big electric loco smoothly pulled us out of the station; I was alone at my table for two.

Very shortly after, a printed menu in a leather folder was handed to me, a menu to suit all religious tastes and, as the waiter was obviously an Anglo, I felt quite happy about ordering bacon and two poached eggs. The tea soon arrived in a silver pot, then the bacon and eggs on a red-hot plate, followed by a regular supply of hot toast and a fresh pot of tea. By this point, we were clickety-clicking through a valley in the Ghats. The sunshine of Poona had been left behind; it was raining and, at times, we were engulfed in mist. Then, the side of the train would be drenched in water as we passed a waterfall crashing down the near-vertical side of the valley. Well-fed, I decided to have a stroll to take a look at the lounge. Some passengers remained at their tables and were playing cards (presumably bridge); others were looking important, reading files of papers. In the lounge car, I found that the passengers with the darkest skin were the most affable, responding readily to smile and a nod and prepared to 'pass the time of day', but, at the other extreme, the chinless white ones would look through a junior officer as if he were not there. I had a short conversation with one falling somewhere in between; he inquired whether I knew Bombay and when I told him that I was visiting the manager of the insurance company for whom I worked in England, he informed me he was a banker.

It did not seem to be as long as three hours when I realised the noise of the train wheels had stopped and we were on the jointless track running in to Bombay. It had actually stopped raining but was heavily overcast; before long, we were coming to rest in Victoria Terminus and it felt ever so oppressive and sticky. Off the platform, then through the crowds of beggars, past the rickshaw and *gharry wallahs* all shouting for custom and out into the chaos of the noisy street, motor horns, and policemen's whistles. I had half an hour to spare, in fact more like an hour, so I decided to stroll round to the office and savour the atmosphere on the way.

No sooner had I been ushered into Charlie's office than the inevitable tea arrived. We talked about folks in York; I asked him what it was like doing business out here, then he took me around the office, introducing me as 'from the head office in York'. Most of the staff seemed very fussy and eager to shake hands, then. Back in his office, he phoned for someone to bring his car around and told us that we would have tiffin at the Yacht Club. Soon, Charlie and I were in the back of a big black Austin, being driven to the harbour and into the immaculate gardens of the Bombay Yacht Club. I could not see a single yacht, just a big, low, white building.

This was obviously a European-only club, with the usual mass of turbaned bearers hanging around ready to leap into action at a clap of the hand. Charlie was obviously well-known but pointed out one group as being 'civil servants', as if they were a breed apart. After a couple of gin and tonics, we had tiffin; I chose a vindaloo curry but had no idea how hot it was going to be, and some little red balls in the spices were dynamite, making perspiration trickle through my hair from the top of my head until you quenched them with a gulp of water. After tiffin, sweet meats and brandy were taken on the terrace. Charlie said they did not know how to make coffee out there and the bearers made us look like a couple of invalids, adjusting the back of the lounger chairs to our satisfaction and fitting foot rests on to which they lifted our legs.

It was about three o'clock by the time we had finished tiffin, talking and looking round the club. Charlie did not seem in any hurry to get back to work and ordered tea. The bearer inquired, 'Which kind of tea, *sahib?*' Charlie replied 'Darjeeling'. I nodded in agreement. I did not know one kind of tea from another, but now I knew what to say if I was asked the same question, without looking silly (or maybe the next time, I could try something else). The tea arrived in a very fancy silver teapot, mounted on a stand, perfectly balanced so that to pour, you merely tilted the pot forward and on release, it swung back level. The bearer lit a little meths flame under the pot to keep it warm. Talk about being lazy—you did not even have to lift the pot.

It was raining, so the driver (after dropping Charlie at his office) took me to Victoria Terminus. With about an hour to wait before *The Deccan Queen* departed, I had a look around this grand old building, dropped a few *baksheesh* in front of particularly pitiful-looking beggars (because in spite of what they say, you cannot help feeling for them in this land of such extremes), then, as the train was in, I decided to get aboard and continue reading a *Times of India*. It sounded as if we were beginning to make some headway on pushing the Japanese back. We had taken a place called Mogaung and the road between Imphal, Kohima, and India had been re-opened; there was fighting somewhere between Tiddim and Kalemyo, but the only places I had heard of before were Imphal and Kohima. I recognised some of the same chaps getting in the train but as I was in the same seat as this morning, I knew I was OK. Dead on 5.30 p.m., we glided out of the station. I thought I may as well make the best of this 'high living' while I had the chance, so I made my way to the lounge, sat down, and ordered a gin and tonic.

I had a good tiffin, but what the hell—I had seen what they were offering for dinner. I saw my banker friend again; he inquired about my day and I invited him to join me for dinner, which, to my pleasure, he accepted. There was no deep conversation, just a little light chat, and he seemed interested to know about York, which he knew had 'a very magnificent Temple—I believe you call it a Minster'. It was another fine meal—soup, then grilled fish on a red-hot plate (I did not have beef in case my friend was a Hindu), followed by fresh fruit and cheese, all washed down with a bottle of white wine of unknown origin, then a brandy. I fell for a cigar when the *abdar* came around offering a choice from three cigar boxes. To hell with those straight-faced white chaps on the next table, I was enjoying chatting to my friend, the Indian banker even if, maybe, he was only a chief clerk. Before we arrived at Poona the sun had set, the velvet curtains had been drawn as if we were in *purdah* and the scene inside was like something I had only previously seen on the films, maybe a bit like the Orient Express. The whole meal and drinks, plus the cigar, was amazingly cheap—twelve rupees, less than a pound.

There was no need to rush back to the station, so I decided to stroll so far and then tried to pick up a *gharry* or a *tonga*. It was a lovely warm, still night, with crickets (or whatever they are out here) making a hell of a noise and glow-worms flashing brilliant little lights from the bottom of bushes. I stopped on the river bridge for a while, listening to the noise of the weir and smiled when I thought of Eric's escapade. Downstream, at the other side of the bridge, there were three or four fires on the bank, almost burning themselves out; they could be dying funeral pyres. I spent a while watching the reflections of the fires on the water and thought over the day; I had seen another side of India. I wished Peggy were here; I didn't think she would like Bombay, but she would love Poona. I wondered how long it would be until I saw her again and wondered what she was doing. It would only be mid-afternoon there, so she would have been at work. I hoped she was all right. I would write when I got back. I wondered what it would be like when we got to Burma; I did not think I would tell her where I was and would instead let her think I was still here.

I heard a horse trotting along the road, then little bells tinkling. They slowed down. A *tonga* pulled up beside me, and the driver said '*Salaam, sahib*. Very good *tonga, sahib*. I take you to town or RAF station, two rupees'. I replied, 'RAF Station, two rupees no, RAF Station one rupee, *Thik hai?*' In the light of the two candle lamps, I saw him nodding his head from side to side; he came back, '*Thik hai*, RAF Station, one rupee'. I got in. He shouted '*Jaldi-jao*' at the horse, then we turned around and set off at damn nearly a gallop; I was rocking backwards and forwards in this two-wheel trap as the *tonga wallah* stuck up on his perch and drove the horse into the darkness. However, the horse must have known its way for we soon pulled up at the lights of the airfield gates. As I sought through my change, the *tonga wallah* said, 'I told you, very good *tonga, sahib*. Very quick'. I gave him a rupee. He put his hand to his head in a sort of salute and then I gave him another eight annas, saying, 'This is for the horse—very good horse'. His nodding head said, 'You very good, *sahib*. *Namaste*,' and they shot off into the darkness.

14

The Wettest Place on Earth

'Thanks for all the tips, Brian. We'll try not to forget them'.

'All the best. May meet up with you again but, forty-what Squadron did you say, 'cause, far as I remember, 45 were on Vengeances, talk of them getting Beaus; it was 47 on Beaus, they brought them from the Middle East. KG is a strip they made on a tea plantation in Assam—it'll be bloody wet', Brian replied.

So, Douggie and I (along with Eric, his observer, and another crew) were off to Calcutta, where we would get further instructions on how to get to Khumbirgram (KG). This first leg was going to take about three days and two nights on the train, or rather on three trains, but it did not matter to us how long it took. I had only been in the country about six weeks, the last four being at Poona, but I had already become well-attuned to the pace of Indian life and realised there was no point in trying to rush anything. I felt as if I had lived here for years.

We loaded up with all our kit (tin trunks, suitcases, and bedrolls) and we left Poona for the short—a 90-mile ride through the Ghats (and the rain) to Kalyan junction, where we transferred to the Great Indian Peninsular train, which had come out of Bombay. There was the usual chaos over our reservations when the train came in—officials were waving bits of paper around, shouting, and gesticulating at each other—until an Army RTO sorted the job out. Two chaps were pulled out of a compartment reserved for four of us, and then we made sure that Douggie and Jake (Eric's observer, who was also an NCO) were fixed up OK before we had all our kit put aboard. Fortunately, there was never any need to rush on an Indian station as the trains seemed to stop for a long time while folks argued, left the train for some food, or just went for a walk. All the time, folks were climbing about on the third-class coaches at the rear of the train, trying to get on while those already on tried to push them off; even as trains moved off, chaps would be getting pushed off or try to stand on the buffers.

It was not a bad coach (nothing like *The Deccan Queen*), but there was plenty of room, even with all our kit, and the private washroom/toilet was very clean and roomy. The green leather-covered seats were a bit 'firm'. We had quite a long run—must have been a good hour—without a stop, heading north-eastwards through the Ghats, then we stopped at Deolali, where there were lots of Army chaps on the platform. The RTO put an officer in with us, telling us that he was only going as far as Jalgaon, and we should be there soon after 6 p.m. so he would not be with us for the night. We learnt from this chap that there was a big military hospital at Deolali with a unit for chaps who 'got a touch of the sun', so if you 'went round the bend' or got 'the Deolali Tap', you could finish up there, hence the expression 'he's gone Deolali' (doolally). I hoped we would not finish up there, and I did not know whether this chap had been a patient or worked there.

We trundled along, sometimes maybe even touching 40 miles an hour. We were out of the rain and it was getting a bit hot, but it would be dark in a couple of hours and we were wondering what the score was about some food. Then, after several stops, we arrived at a busy little junction and a chap came around to take orders for dinner, which would be in about another hour, at Jalgaon, so we ordered curries. Our Army chap left us there; he was going up to Jubbulpore. Our meals were ready when we got in the restaurant; they were exactly what we had ordered—must give full marks to the ordering of meals over the telegraph. This seemed quite a busy little place, with bags of noise and shouting and blokes trying to cram on to the third-class coaches, which had no glass in the sides and just wooden seats. After dinner, we got the bedrolls out, had a couple of 'Mariners' gins (India made gin with a seaman in oilskins clutching a ship's wheel, on the label, which was not at all bad), and tried to get to sleep. We kept being woken up by juddering to a halt, followed by lots of chatter outside, and so in the early hours, we got up to have a look out as there was such a racket going on. I think it was called Akola and it seemed as if it were a pretty big place and even at that time in the morning there was a *chai wallah*; as soon as he saw our window being opened, we all had a cup of tea.

We were due in Nagpur about 8 a.m. and arrived almost on the dot. We had to get everything out as we changed trains here. My, this really was a busy station. The *coolies* soon had our kit on the platform and we found the RTO. Yes, he had a signal to say we were coming; our compartments were reserved on the Bengal and Nagpur Railway train, which started off from here in about an hour and a half. He would see to putting our kit on board and would see us after breakfast, which could not have been better. After a good breakfast, little lads pestered us to buy cotton goods, but they were so cheap that I bought a couple of cotton sports shirts. Charlie Agar mentioned something about the Empress Cotton Mill at Nagpur. Looking at a map on the station, it appeared that we were almost slap bang in the middle of India. We had a long way to go yet—two days and a night on this train.

It looked well cultivated round here. It was an interesting country, with bullock carts, folks working in the (perhaps cotton) fields, but it was getting bloody hot and after an hour or so, we were glad when a big block of ice was shoved into our compartment, even though it did mean having to get everything off the floor, which we knew would soon be swimming with water. Tiffin ordered for Raipur, which turned out to be another big place and a busy junction. The land was still well-cultivated around here. We seemed to be near a river; there were also some densely wooded areas but by Jove, it was stinking hot. We tried the windows down, then blinds down, then blinds up, and windows up—every combination we could think of, but it was still boiling. We seemed to stop for ages at Bilaspur, where we had lots of tea and more lads and women tried to sell us not only cottons, but silks as well. We changed engines here with a lot of bumping about. It must have been hot work for the engine driver and the gang of about three he had on the footplate with him; I supposed they all took turns at shovelling—rather them than me.

At one stop, a ticket inspector came aboard to punch holes in our rail warrants. The train started to move while he was with us so he had to travel with us to the next stop, a smart chap in a white suit, obviously an Anglo, who spoke perfect English in a delightful lilting accent, his head nodding from side to side in rhythm with his speech. We asked him how he got on with all the folks in third class—did they all have tickets? We gathered that all they could do was to push their way around as best they could and try to see that those without tickets got off at the next stop but, it was all pretty hopeless because they would jump on again after the train had started off and they were not allowed to push people off when the train was in motion, although other passengers might. The arguments arose mainly at stations when folks with tickets could not get on, and then they had to try to root out those who did not have tickets to make room for those who did. Some people did fall off the outside, or get pushed off, when the train was going; he admitted that it was 'most unfortunate' that sometimes someone got killed. He also thought it was 'most unfortunate' that some 'ignorant peasants' do not seem to think that trains run at night and sleep on the track, using a sleeper as a bed and the rail as a pillow. The driver cannot see them in the dark. The 'cow catcher' is too high to push them aside clearly so they are killed. In reply to one of our questions, he admitted that the driver would slap the brakes hard on if he saw a sacred cow on the line but would merely blow his whistle for a peasant. He was very proud of the Bengal Nagpur Railway, saying it was much better than the Great Indian Peninsula Railway; our impression was the opposite, but it was nice to talk to a loyal employee.

We learned that the total length of our journey was just over 1,200 miles; he reckoned we would be in Calcutta at about 5 p.m. the next day, but some of the engines were getting 'a bit tired' with all the extra work they were having to do because of the war. He told us that we would be having dinner at Jharsuguda and he promised to see that our orders were sent ahead, so we agreed on six meat curries, two for Douggie and Jake, who were not in our compartment. He smiled and nodded his head when we complimented him on the 'telegraph' service for ordering meals ahead. He told us the area through which we were passing was a good area for rice and mulberry trees for the silkworms. We clanked to a stop and our ticket collector left us, confirming that the dinners would be OK. We patronised the *chai wallah*, had a stroll on the platform, and told Douggie and Jake that their dinners were ordered—the place was Raigarh. The engine was taking on fuel and water while someone was pouring oil in a box and squirting oil on the connecting rods. It was getting cooler now; there was a river and it was quite hilly.

We were ready for dinner by the time we arrived at Jharsuguda. It was dark—it got dark very quickly out there, with very little twilight, but before going to the restaurant, we organised someone to sweep the remains of the block of ice out of the compartment and mop up the floor, ready for the night.

We were soon settled in our bunks but kept being woken by juddering to a halt, followed by lots of noise outside, then a lurch as we moved off. We had to wait until about 10 a.m. to get our breakfast, by which time it was getting hot again and a block of ice was bundled into the compartment. What the hell the train was burning that morning, God knows. The engine was chucking out clouds of black smoke and showers of sparks, which seemed determined to swirl around our compartment, so we had to keep everything shut on both sides. Even so, we were getting filthy and the water in the wash place ran out, so while we had tiffin at Kharagpur, we made sure the water tank was filled up. After tiffin, we came into the flat plain (which was flat as a pancake but well-cultivated). We rattled on between stops, the engine having spasms of ejecting thick black smoke; eventually, the sun faded away and it was overcast. We crossed a fairly wide river, then another a lot wider, and then there was another river on our right and many more people around. It had begun to rain and was much busier outside with lots of shacks and buildings.

We pulled into Howrah station but it looked more like a big doss-house. The platform was covered with hordes of folk—some standing up; others squatting staring vacantly ahead; some were sitting around a cooking stove; others eating; some stretched out asleep; others were entirely covered under a white cloth—we hoped they were only asleep. There did not seem to be a square foot of spare platform space. Bombay's Victoria Terminus was a palace compared with this.

We decided to stay put for a while. Some *coolies* wearing official armbands pushed their way to our compartment; we told them to wait. After a while, an Army sergeant wearing an RTO arm-band pushed his way towards us and we explained who we were. The *coolies* got our tin trunks on their heads, others carrying the rest of our kit; we followed this sergeant to the RTO's office. The *coolies* bashed people out of the way, stepping on prone bodies, some of which did not even move, while others looked up. Beggars were asking for *baksheesh* and youths were trying to sell us things, but we had to just push them out of the way, otherwise we would have become separated from the sergeant. The RTO arranged to send us to a hotel that he said had been taken over for officers; he agreed that Douggie and Jake could come too, and, after a while, a driver appeared and led us out to a truck. Outside, it was almost as packed with people as it was in the station. The driver told us that the station had a permanent population; they had nowhere else to go.

Soon, we were driving over a bridge, which must have been three-quarters of a mile long, over the River Hooghly, to Calcutta proper, which is on the eastern side. The road was crammed full of cars, lorries, bullock carts, rickshaws, bikes, and anything else that would move on wheels. We weaved in and out, with plenty of horn-blowing and shouting. The river below was flowing pretty fast and it looked a mucky brown colour. By then, it was raining and nearly dark. Eric and I were in the front with the driver, a cheerful bloke, who told us, 'You get all sorts coming down this river. I've heard tell that the old hospital, just a bit of a way up on that bank, had a chute down to the river and after dark they used to send the day's corpses down it. You still see the odd body floating by. This bridge was only opened about a couple of years ago'. 'It must have been a bugger before that', I thought.

On arrival at this big, old-fashioned, run-down hotel, the first thing we were asked was, 'Can I see your Medical Cards, please, to see if all your jabs are in order. We've had cholera here and we don't want you to be getting it, do we? Careful with what you drink, don't touch the water or have any ice in your drinks'. I could not quite make out what went on at this hotel; I think it was called 'The Grand'. Some Army and Air Force units seemed to be actually based here judging by the notices on some of the doors, some chaps were in transit, one or two seemed to be on leave, but all we were concerned about was getting a room and a bath to get rid of the grime from all the engine smoke before dinner. It was a big place, with 300 or more rooms, all of which were very old-fashioned and a bit run-down.

After dinner, we were pleased to find that we could get bottled beer—some Indian brew, but it was OK and a welcome change from gin. Some chaps told us that in 1942, a Hurricane squadron was actually based in this hotel and used a wide road in the town, about 1 mile long, as a runway when the Japanese started dropping a few bombs around Calcutta. It was a damp, humid, and hot night. There seemed to be no air inside the mosquito net, but the few beers helped me drop off to sleep, wondering what sort of place I had come to.

Not unexpectedly, there was some confusion when we called on the movements chap next morning. 'Which Group are you attached to, 221 or 224?' We did not know. It seemed they were both based in Calcutta. We chatted to someone about 'Eastern Air Command' and 'Third Tactical Air Force' while Eric remarked to me, 'Shall we really confuse him and ask where the Torbeau Squadron is?' To this, I quickly replied 'No'. This movements chap started going through a pile of 'signals', but he obviously could not find what he was looking for, so he suggested that we should come back about 6 p.m. and he should have more gen for us then. The rain seemed to have eased up, so we set off to have a look at the town. We only saw a tiny part of this vast town but what contrasts—big open spaces, wide streets, great big ugly buildings, and some rather splendid ones were mixed with areas of utter squalor and poverty.

The movements officer had made some progress. He found some confirmation that we were to go to 'KG'. The nearest 'railhead' was at Sylhet or Silchar, but the way things were on the Assam Bengal Railway, it might take a week to get through, but it was doubtful if we would get through due to damage caused by the rains. He had therefore been on to 229 Group (the transport group) and they would get us there by Dakota. There was no promise when this would be, but we were to be at Dum Dum airfield by 8 a.m. in the morning and they would take us when they could. He would make arrangements for us to be picked up at 7 a.m. and for an early breakfast.

That evening, we heard on the news from England that we had secured our position in Normandy and that Allied Forces were pressing on towards Paris; they also said that there was some sort of uprising in Paris by the partisans, so that sounded a good thing. We expressed surprise at seeing so many Yanks in Calcutta and asked what they were doing out here. A chap told us that they were fighting a completely different campaign from the one we were fighting. They were up in north-east Burma, along with some Chinese, and all they were concerned about was opening up the Ledo Road from Assam through to China. They wanted to get stuff through to China from where, with those new 'Super Fortresses' they had, they would be able to bomb Japan.

They also reckoned that if they could get stuff through to China, old Chan would join with them in attacking Japan. They wanted to get a road and a pipeline through—that was what they were after; they were not bothered about our side of Burma and clearing the Japanese out of Mandalay and Rangoon. They had a lot of transport aircraft out here and were doing a run 'over the hump' to China. It was a hell of a route, through bloody great mountains and damn all aids to speak of; some of our chaps, RAF, and Canadians were on that run too. The trouble was, we were short of transport aircraft as we needed them to drop supplies to the Army lads who had been taken into Burma in gliders;

it was the only way we could get anything to them, poor devils, but we had to rely on the Yanks letting us have the aircraft. It seemed that early in the war, when it became obvious that we could not build all the aircraft that we would need, we would have to rely on getting aircraft from America.

It was agreed that we should concentrate on building only fighters and bombers and the Yanks would provide all the transport aircraft: the Daks. When they found themselves drawn into the war, they needed all the transport aircraft they could lay their hands on, so our supply started to dry up and we had to go pleading to them when we needed more aircraft; sometimes, I believe the top brass had a hell of a job getting enough Daks to keep our lads supplied, as the Yanks reckoned it was more important to get through to China than clearing the Burma plain. The Americans were not daft; when the war was over and civil flying got going again, they would be the only people with any transport aircraft on the drawing board. Individually, however, they were great blokes—very friendly and generous.

So, on a dull, damp morning we drove out to the airfield at Dum Dum. An ammunition factory here used to make the now outlawed 'dumdum' bullets. There was no promise as to when we would get away, except that they would try to persuade a Dak crew to drop us off, provided they had room. They seemed to expect three or four Daks to be going east during the course of the day. We hung around, drinking tea, and looking at maps, posters, and other notices stuck up on the walls. There were posters warning about 'cu-nims', showing sketches of different colours (grey ones, brown ones, and black ones) with notes underneath such as, 'No aircraft will survive if you get in one of these'; under another, 'If you get in one of these do not try to turn back—carry on and hope you come out'; and in big letters, 'Avoid all cu-nims'.

Notices gave gen on the state of various airstrips such as, 'Very wet—do not leave the all-weather strip', 'South end of strip waterlogged', 'Closed—waterlogged', and 'Open with extreme care'. The names of these strips meant little to us and we did not know where they were. We looked at the map to try and get an idea where we were going; it all looked very hilly. We followed the big wide River Brahmaputra, in which there seemed to be many quite large islands, running roughly from east to west through Assam, until it turned south to become known as the Jamuna and finally join the Ganges to flow south eastwards into the sea some 150 miles east of Calcutta. Between

Calcutta and the mouth of the Ganges, there seemed to be a huge delta, but the big rivers did not flow into this; this seemed to be a whole lot of smaller rivers. While we were looking at this, one chap informed us that the Brahmaputra was at present about 40 feet above its normal level, so the course shown on the map did not mean very much. By this time, a Dak had come in but there would be no room on it for us and a US Dak had said that they could have taken two but were not allowed to put down at KG. It was beginning to look as if we would be here for the night, which, indeed, we were, bedding down in a transit place, but it did not matter much where we were as we had our bedrolls with us.

The next day, we got away with a Canadian crew—grand, cheery chaps they were. The plane already seemed to be fully loaded when we got in, with boxes and crates all lashed down. There were no seats, of course, and the skipper asked us to lash our gear down too as, 'We don't want tin trunks flying around if it gets a bit bumpy, do we?' Perched on our bedrolls, we were ready for the off, but it seemed ages and ages before the tail started to come up and we were in a sensible position. There was no surge of power as in the Beau, just the sound of two rather weak engines tearing their guts out and no impression of gaining any speed. Then, we felt that we were off—it seemed to take a hell of a long time—but the engines were still going flat out. At long last, we heard the power being reduced and we seemed to be flying level, but wallowing about and I moved a bit to see out of a side window. For the best part of an hour, we were at 1,500 feet and, except when bits of grey cloud passed by, I saw we were flying over floods. There was mile after mile of flood water with just isolated bits of dry land, like islands, on which there were people and cattle and little huts. We then seemed to enter solid cloud, the engines increased power and we were climbing, still wallowing and now bouncing up and down as well.

For half an hour or so, we kept on climbing, then in about another half an hour, we sensed that we had reduced power and were losing height. We were making several turns, first this way and then the other. It was raining like hell outside. A light flashed, which we assumed is to warn us that we were coming in to land, but there was still cloud and rain outside. A little thump was assumed to be the undercarriage coming down, then some power was put on; we rocked about a bit as some trees appeared out of the murk. We were quite low, so I sat on my bed-roll for the landing. The power came off, there was a gentle bump, and we were clattering along the strip.

The skipper came back for a word with us. We complimented him on the landing in all this muck, but it seemed to mean nothing to him; he said 'It's always like this at this time of the year'. He was pushing on to Chabua (wherever that may be, presumably further east) and would be off as soon as we got our things. We opened the door to be greeted by torrential rain, ruddy great puddles, and mud. One airman was standing there wearing just a pair of long shorts, socks, and a pair of big black muddy boots; another wore the same plus a battered bush hat; and the third looked dejected under a cape and bush hat. They soon got cracking and hauled our kit out into a couple of Jeeps (which fortunately had canvas covers); we squeezed on ourselves and were driven, splashing our way, to some buildings. On the way, we saw some tents and hoped that these were not for us; the 'buildings' were mainly bamboo and matting '*bashas*'. We had arrived at KG, Assam. Douggie remarked, 'Happen we won't be doing much flying while the weather is like this'. How wrong he was to be.

Coming home to North Coates after a raid.

The Fleece, North Coates, 2018 (no longer a pub).

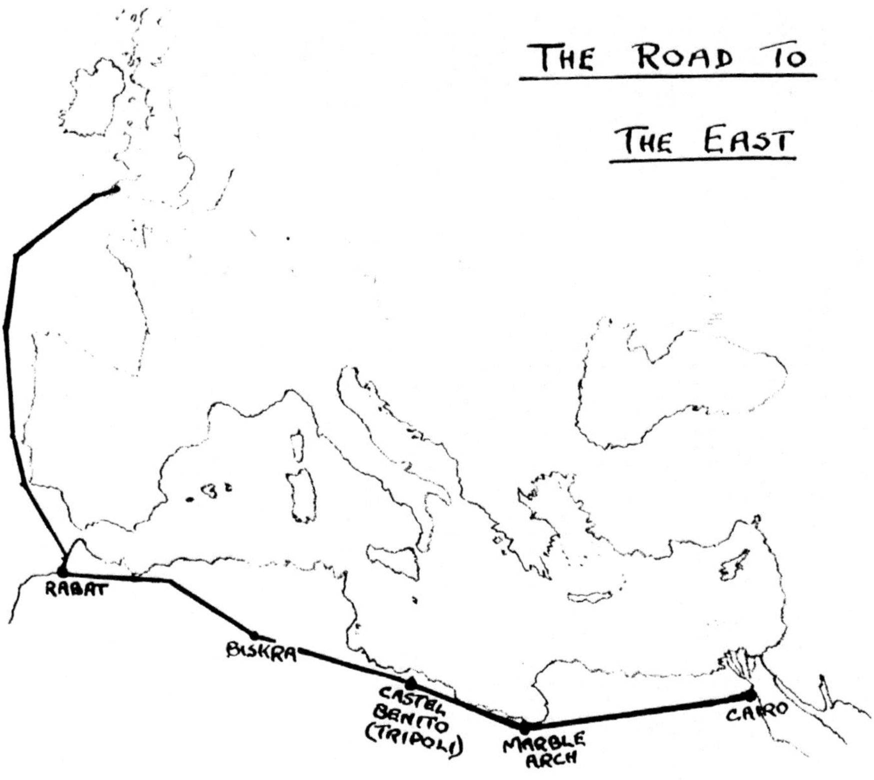

THE ROAD TO THE EAST

Above: The route to Cairo.

Left: Cairo—a street scene.

The Sphinx and pyramids, Cairo.

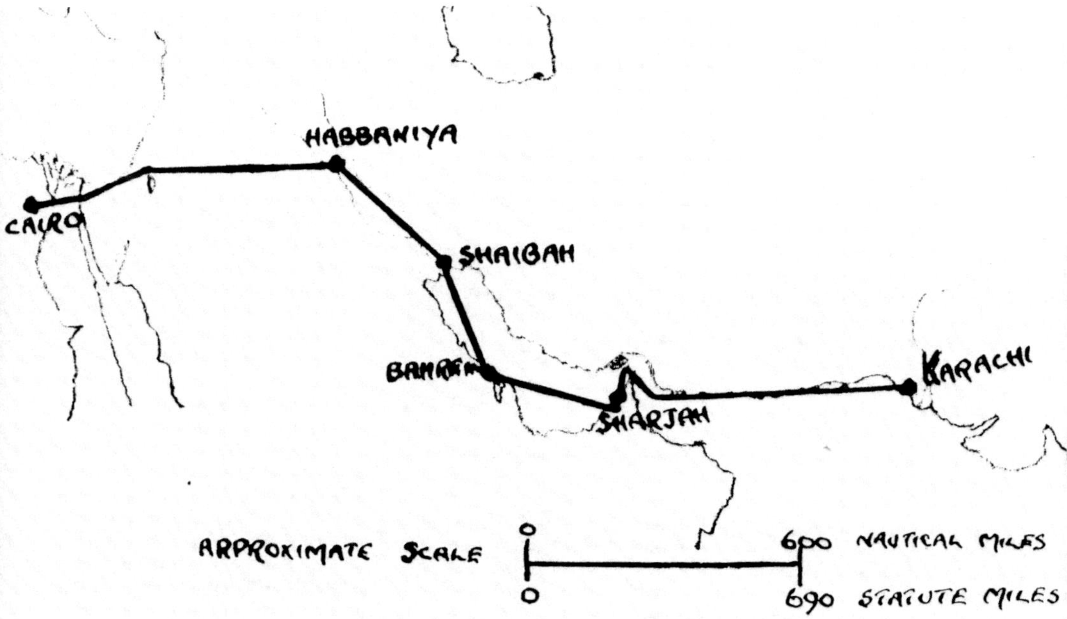

Cairo to Karachi.

The gateway to India—Bombay.

Bombay Museum.

Right: Jack and Douggie in Poona.

Below: Eric's Weir, Poona.

Left: A cheeky chappie.

Below: Jack, Bill, and Buck in Assam.

Right: Burma—rivers and railways.

Below: Before the attack.

Above: After the attack.

Left: The reunion of Jack with his trainer, Harry Guest.

A typical target in Burma.

A rural railway station.

Water buffalo.

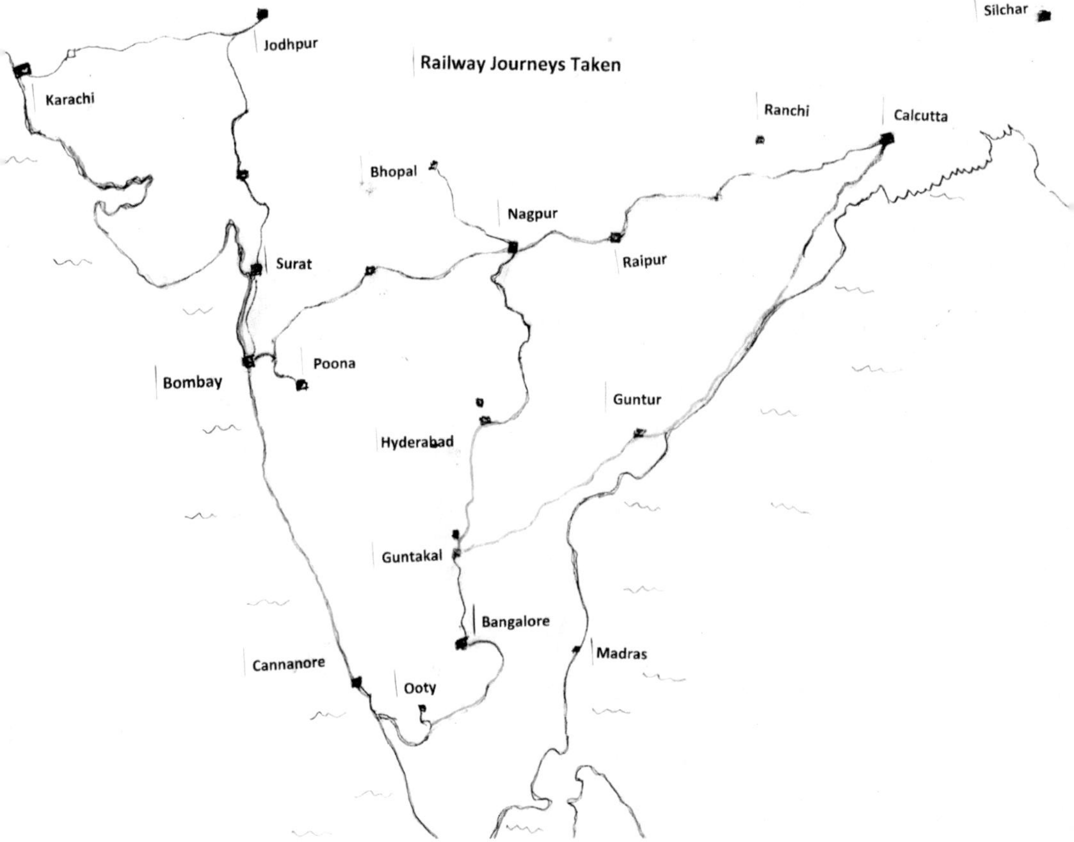

Sketch of Indian railway journeys taken.

The BUS Club.

Above left: David, Jack's loyal bearer.

Above right: Yellow, red, and grey.

Cannanore beach.

Bullock carts.

Above left: Jack with Ginny.

Above right: Eric with Tonic.

Above left: Jack with Gin and Tonic.

Above right: Ginny on guard.

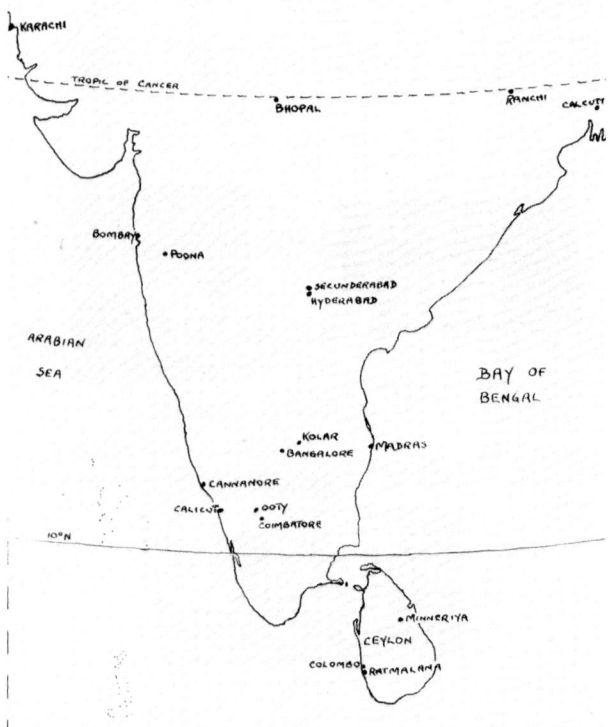

Above: The wedding season.

Left: Tropical India.

Above left: Jack at Poona—Postings.

Above right: The memsahib.

Below: The Tabriz rug.

Above: With Peter and Richard, Scarborough.

Below left: Oosterbeek War Graves.

Below right: Henry Everest Colman, aged nineteen.

15

Bill Briefs Us for Battle

As we half expected, this posting was another 'cock-up'. The squadron to which we had been posted were flying Vengeances, as Brian had thought. We were determined that there was no way they were going to get us to fly Vengeances—American single-engined dive bombers. None of us had flown single-engined aircraft since elementary flying school, none of us had any dive-bombing experience, and, to be perfectly honest, I would have been shit scared trying to fly an aircraft, especially a single-engined one, on which I had no experience, in conditions like this. There was, fortunately, a Beaufighter squadron here as well. They had a squadron leader from New Zealand—a great character called Bill. He was a bit of a rebel in that he never wore his wings or his decorations; as often as not, he never wore his squadron leader's rings either. He had big leather buttons on his 'bush jacket', a big black 'tache (moustache) and black hair with the Brylcreem look. He came over to talk to us in the mess that night and introduced us to his pal—'Buck'—another New Zealander, a flight lieutenant.

In some ways, Buck was a complete contrast to Bill—tall, good-looking, and his dress immaculate, wearing a very natty silk scarf—but they were both great, cheerful, and friendly blokes. When they heard about the cock-up with our postings, Bill asked us what we had done before, then ordered a round of drinks; when they arrived, he said, 'Right, fellas, here's to you three joining us. That OK with you Buck?' Buck raised his glass and said, 'Sure, sounds great to me'. We asked Bill if he had really meant he could get us into his squadron; he assured us there would be no problem as they wanted two more crews anyway (it was only later we learned that two had gone adrift a few days ago) and he would send a signal off in the morning telling them he had now got us. We were to just leave it to him; he would fix it. One thing about these Commonwealth types was that they would not be bothered about red tape. I felt elated to think I had got on a squadron with a chap like Bill; from utter dejection, I felt on top of the world in the space of an hour. The rain was coming down now like 'stair rods', wind was whistling through the mess, thunder seemed to be rumbling all around us, water was creeping in on the floor, and, now and again, there seemed to be a crack right over our heads; however, no one seemed to mind. When it seemed to have eased off a bit, I put a cape over my head and splashed my way over to my *basha*; it was perfectly dry inside and I soon went out like a light.

In a couple of days, all seemed to be sorted out. Bill had managed to get us on his squadron; he was not the CO as we at first assumed, but one of the flight commanders. We met the CO and it was arranged that Eric and I would be in Bill's flight and the other crew in the other flight. It seemed to be raining 90 per cent of the time—sometimes heavily, sometimes less heavily, sometimes just a damp drizzle, and, for brief periods, just damp and sticky. Three or four Beaus had been off on trips although, back home, I doubted whether anyone would have considered taking off in weather like this. It was arranged that we would see the intelligence officer who would give us a run-down on what was going on out here.

Gathered round a large wall map, the IO pointed places out to us with a bamboo stick, as he briefed us on the present situation.

> The Japs have pushed right up the coast, into the Arakan, to beyond Akyab and we have contained them roughly along this line here. They are using the airfields at Akyab and Ramree.
>
> In March '44 they occupied virtually the whole of Burma and pushed on into Assam around Imphal and Kohima. Imphal was surrounded by three Jap Divisions—they had hoped to get into India before the rains broke so that they would be able to get food and supplies from India. There was some very bitter fighting around Imphal and Kohima but we managed to hold them there. The 14th Army have now shifted the Japs from around here and the road between Imphal and Kohima was re-opened towards the end of June but all these rains won't be doing it much good. The 14th Army have

now set about driving the Japs out of these hills, their aim is to get to this big river here, the Chindwin, and secure positions on the west bank by the end of the rains—about the middle of October—so that, as soon as the roads dry up, they can make a big push, over the river and into the plains of Central Burma. Unfortunately, the rains are particularly bad this year and this is devilish country, so progress is necessarily slow.

There is a continuous chain of jungle covered mountains and deep sheer valleys from north of Kohima running roughly south to damn near the Arakan coast—they have fancy names, The Naga Hills, Manipur Hills, Lushai Hills, Chin Hills, and Arakan Hill Tracts but, take it from me, they are not what you think of as hills, they are bloody rugged mountains, rent by deep valleys with steep sides. You will have to fly over them to get to your targets, but think of the poor Army chaps having to hack their way through on foot, their equipment on mules, all bogged down on muddy mountain tracks and relying on supplies being dropped to them from Daks. We hear that the ground is so wet and muddy that some of them are having to hack down trees so that they can lay logs on the ground in order to make any progress at all, and, all the time there may be some Japs waiting to ambush them. They don't return to a dry charpoy every day, they just have to bivouac the best they can, sleeping in mud-caked gear, in the rain, in mosquito-ridden areas and hope the weather will permit the next day's supply drop. Some of our Hurricane pilots, on a so-called 'rest', all volunteers, are with these Army units, running the R/T for communicating with and directing the Air Support.

We get very good reports from the Army on their progress. Most units set up W/T communications when they bivouac. It seems that, about ten days ago they secured this place—Tamu—just over the border. There has been a big engagement on this track here, running down this valley to Tiddim—Hurri-bombers have being spraying D.D.T. around here which is reported to be the worst malarial area in the world. They are now trying to make progress up here to Pyinbon Sakan and encountering stiff resistance so the Hurri-bombers are at it all day long. It seems that some advance columns are closing in on Sittaung while others are pressing on towards Kalewa but they have a long way to go yet. Most of these spots are only little villages, they may contain some friendly Burmese, or some who would give us away to the Japs, or they may be Japs only or Burmese only so, you will see that they always have to be very careful when they come into a village.

You will have heard of Wingate and his Chindits. Well, his second expedition, or Long Range Penetration Force, to give them their correct name, were flown in, in Daks and gliders in March, to several places in this area here, to the SSW of Myitkyina. These crosses marked Broadway, Chowringhee and Aberdeen are where they were landed and this spot here marked Blackpool was a strongpoint they set up with a landing strip. Wingate himself was killed in an air crash over the mountains, on 24 March, when he was flying back to liaise with HQ. They operated as several units right in among the Japs, cutting communications and causing as much havoc as they could. They had to rely on everything being dropped from Daks or being landed on quickly made airstrips, with light aircraft picking up the sick and wounded. Some of them were in there until last month. Those who survived have been got out now, some of them finished up being dragged into assisting the Americans and Chinese around Mogaung.

Yes, there are some Americans and Chinese in north-east Burma, under Stilwell, but their objective seems to be quite different from ours. We are concerned with clearing the Japs out of Burma – the Americans are concerned only with opening up a road from Ledo, down through north-east Burma and into China, so that they can get supplies into China through the back door. They hope that Chiang Kai-shek will use these supplies against Japan and they also want to set up bases in China so that their Super Fortresses will be able to bomb the Japanese mainland. At present they are flying supplies into China 'over the hump'—a very hazardous route over mountains with very few navigation aids—and there are some of our chaps on that run too. There is always a tussle to get Daks out here. The Yanks have nearly all of them—we need them to keep Slim's 14th Army supplied and they want them on their China run. Anyway, Stilwell's lot took the airfield at Myitkyina in May and secured the town earlier this month. They also have Mogaung. What the Yanks plan to do now we do not know—probably concentrate on building their road as they don't show any sign of pressing on towards Mandalay.

Most of the close support work for the 14th Army is done by Hurri-bombers and Vengeances, with Daks dropping supplies and little Stinsons picking up sick and wounded. Your job in the Beaus is to disrupt communications, attack installations and dumps plus any special jobs requested by the Army. The communications will be trains, either on the move or hidden in jungle sidings, army trucks and transport, airfields, bridges and anything on the banks of the Chindwin—barges and paddle steamers. At this time of the year it will only be possible to operate by day but when the rain is clear, night trips with the moon should be most profitable.

I suggest that you study these maps, aerial photographs, noting the mountain ranges, rivers, tracks, railways and airfields until you can visualise them in your sleep. It will be mainly map reading at low level and, for the next few weeks will be in rain or mist. Don't forget you will probably have a compass error on return if you have fired your cannons. Take note of the few alternate landing strips—those with 'all-weather strips', because the emergency-rolled paddy fields aren't any good in the rains. Gen up on the direction finding (D/F) stations. MF D/F is pretty good when well above the mountains on the way home, but no good at low level in your Op areas. The Observers should also gen up on the call-signs and frequencies and all of you have a good look at the silhouettes of the Jap aircraft and their speeds.

We spent a lot of time studying maps and pictures of our 'hunting ground' over the next couple of days. Douggie came to the conclusion, 'Happen, it's going to be a bugger, especially while it keeps on raining'. We got roped in for doing a ground compass swing and Bill informed us that when the clouds lifted a bit we should get up for an hour or so to have a look around locally and familiarise ourselves with the local terrain and note a few landmarks. Also, Eric and I would each do a couple of trips standing behind him or behind Buck, so that they could show us how it was done and show us some useful pin-points.

The next day, Buck had to do an air test, so he took me along with him so that I could stand behind him while we flew round for an hour or so while he tried to point out the local features. Visibility was awful due to rain, low cloud, and mist. Tree-covered hills disappeared into a murky abyss as we crossed deep valleys; he rattled off heights as he seemed to scrape over the tops of ridges. We had a look at Silchar, our nearest railhead, but could not see very much, then headed due east for twenty-five minutes or so to Imphal. Buck remarked that the hills around there were supposed to be full of leopards, tigers, and black bears. Columns of spray were rising from waterfalls cascading down sheer hillsides and a blue mist arose from the valleys to meet the rain, which was coming down in sheets; visibility at times was almost nil. We spoke to the airfield at Imphal and flew over so that I could have a look; I noticed a couple of Dakotas on the ground but saw nothing resembling a town. Buck warned me about the little hills surrounding this airfield, then headed south and we dived down into a misty valley. 'Must keep the ground in sight, or you'll finish up in trouble. This is the Manipur Valley—in a minute we'll pick up the Manipur River'. We seemed to be skimming over terraces of paddy fields—mile after mile of them—then the river, which was a mucky brown affair, flowing like the clappers.

We left the river on our port and picked up a big lake; soon after crossing this, we picked up the river again. Buck remarked, 'This is the valley the 14th Army have gone down—now I'll show you how to get home. Check your gyro on this straight stretch of river in case you've buggered the compass up by firing the cannons—now full power and take up to 9,000'. At 9,000 feet, we did a 180-degree tight turn and continued up to 11,000 feet with oxygen on, where we came out of cloud and saw the sun for the first time since I had arrived in Assam. We now set course for home, getting QDMs from KG and Imphal; these came through very well and, for good measure, we also got a bearing from Agartala. We came over KG on QDMs, then let down into the thick dark cloud, flying a pattern to the south of the airfield. The final approach was on QDMs; at about 400 feet, trees appeared out of the murk and we were home. Buck was really some flyer and after that trip, I knew I must keep studying those maps so that I would know the country like the back of my hand.

The following day, Douggie and I were given an aircraft so that we could have a couple of hours doing practice approaches using QDMs and D/F. It was good practice for both of us and as luck would have it; it was hardly raining—just fairly low cloud and a bit of drizzle. To get in as much practice as possible, we overshot when the runway came into sight, although once we saw no runway—just bloody trees—and I did not enjoy that.

Bill had been having several chats with us 'new boys':

Be professional. No point in being foolhardy and getting killed unnecessarily, that's no way to win a war, leave the suicide stuff to the Nips. Our job is to rub out Nips and disrupt their supplies and come back so that we can keep on doing it again and again. We have a big advantage—we've got the best aircraft in the world for doing the job—perfect forward vision—strong as a bloody ox if you clip the odd tree but watch out for dead teak trees left standing to season, can't see them too well—just like poles and bloody solid. Biggest plus is that they don't hear us coming, if you can't make a telling attack first time don't mill around after they know you are there, clear off for a while, then return from another direction—strike and be off like an elusive phantom—that keeps them on tenterhooks. Don't waste any rockets or shells—make every one tell. Don't blast away at a village unless you know it is a Nip base or depot—it may be occupied by friendly Burmese, or even our own troops. Listen out on the VHF Air Support frequency. Keep very low—the Nips are red-hot with their light Ack-Ack and small arms fire. Don't fly straight and level in open areas, zig-zag, skid or gently corkscrew. Always be alert to trip wires in narrow valleys and visualise areas where there may be land mines set off remotely to catch low flying aircraft. The Nip fighters are all radial-engined and have to depress the nose slightly to bring their guns to bear so, if you get one on your tail, try to get him down to your level, then, when he fires his guns he'll probably fly into the deck – or try to lead him into a hillock. Don't get mesmerised by your rockets and follow them in to the deck but pull away to avoid the explosion and debris. Watch out for cu-nims over the mountains on the way back and if you get in one, for Christ's sake do not try to turn back—open the throttles, try to keep the nose down a bit and everything central, close your eyes and pray—don't look at your instruments.

By now, I felt as if I had been at this station much longer than a mere couple of weeks. I would be glad when I had done my first Op, but the lads were such a cheerful, friendly bunch that I felt as if I had known them for months. There was nowhere else to go, so our little mess was always in full swing—someone always thought up some excuse for a party, maybe the birthday of someone's distant relation, maybe to celebrate another tenth of an inch on Bill's 'tache, or to thank Oscar (a little lizard who scampered around the roof) for keeping the flies down. By now, it was just routine to sweep out water that crept in on the floor and the thunder that rumbled around was taken for granted.

I recalled that during the year I was in Iceland, I do not remember one single thunderstorm, but here, it seemed to rattle around most evenings although the lads said they were usually worse at the beginning of the rainy season.

We could pick up the BBC News reasonably well and heard that Brussels had been liberated—there was lots of news about progress in Europe, Finland, Rumania, Bulgaria, and the progress of the Yanks in the Pacific but never a bloody word about Southeast Asia; maybe no one knew we were there. Perhaps it was just as well; there was no point letting the Japanese know the 14th Army were pressing on towards the Chindwin in pissing rain and going to cross somewhere near Kalewa when the rains stopped.

16

The Fright of My Life

It was just beginning to get light on a warm, sticky, and wet morning as I hung on to the roof rails, feet astride across the hatch, looking over Bill's shoulder as we roared off into the murk. I was about to get my first glimpse of Burma. I was all decked up in my jungle suit, revolver around my waist, knife tucked down my boot, map stuffed into one pocket, some emergency rations in other pockets, and wearing Douggie's parachute harness as, with having to stand up, I could not use my own sit-on harness. Our job was to pick up the River Chindwin at a river junction just north of Kindat, fly south down the river for about 200 miles to Monywa, then cover a stretch of railway from just west of Mandalay up to Ye-U, attacking anything we could find. Bill kept giving me a running commentary over the intercom. He seemed to know exactly where we were; he kept half turning his head as he spoke to me, just as if he were out on a Sunday afternoon drive and I hoped that he could see out better than I could as trees appeared out of the mist and flashed by our starboard wing. I thanked the Lord that I was a pilot and would soon be in the pilot's seat myself as, although I knew Bill was a damned good pilot, I did not like flying passenger; I supposed chaps in other aircrew categories got used to it as they had their own jobs to think about. He said:

> We've got three ranges to cross. Next one is the Manipur Valley coming down from Imphal—this rain should ease up when we get down into the plain—somewhere down there is a muddy track to Tamu—there seemed a bit of doubt as to where the Army were—

some of them got to Tamu a couple of weeks ago but they don't seem to have cleared the Nips out yet—that's why they want us to cover this stretch of the river.

I tried to look at my map but it was difficult as I had to keep hanging on with one hand and keep moving my legs so that they did not get stiff; gosh, it was warm and sticky under all that clobber. He continued:

Hang on—we'll sidle down the side of the valley to pick up the river—never let the ground get out of sight and hug the hill-side for cover—not that that matters much in this weather but when it's clear you don't want to be silhouetted against the sky-line.

He checked with his observer that the cannons were cocked and then he selected 'pairs' for the rockets. We picked up the river, which was flowing fast like a raging torrent, then we joined another (a very wide one), the Chindwin. It was flowing like the clappers—a muddy brown, swirling in whirlpools and carrying floating trees and bits of debris. I cannot visualise any river traffic in these conditions; no boat would be able to make any headway against this current. It was still overcast and misty but not raining—just miserable and sticky—as we weaved from side to side of the river looking for any sign of life. To the east of the river, the ground was flat, dotted with isolated trees and just faded away into the mist. We paid special attention to a little place on the west bank called Mawlaik, but Bill decided there was nothing doing there. After another seven minutes or so another river appeared through a gap in the hills to the west and we turned to starboard up here for a mile or two to Kalewa, but there was no sign of anything moving, so we went back to the Chindwin where a road bridge was missing: 'Got to keep a good eye on this area as the 14th Army is making for the river around here'.

We moved on down the Chindwin for the best part of another hour, weaving about and scanning both banks, with Bill taking the port and his observer the starboard while I looked out as best I could, hanging on and flexing my knees; it was like being on the Big Dipper. Then Bill increased the power; we came to another demolished bridge, turning sharply to port we left the river and followed a track for a mile or so to Monywa, where we nearly took the roofs off some buildings, bobbed up for a look at the railway then down behind some trees, turned around, back over the railway station, which Bill raked with a couple of seconds of cannon fire (although there was no train to be seen). We then went on towards Mandalay, weaving across the railway and a road, which ran parallel to each other; it was flat around here. My arms were stiff and tired but I could not let go. Next, we came to another flooded river coming down from the north to join the Irrawaddy—the River Mu. The rail bridge was down here, but Bill said they looked to have made some repairs at one end so we did a bit of a scurrying around in a big arc, came in at an angle, and he released a pair of rockets then raked some *bashas* with the cannons. While I was coughing from the cordite fumes, Bill remarked, 'The bomber boys have made a good job of these bridges—bombs are better than rockets for that job'. It was the first time I had seen a rocket with a high-explosive warhead; they were certainly very effective as wood and rubbish went flying through the air.

We went up the Mu to another bridge, which was either demolished or washed away, then in a roundabout way following a muddy track, to back near Monywa, then up north, criss-crossing the railway and a parallel road up towards the end of the line at Ye-U. Suddenly, Bill noticed a siding surrounded by dense trees. We were in a tight turn, and I was forced against one side of the aircraft, trying to see where the ground was; then, I saw we were heading down on a line of wagons, like boxcars; the cannons rattled, and I heard a whoosh as a pair of rockets sailed ahead of us. We pulled away to starboard, skimming the trees and away. We did not go back to investigate.

The observer reported some smoke rising out of the trees, but Bill was muttering about there being no engine, just a line of trucks, but at least they would not use some of them again. At the railhead, all seemed quiet and deserted so Bill decided to hang on to the remaining four rockets to see if we could catch anything on the track from here to Kalewa. This was a hair-raising stretch, following a muddy track for nearly 100 miles, back into hilly country. Then, we went back over the Chindwin, into the tree-covered valley towards Kalemyo, and then 'bingo'—Bill's idea paid off. On the track, which was just like a cutting in the trees, were three big, brown covered trucks that seemed to be stuck in the mud because there were blokes standing around them. Bill yanked the wheel back then down with the nose. Cannon shells were kicking up the mud in front of this column, and the two pairs of rockets whooshed away in rapid succession. As we rushed by at one side, almost clipping the treetops, black smoke was rising. We did a complete circle and came over again from the same direction; flames were now rising in the middle of the smoke and Bill pressed the cannon button again, but after two or three rattles, we had run out of ammo. We turned north at Kalemyo, up the valley and climbed up into the rain-laden clouds, heading for home. Bill seemed satisfied with the day's work, and I was able to relax my grip and exercise my arms as we steadily climbed. Bill produced a bar of chocolate and handed it to me over his shoulder; it was all soft and sticky, almost running out of the wrapper. We were back at KG in time for lunch; we had been away four and a half hours.

This trip with Bill made me realise more than ever that there was no chance of more than a very quick glance at a map when over Japanese territory. So, I studied the maps and photographs even more closely, trying to commit the rivers, railways, roads, and tracks to memory, along with the positions of towns, villages, airfields, and defended areas, while Douggie concentrated on their heights. We made sketches and then checked them against the maps. We built up a reasonable mental picture of central Burma. The intelligence officer and the other lads were very helpful in pointing out which areas were thickly wooded, which were flat open plain, and where we may find sidings or depots tucked away in the trees.

The picture soon built up. There was a big river—the Irrawaddy— flowing almost due south till passing Mandalay on its east bank; it then began a long bend to the west, passing Sagaing on its northern bank, then headed straight for about 40 miles, where it was joined by the River Mu from the north and began a long gentle sweep to the south to Myingyan. It then went south-west to Pakokku, where it was joined by the other big river—the Chindwin—and then wound its way down to Rangoon. The Chindwin had meandered its way south through the mountains of northern Burma, then along the foothills of the mountains between us and the central plain. There were dozens and dozens of smaller feeder rivers, some of which did not even seem to have a name. Between these two big rivers and covering some 150 miles by 70 miles was the central plain—a flat area about 500 feet above sea level to the north and west of Mandalay.

A railway came down from Myitkyina (which was now held by Stilwell's lot) through Wuntho and Shwebo (which is in the plain) to Sagaing, just across the Irrawaddy from Mandalay. From Sagaing, another line went west, then north to Monywa on the Chindwin, and then continued north up the plane to Ye-U. These were the only lines west of the Irrawaddy, but on the east side, there were four radiating from Mandalay—a short line due north to Madaya; another going north-east to Lashio; the 'main' line going south to Rangoon; and, what we called the 'loop line', setting off to the south-west towards Myingyan on the Irrawaddy then looping back to join the main line at Thazi Junction.

This loop line was quite a 'hot spot' as 7 or 8 miles up this loop from Thazi was Meiktila with a Japanese airfield and another 10 miles away was a Japanese strongpoint at Thabutkon. From Thazi Junction, another line ran east into the hills to Heho, where there was another Jap airfield. Some 80 miles down the main line from Thazi was Pyinmana, where the Japanese had a training centre, and from here, a line branched off to the west and then turned north to Kyaukpadaung, which was about on the same latitude as Meiktila and about 30 miles from the Irrawaddy. We tried to memorise the main roads too but could not possibly remember all the tracks; some of them would not be on the maps anyway.

My name appeared on the Ops board. Bill had decided that there was no point in me doing another trip 'riding shotgun' and I was glad about that; I would be able to sit down and see where I was going. It was another early morning take-off and not raining for a change. There were no stars to be seen, so obviously still overcast, though it seemed very warm. The briefing was to pay close attention to the banks of the Chindwin from north of Kindat right down to Pakokku and then, if we had not used our weapons, to follow a road west to Pauk and Tilin and up the narrow Gangaw Valley to Kalemyo.

We were warned that some of our troops may be getting near to Kalemyo from the north and also warned of possible Dakota supply-dropping areas to avoid on our way home. It began to get light as we were over the wooded mountains; it was not raining but dull, drab, and misty with little 'scud' clouds sitting on the treetops here and there. Looking down, it was hard to believe that somewhere in those trees there could be hundreds (even thousands) of men of the 14th Army making their tortuous way to the Chindwin. Maybe some of them would hear us as we brushed over the treetops and it would give them a bit of moral support—God knows, they deserved it; thank goodness I got into the Air Force. Douggie cocked the cannons, while I switched on the rocket master switch and selected 'Pairs', checked the fuel and changed over the tanks, and gave a little tug to make sure my harness was tight; we then sidled down to the river. I could not imagine how the Army were ever going to cross this river. When the rains stopped, it would surely stop flowing so fast, but it would still be bloody wide and they surely could not be bringing heavy equipment with them through the mountains on those muddy and washed away tracks? Also, big stuff could not be dropped from Dakotas; they would have to land, but the problem was where. Also, you could not get tanks in Dakotas; maybe they would use more gliders.

I felt like a great fat Buddha sitting there, weaving from side to side of the river, searching the banks for any sign of movement or anything to blast away at; somehow, I did not seem to be in an aeroplane; the view was so good and the Beau seemed to just be an extension of my own body. Everything was so easily to hand and flying the Beau was just like having slipped into a comfortable old sports jacket. The weather down there was quite good—not sunny but visibility was OK, although it was bloody warm and I was sweating like a pig under my jungle suit; thank goodness, I had my Aertex helmet instead of the leather sort, even though my hair was soaking and perspiration running into my eyes made them smart. We had weaved our way down the river for some 250 miles without seeing a damned thing, although I had used the cannon on what looked to me to be a small boat up an inlet near Monywa and covered over with tree branches. This is when I found that two cannons were not working as the racket was not as loud as usual; Douggie came forward to investigate and reckoned and that one had not fired at all and another had fired a few rounds and then jammed. Remembering what happened in Scotland when a round stuck and we blew a hole in the bottom of the aircraft, I told him to make these two 'safe' to avoid possible future trouble. As we approached Pakokku, we kept an extra special look-out for Japanese aircraft, knowing that we would not be far from Meiktila (a Japanese airfield).

At Pakokku, the two big rivers met in a great big swirling mass of brown water, more like being over a lake than a river, except lakes do not usually flow at this speed. Here, we shot off to the west, into the high ground and picked up the track to Pauk. After that, we followed this track over a high ridge and dropped quickly down into a narrow valley with steep sides. It was very damp and misty down there, raining a little bit and the smell of wet, rancid vegetation even penetrated the cockpit. The mist seemed to be blue and the rain a bit heavier; I went up a little but did not want to lose sight of the ground. It was just beginning to look as if we would have to pull up out of this narrow valley if visibility got any worse when lo and behold, the river crossed the road and there were three or four covered trucks all stationary with chaps all over the road. I was over them before I could think of getting my sight on them and they did not seem to look up. 'How wide is this bloody valley? Let them think I haven't seen them. Carry on a minute or two. Then a bloody tight turn and pick up the river again. Up as high as I can in this mist without losing the ground. Put the rockets on the "Salvo" and let them have the lot'.

There they were, still chaps all over the road—they seemed to be working out how to cross the river. I pushed the cannon button so hard I nearly pushed it off the wheel. Shells rushed up to the first truck. I slipped over to the RP button and eight trails of smoke rushed ahead of us as I slid to one side at full throttle and away, skimming the trees. It was a pity all four cannons were not firing, but after we turned around and flew back to one side, low over the trees so that they could not see us, there was plenty of black smoke hanging around in the mist. I was not going to have a closer look because any survivors could be rather angry by now and I thought of what Bill had said about being a professional. We followed this valley almost to Kalemyo then climbed rapidly up into the clouds and headed for home. With the help of a couple of QDMs, we were back over base and felt chuffed to have bagged something on our first Op. We found that the cannon that did not fire at all had dirt in the breech and the one that jammed was due to an oversized round; fortunately, the nose camera worked OK and although the light in the valley was not good, it showed the trucks clearly—even the big white metal star on the front and the shells going in.

By the beginning of October, Douggie and I had carried out four Ops. It seemed a shame that we were in different messes as we had a great relationship in the air yet could not socialise together, except for having cups of char over at the 'flight'. The Canadians surely had the right idea by commissioning all their aircrew when they went overseas. My promotion to flying officer had just come through and it was rather nice to get off the bottom rung of the ladder. Eric had also had a step up—back to flight lieutenant; we hoped he would not slip back again this time, though there was not much chance of him misbehaving himself in Khumbirgram (KG).

We heard from the BBC that Allied airborne troops had landed near Arnhem in Holland, but they did not sound to be having it all their own way; in fact, it was very much the opposite. We heard that Allied forces were somewhere within Reich territory and that the Americans were engaged in the Philippines, but there was not a word about Burma (which was probably just as well). Although there was no mention on the BBC, we heard that some new-type rockets had been falling on south-east England; it seemed that those things that were being sent over just before we left England were not rockets as we understood but flying bomb, or doodlebugs—small pilotless jet aircraft, packed with explosives, which came down when the fuel ran out. These later things were actually rockets—more accurate and packed with more explosive. I hoped that they could not reach the north of England and that Peggy was OK. I had just received some letters from Peggy, which had eventually caught up with me. She seemed alright and talked about some lovely sunny days and how she hoped I was enjoying the weather in India. She had been harvesting somewhere near Askham Richard and was shortly going to do some potato picking. It was difficult to know what to tell her in my letters, except to keep on saying that I loved her, how we were enjoying ourselves, and what we would do when I got home.

The weather was beginning to change and was better already on the Burma plain, but there was still a great build-up of cloud and plenty of rain over the hills. Another four weeks saw the end of the wet monsoon. The air seemed to be getting more unstable; I supposed the monsoon was thinking about changing direction and getting a bit confused. From June to the middle of October, the hot air rising over the land mass sucked masses of warm, wet air up from the south-west; when this wet air hit the Ghats on the west coast of India, or the high ground of Assam and Burma, it was forced up, cools forming great masses of cloud and torrential rain. By the end of October, the land had cooled quicker than the sea so the reverse took place and the monsoon rushed back the other way. This gave nice, dry weather to western India, Assam, and Burma but dropped a fair bit of rain on the Madras coast in October, November, December, and early January.

Apart from our first Op, you could not say that our first four Ops had been very productive. On two of them, it was so wet and misty that we could hardly see a thing and all we did was to 'paste' the buildings of a little railway station on the plain, although there was no sign of a train or even any trucks; on another, we blew up a small building with the rockets, which looked as if it may have been a store of some sort. However, trip number five was the most frightening experience of my life and one which I never want to experience again.

Returning from a 'rhubarb' (our name for a trip looking for trains) on the Meiktila–Myingyan–Sagaing loop, where we had been lucky and blown a stationary train right off the rails, it got dark as we were heading home over the mountains. It got dark very quickly out there, with only a very short twilight. I was carefully watching the fuel as you can use a hell of a lot in a short time while at high revs and boost on a 'rhubarb'. We were OK, but I also had to think of the fuel we would use if we went very high over the mountains, yet I wanted to get above this bumpy cloud if I could. I told Douggie to get his oxygen set up and with the supercharger in high gear, we seemed to be in a layer of clear air at about 9,000 feet.

In the distance, I could see flashes of sheet lightning to the west and ahead; I thought to myself that it would be forked lightning diffused by cloud. Douggie told me he was getting a lot of static on the W/T but had managed to get the bearing from Agartala and another from KG, but he would try to get some more as the bearing from Agartala would put us further south than he reckoned we should be; we seemed to have an unusual headwind. It looked as if there were lightning flashes that were all around us in a semi-circle and between us and KG. In the light of the flashes, I tried to pick out the clouds; if only the sky had been clear above and there had been a moon, I would then have been able to see them and pick my way through but it was as black as ink except for those eerie pink flashes. There followed some very heavy showers followed by a vivid fork of lightning, which, for seemingly several seconds seemed to light us up like day and lit up some horrible clouds—the dreaded cu-nims.

After the flash had gone, I could still see it; it seemed to have affected my eyes. Instinctively, I told Douggie to see his oxygen was on and to tighten his harness. We had to go on as there was nowhere we could land if we went back; we could not get around them as they were around us in a great big semi-circle, between us and KG or Agartala, or Imphal for that matter and we did not have enough fuel to bugger about for too long. I prayed for another flash, which might enable me to see a gap I could aim for; if the gods were with us, maybe the next flash would be behind us. I was sweating like a pig as I increased the revs a bit, grabbed the wheel with one hand, and clung onto the throttles with the other, peering intently into the pitch darkness so as to see as much as I could from the next flash. Then, what happened next was a nightmare.

We dropped like a stone. I was dragged down by the harness over my shoulders and thrown over to starboard; my knees wanted to come up and my feet were only kept down by being tucked well under the straps on the rubber pedals. My left hand flew off the throttles so I grabbed the wheel with both hands and tried to stop it wagging about. Then, with a great thump and a noise as if we were being bombarded with marbles, I slumped down into the seat and was forced over to the port side; we were then going up like in a lift. With an effort, I raised a hand to the throttles and pushed them right forward; then, with both hands back on the wheel, I tried to stop it shaking about and force it forward. I felt as if we were on our side and going straight upwards, so I tried to force on some starboard rudder, though what the hell the instruments were showing I had no idea; it just flashed through my mind to 'keep the nose down and keep straight ahead', which was all very well if you knew which way you were facing and which way up you were, but I did not have a clue—all I knew was that I was hunched up and felt to be on my side, the wheel and the rudder pedals wanted to thrash about all over the place, and there was a terrible racket outside as if we were being peppered by marbles. This seemed to go on and on and there was nothing I could do, other than try to hold the controls as firmly as I could; it probably only lasted a few seconds but it seemed a lifetime.

Then, just as suddenly as we started coming up, we fell again. I was snatched down by my harness and flung back to the starboard side; the props started to scream as if they were over-revving and, in a couple of seconds, we were thrown out of the cloud. It went quiet, except for the noise of the engines, and I could see some stars. For an instant, I thought, 'we'd had it' and this was a sight of the other world, but where were we? It felt as if we were still losing height. I took a look at the instruments—the artificial horizon was at an angle and it did not move as I moved the wheel, and the directional gyro was spinning, even when I held the rudder central, meaning the gyros must have toppled. The airspeed was way up, so at least we were not going to stall—not yet anyway. The stars were moving around and around, and my mind told me that if I could line up pointing to a star, at least I knew there was nothing between me and the star so that I would not get back in that bloody cloud. I caged the directional gyro so that it would not put me off with it spinning round. Then I saw a little crescent moon and that made me think I was still on my side. I managed to keep one star almost dead ahead and bring the rate of descent indicator back on the clock at 400 feet a minute, so that looked better, and I gave Douggie a shout. To my relief, he replied.

I took further stock and saw we were at about 14,000 feet, which was above the normal ceiling for the Mark X Beau, so it was no wonder we were losing height and I had very little boost, even with the throttles nearly fully open and high-speed blower. Anyway, we were out of that cloud, and we hoped we were on the right side. Douggie got a bearing from KG and it looked as if we were OK. I turned on to this as well as I could, using just the magnetic compass, hoping that it was not too much out. We went down to 10,000 feet and the artificial horizon showed signs of working again, so the gyro must have got going again. I tried the directional gyro and this seemed OK too. Then I realised why the crescent moon had been confusing me; in these tropical latitudes, the crescent is damn nearly at the bottom, instead of roughly at the side like it is further north. My mind also flashed back to that chap who took me on my instrument test at Ferry Command and kept covering up various instruments. Another bearing showed that we were now going in the right direction. Very soon, I was able to get QDMs on the VHF; they changed rapidly, showing that we were nearly there, then, a rapid change showed that we were over the top.

On our let-down pattern, I did not seem to be flying as accurately as I knew I could; I put it down to being a bit 'shaken'. I wondered whether the undercarriage may have suffered some strain with all that buffeting and not come down properly, so I put it down in good time and the indicators looked as if it was OK. The last 1,000 feet was through cloud but, Jesus it was great to see the flarepath and I thumped her down—it was more of an 'arrival' than a landing.

Of course, it was raining. When we pulled up at the dispersal and I cut the engines, I just sat there for a while. I heard someone open the hatch. Then someone climbed in to see why I was so long. It was Little Ernie, one of our cheerful ground crew. 'You all right sir? Not a very nice night for flying. Glad you got back without any bother. We said you would when we heard all that thunder racketing around'. 'Thanks, Ernie. I'd give her a good check in the morning. She's had a bit of a rough ride but, by Jove, she's a good un'.'

I was most concerned about Douggie. He seemed OK but a bit pale, as usual. However, his ears had not given him any bother, which was the main thing. The first thing I wanted at debriefing was a good big mug of char. The debriefing officer must have soon realised that we were both a bit shaken and did not keep us very long. We had almost forgotten about the train. He said he would see us again in the morning about that, when they would have developed the pictures from the nose camera.

We were driven round to our *bashas*. I stretched out on my charpoy and was all for turning in when Bill came across to say he had heard I had had a rough trip, that it sounded as if I had been in a cu-nim. He suggested I had better come over to the mess for a meal and he waited for me to get ready. It must have been after 10 p.m. I had a meal then one drink, but I found my hand kept shaking as I picked up the glass, so I decided to get to bed. The MO was in the mess. He told me to stay in bed in the morning till he came over to have a look at me. Bill walked over to the *basha* with me and shouted to the *chai wallah* to bring us, 'Two char–*jaldi*'. Bill stayed until I was safely inside my mosquito net. 'Quite a day you've had. First a train then you tackle a cu-nim. We'll have a look at the pictures in the morning'. It was a warm night, but I felt cold and shivery before I dropped off to sleep. The next thing I remember was Buck coming in in the morning with a mug of hot char. Then came the MO, who took my temperature and said I was OK but I may as well stay in bed till tiffin.

Bill came in the mess at tiffin, beaming from ear to ear, saying 'You got some wizzo pictures of that train. Pranged the bugger good and proper but what have you done to your aeroplane? The tail-plane has a bloody hole in it, the whole tail is twisted, one aileron is damaged, the cowlings are dented and there is a bad oil leak. It looks as if she'll need a new stern frame. Bloody good job you were in a Beaufighter'. Eric and another crew were out; we hoped the cu-nims did not return that night as they were supposed to be at their worst at the beginning of the monsoon, but it looked as if they were having a last fling before the season changed. I mused on those posters I had seen at Dum Dum about three different colours of cu-nim—how the hell can you tell the colour when it is pitch dark?

17

The Rains Ease Up

By the end of October, things were beginning to change. The rains had not finished but had begun to ease up; the weather was OK down in the plain, although very hot and sticky; and the rivers did not seem to be running quite so fast, or was it that we were just getting used to them?

We were trying to keep at least six aircraft over the plain every day during daylight so that at all times during the day, there would be a couple of Beaus somewhere over the railways or rivers, but we were a bit hard pressed at times as, at one stage we had several aircraft out of service. Mine was waiting for a new stern frame; another had all the spark plugs welded into the cylinders as one chap had had to run at full combat power for too long to get away from trouble near Meiktila airfield. Eric had excelled himself by clipping the ground and bending his prop tips, although he got back OK with a lot of vibration and noise; another chap had lost his IFF aerial when he brushed a tree with the result that our own Ack-Ack lads had put a hole in the wing as he was making his approach to land. On top of this, there were usually one or two aircrew off sick with the 'squitters' and most of us had big purple stains of gentian violet somewhere on our anatomy to relieve the 'prickly heat'.

Douggie and I clocked up thirteen Ops, mostly along the railway lines and roads in the plain and south of Mandalay. We managed another train and several trucks on the roads and sprayed a couple of aircraft on the ground in a quick dash over Meiktila. We never brought our rockets back; if we had not seen anything by the end of our time, we would at least belt them off into the railway track or make a big hole in a road, somewhere where they would have difficulty in getting around it.

There were some new aircraft on the scene. Some of the Hurri-bomber boys had converted to an American dive bomber—the Republic F- 47 Thunderbolt. This was a hell of a size for a single-engined aircraft; it was a flat, deep fuselage with a huge radial engine, a Pratt and Whitney Double Wasp of 2535 hp. Empty, it weighed about 10,000 lb but had a maximum loaded weight of over 17,000 lb. Its range was nearly 600 miles. It had a hell of a ceiling and was supposed to do over 430 mph at 30,000 feet, with the help of a water-injection system. It carried eight 0.5-inch machine guns and either three 500-lb bombs or ten rockets. It looked as if it would be a brute to fly but the ex-Hurricane lads seemed to like it. I never failed to marvel at the dexterity of those Hurricane lads; they seemed to be a race apart.

Even when they became due for a rest, they volunteered for such things as wandering around the jungle with Army units to act as air liaison officers or, in earlier days, as pilots on Hurricats, to be catapulted from the bow of a merchant ship in mid-Atlantic to drive off, or shoot down, an attacking aircraft, after which they bailed out and hoped to be picked up, unless they were lucky enough to be able to make land. Their role here with the Thunderbolts was to fly a 'Cab Rank' (a flying reserve of fighter-bomber aircraft that can be called in to provide close air support), over Army positions, waiting to be directed onto targets by the air liaison officer on the ground, same as they had been doing with the Hurri-bombers. There was also talk that the Vengeance squadron was shortly to be withdrawn for a quick conversion on to Mosquitoes. We did not want to be involved with any new aircraft; we were quite content with our ugly, dented, and tough Beaufighters.

During the month, we learned that the Army had secured Tiddim and that although Kalemyo had not yet been occupied, some troops had bypassed it and were moving south near the west bank of the Chindwin while other units were nearing the Chindwin further north. Mawlaik, on the Upper Chindwin, had been bombed and we had dropped leaflets over some of the Japanese-held areas, telling them we would not shoot them if they surrendered but would give them food and safety.

Our wonderful ground crews were doing a marvellous job. There were no hangars out here, just any sort of shelter they could rig up. Tarpaulins were draped over ropes tied to trees or propped up with bamboo poles, with water running down the sides. There were puddles all around the place, but there was also always a *chai wallah* popping up with an urn of stewed chai, which never failed to cheer. A cup of 'char' with the erks was always time for a good laugh and a joke. It was funny how the worse the conditions, the better the spirit seemed to be when there was a job to get on with. We really had a grand lot of lads, and they seemed to be able to get on with jobs that you would have thought impossible in the conditions. When I took up the Beau with the new stern frame for its air test, three or four of them wanted to come with me and it was perfect; it only required the smallest adjustment to one of the trimming tabs.

Some nights in the mess turned out to be rather hectic, depending on who was in and not flying first thing in the morning. On the other hand, we had a couple of sombre nights when chaps were well overdue and nothing had been heard from them; as time passed by, we realised they were not coming back. Another day, one crew reported that they were in trouble and could not make the hills so were hoping to put down in the paddy in Imphal Valley; someone overflew the area and spotted the pranged Beau, which looked to be in one piece and, in due course, they got back by road.

The 'hectic' nights usually finished off with singing, which always included a rather bawdy version of Lili Marlene, all about a Little Burmese Maiden and a rendering of 'On the road to Mandalay' in which, at the words 'and the dawn comes up like thunder', everyone made as much noise as they could by banging and bashing everything they could lay their hands on. Another was a new tune by the Ink Spots, which we had heard on the wireless: 'Into Each Life Some Rain Must Fall'; this was a dangerous one because you knew that towards the end, somebody was going to get a bucket of water thrown over them.

Eventually, we moved into November, and we were looking forward to seeing some sunshine and getting rid of all these clouds and rain. We soon found we had two other things to contend with—the Japanese planes became more active and there were bloody big birds. We called them 'shitehawks', and they were some sort of hawk which hung around over anywhere where there was food or rubbish or suddenly appeared out of the trees. There were big black vultures, too. Maybe they did us a good turn in hovering over something that may be worth investigating, but it made you jump when one flashed past or thumped against the aircraft; fortunately, a Beau was tough enough to stand it, but we collected a few dents that did not affect anything so they were just left, although if a bird stuck in the front of an engine, it could cause some of the cylinders to overheat.

We received some replacement aircraft and crews. The crews were all experienced lads, having previously been on Beaus in the Middle East, Italy, or around the Greek islands. Some had done their training in South Africa or Rhodesia and not been back to the UK since they left for training. We were a mixed lot—a handful from the UK, the rest from various parts of the Commonwealth, even one chap from Brazil; how he came to be in the RAF, I do not know. We had no Canadians or Australians, however; they would be in their own squadrons.

There was talk that we would soon be doing some Ops at night. The clouds should be away in another week. It was already clear down on the plain and the moon would be showing up in about ten days. There had not been a lot of movement on the plain recently, so it was assumed that the Japanese must be moving as much as possible by night. We discussed our plans. If the rivers looked to be fit for the paddle steamers and boats to get moving, we would try to catch them as they passed through the 'moon-path' on the river; we would look for light from the fire boxes on the railway engines, or the light shining on the smoke; we would look for the lights on lorries or cars. We worked out ahead, the time of moonrise and moonset along with the take-off times for arriving at various places at the best time. We decided to reduce the number of tracer rounds in the cannon ammo so that the light from these would not blind us in the dark.

The first four Ops of the month were by day. One was down the river, past Pakokku to Pagan on the Irrawaddy. We had strict instructions not to damage the little town where we had caught a glimpse of some fancy temples with gold or gilded Pagodas. They looked a real picture by the side of the river which became very wide here with several large islands and no sign of river traffic, but we pranged some vehicles on the way back near a village on the west side of the Chindwin. On another trip, we were given a specific two-storey *basha*-type building to deal with, right by the side of the track through a village, surrounded by trees in a gently rolling part of the plain with a steepish hill close by to the north. How we knew there was something in the building I do not know—maybe some friendly guerrilla in the village. The weather was perfect, with a bit of cloud around but the sun was shining brightly as we approached from the south-south-east, and the odd big bird hanging around as we skimmed over the trees, following this well-defined whitish winding track. Suddenly, I saw a little clearing with *bashas* dotted around and, bang on the right-hand side of the roads, standing more or less on its own, was this taller building, a bit bigger than the rest. I could see it in time to pull up and bring my sight onto it without having to do any manoeuvring and plonked two pairs of rockets right into the heart of it, then I went away down the track. We disappeared around the hill, then, hugging the treetops, we skirted around the hill and up to have a look; the building was in flames with a column of smoke rising vertically in the still air. We decided that 'that would do' and popped back among the trees and away. Douggie was trying out a hand-held camera and he got a lovely picture. We did not see a living soul in the village but further down the track, a smaller rough track led us to some vehicles parked in a clearing and we used the other rockets and most of the cannon ammo on these, still without seeing any sign of life. The last of the cannon ammo I just sprayed into the nearby trees, in case there were any Japanese around.

Some railway wagons near Thazi junction completed our tally for the first half of November. The weather was certainly on the change now. Instead of constant mist over the trees, you could actually see down into them clearly; the waterfalls were less spectacular, the rivers were slowing down a bit, and the early morning mist was soon driven away by the sun; with more sunshine, it seemed to be getting much hotter.

Although it was November, it did not seem to get darker any earlier; it seemed to get dark about 7 p.m. whatever the season. With the rains almost over, we were able to smarten ourselves up bit; instead of dashing around under a cape between our *bashas* and the mess and wearing muddy boots, we were able to put on clean gear to go for dinner and stood outside having our pre-dinner '*chota peg*' (a half-sized serving of whisky). Unless we were 'working', the thirty minutes before sundown became quite a ritual—donning long slacks and mosquito boots, rolling down your sleeves to keep off the mozzies and, gathering outside the mess until the sun went down when, it became in order to have the first drink. It was also a pleasant change to be able to stroll back to the *basha*, instead of running and splashing in muddy puddles, and to find on arrival at your *basha* that the matches would work when you wanted to light the hurricane lamp, instead of being damp because you had forgotten to put them back in the little tin box. Peggy's picture on the wall always looked nice in the light of the hurricane lamp.

18

Two Important Visitors

The Supreme Allied Commander for Southeast Asia was coming to see us. We only learned the previous evening that Lord Louis Mountbatten was to pay us a 'flying visit'. There was chaos in the morning, trying to organise an undisciplined lot of ground crew and aircrew into squads of three columns and getting the NCOs and officers in the right places. None of us had done this sort of thing for years, and we only hoped there would be no need for us to march, otherwise, God knows what would have happened.

Anyhow, we got ourselves organised in a fashion just as the Supremo's aircraft appeared overhead in the bright sunlight and just finished 'dressing by the right' as the plane taxied in front of us and cut engines. As the door opened, the CO called, 'Parade—attention', though not everyone heard him; over the next seven or eight seconds, there were ripples of movement as we realised that we ought to be doing something.

Then, out of the aircraft, emerged this very tall, slim man, wearing an immaculate Persil-white admiral's uniform—white cap, the peak covered in 'scrambled egg'; a gold lanyard affair around one shoulder, from which hung a tassel; rows of medal ribbons; and a big smile. He returned our CO's salute with a flamboyant one in the Navy fashion and strode briskly towards us. In his dazzling white uniform and with the sun shining down on him, there seemed to be some sort of aurora around him. As he neared us, he stopped and asked in a loud voice if there was a crate or an oil drum around. A crate was soon produced. Lord Louis then sprung up on to this crate and told us to gather around in a semi-circle so that we could all hear. With a big smile on his face, he said something like the following:

> I have come to thank you men for what you have already done and to let you know I can rely on you in the important days which are ahead of us. The Japanese never expected us to fight and fly in the rainy season, but we have shown them it can be done and that we can beat them in jungle warfare. Not only have we driven them back from our very doorstep at Kohima and Imphal, we have virtually cleared them out of the hills and now, the gallant 14th Army, after five months of hard slog through some of the most inhospitable country in the world, are poised on the banks of the Chindwin, ready to cross into the Burma plain. We will have cleared central Burma and taken Mandalay by February and then move south to clear the rest of Burma and be in Rangoon before the onset of the rainy season in June. We will also mount an operation to re-take the Arakan. Our victory in Burma will go down as a victory for co-operation between the Army and the Air forces, the like of which has never been seen before. Your supply squadrons are the Army's life-line, Dakotas dropping vital supplies or landing on roughly made strips; light aircraft picking up the sick and wounded; your Hurricanes, Vengeances and Thunderbolts giving close support to the Army and bombing strategic targets; and, by no means least, your Beaufighters, ranging far into central Burma causing chaos among the Japanese communications. You have had it rough during the rains, the rains are now over and the big battle to re-take Burma is about to begin. I know I can rely on you all to do your jobs as effectively as you have done in the past. The sooner this job is over, the sooner some of us can go home. I can tell you that some of your Wellington Squadrons are being re-equipped with Liberators which will mean that we can carry the offensive against transport and communications well into Siam, to cut off the Japanese escape route. Very soon we will have more Mosquitoes; we are getting the Fighter/Bomber version.

Lord Louis announced that he was sorry that he could not spend more time with us but he had several more calls to make. Someone instinctively shouted, 'Three cheers for our Supreme Commander'. Three cheers rang out. Lord Louis raised his cap and waved it in the air. Then, he jumped down like a two-year-old and made for his aircraft.

Someone tried to call us to 'Attention'; he paused at the aircraft and gave us another flamboyant salute before jumping aboard and he was gone. We were all left speechless—what a chap, what a pep-talk. We all felt we had a bloody good supreme commander.

We then started the night Ops. Actually, they were a pleasant change. I always liked flying at night, especially when there was a moon. There was no need to fly so low and no need to keep weaving and bobbing up and down because we felt that they could not see us and they could not hear the beautiful Beau coming anyway. It was far less tiring, so long as you kept some skyline in front of you to make sure you did not fly into a hill. We all seemed to have success, in varying degrees, on these night rhubarbs. Bill was the first to get a big one; he spotted the light from a train that he reckoned was travelling like the clappers, and he came up behind it slowly. He reckoned he was hardly gaining on it so that he was able to plonk his rockets right into the open firebox; they did not even touch the sides, and there was one enormous explosion. He then came back and raked the rest of the train with cannon fire. He reckoned it was as light as day when he ran over the second time and chaps were falling about all over the trackside. Mind you, Bill often did embellish a bit. We spotted a line of lights on the road on our first trip, but I was not in a position to get the sight on them first time so I went around again, by which time the lights had gone out, so they must have heard us. However, I belted cannon shells in the area as near as I could judge and we saw two small fires.

At least at night, you did not have to worry about hitting birds as I had convinced myself that they would all be sleeping. On our second night job, I was doing a wide turn to investigate what I took to be the glow from a railway engine when suddenly, a pyrotechnic display started all around us and there, almost dead ahead, shining as clear as you like in the moonlight, was the runway of Meiktila airfield with aircraft parked in little compounds. I just pushed the nose down, pressed both tits as things seemed to be coming into the sight, and shot off at full power hugging the ground as tight as I dare. I had no ammo left and thought that was enough war for one night, so we made our way home. I do not know whether we actually did any damage but at least, if it put the shits up the Japanese half as much as it did me, it was a job well done. It was our fourth night job before we caught a train; it was not as spectacular as Bill's sounded, but at least we spotted it and after the attack, there was white steam or smoke billowing all around it in the moonlight. We raked the wagons too, but nothing blew up, just a few flames.

We were getting to the end of the moon period, so it would be day Ops only for the following couple of weeks or so. We got news that Kalemyo had been taken and that the Army were ready to cross the Chindwin near Sittaung, Kalewa, and Mawlaik. Although we had noticed that the river had now settled down a lot, I still wondered how they were going to cross that big, wide river. We also heard that somewhere in Assam, 500 inches of rain had been recorded during the monsoon period; it made you realise why the rivers had been flowing so fast. That was over 40 feet of rain, all in the space of a few months. The average rainfall over England was only 35 inches spread over the whole year—quite a difference. Down on the Burma plain, however, they reckoned it would have been a lot less, probably around 150 inches.

Sitting quietly in the mess one afternoon, censoring a pile of letters, I heard, 'Jacko, you goddamned son of a bitch. What the hell are you doing here?' I knew that voice; it could only be Harry Guest, my instructor on Ansons in Canada. It sure was; he was a flight lieutenant, but just the same old Harry. He had flown a Dakota in with some supplies and spare parts but had some trouble with one of the engines so he would be spending the night with us, while it was fixed. It was great to see him again and he seemed delighted too that he had come across one of his old pupils. We nattered about the lads on that course. He reckoned we were one of the best courses he had had. He particularly wanted to know about Peter, saying, 'That pal of yours, Peter, such a quiet pair of sons of bitches you were, but that lad Peter, he could fly the goddamned Anson better than I could, a real natural he was'. I had to tell him that Cyril and St John had both 'bought it'.

We chatted away about folks we knew and places we had been to. He got off instructing shortly after we left and went on Dakotas and had been on them ever since. He had been to several areas but had been around India, Assam, and Burma for nearly a year. He seemed to love the old Dakota, saying you could do anything with them (just like overgrown Ansons)—put them down on rough strips and load them up with freight until there was hardly any room to get in—but he was very keen to see if I could organise a trip in a Beau.

Before dinner, he came around to my *basha*, wearing only a towel he had nicked from Canadian Pacific and insisted we found someone to take a photograph of us together. In the mess, he was in fine spirits and told everyone we spoke to that he had 'taught this young son of a bitch to fly'. Bill agreed that in the morning, there would be an aircraft needing an air test and that I could do it and take Harry with me. He seemed genuinely excited about that. After dinner, he related some of his experiences out here.

The most hair-raising seemed to be earlier this year, in March when he towed gliders from Lalaghat, taking the Chindits to Broadway, in north-east Burma. Quite a lot of aircraft never got up properly and crashed over the hills but the way Harry told it made the whole serious affair sound even amusing. He told of the old Dak wallowing around, just above stalling speed in spite of almost full power, with the glider snatching at the tail as the tow rope became slack and then suddenly whipped taut; sometimes, the glider would start cork screwing, dragging your tail round in tight circles. All the time, you were trying to keep the thing in the air and wrestling with the controls. He told us about landing on rough clearings and taking on mules. It was bad enough getting some of them to get aboard. The handlers tried to keep them in pens made out of bamboo, but sometimes, they got restless and tried to kick out the side of the aircraft. The big American mules could break loose and start stamping around the aircraft. He told us about snatching gliders up off the ground and dropping supplies.

He had done a few trips 'over the hump' to China, on which the navigation aids were absolutely nil and they were a grumpy lot when you got there; there was never a word of thanks and they looked on you with suspicion. Harry kept us all enthralled with his experiences and his enthusiasm. Drinks kept coming from one source or another, and before long, we were all toasting the 'transport crews'. One often tends to think of transport squadrons not really being 'operational' but, by Jove, the lads out here had it just as rough as any operational squadron. We asked him how the army could get heavy equipment, and when he told us that he had taken bulldozers and Ack-Ack guns into jungle strips with bullets whizzing all around the perimeter at a spot called 'Blackpool', we realised what a grand old kite the Dakota must be. Harry and I walked, or staggered, back to our *bashas* with our arms around each other, Harry mumbling, 'and I taught you to fly, you son of a bitch. Tomorrow, you can take me up in a Beaufighter'.

Sure enough, Bill fixed me up with an air test in the morning. This was to include checking the cannons. With Harry standing behind me, plugged into the intercom, I started the engines, and this impressed

Harry for a start. Actually, I always got quite a kick myself when the big Hercules started and everything seemed to come to life; the Beau was no longer just a piece of machinery but something alive and it seemed to become part of your own body. I told Harry to hang on tight as we turned onto the strip for take-off; as the throttles went through the gate, I heard over the intercom, 'Jesus, oh boy, sure got some surge there'. I put on a bit of a show for Harry, showed him how well she would trim and fly 'hands off'; did a few really steep turns that nearly had him on the floor; and did a bit of really low flying at nearly full power. We then headed for the area where we fired the cannons. Douggie had confirmed that they were loaded and cocked. I warned Harry to hang on tight, climbed up, then dived on our makeshift target and fired about a four-second burst, levelling out pretty quickly, as usual. There was no reaction from Harry, so I looked over my shoulder to see him just appearing from down in the well. His intercom jack had pulled out and he was coughing and red in the face. He soon sorted himself out and got plugged in again; I heard, 'Are you trying to kill me, you son of a bitch? Bloody marvellous. Jeese, I'd like to fly one of these things'. Pity was there was no way we could change places in a Beau, not without being plain stupid; otherwise, I would have loved to have let him have a go.

On our return, we went to see how they were getting on with Harry's Dak. It was not ready yet and there seemed to be no hope of it being ready till tomorrow. We went inside and he showed me the layout of the cockpit. He asked if I had any Dakota time in my logbook, I told him only as a passenger between Rabat and the UK and from Dum Dum to here. He promised he would take me on his air test if I were free when it was ready.

By about 5 p.m., an erk came around to say that the Dak seemed OK and would he like to take it on an air test. Harry said, 'Right, we'll go over now, just nice time before dinner'. So, with me in the second dickie's seat, Harry got the engines started; they belched out clouds of black smoke and sounded very weak compared with the Hercules. Harry carefully did his cockpit checks, paying particular attention to the engine, which had been giving trouble; he then waved the chocks away and we taxied out. We seemed to be sitting a long way above the runway, much higher than in a Beau or a Lib. Then, we started the take-off run. We seemed to be taking ages to gather any speed, yet the engines were going flat out. We were not loaded, so it must have been a frighteningly long job fully loaded. Then we seemed to just float off, but we were wallowing around; it all seemed very sluggish. Eventually, Harry throttled back, putting the palms of his hands upwards, then pointed to the wheel and said, 'You've got her. Think of her as a big Anson. Not like that thing of yours.' We seemed to wallow along, the controls feeling sloppy, but she trimmed nicely. Harry kept telling me a few things about airspeed, boost and revs, alteration of trim when wheels and flaps come down, points out the brakes, and a few other odds and ends. I brought us back over the strip and Harry took over for the landing. He then said that we would do another take-off and as we were at the end of the strip, he said, 'OK we'll change seats and you can have a go'.

So, off we went. Throttles were fully open; there was no sign of a swing but we did not seem to be making much progress and the tail did not seem to want to come up. Then, gradually, it came up. We were level and picked up a bit more speed. I held her like that, as she did not seem to be going fast enough to lift off when Harry said, 'OK let her come up'. I eased back a little and she just seemed to float off. We flew around for a few minutes then back over the strip, and I commenced a circuit. Harry told me the revs and boosts to set, the airspeed I wanted, when to drop the wheels, fine pitch, airspeed, how much flap, airspeed, full flap, and she floated in for a reasonable wheel landing. The tail seemed to take ages to settle down. Harry considered we had time for another circuit before dinner and then he would push off in the morning. So, we did another rather extended circuit; this time, he did not say much. This thing almost wanted to fly itself as long as you pointed it in the right direction and you did not get worried about it being so sluggish.

That night in the mess, Harry was enthusing about his trip in the Beau with his old pupil, about me chucking him on the floor and then trying to poison him with cordite fumes. He also told how, for old times' sake, he had taken me up in the Dak. As we were leaving the mess, he asked to see my logbook. We entered the Dak trips as three separate trips and then Harry wrote 'Certified that the Flying Officer named above is qualified on C47A Dakota Aircraft. H. Guest Flt Lt.'

Harry's unexpected visit was a very pleasant interlude. I am sure he enjoyed it as much as I did, and he certainly left us all with a very high regard for 'the Transport lads'.

19

The Beau Bows Out in Style

The end of November saw the news that the Army were across the Chindwin at three places. We also heard that the Air Chief Marshal Sir Leigh Mallory (who was coming out to take over as Air Officer Commanding, Southeast Asia) had been killed in an air crash *en route*. The Vengeances had disappeared and been replaced by a squadron of Mosquitoes. It was drying up now; some of the roads and tracks on the plain were even throwing up dust and it was dashed hot for November. We heard that the Army were bringing up armour and concentrating in the Shwebo plain, but how the devil they got it there seemed to be a miracle. The Hurri-bombers and Thunderbolts were in the air all hours of the day, giving close support to the Army, while the Daks were dropping supplies and our Beaus were ranging far and wide from Mawlaik and Wuntho in the north to Yamethin and Magwe in the south, pranging anything moving on rail, road, and river. The Mosquitoes were paying special attention to the Japanese airfields. We always found something to have a go at.

Early in December, we passed by Kalewa and could hardly believe our eyes. There was a great, long bridge floating across the river with lorries passing over and 'ducks' (amphibian aircraft) buzzing around on the water. It seemed incredible how they had got all that stuff there. Hurri-bombers were buzzing around, spraying white powder over the trees; we later learned that this was DDT to try to kill the mosquitoes. Then we had our most spectacular success: Op. No. 24.

We were weaving down the Irrawaddy, south of Pagan. The river became very wide here and flowed around several islands, some of which were 7 or more miles long and quite wide, with a flat plain on the east bank with some rising, wooded, trackless ground on the other. Douggie was sitting facing the tail to keep a good look-out for Japanese fighters, which were quite a lot faster than we were.

If any had appeared, I would have led them into the woods on the west bank and away from their base at Meiktila, which was about 70 miles to the east. Then, as we weaved close to the west bank, I saw very clearly, under what at first sight seemed to be an outcrop of fallen trees, part of a big barge or paddle river steamer with a net draped over the side, which was dangling in the water. I was past it in a flash, looking around to pick a prominent landmark—a particularly noticeable mound in the trees—while at the same time shouting to Douggie to fix his eyes on that hump on the west bank: 'there's a barge under there—keep looking back at it so you know what it looks like on the way back'. I resisted the temptation to swing straight back, remembering what Bill had told me about shoving off for a little while and then coming back to catch them unawares.

The boat could not go anywhere anyway. If it came out into the open, we would catch it on the river; however, they would have heard us by now and been ready for us. So, I carried on as if we had not seen them. I told Douggie to go back to watching the sky while I carried on weaving down the river and around the islands; I thought, 'which is the best way to come in? Shall I make the best approach for the cannons or for the rockets? How long shall we give them? Wonder how long it will be before they relax and assume we didn't see them?' I decided to come in obliquely across the river from behind one of the islands, pulling up for a rocket attack, but if I could not see the outline clearly, I could use the cannons as I could keep them going and cover a bigger area. 'What rockets shall I use, pairs or salvo? Wish we had an arrangement for two separate lots of two pairs. Shit or bust, I'll select "Salvo". If we miss, we'll just have to risk coming around again and using the cannons. Half an hour should be enough'.

We kept close to the east bank on the way back north, passing the first big island; the adrenaline was starting to flow. A second big island was coming up. We then turned over this island just south of its northern tip, then smartly to starboard following a right-hand curve in the river. There were those funny-shaped trees; just beyond them should be those fallen trees. I could see it, so I slowly pushed the throttles open, lifted the nose, and came up a bit early; I felt a bit exposed up here, then aimed the nose down, with the target coming in the ring. Eight smoke trails forged ahead of us and, still diving, I more or less skidded her to starboard so as not to expose too much of my belly to the target; as I levelled off, there was the most enormous explosion—it seemed to be just beyond my port wing tip.

Douggie reported a great billowing cloud of black smoke going up for hundreds of feet as we skimmed away uphill at treetop height. Then we did the thing we would not normally do—we did a 360-degree turn to have a look. As we did so, a great column of flame shot into the air, which became capped with a big burning ball and black smoke was floating away in a dense cloud. That would do. We were not going back anymore. 'The Whispering Death' had struck and, as Bill had told me, been in and out like a phantom. Feeling rather pleased with ourselves because we realised that that barge must have been bringing stocks of fuel and had hidden for the day ready to move again after dark, we popped over rising ground and dropped down into the valley near Pauk, then followed the track over the hills and dropped down into the Gangaw Valley. We knew this valley from the days when it was wet and misty; it looked very different now as you could see clearly down into the trees and the track stood out clearly instead of merely being a muddy mess. Near Tilin, we had some more luck. A group of Japanese and their vehicles were resting by the river. We wheeled over them three times and got rid of all our cannon shells. Chaps were falling about all over the place and at least some of the vehicles were wrecked. After Gangaw, we thought it prudent to climb up and make for home. We knew the Army were at Kalemyo, at the head of the valley; some might have been coming down this way and we did not want to get mixed up with them. They might not recognise us as being a Beaufighter. We had had a good day, which was duly celebrated in the mess.

There was a rumour that we were to be withdrawn for conversion to Mosquitoes. We were not at all enthusiastic about this as we liked our rugged, whispering Beaufighters. The new moon was with us and after one more trip—a night one, to our old stamping grounds around Meiktila, one on which we saw absolutely nothing—the rumour was confirmed. We were being broken up. Bill and Buck were to go to Poona and would be coming off Ops for a while. Two other crews were also going to India for a rest. The rest of us were to take our Beaus to a place about 200 miles west of Calcutta where we would convert to Mosquitoes. A squadron already on Mosquitoes would take our place here.

Until now, I had no idea how many Ops constituted a 'tour' on this job. Only one or two crews seemed to have left us for 'a rest' during the time I had been there; the odd crew had been sent back to India due to sickness, but our newcomers had mainly been to replace those lads who had been unlucky. It seemed to be tempting providence to inquire the number of Ops we were expected to do. Anyway, we found out that, generally speaking, the tour was thirty Ops, provided replacements were available. As I had already done twenty-five, I asked if I could go on another Beaufighter squadron to complete the other five rather than 'put the country to the expense of converting me to Mosquitoes for the sake of another five trips', but it was to no avail. A few days later, Douggie and I managed to get all our gear into a Beau (though the tin trunks were a bit of a problem), and we set off for Ranchi. The day before we left, there was a bit of a panic as, without any warning, the Yanks had withdrawn three of their Dakota squadrons from taking supplies to the 14th Army to use on the China run.

20

The Mozzie: Wood, Glue, and a Silly Stick

We found ourselves on another squadron, which was actually the one I was originally posted to but had turned out to be on Vengeances. We were quite a mixture—some lads who had been on Vengeances and had just completed a conversion course on to twin-engined Oxfords in central or southern India; some who had been on Mosquitoes in Malta, operating over Sicily and Italy; and those of us who had been on Beaus.

We had seen Mosquitoes before but not paid a lot of attention to them. When we had a close look, we were horrified, having no desire at all to do the same type of Ops in these as we did in the Beaus, if that was what they had in mind for us. They looked OK for taking photographs from 20,000 or 30,000 feet, or medium to high level bombing or even as a night-fighter, but not for scurrying about near the treetops, clipping the odd branch, or collecting the odd shitehawk. Also, there was no rear vision for the observer; he was upfront, sitting beside and very slightly behind the pilot, and he could not move about to get at anything whereas in the Beau, he could crawl about and get at equipment, like the radio, if something went wrong.

Getting in and out looked difficult, too—it was via a tiny door in the side of the fuselage, squeezed between the leading edge of the wing and the tip of the prop. It hinged forward, so there would be no chance of opening against the slipstream in the air; even if you could, you would probably be clobbered by the prop. So, the only way out in a hurry would be to jettison the port half of the canopy, turn the thing upside down, and hope you could both drop clear. It looked like a sleek greyhound—smooth skin with no rows of rivet heads, a flimsy-looking undercarriage, and two long pointed engines. Looking at the engines, one of the lads who had come with us from the squadron (and incidentally came from Glasgow) said, 'Just look at her, she's only got bloody long nipples, no nice big boobs. If we are going to carry on what we've all been doing, it will be as daft as putting a prima donna on at the Glasgow Empire on a Saturday night'.

The lads off Vengeances were full of excitement about getting on Mozzies and those who had been on them before thought she was the 'bee's knees', but we thought otherwise and looked longingly across at our Beaus, standing there looking so forlorn, as if we had abandoned them in their middle age for some flashy young flapper. We inquired what was going to happen to them. We gathered that they were to go to a squadron that would be using them against shipping off the Arakan Coast and down towards Rangoon; immediately, Eric and I found the CO and told him of our coastal experience and that we were originally sent out here to go to a Torbeau squadron, so we asked if we could stay with our Beaus, but he would not hear of it.

We noticed that you could hear these Mozzies approaching from miles away. It was an unpleasant drone, then a shattering crescendo as they whizzed overhead. However, we did not like the idea that you could hear them approaching. Our first lecture on the Mozzie did not exactly impress us—at least, not favourably. The whole fuselage and wing were made of wood. The fuselage was made out of a balsa wood, sandwiched between two layers of plywood; it was made in two halves so that all the gear could be put inside and then the two halves were stuck together, from front to rear, around six or seven bulkheads. The wing had a wooden main spar running all the way across and two plywood skins kept apart by a lot of little stringers. The undercarriage had some sort of rubber compression rings, instead of an oleo-pneumatic shock absorber, so it could bounce a bit on a heavy landing.

This bloke—who I reckon worked for de Havilland as he would have made a bloody good salesman—went on to expound the wonders of the Mosquito Mark VI Fighter/Bomber and its Rolls-Royce Merlin '25' engine. I had only flown with a Merlin on that short trip in a clapped-out Beau from York to Melton Mowbray, and I did not think much of that, but I supposed this would be a much later model; I certainly hoped so. After all this chap's effort to convince us that a Mozzie was so superior to the Beau, we were left not really convinced at all. He harped on about its single-engine performance, telling us that she would get back over the mountains if we lost an engine, whereas the Beau Mark X would not; that she would do 336 mph at sea level, 360 mph at 5,500 feet, and 380 mph at 13,000 feet; and that the maximum for continuous cruising was 296 mph or 250 mph for maximum range, which at the heights we were interested in was, admittedly, about 40 mph faster. Also, the range was no better at about 1,400 miles, although, in both cases, it depended on what variation you had as between extra fuel tanks and guns; she was lighter than the Beau, both loaded and empty, and could tuck two 500-lb bombs in the bomb bay as well as carrying eight rockets under the wings, whereas the Beau could not carry both together. The Merlin was only rated at 1,635 hp instead of 1,700 hp for the Hercules, and the power available for take-off was 1,620 against the Beau's 1,665. We had to admit that the Mozzie was faster, had a better single-engined performance, could fly higher, and carry both bombs and rockets, but we then battered him with questions and arguments.

'What about the glue? Can it stand the heat and wet we get in these regions?' He admitted that at first, when they used casein glue, it was not very satisfactory, but they had changed to using something much better—formaldehyde cement. They had had a couple of aircraft parked somewhere during the heat and through a monsoon, and it had been perfectly airtight. Moisture did not affect it and it did not crack with heat. 'Surely wood will swell and shrink, twist and warp with the heat and wet?' He reckoned that this wood would not.

'But how about insects?' we thought. 'If a colony of termites set about an airframe in the night, by morning, all the wood would have gone and you would be left with a couple of engines and other bits of metal in a heap on the ground. Worse still, what if some other wood-eating insect moved in and made a meal out of the main spar, reducing it to powder?' He reckoned that all these things had been thought of and inspection of the aircraft that had been left out on test had not revealed any ill effects.

'All this stress you put on her single-engined performance, sounds as if it's nothing unusual to lose an engine. The Hercules would keep going even with a couple of pots damaged but one sniper's round into the Merlin and you could lose all your coolant so is there any protection for the cooling system? Also, there seems to be a big open slot on the leading edge between the fuselage and the engine for the oil and coolant radiators. What happens if this gets bunged up with a shite hawk?' He had no answer to this, except to say that an outer grill is fitted in the hope that this will help but admitted a big bird lodged in there would cause the engine to overheat.

A bit later on, when we went to examine an aircraft, we noticed some elastic bands coming out of a drum in the undercarriage bay. We were told that they were holding the undercarriage doors closed. What with that, the cheap-looking compression legs on the undercarriage, and the fact that she was all wood, we thought that 'this looks as if she has been made for cheapness, not toughness'.

Inside did not impress us much either. Sitting on the left-hand side of this little cockpit did not give you much feeling of being part of the aircraft, not like you felt in a Beau. The view did not seem as good—it was nothing like we had in a Beau. Yet what I disliked even more than the view and the position was a bloody silly little 'stick' instead of a decent wheel. It was 'cranked' towards the top, with the bottom part moving backwards and forwards for the elevators and the top bit moving from side to side for the ailerons. Yet the top bit was not vertical when the ailerons were level; it was at an angle over to the right. I thought there was something wrong when I held the top bit vertical and looked out at the ailerons and saw the one on my side was stuck up in the air, but I was told this was how it should be.

We had a few beers (they had some Indian beer here) in the mess that night while we nattered over what we looked to be in for—flying an aeroplane with a bloody funny stick, made of wood and stuck together with cement, probably being chewed away by insects, a bugger to get out of in a hurry, engines that would over-heat and seize up if a bullet punctures the cooling system or a shite hawk bunged up the cooling rads, and partly held together with elastic bands.

The next day was spent mooching around the aircraft, studying the pilots' notes (although there were not enough copies for us to have one each), and memorising the various engine settings, speeds, and what have you. Then, the day after, a flight lieutenant took me for a couple of 'demonstration flights' of fifty minutes each, after which I went off on my own for forty-five minutes, followed by another hour and ten minutes local flying and a couple more landings. I was still not very impressed, not like I was on my first trip in a Beau. The engines did not seem to want to get going. I had been told not to open them up too quickly, otherwise they may 'surge'. It was very tempting to want to push the throttles forward quicker as we really seemed to be a hell of a time building up speed; there was no nice kick in the back as with the good old Hercules.

Then, as you lifted off, there seemed to be a surge of power and she felt as if she wanted to go into a slow roll. Maybe that was partly because of the funny stick and getting used to where to hold it to keep the wings level. Like one smart lad said, 'when you manage to keep the wings level, have a good look at the stick. You may want to fly level again sometime'. The response from those Merlins seemed to be so slow, especially when you wanted a bit more power on the final approach. The Hercules responded so quickly that you could make up for poor judgement by using a bit of brute power, but I could see that on these Mozzies I would have to get back to being more precise. It seemed funny flying with just one hand on the stick, unless needed for the throttles or something else; I did not know what to do with my left hand. You could not hold the stick in your left hand with the top being cranked over to the right, so you did not have a hand you could write with, should you want to make some notes, unless you were left-handed. I preferred to have a decent wheel, or at least a 'pair of spectacles' that you could get hold of with either or both hands, but maybe, if you yanked back on the stick of this thing with both hands, you would break the dainty little tail off. To me, this did not seem the kind of machine to go weaving among the treetops with.

After another day, starting with another hour's solo flying, they seemed to decide that I was not going to kill myself, so they let Douggie come up with me. He did not like the cramped feeling and not being able to move from his seat. He tried shuffling around and kneeling on the seat to see what he could see behind us; there was not a lot. When moving around, he clobbered me in the face so we decided that that was not on if we were at low level. We made a pretty fast low run and by Jove, she certainly seemed to be shifting; however, I did not like the forward view, certainly not down at very low altitude, and it seemed all wrong sitting at one side instead of in the middle. I could not get to feel as if I were as much a part of this plane as I did in a Beau. It seemed natural to be sitting on the left side of the bigger ones, like a Hudson or a Lib, but not in one like this, and only a funny little stick too. I had not flown with a stick since Tiger Moth days. Eric's impressions seemed to be the same as mine; we were only thankful that the Monsoon was over as we would not relish flying these things in the weather we were experiencing until a few weeks ago. Our faithful, scratched, dented, and oil-stained Beaus had now gone to fight on in another role; we felt sad and envious when we saw them, one by one, fly away, to the purr of those trusty Hercules. We felt as if they were paying us back for having jilted them.

They seemed to think that we deserved a day off, so Douggie, Eric, and I went to have a look at the town. We were really in quite a nice place, on the south side of a valley with low hills and jungle away to the north. The setting of the town was rather striking—a bare hillock of black stone in the middle of the town with a temple right on the top. It was flat all around this hillock with a lake at the foot of the hill and two more temples, one at each end of the lake. It seemed 'very Indian'. There were Brahmins strolling around with the mark of Vishnu painted on their foreheads, like two thin white horns rising from the bridge of their nose; the women decked in silver and gold rings, bangles, necklaces, and anklets, some carrying big tall brass water-containers on their heads; sacred cows all over the place; and little lads asking for *baksheesh* and laughing and giggling so much that we actually gave them some, until the crowd got too great. We chatted and joked with some young girls who were getting water from a well, one bonny little lass (probably about twelve years old) chatted away to us in a mixture of Urdu and English and posed for her picture to be taken. They all seemed such nice friendly people and so happy. We found a hotel I think was called the 'Railway'; at least, it was by the station, where we had a delightful meal—curry with all the trimmings and hot, tasty bits. It was a big town with many big and impressive buildings, but the most interesting part was around the bazaar area; everything under the sun was for sale here and all so colourful, even if a bit smelly. There were monkeys doing tricks, lads with snakes in baskets, and one young fellow trying to persuade us to let him take us into the jungle to shoot a tiger: 'Very good Tiger, *sahib*, I show you, only 50 miles. I know good place'.

We were wondering how you would drop bombs from a Mosquito without a bombsight. The bomber version had a Perspex nose, so the observer could crawl down and use a bombsight in the nose; however, in our version, the fighter/bomber, there was no Perspex nose and no way of getting down there anyway as it was taken up with the cannons and maybe machine guns too. We soon learned that the answer was 'dive-bombing'; this sounded ridiculous in a Mosquito, but one of the instructors was going to take me up for a demonstration of how it was done.

'On the first run we'll approach at 1,500 feet'. That sounded a bloody dangerous height to be flying over Burma for a start. 'Make sure you have the cannons cocked and ready to fire. Arm the bombs and set the Selector. Now that's our target, over there. Approach so it is going to be slightly on the port side and disappear from view under the port spinner. Put the cannon sight into fully bright. Alter course a bit to get it tracking under the spinner.' I could not even see the target now, with being in the right-hand seat. 'Right, it's just approaching the spinner. It's gone. Nose down, turn to port, settle the target in the middle of the ring'. We were screaming down towards the target; I could see it OK then. We eased back as the target passed out the bottom of the ring. 'Pause, now. Don't pull back too hard or she will mush. Level off gently and away.' I felt relieved that the tail had not come off.

'Have you got the idea? If you start your diving turn just as the target is passing under the spinner it gives you a good angle of dive, not too steep, not too flat. Then if you let the bombs go, just after you have started to pull out of the dive and the target has just disappeared out of the ring, you fling the bombs out and clear of the aircraft but, don't snatch the stick back, you don't want a high-speed stall, or go mushing down into the deck, so ease her out gently and scamper away as low as you can.'

'Right, I'll do another so you can get an idea of the height to start pulling out—don't want to be too high or your bombs will drop short, or too low or you'll be into the ground. Also, try and pick yourself a way out after the attack, while you are making the level approach. OK, here we go again.'

'This time we'll open the bomb doors and let one of the bombs go. Then we'll do another run from 1,200 feet and get rid of the other one'. We had heard that the deadline had been set for us to be back on the job by the second week in January, so most of us were anxious to get in as much practice as possible before then. We were queuing up to use the bombing range and to study the results. Two chaps, each sitting on a bit of safe high ground near the target, took bearings of our bomb-bursts so that the results could be plotted. They noted the letter on each aircraft and the time; then, in the evenings, we studied our results and tried to assess whether we were making any consistent errors. For a change, we fitted in some rocket firing, using concrete practice rockets; for a bit of relief, we did a few low-level cross-countries to give the observers some practice sitting in their new positions. I still did not think I was ever going to feel as if I were 'part' of this aircraft, and I certainly did not dare fly it as low as I did a Beau. I did not risk skidding it either, and there seemed to be even more birds around here than there were in Burma. A gentle weaving, or corkscrewing, was all I felt it was safe to do, and with this funny control stick, the action was like stirring a pudding. Another thing—these liquid-cooled Merlins would overheat like hell on the ground if you did not get away fairly quickly, so then, it was a case of shutting down and waiting for them to cool.

However, it was decided that everyone would have a day off for Christmas Day. A rugby match was arranged for straight after church parade. We had no kit but a rugby ball was produced and the lads erected some posts on a reasonably well-grassed patch. We first thought of aircrew *v.* ground crew, then officers *v.* others, but neither of these worked out, so an officer and a sergeant were elected 'captains' and took it in turns to pick their teams. One team wore shirts and the others did not. This was the ultimate in 'Coarse Rugby' matches. Half the lads had no idea of the rules. Line-outs were all lifting or holding down, barging, or pushing, and there were knock-ons and forward passes galore; half the team seemed to be offside and the other half forgot which way they were playing. Also, the scrums were just sixteen chaps in a clump, some standing up and others lying on the ground. I had foolishly admitted that I had played at stand-off and on the rare occasions that the ball came in my direction, two of the opposition arrived either at the same time or just before.

Anyway, we had one chap who could run like the wind, who scored two tries when someone flung a long overarm pass in his direction and all the rest of the players were busy looking for the ball under a pile of bodies. It was a good job most of us were wearing plimsolls, with all the wild kicking that went on. By a very clever connivance, the referee blew for 'no side' rather early when the scores were level, much to everyone's relief, except for the Indian servants who had come to watch. I have never seen Indians laugh and jump around so much. They seemed to enjoy seeing the English *sahibs* making fools of themselves. They understood cricket, but I doubt whether they were any wiser as to what rugby was all about.

As we all sat on the ground recovering and resting, someone arrived with some bottles of Indian beer, which went down very well, especially as the temperature was into the 80s. It did not seem like Christmas, and then someone mentioned that they would just be waking up in England; they were five hours behind us and he wondered what his little lad would be finding in his stocking. I think we all then thought of the folks at home.

The next event was for us to serve the dinner in the airmen's mess. The cooks had done jolly well—mostly Indian, with a RAF sergeant in charge; each lad had a whole chicken (only a little Indian chicken, though) with stuffing and all the trimmings, followed by Christmas pudding and very yellow custard, with a couple of bottles of beer. Most of us stayed on in their mess for a while, singing a mixture of Christmas carols and service songs. Then it was back to the *basha* for a couple of hours on the charpoy before going over to our own mess for dinner, a few more drinks, and some singing.

It was back to work on Boxing Day and in the evening, we heard that on Christmas night, the Japanese had sent three bombers over Kharagpur, which was 60 miles this side of Calcutta and that two of them had been shot down. We presumed that they were shot down by aircraft, in which case the night fighter boys must have been in a better state than we were. We presumed that these Japanese must have come up from Akyab or Ramree, off the Arakan Coast, which they still occupied.

Then I got a letter from Peggy—in fact, three letters from Peggy and one from mother. It was great to hear from them, but I was a bit shattered to hear that Cousin Henry had been killed; he had been shot down glider-towing over Arnhem in September. I remembered how proud Uncle Leslie had been to tell me that Henry had just got his wings with the Canadian Air Force. When I saw him in Toronto, he looked such a young lad—only a schoolboy; it was difficult to imagine him as a pilot. He must have gone straight on Daks as soon as he arrived back in England and glider-towing, too. I thought of what Harry had told me about glider-towing—aircraft damn nearly stalling and the glider snatching your tail about in all directions; it seemed rough for a young lad with hardly any experience to be put on a job like that, which I bet was his first Op. I felt sorry for Mary, too, losing her brother. I had gathered from the news that the Arnhem affair did not go very well [In fact, Jack's understanding of the situation was not quite accurate. See Appendix I].

Time here was nearly up. The bombing had improved a bit. Instead of falling short, I seemed to be pitching most of them on the target by allowing one second to elapse after the target passed out of the bottom of the ring sight. I still found a tendency to go into a roll when you put on full power and the engine decided to respond, but I automatically corrected it; however, this aircraft would never be like a Beau as far as I was concerned—not that feeling of brute force and instant response, and although it will crack on a bit faster, everyone can hear you coming.

It was now time for us to move back east. It was quite an operation. We could hardly carry anything in the Mozzies. We managed a small bag each, with our two bedrolls tied up in the bomb bay. The rest of our gear had to be ferried over in a couple of Dakotas along with the ground crew, spares, and all the other squadron tackle, spares, and what have you. The Daks had to make several trips, but we were sorted out in three days and catching up with events during our absence.

21
Mozzie Out: Stinson Back

Back in the hills, it was pleasantly cool, dropping down to about 50 degrees after sundown. The Army were really across the Chindwin in strength and had occupied Wuntho on the main railway line some 150 miles north of Mandalay. Things were happening in the Arakan, too. We had landed stores and men by ships at Akyab; six Japanese fighters (Oscars), which were about to attack our ships, were shot down by the newly arrived Spitfires, and we now occupied Akyab airfield. The next objective was to be a landing on Ramree Island, about 100 miles south of Akyab and to take over the airfield there. This would then give us an airfield only 200 miles or so away from Rangoon, handy for attacking south Burma, by just crossing over the Arakan Yoma—the tail end of a long range of hills, not as high or as wide as the hills in the north. We speculated that we could well get moved there in due course.

However, we did not have a very auspicious return to the fray as the squadron had only flown three Ops when the aircraft were grounded. The story we heard was that someone from another Mozzie squadron was seen to do a roll over the airfield on his return and nosedived into the ground where they blew up. Someone thought they saw something fly off the aircraft and hit the tail, which was probably partly knocked off. It was thought that the thing that flew off was an undercarriage door. All our aircraft were being examined and some sort of hook fastened to the undercarriage, which would engage on the door and hold it positively shut when the undercarriage was up.

This gave us time to study the maps and aerial photographs of the area further south than the area we had got to know well and also further east, down the other big river of Burma, the Sittang, although this was only a stream compared with the Irrawaddy. It was clear that our role was going to be rather different from the one we had played in the Beaus. Instead of roving about in a given area looking for anything on the move, we were going to be given specific targets, so at least this would mean we always had something specific on which to get rid of our load, and there would be no need to keep on looking for something to hit before turning around for home.

For a few days, we had to content ourselves just picking up bits of 'gen' from the intelligence officer about Liberators doing 1,000-mile trips to prang bridges on the railway line coming up from Bangkok in Siam to Moulmein in Burma. There were said to be hundreds of bridges on this 244-mile stretch of railway through the jungle, and the Libs and Mitchells were knocking them down faster than the Japanese could rebuild them. We also heard about a new 'Azon' bomb that the Libs and Mitchells were using, which could be controlled by radio from the air; about some new 'bomb' that we might get called 'Perafix', which, when dropped, sounded like rifle fire and hand grenades going off, to confuse the opposition; and the activities of some lucky lads who were still attacking the railways in Beaus.

Our CO seemed to fancy the idea of us going out in pairs. The Beau lads had told us that they used to go in pairs at one time but found it better to go singly. We talked about this; we felt that if you were flying really low, you had enough to watch without having to keep an eye on another aircraft. It was decided that we would try some 'loose pairs' and see how it went.

At last, we were cleared to take to the air again, and I got a 'loose pair' job with a chap we all called Shirley, for a blow-up of Heho airfield. I had not been there before; it was about 60 miles east of Meiktila and surrounded by hills. We looked at the maps and decided which way we would go as there was no point in getting too near Meiktila; we also decided from which direction we would attack and which way we would come home. The intelligence officer produced two quite good pictures of the airfield so we could select which looked to be the best targets. The CO kindly gave us an alternative target—the Japanese-occupied town of Thabutkon—if Heho was 'out' through low cloud. Shirley and I decided to just keep each other in sight on the way out, then close up to half a mile or so as we approached up the railway line from the south. One of us would then go around the airfield at one side and one the other, then tight turns would bring us back over the airfield; we would then climb up, attack, and get the hell out of it, low down, back the way we came but we would not hang around looking for each other. We would be listening out for each other but would not chat unless there was any need to.

The outward trip was uneventful. Once over the plain, I kept gently weaving, but I still did not like flying with one hand all the time, like gently stirring a pudding, and all the time I was aware that if there was anyone about, they would hear us coming; however, we had picked our route to avoid possible trouble spots as far as we could. It was getting jolly hot down in the plain, or was it just me sweating under my jungle suit? Douggie kept trying to twist around to look out the rear as we knew these Japanese fighters were as fast, or even faster, than we were. At the same time, I was a bit scared of getting too low as I did not fancy the chances of balsa and plywood if we hit a teak stump. There were no nice round engines to look at for comfort either.

Up the little railway line, we went; it was a twisty valley with not a lot of room. We went over a little ridge, like two valleys crossing, then, there it was—I went around on the port side, which was the worst side to go as I could not see to starboard properly sitting on the left. I had to pull up because of the hills. They must have seen or heard us, so we made a steep turn to starboard, checked bombs and cannon were set (we had no rockets) and with the target ahead, the bomb doors were opened as we spotted two twin-engined aircraft in pens with two buildings more or less in line.

'Shirley, you take runway'. I dived on the first aircraft with the cannon, raking through it onto the second while trying to twist onto the building; a second after it passed out of the bottom of the sight, I pressed the bomb release as Shirley came on, 'I'm behind you, Jacko'. I pissed off, fast as I could, hoping that the mirror camera fixed in the back had got some decent photos. I gave Shirley a quick call, 'You all right, Shirley?' He was. I had no idea what sort of communications the Japanese had; it crossed my mind that if they were able to let Meiktila know about us, they may try to intercept us, so I told Douggie to keep looking out all the time. We crossed the Irrawaddy well south of Pagan, by which time Shirley was back with us, so it was then just up into the hills and after a while, we climbed up and relaxed. I then realised how tired my right arm was; why the devil could they not put a decent control wheel on these things instead of this stupid stick, which you can only use with the right hand (try to use your left and you automatically pull the thing into a steep left-hand turn)? Shirley reckoned that there had been some Ack-Ack fire from one side of the airfield, but I never saw it, or maybe I was through before they started; he also reckoned that one of the aircraft I had a go at collapsed and that one, maybe both, of my bombs went in one of the buildings as the roof was taking off as he went by.

We heard that our bombers have been over Mandalay. Up to then, we seemed to have left the town of Mandalay alone as we did not want to damage their fine Buddhist temples and pagodas. Every day, we had several aircraft on targets at Thazi Junction, Thabutkon, and Meiktila as in addition to the airfield, this area was the centre for Japanese communications and supply depots. After three or four days of this without suffering any damage, we were getting a bit cocky, till two crews did not return; what happened, we will never know, maybe Ack-Ack, maybe fighters, or maybe they just misjudged something. On our two trips, we were lucky; each time, we had two targets—one for cannon and bombs and one for cannon and rockets. The town of Thabutkon already seemed to be in ruins. We knew there were no Burmese there, only Japanese, so anything standing was a legitimate target, but there was not much left standing; it was a sad-looking place. The Japanese soon seemed to get the holes in the airfield runway patched up and put up quite a lot of flak from the airfield perimeter. The most disturbing thing, however, was the realisation that folks could hear you coming. In the Beau, you would see folks nonchalantly strolling in the paddy until they disappeared right under the nose, but in these Mozzies, you would see them start running and falling down several hundred yards ahead of us as they heard you coming. I must admit the Mozzie was quite a bit faster—you could wind her up to 330 for short periods—but I did not feel happy taking her quite as low as a Beau as apart from always being aware that she was made of wood, the forward view was not as good so you did not get the impression of being any faster.

By the third week in January, we heard that Ramree Island off the Arakan coast had been occupied. On our side of the hills, the Army had swept across the Shwebo plain, crossed the River Mu, and were heading for the Irrawaddy some 60 miles north of Mandalay but the Japanese still held Monywa to the south on the east bank of the Chindwin. Some of the Army, still on the west bank of the Chindwin, were moving south down the Gangaw Valley; they sounded to be somewhere between Tilin and Pauk (in the valley which we had got to know quite well), presumably planning to cross the Irrawaddy somewhere south of Pakokku (after the two big rivers had joined) and then make for Meiktila to cut off the Japanese south of Mandalay.

For a change, we got a fairly long trip—just over 500 miles each way—to a little village on the bank of the Irrawaddy, south of Prome, where the river snaked around some big flat islands. At the briefing, no one let on how they got the information, but we were told exactly which building to hit; that there were little *bashas* around occupied by the Burmese; that there was no Ack-Ack so that we could have a good look first; to make sure we got the right building, although this would not be difficult as it was the biggest place in the village—of the four big buildings facing onto the river and two others at right angles to them, the buildings facing the river were the ones we wanted. I reckoned we must have had a guerrilla in that village, especially as we were given a period in which we should make the attack and we were to use rockets (rather than bombs, but they could be used if we could not fire it with our rockets. I noted that we would be about 70 miles from the Japanese airfield at Toungoo. We cruised down at 250 mph (why these airspeed indicators were calibrated in mph instead of knots I do not know, unless it was to make you think you were going faster), meeting the Irrawaddy south of Pagan, then roughly followed the river, taking care to avoid possible trouble spots.

There certainly were a lot of islands as we approached the target area; the big, wide river seemed to split up into lots of snaking rivers and little streams, some suddenly bending at right angles. It was very flat land, with lots of paddy, a few clumps of trees, and isolated palms. I thought, 'Christ, we can be looking all round for this village,' but Douggie was sure we were heading up the right bit of water; then we saw it. There was a little, single-masted boat on the river. We flew over the building; it was just as we had been told it would be. On the one side, there were two rows of *bashas*—one along the riverbank and one along the edge of the stream, which ran roughly parallel to the river and then turned at right angles to join the river just by that big building. The run in to give me the 'longest' target and not damage the *bashas* if I overshot, meant coming in over the paddy, between the rows of *bashas* and out over the river. Everything looked so quiet, with not a soul in sight, only that little boat on the river. So, round we went, launched the rockets, and pulled to one side as the eight smoke trails were about to enter the roof. This time, we circled around to see if there was any need to use the bombs, but the building was now partially obscured by black smoke and flames were leaping up; they would soon have spread to the whole of the bamboo and rush building. As we turned for home, we noticed a chap in the boat waving both arms in the air. Was he annoyed or was he our guerrilla? We got some good photos. The trip was four hours and ten minutes.

When we were nearly home, flying high over the hills, I began to think that these Mozzies would be quite nice aircraft for high-level work, if only they had a wheel instead of a silly one-handed stick, but you cannot beat a Beau for low-level work. Douggie preferred the Beau, too, as he was so cramped in the Mozzie.

Into February, Monywa (on the east bank of the Chindwin) had now been occupied with bridgeheads secured across the Irrawaddy at Thabeikkyin and Singu, north of Mandalay. The Army were, however, having a hard time west of the Irrawaddy near Sagaing, opposite Mandalay, where the river does a long sweeping right-hand bend. Twice we were called on to bomb and rocket some positions here on a bit of rising ground. On one trip, as I was watching the target creep up to the spinner before commencing our dive, I saw a line of bomb bursts across the target, which were from a Liberator flying above us; either he was early or we were late. All sorts of aircraft were keeping up an offensive on this area—Libs, Mitchells, Hurries, and Thunderbolts. The Hurries were operating from a quickly made strip not far away, and the air support officer was just calling in some Thunderbolts off the 'cab rank' as we left. How the hell the Japanese hung on, goodness only knows, but they were like that—stay there until there was not a man left.

The moon had just come right and we got a night job against transport—like old times, but it was not so easy in a Mozzie. We were warned off an area where a Lysander might be landing with some guerrillas; otherwise, it was a case of cannon and rockets on anything that showed a light (no bombs on this trip). Not far away, to the north-east, we saw flashes and fires that were from Libs bombing Madaya, the terminus of the short railway going due north from Mandalay. The air over Burma was getting very busy now; we often wondered where all our aircraft were coming from, and by day, there were Daks all over the place.

We began to wonder how much longer we would be out here. If we had stayed on Beaus, we would probably have completed our 'tour' by then. Eric was still going strong; he had been on two more Ops than I had (he had done thirty-four). The CO had told him that he would be 'rested' when three replacement crews arrived as we were two crews short again. It looked as if we would just carry on unless the replacement crews exceeded our losses, but we were told that some more crews would be along soon as a conversion course in India was nearing completion.

I next found myself on a 'pairs' trip with a big lad from Somerset we all called 'Long John'. We were to deal with an Army camp not far from Pagan. L. J. had been on a Mozzie squadron in the Middle East; he was a very experienced lad who had a better view out of a Mozzie than most of us as his head was almost touching the canopy, which meant he had to work out his own bombing technique. We took the Gangaw Valley route and actually spotted some of our Army lads round about Pauk, within about 50 miles of the river. We cut across to pick up the river, crossed it south of the target area, and then turned north to come up to the target.

The land was flat, with scattered dense clumps of trees, isolated palms, and a criss-cross of tracks between paddy. At first, we could not find what we wanted, so we opened out and went around again. Then, Long John came over the R/T: 'It's here, on your starboard'. I saw him pulling up to attack, near to a very big clump of trees; so, turning and climbing, I approached at roughly 90 degrees to him. In a big clearing in the middle of those trees, there were *bashas* and all sorts of vehicles. We gave them cannons and bombs first, then wheeled around and coming in at a much flatter angle, fired the rest of the cannon shells and a salvo of eight rockets. We then pulled away, very low over the trees; that is when we came unstuck.

Something—it can only have been a damn big bird—hit the windscreen with an almighty crack, right in front of my eyes. Instinctively, I must have ducked and, in so doing, lowered my right hand, dipping the right wing right into the trees. There was a hell of a jolt; we seemed to be snatched to starboard. I wrenched the stick back and hard over to the left. We cleared the trees but were still turning to starboard. I had to bring the port throttle back to hold it, but at least we were still flying; the speed had dropped and it needed a lot of left rudder and the stick well over to the left to keep straight. Douggie said something like, 'There's a bloody wire round the wing'. Easing myself up a bit while still holding pressure on the rudder and stick, I looked to starboard and there, just outboard of the engine, I could see a wire draped over the top of the wing, jammed in a slot 4 or 5 inches deep, which it had cut for itself in the leading edge.

I told Douggie to keep his eyes on it and shout if the slot looked to be getting any deeper. I knew it must be up against the main spar and wondered how thick it was; I did not know, but thought 'I'll never get home with this on'. Luckily, I had a good mental picture of the area. 'I'll pick up the Chindwin and try to get up near Monywa as our lads are up there and then put her down on the water—daren't try putting her down on land as this bloody wire will snag up on anything and snatch the wing off.' I called Long John to tell him what had happened and what I was doing. Boy, was I glad to hear his Somerset voice, clearly saying that he would find me and stick with me, although I knew he could not help.

My mind was working overtime as I was only maintaining 190 and still had full power on the starboard engine. It was already getting hot, but oil pressure was OK. I wondered 'What will the stalling speed be? Dare I use flap? If the wire has damaged the flaps and only one side comes down we will turn right over. How long is the wire? It feels to be bloody heavy. Will she keep flying for another twenty minutes?' We were over the river now. I felt better, especially when Long John said he was with us and then flashed past, went around, and came up beside me. However, I was having to work really hard now to keep her level and straight. I asked Long John how long the wire was, but he said he could not see the end properly. I realised that it was beginning to oscillate, like that trailing aerial on the Lib used to do, so I had to stop it somehow, otherwise I would not be able to hold it. I told Long John that I was going to try to dip it in the water to stop it spinning, so I asked him if he would tell me as soon as it touched. Gingerly, I went down until he shouted, 'Splashing'. I tried to hold her steady, but she was wanting to rock and slew, then he shouted, 'Take her up' and thank goodness, she felt a lot better.

Still with lots of rudder and stick well over, we were making good progress, although the coolant temperature was just on the danger mark as I still needed full power on that starboard engine. If she would keep going for another five minutes, I would know where I wanted to be—on the inside of that curve near Monywa, where the river would be shallowest and slow running and there might be some exposed mudbanks. I told Douggie to press the 'Destruct' button for the IFF (friend or foe system), then to jettison the cockpit canopy (hoping like hell that it did not hit the tail), and then tighten his harness and 'watch his head'. I did not really know what was going to happen when we got down near the water. It was bloody noisy with the canopy off. I saw the bend coming up. Still with the power on, I went lower and lower.

Long John told me the wire was trailing through the water, so I closed the port throttle but left the other almost fully open; this seemed to be keeping her straight. We were losing speed and sinking. I had the stick right back, trying to hold her off. The ripples on the water were just a blur, then we touched the water and I whipped the throttles back and reached for the switches; for a split second, the water seemed to cascade in front of us, then we were flung to port and a huge curtain of water seemed to rise at the port side of the aircraft, coming crashing down on top of me through the open canopy. Then there was silence. We had stopped, but we were not sinking. We were firmly settled on a mudbank. The port wing was half out of the water, the starboard wing underwater. We were sitting in warm water, completely soaked from the water that came in through the canopy.

For a moment, neither Douggie nor I thought of getting out. We just sat there, burst out laughing and he then punched me on the shoulder. We saw that we had completely turned around and were facing the way from which we came, only about 30 yards from the bank. Long John flew over so we both climbed out, sat astride the fuselage, and waved at him when he flew over again. We did not really know what to do next. The water was clearing now, the slow currents had shifted the mud we stirred up, and we could see the starboard wing under the water. We paddled out on the wing to look at the wire but it had gone. The leading edge, outboard of the slot that the wire had made for itself, was stripped away right to the wing tip. The drag of the wire in the water must have whipped us right around and snatched the wire away sideways, peeling off the leading edge and all the little stringers as it went; it was a bloody good job we were on water.

We felt down in the water and could feel an indentation in the spar where the wire would have been resting, so maybe these Mozzies were stronger than we thought and we were left to speculate whether the wire would have slipped harmlessly off the metal wing of a Beau. We also wondered whether the wire had been fastened at each end or just slung between trees because if it had been firmly fastened, we reckoned it would have torn our wing off.

However, we could not just stop here; we knew we had better find somebody, so I popped back inside, passing out our parachutes (as they would be nice to sleep in), the emergency rations, and Douggie's nav. bag. Shortly after, Long John flew over again, then twice set off in the same direction, finally flying over while rocking his wings. We realised he was off but must have been indicating to us the way to go. We paddled ashore, the water barely coming up to our waist, although the mud nearly sucked our boots off; we then sorted ourselves out on the bank. It was hot and sunny, so we soon got dry. We decided there was no point wondering about trying to find somebody. Long John would tell them we were OK and where we were, so there was no danger of them telling the folks at home that we were missing. It was only about 3 p.m., so there was plenty of daylight yet. There was plenty of shade there, plenty of water, and the parachutes would be dry inside, so they would make nice 'sheets', even if we spent the night there. The rations would be OK for a couple of days; we opened them as there were some fags in there and decided we would let somebody find us.

Our experience of 'survival' was very short because at about 6 p.m., we heard a vehicle. It looked to be a Jeep followed by a big cloud of dust making its way across the scrub. We stood up, waved, and then wondered whether we had done the right thing as they were not white men. I undid the flap on my revolver holster as we watched them approach. They did not look like Japanese, but who were they? They seemed friendly all right. They turned out to be Nigerians, part of the East African Corps. They had been sent out to get us, so good old Long John must have got a message through to the Air Support folks who had passed it on. It was all very efficient.

We boarded the Jeep, which was a bit crowded, and set off to their camp just near Monywa, only 2 or 3 miles away. They were a grand lot of happy-go-lucky lads, joking and laughing and giving us cigarettes. Their officer promised to make arrangements for us to be 'taken out' in a few days' time and that he would make arrangements to billet us in the village. It was dark, but after a big mug of thick stewed tea, this officer took us to the village in a Jeep. There we went to a little *basha*, where (in English) he explained to this Burmese chap that he was to look after us for a few days. The Burmese chap spoke perfect English and was excessively polite. He bowed and by the dim light from the smallest of hurricane lamps, he showed us to a little bare room in which there were three charpoys. He promised to get us some food, shortly to reappear with two bowls of rice with something in it (we could not see what it was as the light was too poor), but it was tasteless. He stayed chatting for a while, in perfect 'upper-class' English, telling us how pleased he was to see the English and that he used to work for the Burmese Government. Then, to our surprise, he produced a full packet of Capstan Full Strength Cigarettes, saying he would be pleased if we would accept them, along with a box of matches. I was surprised to see cigarettes in the same brown packets as at home because the cigarettes we got out here were usually in tins. After a good cough over these very strong cigarettes, we decided to turn in. We pulled our parachutes and enshrouded ourselves in copious folds of lovely soft silk. We did not worry about not having mosquito nets and soon fell off to sleep.

We caused quite a stir in this tiny, knocked-about village. The next morning, when we pushed open the wattle 'window', we saw a little crowd outside; silently, they gathered around the window, peering in at us and holding the kiddies up so they could look in too. We felt like animals in a zoo until our host went outside and moved them away. After more rice for breakfast, we went outside and let the people see us as we thought they may then go away. Our host spoke to them, telling us they wanted to see the Englishmen who came out of the sky in a big bird; they were our friends. We smiled at them and put our hands together as the Indians do, but I am not sure whether that was the right thing to do here as they were probably Buddhists, but it seemed to amuse them and they did the same back to us.

Our host explained that before the Japanese came, he was the government tax collector for some area we had not heard of, but he had to flee several times, avoiding the Japanese by taking to the jungle, and had come here from across the river only a week or so earlier, after the British drove the Japanese away. A lot of these people had been with him. He was obviously regarded as the 'Head Man'.

He told us about his job as a tax collector. It seemed to work exactly the opposite way to the way it works in Britain. Those who worked hardest and made the most money paid nothing, or only very little, while those who were lazy and did not work paid the most. He explained that the villagers would each be given roughly the same area of land, but it may be in two lots—one good and one not so good—so that, as far as possible, it was divided fairly. Then, once a year, as tax collector, he would inspect each person's holding. If someone had not done anything with his poor land or just left it growing coconuts so that he could get drunk off the toddy, he would be highly taxed. Someone who had looked after his good land well and had made efforts to improve his poor land may get away without paying any tax at all. It sounded a damn good system.

We had happy memories of these charming people who were trying to get themselves together and knock up a few *bashas* to make a new village before the monsoons paid them another visit. In particular, we remembered the bowls of rice and fish from the river; the pretty little girl who was sent to bathe a cut on my shin by gently wiping it with a leaf she had kept dipping in some suspect water (I had caught my leg on a stone and our hosts noticed a bit of blood on my slacks); the dim hurricane lamp with its sooty glass; the huge leaves on the trees; the smell of cooking; and the seemingly endless supply of Capstan Full Strength (we reckoned our troops had got rid of them on these people).

On day three, we were visited by a British lieutenant who informed us that we were on the 'low priority' list to be picked up by a light aircraft; the sick and wounded chaps had first call, which was how it should be. There was a suitable strip only 4 or 5 miles away, so if we stayed around there, they would collect us when there was an aircraft. We offered him a Capstan Full Strength; he refused, saying he preferred his own and he would not have expected RAF chaps to smoke those things. For another two days, we waited, but we were now getting to know the villagers better, although we could not talk to each other. We made signs and smiled. We helped them tie pieces of wood together to make the frame of a *basha* and tried our hands at a bit of a reed weaving to make a wattle pane. We crouched on the ground with them to have a cup of char and squatted in the bushes to go to the toilet.

On day six, we were collected. We waved goodbye to these nice people who were standing in a group with their hands together and smiling. I think they were having a bit of a joke on us because I never saw them doing this to each other. Covered in dust, we pulled up in a flat scrubby area by a lorry, in the back of which was a chap with a radio. He told us that it would be about forty minutes. He wore no badges of rank, just a pair of shorts and a bush hat. He turned out to be one of those RAF pilots on a 'rest'. Sure enough, a little speck appeared in the sky, which did not grow all that much bigger when it was overhead—a little high wing affair with a fixed undercarriage, making a noise like a motorbike. It was a Sentinel or, as the Americans call them, a Stinson L-5. Out popped a lad with a glorious suntan, wearing shorts and no shirt (strictly against Air Force regulations), slinging a bush hat on his head as he walked over, holding out his hand and saying, 'How do. I'm Dave from Doncaster. Come to give you a lift back'.

I looked at the little plane and asked if he could take us both at once, to which he replied, 'Sure, as long as one of you gets on the stretcher'. Then Dave started discussing the fuel situation with the chap in the lorry. He needed some and there was none here, so the Jeep was sent somewhere to get some in tins; it was to take about an hour. Dave told us he had been on this job for over a year, evacuating chaps from the Chindit expeditions and from around Imphal and Kohima, first on Puss Moths or Leopard Moths and now on these American Sentinels. He seemed to love the job but only one engine of 185 hp and a maximum speed of under 120 mph was not exactly my 'cup of char'. He said he would be cruising at about 90 mph; we would go to Imphal, which was about 200 miles, but if he could not get enough fuel here, he would put down at Wangjin or a rolled paddy field at Tulihull.

In due course, some petrol cans arrived and fuel was poured in; Douggie volunteered to lay on the stretcher and I squeezed in beside Dave. The little motor was started, then there was a quick run-up and almost as soon as we started to move, we had risen into the air, although we hardly seemed to be moving. We were bouncing about in the hot air, up and down like a whore's drawers; I would not have been at all surprised if I was sick, and I reckoned Douggie had the best place.

We were at about 1,000 feet. This was all friendly territory and there was no need to keep low. The ground seemed to be passing below painfully slowly; in fact, if you looked well ahead, we did not appear to be moving. The one propeller was whirling around just in front of us; I never was very struck on single-engined aircraft and a glance at the airspeed indicator showing 85 was not exactly comforting as I had become used to expecting an aircraft to stall if the needle approached the 100 mark. Fortunately, my 'mike jack' fitted the socket, so I was able to talk to Dave, who was sitting there with his bush hat on top of his helmet, looking for all the world like one of the original aviation pioneers in his shorts and canvas boots. There was no need to bother with maps; he knew the country as if it were his own backyard. He was telling me that these Sentinels had a bigger engine than an Auster or the Puss Moth and Leopard Moth, but they were slower; on the other hand, they could carry more and get in more confined spaces.

Douggie seemed to be OK stretched out behind us, surrounded by billowing parachute material, as we could not stuff it all back like the parachute packers are able to do; we just gathered it up in a bundle and stuffed it in. We were in two minds about leaving it for our Burmese hosts as it would have been a priceless luxury to them, but we did not think the Air Force would approve. Every time we crossed a bit of water or passed from over baked dry land to a clump of trees, we seemed to either drop or shoot up about 20 feet, but nonchalant Dave soon inspired confidence.

After nearly two hours, we were making our way up the Imphal Valley near Tiddim; I had plenty of time to look at the area that we had got to know quite well from a much lower level. There were some areas of very colourful trees. Dave decided that in another twenty-five minutes, he would put down at (I think it was) Wangjin for some fuel. We duly put down on this rough little rolled strip and got out to stretch our legs while Dave met some chaps who had emerged from a *basha* under some trees. He beckoned us to follow him to the *basha*; he obviously knew all these guys. There seemed to be five of them and in no time, we were all drinking tea out of chipped enamel mugs. They were talking about so-and-so having been through and 'have you seen so-and-so lately?' He told them that we had ditched a Mozzie in the river, then got around to talking about fuel. They said he could have as much as he wanted and two of the chaps went to load some cans in a Jeep. Then Dave looked at his watch, worked out how much daylight was left, and said he may as well take us 'over the top' and straight home as this would still give him time to get back to his base at Imphal before sundown. One of the chaps said he would tell Imphal on the W/T what he was doing and we followed the Jeep with the fuel cans out to the aircraft. The cans were handed out and the contents poured into the tank through a funnel and a strainer, which looked like a piece of a lady's stocking, while Dave remarked that he did not need high octane stuff like we did. Some of the lads gave Dave some letters to post as we climbed in. Dave started the engine as the lads waved; then, Dave just opened up and we were off.

We laboured up and up in this wide valley, a mere 70 showing on the clock. The river far below looked like a mere stream and ahead, but seemingly getting no closer, was the big lake south of Imphal. We were now just about level with the top of the mountain ridge on our port when Dave turned to the north-west. We slowly crossed over one jagged ridge and the ground fell steeply away into the next valley; although the little engine was whirling away, the ridge at the other side of the valley did not seem to be getting any nearer. Then we were over it and looking down into the next steep valley. This time, I knew that after the next ridge, we would be home.

I invited Dave to stay for some food but he declined, pushing off as soon as we had disembarked, having filled our arms with the parachute material, saying, 'Good luck—it's all part of the service'. Some ground crew lads came running up, saying it was good to see us back and we apologised for leaving their aeroplane behind. We got a lift over to the flight office. The CO soon put in an appearance; he said he was glad to see us back and that Long John had told him all about it, but he nearly 'went spare' about us having pulled the parachutes. It was a good job we had not left them behind. He said there were some forms to complete, but we could see about that in the morning as it was about time we had a shave.

Upon going over to the mess, someone told us that Eric 'had gone'. 'Gone where?' I asked, thinking they meant he had 'gone for a Burton', but I was relieved when they told me he had gone back to India as three new crews had arrived. We had a night yarning and line-shooting. Long John had told them all about my escapade. He said that as I went down, there was this splash on the water behind me, which caught up with me like the wash from a speed boat, followed by a big splash under the aircraft when, suddenly, I seemed to slew round and was completely obscured in spray. When he came around again, we were sitting there half out of the water but facing the other way and damn nearly touching the bank. The next time he came around, he saw no movement, but on his third run over, we were sitting on top of the fuselage. I told him what a difference it made knowing he was around, particularly when we were OK, as we did not worry then about being thought to be missing. We both then proceeded to get rather pissed.

The next morning, we had to fill in forms about the 'Loss of one of His Majesty's Aircraft'. Some of the questions seemed to infer that we had done it on purpose and when the CO remarked that 'You ex-Beau types seem to think you can go around barging into things', I let him see that I did not think that remark was funny. Anyway, I was next on the list to be rested when another crew arrived but with being away for a week, I was at the top of the Ops roster; as there was still a bit of the moon period left, I could do a night Op against 'transport' that night.

A lot had happened while we had been away. An Army corps had made another crossing of the Irrawaddy just south of Mandalay, and another corps was just crossing, down near Pagan (almost where we had been on our last trip), so they had made jolly good progress.

The night Op went off without any bother. I told myself that big birds would not be flying around in the dark. We were down near Kyaukpadaung, across the Irrawaddy, south-east of Pagan. There were lots of lights around which seemed to be on vehicles, but the Japanese must have heard us as they kept going out as we were getting ready to pounce on them. We caught two lots, who got the full benefit of our cannons and rockets. On the way back, we dropped some 'Perafix' in a given area; the stuff was supposed to make a noise like the sound of hand grenades and rifle fire to confuse the Japanese. It was a nice ride home. The moon had gone by the time we landed at about 4 a.m.

I slept for most of the day and saw some new faces in the mess when I went over at about 6 p.m. Four new crews had arrived; two of them had already done a tour on Mozzies in Italy, so I reckoned that they should be going on to Ops straight away, in which case I may get away for a rest. The CO confirmed this when he came in the mess for dinner. I went over to find Douggie and tell him that 'we were off'.

In a couple of days, we were away. Our tin trunks were packed the day before. We thumbed a lift to Imphal in a Dak. Imphal was buzzing with Daks. We got another Dak later in the day to take us to Dum Dum, from where we would get the train to a place called Yelahanka, just north of Bangalore in southern India. We were going to a Mosquito conversion unit, but what we would be doing there we did not know. Some lads had told us it was a grand spot with a lovely climate, so we were not much bothered about what we would be doing as long as we got a bit of flying.

The weather was a lot different from what it was when we came the other way in a Dak. This time, we could see the ground. We looked out at acres of bright green tea plantations, studded with the scarlet dress of the plantation workers as they moved among the waist-high bushes; later, we looked at the flat, dried-up plain, which had previously been covered with a great flood, but was now only criss-crossed by tiny streams. Then the great sprawling eyesore of Calcutta on our port was beginning to show a few lights as it was nearly sundown. As we touched down at Dum Dum, Douggie gave me another punch on the shoulder, saying, 'Happen we've made it, then'. That said it all.

22

We Leave the War Behind

I was glad we were able to get away from Calcutta after only one day. It was hot, well over 80 degrees, although there was a light shower of rain. It was noisy, smelly, and nowhere in the world can there be so many folks packed together, seemingly all shouting and arguing with each other. We had a journey of over 1,000 miles ahead of us, which looked like taking about four days, but time did not matter when travelling in this country; the main thing was not to worry when the train kept stopping for no apparent reason, just to enjoy the journey and look forward to the next meal. I expected a train right through to Madras and then another to Bangalore, but the RTO had other ideas—five changes of train and two different railways, including the Bengal Nagpur Railway and then the MSMR (which stood for 'Madras' and something else). Getting to Howrah Station over the Hooghly Bridge, we were held up in a traffic jam for a good half an hour as some bullock carts had shed their load all over the road, horns were blowing, bells ringing, and whistles being blown until you could not hear yourself speak. The station platform was out of sight below white-clad bodies squatting around cooking stoves, yet the official *coolies* with their red armbands and our tin trunks on their heads strode over them as if they were not there. Once on board the train, we could relax.

It was uninteresting country to start with, but the next day, we were running down a lush coastal belt with pretty high hills just inland. It was a very hot day with the water from the melting ice running all over the floor. Our first change of train was at Rajahmundry in the evening; we were well in from the coast here on a very wide river. The next morning, we were only about 70 miles away at Bezawada, on another big river: the Kistna. Here, I was joined by a very interesting Hindu gentleman who very politely asked if he could come in my compartment; I was delighted as I was now alone. We were soon talking and his use of the English language was far more eloquent than mine.

We soon knew each other's names, where we came from, our wife's names (he showed me a photo of his wife and I did the same), where we were going, and that he was the editor of some Hindu newspaper. He began to explain aspects of Hinduism, the significance of the River Ganges, and the sacred city of Benares. He explained why the cow was sacred, being so because it gives the Hindu the five essentials for life— milk, curds, ghee, dung, and urine. The first two were pretty obvious, but I asked about the other three. The ghee is a sort of clarified butter used for cooking and also used, by those who could afford it, on the funeral pyre; the dung is used as fuel by making bricks out of dung pats or for making dung huts; and the urine is an ingredient in many Hindu medicines. Jesus, I hoped I would never be treated by a Hindu doctor. He told me lots more about different Indian peoples, but it all got a bit confusing. We had dinner together that evening, but out of respect for this charming and delightful companion, I did not order meat, choosing a vegetable curry. I could not help wondering whether he had ever taken cow's urine; if so, it had not done him any harm.

The next day, I had the rather uninteresting company of a couple of British Army officers who seemed to regard all Indians as servants to be shouted at; I thought, 'they are missing a lot in this interesting country'.

On the fourth day, we were in our fourth train, moving a bit and stopping a bit as we slowly and surely made our way due south from Guntakal Junction towards Bangalore. The scenery was not particularly impressive—a flat plateau with odd-shaped outcrops of rock as far as the eye could see in all directions and shimmering as the morning became hotter. This leg was about 150 miles, so we would be in Yelahanka by about 4 p.m. We kept stopping in the country, where the third-class passengers all seemed to get out to relieve themselves— men and women side-by-side in a line at the side of the track. Folks would appear in the distance, running towards us, and those who made it before the train moved off would try to sell us something. We stopped at little stations where the *chai wallahs* had already brewed up in anticipation of our arrival or our pre-ordered meal was waiting.

For the last half of the journey, we seemed to be running either parallel to or criss-crossing a road that was quite busy in places with slow moving bullock carts. Although I saw no river, we came across some areas of lush green vegetation, trees, and colourful flowers, as well as pools covered with what looked to be blue water-lilies. Then came the monkeys—to start with just a few, then dozens, and then hundreds of them. They were swinging in the trees and hanging on the roof of the train with one hand, hanging down and putting the other hand inside the open window. While watching the monkeys, I almost failed to notice that we were pulling into Yelahanka (just north of Bangalore). The monkeys were everywhere, on top of the train, swinging on the station lamp posts and pillars, hanging from the arms of the signals and even on the platform.

This seemed a nice place—sunny and hot, but not too hot—and we certainly had an interesting reception. The RTO soon had us fixed up with transport and we were on our way to the airfield.

23

The Good Life, Even in Hospital

At least the folks at Yelahanka knew we were coming, so that was a good start. The adjutant gave us a nice welcome, saying the first thing to do was to get us fixed up with *bashas* and to find me a bearer. He thought a bearer called David was still around as the officer he was looking after only left the day before; he was a good man, so he would send someone to see if they could find him, and if so, he would send him round to me so I could have a look at him and take him on if I liked but, 'don't pay him more than two rupees a week, unless he does anything special for you'.

The *basha* was similar to the one in Poona, only a bit bigger, with one room at the front and two smaller rooms at the rear for the wash place and thunderbox, and doors at the front and another at the back, both leading onto verandas; there were also brick walls up to about 3 feet with rush matting above. There was a chest of drawers, table, easy chair, and a charpoy. In the back was another table with a metal washbasin, two metal jugs, and (most importantly) the thunderbox. There was a rush mat on the floor and a lounger type of deckchair on the veranda; a Tilley lamp for lighting; and an earthenware '*chatti*' for cold drinking water.

I had my trunks and bedroll dumped in the *basha*, then wandered out to see if I could see Eric, as the adjutant had confirmed that he was here. I found him only two doors away in the same block. There he was, stretched out on his charpoy: 'Jacko, my old pal. Last I heard of you, you were thumbing your way back from the Irrawaddy, you old bugger. How are you? Great to see you'.

After catching up on the chat, I asked him what we would be doing here. 'It's a great place. We get these chaps coming to convert on to Mozzies. They've all had plenty of experience but some of them haven't flown twins before, so we give them a bit of dual on Oxfords, then a few demos on Mozzies and that's about it. The CO may want you to give them a few talks on something but we sort out who is doing what among ourselves. But, there's a jolly good club in town, only takes forty-five minutes to get there and there are some cracking popsies at the Bus club, mostly QAs'.

'Bus club,' I remarked, 'that's a funny name for a club, sounds as if it's for bus drivers, and who are these QAs?' 'The BUS Club is Bangalore's United Services Club, like the Poona Club, but better and not so stuck-up. The QAs are Queen Alexandra's Imperial Military Nursing Services—all Sisters at the hospital in Bangalore, so they know what they are on about. There's a dance at the club tomorrow night—Saturday—we'll go along and I'll get you signed up'. Yelahanka and Bangalore were starting to sound OK, but I was not going to get myself tied up with a nursing sister; as long as we were in a crowd, that was all right.

As I made my way back along the veranda, I saw an Indian sitting outside my door. On seeing me, he jumped up, smartly saluted, then put his hands together, nodded his head from side to side, '*Namaste, sahib*. My name is David'. He was obviously Hindu from his greeting and the *dhoti* he was wearing (white cloth tied around his waist and somehow gathered up between his legs to form a pair of trousers), but his bearing and erectness was more like a Rajput warrior. He was so dark that I could hardly see his features, but his stubble was white, so I assumed he was getting on in years. He wore a loosely wound white '*pugri*' (or turban), around which, at a jaunty angle, was a belt, like we used to wear as a schoolboy, in RAF colours, fastened with a snake clasp.

'Yes, David,' I said, 'come inside'. He stood firmly at attention, showed me his official services identity card bearing his photo, thumbprint, and name (both Indian and 'David'). Nodding his head from side to side, he explained that David was his 'British name', that he had worked for the Army and Air Force for many years, and that he liked Air Force *sahibs* as they were very good *sahibs*. He explained that he also had British white trousers and a long white British coat as some *sahibs* wanted him to attend them in the mess. He would look after all the other servants that I would need, the *bhisti*, the sweepers; he would bring me *chota hazri* (early morning tea) from the *chai wallah* and see to all my *dhobi* and have my clothes laid out ready for me. We agreed terms, whereupon he saluted, then put his hands together and, still nodding his head, said he would look well after me. Then he inquired whether I had any boxes that I did not wish him to go into; as soon as I told him, 'No', he went to the door, shouted for the *bhisti* to bring the water for my bath, then set about emptying my trunks.

By the time I had had my bath, he had decided which drawers things were to go in, which things stayed in the tin trunks because of the ants and termites, and which clothes were going to the *dhobi*; the clothes I was to wear for dinner were laid out on the charpoy. He also informed me that I should get some new shirts and a bush jacket; I could also do with some new slacks as all these had got very bad and he always like to make sure his *sahibs* were very well turned out. He promised that while I was at dinner, he would tighten up the webbing on my charpoy and erect a mosquito net, then, looking at Peggy's picture, which he had taken out of the trunk and placed on top of the drawers, he inquired, 'Is that *memsahib*?' 'Yes, David,' I replied, 'that is my *memsahib*'. Still nodding, he smiled, put his hands together, and looked at the photos, saying, 'Oh *Sahib, memsahib*, she is very beautiful'. That reminded me to write to Peggy and give her my new address after dinner, then I would get my mail a lot quicker. I hoped she was all right and wished she were here with me.

The mess was a nice place, too, it being a *basha* but three rooms with plenty of comfortable chairs, an attractive little bar, and some real friendly chaps. I met the CO, who said I should see him on Monday; it was Saturday the next day and there was no point in bothering over the weekend as the chaps on the course would be doing some flying but there's nothing for us to do. On overhearing this, Eric inquired if he would be OK to spend the following night at the club, and the answer was, 'That's OK as long as you are here Monday morning'. What a change. As I walked over to my *basha*, a white-clad figure leapt to his feet besides my door. It was David, who nipped inside to light the Tilley lamp. I did not write to Peggy as I had had too many gins. I got into bed and had a look around to see if I had trapped anything inside the mosquito net. Satisfied I was alone, I called David to put out the light; he then settled down on his rush mat outside my door. I thought I was lucky to get posted here.

On Saturday morning, I got my letters written. David seemed to have whipped all my clothes away and sent them to the *dhobi* so I decided I really must try and get some new ones in Bangalore. Eric suggested that we should get a lift into town straight after tiffin, call at the club, get me signed up, and book a room for the night, otherwise we would be in a tent. It seemed that as there were more officers around than there were in peacetime, the rooms soon got booked up, so they had erected bell tents in parts of the grounds where folks could stop the night if all the rooms were taken. We got a lift, even though it was sitting in the back of an open 15-cwt truck. It was a tree-lined road, and the monkeys were thick in the trees, cascading around and jumping down onto passing bullock carts to see what they could pinch, while the bullock carts clanked along, the driver looking to be fast asleep and white birds perched on the backs of the bullocks. It was a good road, only narrow but OK.

In forty-five minutes, we were entering Bangalore. It looked a very clean place with lots of trees, and the roads became quite wide. The club was a single-storey building, brilliant white, standing in lovely grounds of green lawns and beds of brilliant flowers, mostly bright red; they looked like gladioli, dahlias, zinnias, and salvias. There were lots of trees, too. Formalities completed and a room obtained, we deposited our toilet kit, had a quick look around at the lounge, snooker room, drinking room, reading room, ballroom, and outside swimming pool, and then took a *gharry* into the shopping area. This seemed very posh for an Indian town. I fixed myself up with a new outfit at a very posh military tailors, then we went back to the club for tea, sat in the garden for a while, then headed to our room for a snooze before having a bath and shave and getting ready for the fray.

One would have thought that Eric had been here for months instead of a mere ten days as he had everything organised. Before taking dinner, he reserved a table in the ballroom, right by the glass doors leading onto the patio beside the pool. He instructed the *abdar* (wine-waiter) to place a bottle of gin, a jug of ice-cold fresh lime juice, some bottles of tonic water, and some glasses on the table; he told me it was best to buy gin by the bottle here as it was cheaper than ordering tots and that it also saved a lot of time not signing separate chits. You never paid cash for drinks out there, either in the mess or in these clubs; it was all done on the chitty system and you settled the bill at the office, either at the end of the night or the end of the month.

After dinner, we took our place at the table. Eric invited a couple of our RAF chaps to join us. After a while, Eric announced, 'The girls are here', and he went over to a group of six girls and brought them over to join us. They were a bright, lively lot, and it seemed a long time since I had seen girls in evening dress. Eric introduced everyone and called a waiter over to start pouring the drinks, by which time the room was filling up and a pretty big band had started some lively music—damn good they were. We were soon all chatting, dancing, drinking, and laughing. Chaps kept coming over and asking one of our girls to dance, but they always came back to our table. Another bottle of gin was called for, then another.

It got hotter and hotter, even with the windows to the patio wide open, so we moved out onto the patio, the girls throwing scarves over their shoulders to keep the mosquitoes off their bare backs and shoulders. The gardens were floodlit. It was an unforgettable setting—the brilliant red flowers and snow-white walls at the side of the swimming pool looked to be suspended in the blackness, the white diving board at the pool stood out like a big dinosaur, and ripples on the water twinkled like stars. Music was drifting out of the ballroom into the warm air night air. What a difference to the previous Saturday night, but in spite of the pleasant company, it made me feel further from home than ever before. I thought, 'it will be only about six o'clock at home, perhaps just getting dark, then they will have the blackout, maybe air-raids, I wonder what Peggy is doing. I do hope she is all right and that I will be home soon'. I also realised that 'having been so involved with our own war out here, I had hardly spared a thought as to how they were getting on in Europe so, we couldn't really expect them to have a great deal of interest in what was happening out here. At the moment, it's probably just as well they don't know'.

At about 2 a.m., things came to an end. Following polite kisses all round, the girls donned their grey uniform coats with scarlet-lined capes and boarded the transport, which had been sent for them from the hospital; with promises to see them next week, we waved them goodbye. Eric and I made our way to our room. Eric seemed to think he had made some progress with one of them and that he would 'crack it' before long. David was sitting on his mat outside my door when we returned at about four o'clock on Sunday and seemed to be pleased that I had bought some new clothes. Nodding his head from side to side and hands together, he eyed me up and down and said, '*sahib* looks very good'.

On Monday, I learned officially what my job was to be. There were eight of us here, all Mozzie pilots. The chaps on the courses were all pretty experienced. We would give them all a bit of dual on Oxfords—how much would depend on what they had flown before and what they had been doing. When they were OK on the Oxford, we would take them on low flying and formation demonstrations and the odd low-level cross-country (for the benefit of the observers). After that, we would take the pilots on demonstration flights in a Mozzie, after which they would go on their own, and then we would give them a couple of demo trips on bombing and using the cannons. Actually, we would not need to do an awful lot of flying ourselves, unless someone was having a bit of difficulty. We may also be called on to give them a few talks on techniques and the like.

The CO showed me a training schedule, showing what dual, demonstrations, and exercises a pupil was required to complete, and also a chart that he put up and 'you staff lads mark in which exercises you will do. You usually work it out among yourselves, without me having to detail anybody'. There was going to be even less for Douggie to do.

'Only one thing,' I said. 'I haven't flown an Oxford'. He did not seem to think that that mattered. 'Nice aircraft to fly,' he said, 'borrow some Pilots' Notes and take one up for an hour or so in the morning. Get one of the other lads to come up with you if you like'. I then studied the local map, noting places to avoid, such as the Maharajah's Palace at Mysore and the surrounding city, various temples and holy places; the position of the firing and bombing ranges; the approved low-flying and cross-country routes and other airfields.

I was rather pleased to be flying an Oxford because it was made by Airspeed, the firm who started up in that bus garage in York and I had flown in their very first aircraft—the old 'Ferry'. They must have built hundreds of these Oxfords for training aircraft. They were supposed to be better training aircraft than the old Anson because the Anson was so docile that it almost flew and landed itself, whereas the Oxford had a few vices more like an operational aircraft and it was therefore not such a big jump when a student moved on to something else. For one thing, it would drop a wing sharply in a stall whereas the Anson just kept on mushing down and recovering on its own. I read the notes for the Mark III—two 425-hp Armstrong Siddeley Cheetah XV engines (radials, of course; I liked that); weight empty: 5,380 lb, weight loaded:

7,600 lb; maximum speed: 182 mph at 8,300 feet; ceiling: 19,200 feet; range: 550 miles; and span: 53 feet 4 inches. I memorised the speeds for take-off; climbing; lowering the undercarriage and flaps; stalling speeds; and landing speed. I was looking forward to the next day.

Douggie was keen to come with me. When we got to the aircraft, we found it was not a Mark III with Cheetah XV engines but a Mark II with Cheetah X 355-hp engines, but this would not matter; perhaps she would need a bit more boost to give the same air speeds. It was really nice to get in an aircraft in which you could move around again, have a bit of room, and not have to stick in the same seat all the time, although, at first, it seemed funny having the throttles in your right hand again, but thank goodness for a proper wheel instead of a silly bent stick. She did tend to have a little swing on take-off—not much but it would give a student an idea of what a swing could be like. It sounded nice and trimmed nicely; the view was good, but not as good as a Beau, and it was nice to look out at radial engines again.

We climbed well up and I tried a stall (one wing did drop away a bit quickly), then another stall with the wheels down, and a third with the wheels and flaps down—that was quite rapid. Then, I let Douggie fly it for a few minutes while I walked back; I just had to walk about in an aircraft again. Finally, I tried a few relatively tight turns to see whether she tightened up or wanted to come out of it, yet she did not seem to mind. We then went in for a landing and did a couple more 'circuits and bumps'. I liked it. The weather was perfect. The country below was nice— real mixture of bare land, green cultivated land, trees, patches of bright colour, little ponds, and a big lake or reservoir. The town of Bangalore looked compact with clean, white buildings, and somewhere in the middle was a big splash of red, like a big garden. I reported to the CO, telling him that I was very happy with the Oxford, but if I was supposed to give demonstrations of formation flying in one, I thought I had better have a bit of practice with another Oxford. He thought this a good idea and suggested I fixed this up with one of the other lads. Naturally, I asked Eric.

The next day, Eric and I pushed off for the best part of a couple of hours' formation flying. I formated on him for most of the time, and after I had got the feel of it, he started doing all sorts of awkward manoeuvres and mucking about with the speed. We had gone due south and came to a huge lake or reservoir, which must have been 15 miles long and 8 miles wide. Eric piped up, 'Do you reckon that's the Dead

The Good Life, Even in Hospital

Sea down there—shall we go down and have a look, this time?' 'OK' I replied, 'it'll be like the old Torbeau days'. Down we went, but it was so flat and glassy that even Eric did not risk going too low, and the impression was nothing like skimming just above the waves as in the Beau. Actually, I found it more difficult to keep in really close formation in the Oxford than I did in a Beau, or even a Mozzie for that matter.

There was not much to do just now as the lads on the course had got past the Oxford stage and were all practising on their own in Mozzies, but another course was expected in about ten days. We were at the beginning of March. We heard that in Burma, the Army had secured the airfield at Thabutkon near Meiktila and that they were on the outskirts of the town; Daks were flying into Thabutkon from Imphal but coming under fire from around the airfield. It was a wonder that there was anything left at Thabutkon because it was bombed and rocketed to buggery. We also got a notice that Air Marshal Sir Keith Park had taken over as Air Officer Commanding Southeast Asia from Sir Guy Garrod. Another bit of news was that the Yanks had opened their Burma Road into China and had been able to get a few lorries through. As far as Europe was concerned, we were a bit out of touch but gathered from the BBC that the Russians were in Warsaw and that our troops were nearing Cologne. It sounded as if those rockets that had been falling on England had stopped.

The station commander was in a bit of a panic because he had arranged a big evening in the mess to entertain some folks from the group headquarters in Bangalore and some of their guests, but he had learned that we were short of gin. Our CO asked if I would take one of the Oxfords to Madras and collect some gin. It appeared that the local gin factory was a few miles south of Madras and the idea was that Douggie and I would take two big empty stone jars to Madras, where it would be laid on that a lorry would meet us, take the jars to the gin factory, then get them filled and brought back for us to fly home. It was all sorted with the folks at St Thomas Mount, the airfield at Madras, and the CO suggested that while we were waiting, we should go to the Connemara Hotel for a meal; he said it was a good place. So, off Douggie and I set, with two pot carboys (each about 40 gallons in capacity) lashed down in the cabin, plus two passengers who wanted a lift to Madras. It was a lovely trip, lasting only an hour and a half. As we neared the coast and dropped down into the coastal plain, the vegetation became very lush—lots of palm trees and bright green fields;

it also got bloody hot. St Thomas Mount was a big airfield, with two long concrete runways and substantial buildings; it seemed a funny name for a place in India, but we were told that it got its name from a nearby hill on which the disciple doubting Thomas preached when he brought Christianity to India. I never knew he was supposed to have come to India, but if he did, he was not very successful. One thing was for sure; it was baking hot—the thermometer in the control office showed 93 degrees. They reckoned it would be three hours before the lorry returned, so we got a lift so far into town and then took a rickshaw to the Connemara for tiffin.

Madras looked a nice town with lots of folks here, but not the hordes of beggars like in Calcutta or Bombay. The people seemed much calmer, maybe because it was not so hot, but they looked different too—thin, brighter people who all seemed to speak very good English. Some did not wear headgear and had curly hair, and most of the men wore the *lungi* (coloured cloth tied around their waist like a skirt) rather than a *dhoti*. We were told that most of them were Tamils. The streets were wide and tree-lined, with lots of palms about, and a most beautiful long beach, fringed with palm trees, but no one was in the water; we were told that there were sharks off-shore. We would have liked more time to look around, but we soon had to take a taxi back to the airfield. We need not have rushed as the lorry was not back, so we had to wait another hour and a half. Signals were coming in from Yelahanka, asking how long we would be. By the time we got away, it looked as if we would not get back before sundown, so we asked for a signal to be sent asking for the flarepath to be on. I speeded things up a bit on the way back and we made it in one hour and twenty minutes, with only the last ten minutes being in the dark. It was delightfully cool at Yelahanka; being 3,000 feet above sea level makes an awful lot of difference. The gin was whistled into the mess through the back door, just in time to get some put into bottles and save the party, which was just getting underway. After a quick bath and change—David had everything ready—I was able to join the party, where the station commander bought me a drink for saving his bacon. However, I missed my dinner.

With nothing to do one day, Douggie and I got a lift into Bangalore. This was always good entertainment because of the monkeys swinging about in the trees, running about on the road, or jumping into the back of the truck. We walked through the Cantonment area. 'Cantonment' strictly means a military station, but it was by no means a barracks full of troops. It was a well set out residential area for Europeans with wide roads, trees, big houses, or bungalows with verandas surrounded by large, English-style gardens. There was no hustle or bustle around here; no smells, except for the scent of flowers; no beggars; and no cow dung on the footpath or bodies being carried to the funeral pyre. The only Indians to be seen were household servants, road sweepers, or the driver of a *gharry*, *tonga*, or rickshaw. You could forget you were in India, save for the fact that some of the trees carried unusual coloured blooms, the birds were colourful, and the sun was beaming down out of the clear blue sky. Coming into the town proper, even this seemed to be clean and tidy compared with other places. There were temples, mosques, and Christian churches but nothing that looked particularly old. The whole place seemed to be orderly laid out.

There were, of course, the usual stalls and craftsmen working—carving cigarette boxes out of sandalwood, making wooden 'Lotus lamps', jewellery, and shoes. I decided to let one of them make me a pair of suede shoes. He carefully drew around my foot on a piece of cardboard, we agreed a price, and the shoes would be ready for me in a week. He was a Muslim; Hindus were not supposed to work with leather as it comes from the cow, but they do not object to wearing the finished product. Then we looked around a little open-fronted shop selling rugs. There were all sorts from little Kashmir rugs to large Persian ones and some which looked like Persian but were made in India. I spotted a lovely blue one hanging up at the back, which looked to be Persian. He told me it was from Tabriz (the capital city of East Azerbaijan) and quoted me several thousand rupees, which I calculated was something like £150. I offered him something in the region of £10; he was ever so polite, merely putting his hands together and, nodding his head from side to side, asked us to 'Please sit down and take coffee'. We squatted on the floor with him and small brass cups of very black coffee soon arrived; he then gave me the sales talk—this rug had come all the way from Tabriz in Russia on a camel train, through the mountains of Afghanistan, and so he could not sell it for less. I stuck to my offer and we left to much nodding and the invitation to see him again the next time we were in town. I told Douggie that, 'if we are here long enough, I'll have that carpet before we go'.

Back in the city, we found a nice little place where Douggie and I could eat together for a change. Then the taxi back to Yelahanka. It was dark and the biggest hazard was the bullock carts on the road.

Suddenly, one would appear with no lights on, with the driver curled up asleep and his *dhoti* pulled over his head. The bullocks seemed to know they were to keep roughly to the left side of the road. The driver would blow his horn and we squeezed by.

On Saturday, there was an air test to be done on an Oxford. I volunteered to do it as I realised that, I had not yet tried any single-engined landings on the 'Ox-box' and it would be a good idea to practise two or three before I had to show somebody else how to do it. Then, after tiffin, with nothing else to do till Monday, I went down to the club with Eric and one of the lads who had joined us there the week before. It was a repeat of the last Saturday night—still six girls but two of them were different from last week. With a bit of encouragement, I could get quite used to this life. This time, Eric did not come back with me to the room. I do not know what time he came in and I never asked him, but I assumed he got on OK. He never bragged about any of his conquests; I respected him for that.

On Sunday afternoon, I took him somewhere he had not been before: the Botanical Gardens. We sat and listened to a military band playing stirring tunes like 'Sons of the Brave' while the *sahibs* and their *memsahibs* paraded under their parasols, and Indian ladies showed off their colourful, gold-embroidered saris. This really was the India of the British Raj; it only wanted elephants to complete the picture, or someone to come along wearing a pith helmet and dragging a tiger.

There was work to be done. Some chaps arrived for a new course. I was dead lucky because the chap I got had flown Bostons and Marauders. I knew that if he had flown the 'Widow Maker', he would be able to fly anything so it seemed a bit of a waste of time and fuel, flying around with him in an Oxford, which he could probably fly better than I could anyway.

We ran through the various routines while I sat in the right-hand seat. I showed him the local features, bombing range, and the like; then we took both Douggie and his observer with us and did a couple of low-level cross-countries, mainly for his observer's benefit. It was all very pleasant, but I started to get a pain around my tummy and kept feeling sick without actually being sick. I also lost my appetite and when not flying, all I wanted to do was to lie around on my charpoy. David noticed that '*sahib* is poorly', but the MO reckoned I had just caught a chill on my tummy and the fact that I was yellow was due to the mepacrine I had been taking. One night, he came up to me in the mess. I had not eaten much and was holding my side, about to go back to my *basha*. He looked at my eyes and remarked, 'By Jove. You've got jaundice'. I told him I reckoned that I had had it for about a week, to which he replied that I was probably over the worst of it by now, but he would get me into sick quarters in the morning.

'Sick quarters' was the hospital in Bangalore where our friends were the Sisters. I was put in a nice little ward, just the three of us, each backing onto one wall, the fourth wall having the windows and a door opening on to a veranda overlooking a garden. A nurse jokingly gave me a pair of pyjamas that were about ten sizes too big. I got into bed, where an Army MO felt my spleen, looked in my mouth and eyes, and took my temperature and a sample of my water. A nurse brought me a cup of char and shortly after, one of the Sisters I knew came bounding in, laughing and saying, 'I heard you were here. Now get into bed, like a good boy'. She tucked me in, saying she would be back. I felt better already. The lad directly opposite me had had his appendix removed, but they were keeping him in because there was a clot of blood working its way around his system and he kept getting a pain in his heart at regular intervals, every time the clot came around. The other lad was recovering from dysentery; he looked pretty grey. The nurses soon christened us 'Red', 'Grey', and 'Yellow'.

For a day or two, I did not feel too good, so I took some pills; I did not feel like eating and was sick once or twice but slept a lot on this comfy bed with a proper mattress. A nurse was always handy if you wanted a drink or escorting to the loo, and they insisted upon a bed bath before lowering the mosquito net at night. At regular intervals, a sister would appear and casually have a chat around the time when they expected Red to have his next flutter. A couple of times, there seemed to be a bit of a panic when they whipped the curtains around his bed and you could hear a bit of activity going on inside. After a few days, however, I was feeling fine. Grey was looking much better too, and Red's 'funny do's' were not as frequent. The Sisters I knew—Sheila, Sue, Betty, Maureen, and Kitty—kept popping in for a chat and a joke. Sheila and Sue were particularly bright sparks. Often, they would tell the nurse that they would see to us in the evening and when it came to putting the nets down, little Sue would always lean right over to tuck the net in at the far side, then lose her balance and fall across the bed. After a bit of a struggle and unhelpful assistance, she would regain her feet and go all round tucking the net under the mattress. We would then call out, 'What about a goodnight kiss, then?' Up would come the net and we got our goodnight kiss. This was some hospital.

After another day or two, Grey and I were allowed up. We sat out on the veranda and Red was allowed out with us but only sitting in a wheelchair. Eric called to see me a couple of times, but I knew it was not really me he came to see; I was just an excuse for him coming to see the girls. Somehow or other, they always seemed to find me the biggest pyjamas they could, and I was always lost in them; the Sisters and nurses used to tease me about them, but the other two always seemed to get ones to fit. On the Saturday night, some of the Sisters came in the ward, all dressed up before leaving for the club. These girls certainly had a good system of therapy, although it made you in no hurry to leave. I seemed perfectly OK after a week, spending the days walking around the garden and reading on the veranda, or writing letters. Then the MO decided I could be discharged, but that he would recommend me for a couple of weeks' leave. He advised me to go steady on the drinking, saying 'the odd whisky or brandy would be OK but avoid the gin for a week or two'. Otherwise, I was to carry on as normal but that with having had a touch of jaundice, I should not offer to give blood.

Back at Yelahanka, I spent a couple of days before asking for my leave, while I collected a bit of information and decided where to go. I would have liked to have gone way up north to see Kashmir and the Himalayas, but when I found it would be nearly 2,000 miles each way, I realised that this was out of the question as it would have taken the two weeks to merely travel there and back. I decided to have a few days at Ootacamund ('Snooty Ooty'), a hill station in the Nilgiri Hills, some 7,500 feet above sea level, and then carry on for a few days on the Malabar Coast, which I knew would be hot but should be interesting.

David sounded disappointed when I told him I was going on leave for a couple of weeks but then I told him he could come and look after me. He sprang to attention and put his hands together, 'Thank you, *sahib*, very good *sahib*. When do we move out?' 'The train from Yelahanka to Bangalore leaves at 10.15 hours tomorrow, David. I'll take the things I want in my parachute bag, so that and my bed-roll will be all I need. I'll give you some rupees for the fare'. I could even detect his face smiling, as he replied, 'No *sahib*. Got plenty rupees. I know what you want to take. I will pack parachute bag in morning'. I thought, maybe he was going to travel on the outside of the train without paying, like a lot of them seem to do.

24

David and I Go on Holiday

It was obvious as soon as we arrived at the station that David was not going to carry any baggage himself. He soon had a couple of *coolies* at his command. I gave him a small handful of anna and half-anna pieces so he could look after the formalities. He then went to get his ticket to Ooty; we would play it by ear after that, even though I had a return warrant to Ooty. The monkeys entertained us as we waited for the train. A chat with the RTO convinced me that we were going to make Ooty in the day. Although it was only about 130 miles in a straight line, there was no direct railway line; it meant doing a big sweep round to the east, changing trains about three times, about 300 miles altogether. Anyhow, it did not matter how long it took. We were on our holidays. I had David to look after me. We had our bedding with us and I enjoyed travelling in these trains. Maybe we would get as far as Coimbatore today, but it did not matter if we did not.

No trouble about getting on the train, David gave orders to the *coolies* in military fashion and then disappeared to his coach. At Bangalore, David quickly appeared outside my compartment and I left everything to him. I bought myself a *Times of India* at the bookstall and by 11.30 a.m., we were on our way, about 50 miles to the east to a place called Bowringpet. Soon, the monkeys were with us again, swinging on the sides and poking their arms in through the open window. We were on a slow train. It took about two hours to do the 50 miles, but the scene was always interesting; the drill seemed to be that the chaps squatted in little groups in the shade of the trees, smoking and chatting, while the women, bent double, scratched about in the fields under the hot sun. At some stops, David would appear outside my compartment and direct a *chai wallah* to pass me a cup of char; I felt like a real *bara sahib*. We had a change of trains and tiffin at Bowringpet. I had nothing to do but stroll out of the train and into the dining room. David took care of the bags and even made the *punkah wallah* pull his rope faster to keep *sahib* cool; it certainly was bloody hot.

The next 50 miles was on a very ordinary type of train, still it was OK and had the usual toilet and loo room but the seats would have been a bit hard to sleep on. At a little junction we changed again. After a wait of about an hour, we boarded a train that had come in from Madras, but only for about 12 miles where we all had to change to another train belonging to another railway—the South India Railway. We did the next 80 miles to Salem in just over two hours, which was jolly good. It was getting cooler. I was hoping that we would have dinner there, but we changed trains again. In half an hour, we were off again, still on the South India Railway but on the Malabar Express, which was going right through to Calicut on the west coast. This was the big main-line train. In my compartment were two Europeans civilians and an Army officer; I think they were rather jealous of the attention that David kept paying to a mere flying officer. Orders were taken for dinner to be taken at Erode, where we still had one hour to go. It had just got dark as we pulled into Erode and as I got out, David asked if I would allow him to walk down to the river; he said it would only take ten minutes, which I told him would be OK. While having dinner, I asked one of my companions if there was anything special about this river. He told me that to the Hindu, this river—the Cauvery—is the sacred river of Southern India, just as the Ganges is the sacred river of Northern India. I was glad I let David go.

On returning to the train, David was waiting by my compartment; he held his hands together, nodded, and said 'Thank you, *sahib*. You are very good'. 'You good man too, David,' I replied. We rattled on in the dark. Two of my companions got their bedrolls down, but the other was getting off with me at Coimbatore. We arrived just after ten o'clock. The station was a little way away from the town, so we took a gharry. David found out from the driver where there was a hotel for me. It was a typical Indian hotel (if there is anything typically Indian), and the chap at the little desk spoke pretty good English. He had a room, I told him that I was on my way to Ooty and he told me that I should take the train early in the morning, at 8 a.m., as the journey up into the 'Blue Mountains' is most beautiful in the morning, when the sun is new and the air is clear. I agree to have *chota hazri* at 6.30 a.m. to get that train. I explained that David was my bearer and asked if could he stay too; the two of them conversed with much animation, but from the nods and smiles, I gathered that this was OK. David soon had my mosquito net erected over the charpoy and my pyjamas laid out, then took up station on his rush mat outside my door. I told him he could put his canvas bag in my room if he wanted, but he declined, indicating that he would use it as his pillow.

As I went to sleep, I thought it was a good job I brought David with me. With my privileges as a European and his local knowledge, we would be able to travel anywhere without any bother. We boarded our little mountain railway for the climb of about 50 miles up to Ooty. The first 20 miles or so were nice, but after that, it really got spectacular.

The carriages were not divided into compartments, so you got a good view all around; the side windows were all down (or maybe there were not any windows), so a pleasant warm breeze was passing through. The high ground was on our left; then we approached a little river and turned to the left, up into the hills. There were tea plantations on the sides of the hills, and the track was twisting and turning as the little engine puffed its way up, belching out thick smoke. There were spectacular views and trees. Then we arrived at a little station—Coonoor—where notices told us we were 5,600 feet above sea level. After a short stop, during which the engine took on more water, we set off to climb another 1,900 feet in some 9 or 10 miles to Ooty. The little train puffed steadily up and up, around bend after bend, and let off what steam it had left in a sigh of relief to announce its arrival at Ootacamund. We had come through acres and acres of forest and tea plantations, but here we seemed to be on lush English-type Downs, with gorse bushes, trees, and acres of grass; however, the flowers were a bit more showy than in England. This looked a posh place. The station staff had very smart uniforms; everywhere was clean and looked to be freshly painted. I had been advised to stay at one of the clubs there, where there were several clubs, so we took a gaily decorated *gharry*. David was sitting rigidly upright as if he were the viceroy in person.

The club fixed me up in a bungalow annex forming three sides of a square around a garden. The room opened onto a nice veranda. With me having my own bearer, I was expected to pay a few annas a day to the bearer who would normally look after that room, but the chap at the desk agreed to David, after he had looked at his identity card. It looked a real posh place, and I began to wonder whether I would find it a bit too 'stiff' here. David soon had my room and gear sorted out, and I went to have a rather late tiffin.

Changed into my casual gear, I then went for a stroll. It was certainly cool up here—only in the 50s, which was the coolest it had been since arriving in the subcontinent. For the following three days, I wandered around; it reminded me of a mixture of the North Yorkshire Moors around Goathland and a London park. There were green 'downs' sprinkled with gorse bushes; houses and bungalows scattered over hillsides among the trees; young girls in smart riding gear cantering on their horses; middle-aged women in jumpers, tweed skirts, and flat brogue shoes, exercising their pedigree dogs; and *ayahs* pushing perambulators.

In the evening, when I saw men arriving at the club wearing white dinner jackets and the ladies their best evening frocks, I decided I had better revert to my uniform. David had caught the atmosphere as well, as I found him in his best regalia—his white trousers and long white coat with a wide belt in RAF colours; he certainly looked a fine figure. He had quickly got the place sorted out, my clothes sent to the *dhobi*, and he assured me he was OK for food and did not need any more money; these fellows seemed to be able to live for a week on just a few annas.

It was interesting watching the 'elite' in the club. The women were smoking their 'Passing Clouds' through long ivory cigarette holders, trying to look gay and talking in affected voices; the men were offering cigarettes from their gold cases—this side Virginia, the other side Turkish—or complaining that the waiter had not cut their cigar properly. Some were utter snobs, like the fat little 'Colonel Blimp' type, who said to me, while I was sitting at the bar with my tonic water, 'Pilot officer is it?' To this, I replied 'No, actually it's flying officer, just a bit wider than a pilot officer'. 'Oh,' was his reply, 'you won't have seen any action yet, young man'. 'Just a couple of tours so far, plus a few trips from England,' I replied. 'The first was over the Atlantic and the Arctic and the other out here; quite a change'. 'You must have been commissioned from the ranks, then'. 'Yes, the top rank, warrant officer'. With that, he walked off. They were not all like that, though; one old boy, who seemed to be on his own, talked to me quite a lot.

I had a couple of nice evenings with this old boy and allowed myself the one brandy the MO said I could have before going to bed. The night got quite chilly, but David said he was warm enough on his rush mat on the veranda. However, I thought it was time I moved on and got back to reality. The station booking clerk was very helpful. The thing to do was to get the Malabar Express, the same train I had come down on, and it would take me all the way to Cannanore, although I may have to change at Calicut. He would book me a sleeping compartment from Coimbatore and I would only have to pay from Coimbatore, as my warrant would cover the ride down from Ooty on the metre gauge, but I was able to fix it all up and I got a ticket for David as well. So, the following night, we would get the last train down to Coimbatore and spend the night on the train. Although these station arrangements always seemed a bit haphazard, they always seemed to work out OK thanks to the telegraph.

On my last day at Ooty, sitting in the gardens, watching the folks pass by, I began to think that it is a little 'two-faced' when Europeans decry the Hindu caste system when we have a such a rigid 'caste system' of our own. One can only be born into this Hindu system and the several rigidly upheld sub-castes. In the European caste system, the viceroy stands alone as representative of the king emperor. Then there is the caste of 'high-borns', otherwise known as the raj—the governors, commissioners, residents, and judges. Below them we have the senior civil servants, army commanders, top politicians, and maybe the top businessmen. The next sub-caste includes Navy, Army, and Air Force commissioned officers, commissioned nursing sisters, the middle administrators, middle businessmen, and ministers of the Anglican Church. Only these castes and their families are allowed to travel first class on the trains; join or be a guest at one of the caste's clubs; or enter the best hotels. A non-commissioned officer or nurse would fall into a lower caste, while those of a lesser rank were thought of little, almost as untouchable, to be gratuitously provided with a little entertainment to keep them quiet. One had to conform, more or less, to this system, but flout it too openly and you would soon be brought to heel.

The only difference between the two systems seemed to be that a Hindu who was born a merchant or a sweeper would remain a merchant or a sweeper for the whole of this life. He knows he cannot move up, so he settles himself down to being a good merchant or a good sweeper, then he may return, in the next incarnation, to a better station in life, but there is no point in being discontented in this one. So, he settles down to get on with his job as contentedly as possible and to living a good life. To try to better his lot in this life would be the very worst thing he could do as that would spoil his chances in the next. This is his doctrine of karma and dharma, yet there is no such thing for those of the European caste. While some are perfectly OK, there are many who are trying to raise their status by affectation and play-acting; using voices and expressions that do not fit their personalities; or trying to impress and becoming frustrated snobs. Now, our supreme commander was not one of these; Lord Louis was a genuine 'highborn'. I bet the Indian boy in the snooker room, who held the 'rest' and passed it to you when required, could tell those who were really *pukka sahibs*—the ones who say *Shukriya* (thank you) and do not feel it necessary to treat him like dirt in order to impress.

The atmosphere of an Indian railway station was, to me, always exciting and Coimbatore at 9 p.m. was no exception. Our train would be another hour, but the efficient Anglo-Indian supervisor had referred to a sheaf of papers on his clipboard and assured me that my compartment was reserved; he even told me the number of the compartment and that he would be there, when the train came in, to see me safely aboard. It was warm down there in spite of the evening hour, but instead of going into the waiting room with its electric fan, I preferred to look around the platform. The station's resident population had already secured their pitches for the night. Some were still having their meal; the most popular seemed to be mostly rice, which they rolled into little balls and tossed into their mouth. They always used the right hand for eating, never the left. Others were packing their utensils away into a wooden box and taking out a rug or a mat to be carefully spread out on the platform as a bed. Some had already gone to bed, covered completely with a sheet, which would be their daytime *dhoti* put to another use. Women were sitting up feeding babies. Some women seemed to be wearing so many golden bangles, bracelets, and jewellery that you wondered why they slept there; surely, they could afford somewhere better, but this was probably their way of life. There did not seem to be any beggars; maybe they had had a good day and gone to bed. The *chai wallah*s, with their 'char' and highly coloured sticky buns, were still at work, as were youths selling cotton shirts and lengths of cloth and the odd fruit seller, selling mainly mangoes and pomegranates.

There was a hubbub of noise. Officious officials ordered or dragged the 'residents' back from the platform edge. Arm-banded *coolies* appeared, in anticipation of the arriving train. The Anglo-Indian supervisor (in his smart, white suit) passed and told me the train would be about ten minutes. The excitement and activity became more intense and then two dim lights showed up in the distant darkness, getting nearer and nearer. We could now see the smoke from the engine picking up the glow from the firebox. The *coolies* jostled for position. Then, into the lights of the station appeared this big, rugged engine, a cow-catcher (or wild animal deflector) on the front, belching clouds of white smoke alternately from each side like a huge dragon. The clanking and hissing got nearer, drowning the hubbub on the platform. As this iron monster was about to pass us, it timed perfectly a big jet of steam right at us. In this cloud, all we could hear was the clanging of the connecting rods; then, as the steam cleared, we saw into the cab, which seemed to be packed with half a dozen chaps. The train slowly moved on, bringing into view coaches festooned with white-clad figures, hanging on the side and out of windows, some jumping off with a big jolt, and the train came to rest. Folks were running about all over the place, but there was no need to panic as it would be there for at least half an hour.

The *chai wallahs* were doing a good trade. The supervisor found me and led me to a compartment, which was exactly the number he had said. David had followed with a *coolie* who he had engaged to carry my bag and bed-roll. I got aboard and David went to find a place. There were two other chaps in the compartment: one European and one Indian officer. They had come from Madras, so as last arrival, I took one of the top bunks. There was a fair bit of banging and shaking, which the Indian smilingly told me was because they were changing the engine. Soon we were on our way and, with a bit of luck, we would be running along the Malabar Coast by the time I got up.

It was light and warm at 8.30 a.m., though being in the top bunk, I could not see outside; however, the chaps below were still in bed and I could not very well get up until they did, which happened half an hour later. We were running up the coast, not far from the blue Arabian Sea, which kept appearing through gaps in the palm trees. We were nearing Calicut, where my companions were getting off and I would have my breakfast. The country looked rather nice, being very lush with lots of fruit trees, coconut palms, tea and rubber plants, and glimpses of the fantastically blue ocean. Calicut turned out to be a rather big, bustling place a port, and there seemed to be a lot of mosques. I could not leave the station, however, as we only had three-quarters of an hour for a leisurely breakfast. It was lovely and warm, almost hot in spite of the early hour. The train was carrying on to Mangalore, but I only had 50 or 60 miles to go to Cannanore, so we would be there shortly after midday. It was a lovely ride.

With the compartment to myself, I could see the sea most of the way and all sorts of trees, fruit trees, flowering trees, and bullock carts on the road, which seemed to be more or less following the railway. We stopped at little stations where people seemed to appear from nowhere to see the train, and *chai wallahs* provided welcome cups of char as it certainly was getting very hot. This was my idea of the tropics; I thought, 'let's hope there's a nice beach. Gosh, I bet Peggy would like this'. Then, at Cannanore, I thought, 'not too big but there looks to be quite a bit here—seems a pretty sleepy place, but I expect everybody is keeping out of the sun as it's so hot'. David even had to wake up a *gharry wallah* to take us to the rest house I had been told about. The chap in the reception place was having a kip, but when he woke up, he was most obliging and soon fixed us up.

What a perfect place for a relaxing tropical seaside holiday. The rest house garden ran right to the cliff edge with a little path down through the palm trees to the beach. The building itself was all on ground level, with white cement walls and a bright red-tiled roof. The public rooms were all in there—dining room, lounges, bar, and snooker room. The guestrooms were in separate six-sided detached blocks, linked to the main building by tiled covered walkways. The chap in charge seemed to be an Anglo-Indian; I think the place was owned either by the government or the railway. It was smart, very clean, and tidy. There was no bullshit here. There were three or four British Army fellows, one or two Indian families (rather well-to-do by the look of them), an elderly English chap on his own, two French nuns, and a Spanish Catholic priest—quite a mixture.

It did not take long to get into a routine—a stroll down the garden, across the brick tennis court and down the palm lined path to the beach after breakfast until it got too hot, then time to retreat into the palms. After tiffin, it was either a rest on the charpoy or on a lounger under the veranda; it was too hot to do anything else. Then, at about 4 p.m., we would go for a walk into town, returning for a bath and change before going out to watch the sunset and thence to dinner. The beach was idyllic—low rocky cliffs, surmounted by clumps of palms, and a quiet little bay of almost white sand, which was washed perfectly clean twice a day. The great expanse of the vivid blue sea met the slightly paler sky at a crystal-clear horizon. Some days, it seemed quite calm as the rollers leisurely broke on the beach; other days, they would be much bigger, breaking a long way out and creating a lot of foaming white surf. On these days, a few locals would appear with surfboards and come shooting right up onto the beach. One day, a young lad offered me his surfboard; it looked so easy. I started walking out with the board under my arm. The water was hardly up to my waist when I saw a late breaker towering above me; before I had time to even panic, my legs were sucked out from under me and the breaker came down on top of me. Then, I was flying about under green water. There seemed to be a hell of a noise and before I knew what the hell was happening, I was being scraped along the sand and the water was rushing back, thankfully leaving me well and truly beached. I did not try that again. The young lads thought it highly amusing; fortunately, the board came back on the next wave. By eleven o'clock, the sand would be too hot to walk on.

David soon had the job sorted, whipping my things off to the *dhobi*, anticipating when I wanted the bath running or what clothes I wanted to wear or when I would like a cup of char—perhaps, he was running my life, which was very pleasant. I found the town was so interesting that I decided to take David with me one day so he could explain some things to me. I knew it would be no use 'asking' him to come, so I 'told' him to come and he enjoyed that. He always kept behind me; when I wanted to ask him something, I had to stop and turn around to talk to him. I soon realised that he did not understand these people's language as when I asked him something, he would try to find out by asking someone else and soon they were trying to understand each other by talking English—the only language they could both understand. It seemed that they mostly spoke Kannada, Telugu, Tamil, or Malayalam; they all had a smattering of English but very little Hindustani. The people's names on the shops or on the church noticeboards all seemed terribly long—a great string of names.

The people looked different, too, and were such a mixture. The women had saris tied in all sorts of different ways, some gathered at the back and some at the front; some drawn tightly between the legs to form tight trousers; some were bare from the waist up, except for a scented frangipani flower stuck in their hair; others, presumably Muslims were in full *purdah*. There were also nuns too in snow-white habits. The men had very mixed attire, some groups selling gaily-coloured cotton cloth in the market, with caste marks on their foreheads just like a runny raw egg and the front half of their scalps shaved bare but long hair hanging down their backs. David showed that he did not think much of them when I asked him who they were; he said they were Brahmins, 'but not pukka Brahmins they were Tamil Brahmins, pukka Brahmins would not look like that and pukka Brahmins would not engage in trade'. Everybody wore bright colours. The pace of life was very slow, with no point in rushing around in the heat; even the pye-dogs were snoozing in the shade. Peacocks walked about, pecking at the ground. A woman was making a cow pat into a round block to take back home to use as fuel on which to cook the dinner; it would soon be dry and ready for burning in this heat. We came across a harbour, but there was little activity here—just a few fishing boats. There seemed to be lots and lots of churches—not just temples and mosques but little wooden ones, painted white—an Anglican and Roman Catholic Mission; a Lutheran church; Methodist Mission hall; and a Syrian Orthodox, with a cross resting on its side, but the crosspiece at an angle instead of at right angles. Some had their little graveyards; two inscriptions in the Anglican one took my eye: 'His Sun Went Down at Noon' and 'He only saw One Monsoon'.

The Spanish Catholic priest gave me quite a lot of local 'gen' during our after-dinner chats; he was also a damn good snooker player. This coast became a very busy trading area after Vasco da Gama landed at Calicut. He came to Cannanore too, and both places became very busy ports. The main export was printed cotton cloth, which became known as 'calico' after the town of Calicut. Then trade extended to sugar cane, rubber, coffee, tea, pepper, betel nut, coconut, and all sorts of spices. The Dutch came, followed by the British. The East India Company gained control of Calicut under a treaty and set up their military headquarters here at Cannanore. However, fifty odd years ago, the military moved out, and Cannanore harbour lost a lot of its trade, which is now all done through Calicut. The people there are different from those in the north or further inland because their ancestors were either tribes from the hills or they came here by sea; they were not affected by the invasions of India from the north.

After seven nights in this delightful and interesting place, it was with some sadness that I stood alone on the cliff top, watching the sun go down for the last time—sorry to be going but sad because Peggy could not be watching the sunset with me. The big crimson sun, which had been almost dead overhead at midday, was just resting on the horizon, a crimson path on the surface of the water from the sun to the edge of the water just below me; swiftly, while rapidly seeming to keep changing shape, it sank below the horizon, and in a matter of seconds, it had gone, making it quite dark. There was very little twilight. The next day, we would be on the train.

25

We Hear of VE Day

'You had better go to the MO and get a jab. They have Bubonic plague in the village, so we all have to be inoculated'. That was my reception on return to Yelahanka. The job was done in two doses, forty-eight hours apart, and I was warned that it made some folks pretty groggy for a few hours. The first jab had no ill effect, so I was rather cocky when I had the second and went to the station cinema after dinner, as I was keeping off the drink. Partway through the film, while Carmen Miranda was wiggling her hips and trying to keep a bowl of fruit on her head, the whole screen started to shimmer, and the next thing I knew, I was waking up on my charpoy the next morning.

A trip down to the hospital in Bangalore saw the MO pronounce me fully recovered from the jaundice and give me a full aircrew medical, which was OK. He did not want to see me anymore and told me just to carry on as normal, although he suggested that I saw the dentist for a filling. Gosh, I think this dentist was a sadist—his drill kept slipping—and as he talked, his foot slowed up on the pedal so the drill nearly stopped; then he would pedal like hell and you could smell the tooth burning from the heat of his drill. I was fully serviced, felt fine, and was ready for the fray. I looked up a couple of the girls before leaving the hospital, then went to chat up the chap at the carpet shop, had another coffee with him, and got him to come down a few rupees.

We were in April and there was good news from Burma. We had taken Mandalay and the Army were moving south towards Rangoon, so I supposed some of our squadron would have moved down from Assam to airfields in Burma itself. Things seem to be going well in

Europe, too. We had taken Cologne and were heading for Berlin; the main concern seemed to be whether the Russians would beat us to it.

Another group of lads had arrived to convert to Mozzies. One or two had flown Beaus in the Middle East, but the chap I put my name against had not flown twins before, although he was experienced on the Vengeance. We had some very pleasant times together in the Oxford. He was impressed by the good view both on the ground and in the air, having been used to having a big radial engine blocking his view. At first, he weaved a lot from side to side when taxiing and kept trying to find the throttles with his left hand, but I did not bother about that as when he got on the Mozzie, they would be on the left again. About the only thing I had to spend much time on was single-engined landings, but after half a dozen or so trips, he was perfectly OK, so we put the rest of the hours in just flying around on cross-countries, with both Douggie and his observer with us. All was very pleasant and the weather was perfect.

I was able to resume the Saturday night routine. It was clear by now that Eric was pretty well organised with Betty; they kept disappearing together into the garden, and once when I popped to our room for something, I found the door locked. Another lad, an observer, working at the Group Headquarters, had become engaged to a QA who I had not met before, and they joined our little circle. I took care to pay equal attention to Sheila, Sue, and Maureen to avoid any bother. The weather was absolutely perfect. It seemed to me that Bangalore had just got it right; 3,000 feet up, the days were pleasantly warm and the evenings balmy. The scent from the flowers drifted across the garden. As the evening progressed, there was invariably a splash as someone was either thrown or dived into the pool to be followed by a dripping chap chasing a girl trying to run in a wet, clinging evening dress and showing much more than she thought.

Music from the band would drift across the gardens; they had a jolly good big band that played tunes like 'Jealousy', 'Up the Lazy River', 'Perfidia', 'Elmer's Tune', 'Paper Doll' (thoughts of Canada), 'Moonlight Serenade', and 'Chattanooga Choo-Choo'—none of the silly sentimental songs we heard on the BBC like Vera Lynn and her 'We'll Meet Again' or 'The White Cliffs of Dover'; Donald Peers singing 'When They Sound the Last All-Clear' or 'The Homecoming Waltz'; or Anne Shelton's ' Coming In On A Wing and A Prayer' and 'A Pair of Silver Wings'. The American Forces Network was much better with its Glen Miller tunes.

Eric turned up one night with a couple of lovely little puppies—short legs, wide bodies, and evenly marked black faces. The only difference was that one had a wider white line running along its head than the other. They had big ears like a spaniel. 'Which one do you want?' he said. I asked what they were. He said they were pedigree Tibetan terriers. An English family in Bangalore had given them to him; what he had done in return, I did not ask. He said they would not grow much bigger, but their coat would grow long and shaggy, a bit like a West Highland terrier. They were both dogs. I chose the one with the wider white mark—real friendly little things they were. Fortunately, David seemed to like them too and said he would look after them when we were not around. Eric suggested that we call them 'Gin' and 'Tonic'. Mine was 'Gin', but I started to call him 'Ginny'—maybe a funny name for a male dog but I could not go around shouting 'Gin' or the bearers would be rushing out with drinks. We got them some food and some dishes. They could play around together, but we decided that we had better make sure they were inside one of our rooms after dark in case any of the jackals that wandered around at night got them. David agreed to make sure about this.

I was now ready to give my 'pupil' his first demonstration on a Mozzie. I had to be careful to refrain from criticising anything about it or making any comparison with the wonderful Beau. I had to make sure he had absolute confidence in his aircraft. I had had several talks with him about the aircraft and sat in one with him in the pilot's seat, showing him the bits and pieces. I had tried to convince him that she was strong, even though made of wood; that the canopy would not hit the tail if it were jettisoned as it had been OK when I had had to do it; that she had a good single-engined performance; that the crank stick was set at a very convenient angle, although I thought it was bloody silly (fortunately, he was used to a stick); that the engines should not overheat if you handled them correctly; and that she should not swing on take-off but watch that she did not want to roll when she surges into full power. He seemed to have learnt the boost and revs settings, the critical speeds, temperatures and pressures, fuel and hydraulic systems, single engine drill and emergency procedures, and fuel consumption; he also knew where the various levers, switches, and tits were to be found. It was funny, but I could sense that like me, he was not overjoyed about a wooden airframe or a liquid-cooled engine, but I tried to put his mind at ease by telling him that these Merlins were well-tried Rolls-Royce engines and not those made in America by the Parkard people. I think I was right.

So off we went on the first demo. I gave him a running commentary on everything I was doing—pointing out the speeds and what I was doing with the trim, wheels up, trim, air speed, boost, flaps up, revs back, trim, climb, airspeed, and so on. We did a few landings and take-offs. After a few, I got him to tell me what to do and I cut in if he forgot anything. A couple of hours was enough for that day. We had a chat afterwards and discussed a few points; he seemed a good bloke, not afraid to ask questions.

The next day, I got him to tell me what to do and he seemed to have got it all off. I kept asking him what so and so should read and he was OK. So I went through the single engine procedures, feathering each engine in turn. Then I whipped one throttle back and told him to tell me what to do. The first time, he forgot about the trim and altering the fuel cocks, so I did it again, this time with the other engine and he got it OK. He seemed happy, so I did a couple of single-engined approaches, getting him to keep telling me what speed I should be doing, and then decided he could go off on his own. I went over to the watch office, so he could talk to me if he wanted to. It gave me a lot of satisfaction when he took off and came back again to make a pretty good landing. I then called him, asking if he would like to do another: 'That one was jolly good'. He said he would and went off again. I now appreciated how Harry seemed to see me as one of his old pupils.

News came in that President Roosevelt had died. We wondered how this would affect America's attitude to the war.

Another few chaps arrived for conversion but only a few at a time; it worked out that we roughly had one instructor to each pupil, so we were not overworked. I had given my Mozzie pupil a couple of demos on bombing and gunnery, and he seemed to be getting good results on the range, so there was nothing more to do with him. The next chap I got was an ex-Beau pilot, so that was easy, although there was no point in trying to kid him that the Merlin was better than the Hercules and he thought the visibility was 'rubbish'.

Excitement was in the air as news came in that a Mozzie pilot, a wing commander, had landed at Mingaladon Airfield in Rangoon and found that the Japanese had all gone. He went to bomb the place but saw it was deserted; flying around, he saw a message painted on the roof of the jail: 'Japs gone. British here'. He had landed, walked into town with his navigator, and could not take off again as he had burst a tyre. The next day, our troops marched in.

Then, most unexpectedly, I was informed that I had been promoted to 'war substantive flight lieutenant'. It all seemed to be happening. Two days later, on 8 May, news came through that the war in Europe was over, and this day was to be VE Day.

This news left us all a bit stunned. The BBC was full of dancing in the streets with bands playing as Hitler had committed suicide. For a moment, my mind flashed back to all those ships crossing the Atlantic and the chaps on them who had faced Atlantic storms and U-boats to get supplies across and keep the war going. Somehow, we had become so conditioned to war, thinking only from day to day or from week to week, that we had given little thought to seeing the end of it. Yet our war was still going on. 'Will they bother much about us now that the war in Europe is over? Maybe we will get a lot more chaps and equipment soon. We'll have to wait and see'.

There were lots of excuses for parties—Rangoon was taken before the monsoon, just as Lord Louis had said, with about three weeks to spare; my promotion to flight lieutenant; victory in Europe; and as well as having the best bearer in India, I also had a dog. The Indians in Bangalore seemed to be having a shindig of their own, throwing much coloured water and perfume over each other to the accompaniment of laughing, singing, and their own style of wailing music. This turned out to be one of their Hindu festivals—the Festival of Holi. It was pretty hot with the sun dead overhead at midday, with refreshing quick showers from white clouds in a deep blue sky. A lot of the earlier flowers had wilted, but they were more than made up for by the wonderful flowering trees, with masses of colour on the bright pink 'Cassia'; the mauve 'Lagerstroemia'; and the yellow, orange, and red 'Ashoka', the striking 'flame of the forest'. There was jasmine and the tall lotus. The ponds were covered in red and white lilies. All the girls, both Indian and European, seemed to have a flower in their hair, and the monkeys, swinging and chattering in the trees, provided free entertainment. We had good nights at the club and so far had avoided pranging any unlit bullock carts on the way back. When in town, I would usually make a point of strolling past the carpet shop, trying to look as if I were not particularly interested. The shopkeeper always seemed to spot me and call me in for a cup of his strong, jet-black coffee. We would sit on the floor and chat, neither of us wanting to make the first move; I had gone up about five rupees and he had come down by a few hundred. He always reckoned that there were other people after it, but in my mind, I felt sure he was keeping it for me.

There was only one 'fly in the ointment'—we got a new station commander. No one knew much about his background, but we came to the conclusion that he had only been in the country five minutes and never been on an operational unit; he was probably an ex-Training Command type. Instead of leaving those of us on the conversion unit to get on with it under our own CO (an arrangement that had been working perfectly well), he wanted to poke his nose into everything. He did not like to see anybody in the mess during the day or on their charpoy during the afternoon. He thought everybody should be banging around the flight, even if they had nothing to do. Then he would think of pointless jobs. We were getting worried in case he decided to have 'Dining-In' nights on a Saturday as he was just the type. Station routine orders appeared on the noticeboard every day instead of about once a week. He wanted to see almost daily reports on each pupil's progress. Then he dropped his big 'clanger'.

After breakfast, one of the NCOs came to my *basha*, thinking he ought to let me know that the CO had said that the IORs (Indian Other Ranks) had 'mutinied' and if they were not back on the job within the hour, they were all to be taken to the guardroom. The IORs were Indian airmen, who worked at the flight on refuelling, polishing the windscreens, helping the fitters and riggers, pulling away the chocks, carrying messages, and such like. I had always found them to be very pleasant and willing blokes, so I could not understand what all this was about. I called Eric and we decided to take off our uniform shirts, put on sports shirts, leave our caps behind, and take the dogs for a stroll down to the *basha* where the IORs lived to make it look as informal as possible and see what was going on. If they were awkward, at least they could then not be accused of not saluting the king's uniform. The IORs always seemed to be either Muslim or Sikh; as we had no Sikhs, the chances were that they were all Muslims. I asked David if today was a Muslim festival, but he did not know. We strolled about a couple of hundred yards towards the IOR's *basha*, it seemed quiet with no one in sight, but the door was open and there was the familiar smell of their cooking. Then Ginny and Tonic both ran inside, and very shortly, one of the lads I knew quite well came outside. He seemed a bit embarrassed. We said, '*Salaam*' and apologised for the dogs going in, saying it would be because of the good smell of their food.

Another lad came out to join us. We asked if it was one of their festival days and he said it was. Then we asked him what this rumour about them not going to work was all about. This lad with his short, spiky black hair, started to explain (while nodding his head and with many hand gestures) that the new CO would not let them have chai when they were on duty; he had inspected their *basha* and told them that they must stop cooking in it, which they all did; he would not allow them to pray at midday, so as it was a festival when they had to be sure to pray at midday, they had decided not to go to work.

We impressed on them that it was a very serious thing not to go to work, and if they would go to work now, we would go and see the CO and make sure that they could cook their food in the *basha* and have time to pray. With this, they said they would tell the others to come out and get over to the flight. We had about ten minutes to the CO's deadline, so we decided to go to his office as we were. The adjutant in the outer office was a bit nonplussed: 'you can't see the old man like that and with those dogs'. 'Just tell him we've stopped this silly talk about a mutiny and it's thanks to these two little dogs'. We were allowed in and we could see that he did not know what to say to us, so Eric got in first and explained what had happened, how the IORs were now back at work and why they were upset. He did not seem to understand the Muslims and their culture, so we told him what good blokes they were if treated right; Eric finished up by telling him that we had only done this for him as when word got around that there had been a mutiny on his station, it would not do him any good and could have far-reaching effects. He said very little throughout, but at the end did say, 'Thank you, gentlemen. I presume you are now going to get dressed properly'. On the way back to our *basha*, Eric remarked jokingly, 'at one stage I thought I may be going back to flying officer again'.

A few days later, some of the chaps in the mess remarked that they had been keeping an eye on the station commander, and they felt sure he was heading for a nervous breakdown. Then Eric and I heard that we were to be detached to Kolar; we would remain on the strength of this station and that this was a temporary attachment. As we were the only two, we wondered whether the station commander had anything to do with it. He assured us he had not, and that the instructions had come from Group. Kolar was a heavy conversion unit about 60 miles east of Bangalore, on the way to Madras, but we had no idea what we would be doing there.

26

Training for What?

A couple of the lads flew us over to Kolar in Oxfords—Eric, Jake, and Tonic in one aircraft; Douggie, Ginny, and I, along with all our kit, in another. Ginny really seemed to like flying, his coat was longer now and hung over his eyes; I had him on my knee and when I held him up so that he could see out, he really seemed to enjoy it. David and Eric's bearer followed by road as they were not allowed to fly. It only took a few minutes but looked to be really 'out in the sticks'—a big concrete runway with a lot of funny markings painted on it, with white stripes across it at each end for 100 yards or so, some more white stripes in the middle, and also some diagonal yellow ones. If this was supposed to be a heavy conversion unit, I would have expected to see some Libs or Halifaxes; as far as I knew they were the only 'heavies' out here, but no, only some Mozzies.

We found two other Mozzie crews there and another two were expected but no one seemed to know what was going on. There were bags of empty *bashas* and only a handful of us in the big mess. We learned that this area's claim to fame was that we were sitting on a gold field. The Kolar gold mine was not far away; it was reputed to be the deepest mine in the world, some 10,600 feet deep, but I could hardly believe that as it seemed a hell of a depth. It seemed that they had been mining gold for centuries there and that most of the gold of the Indian treasures came from the quartz mined here. Production was still going on, but only on a small scale; we had not noticed any sign of mining activity from the air. Apparently, it was a bit to the south. Eric and I looked at the map to assess the possibility of getting to Bangalore for a bit of life, if we were lucky enough to get a couple of days off. We saw that from Kolar town, there appeared to be a main road to Bangalore and it was only about 43 miles; it was the main road from Madras to Bangalore, and we seemed to be about 5 miles from Kolar, so it was only about 48 miles altogether. Another way looked to be to get into Bowringpet and pick up a train, which ran from the gold field to Bangalore; I had done that bit on my leave and it seemed very slow. David and Eric's bearer turned up in the evening, so we soon got organised.

The next day, the other two crews turned up, as did a very 'full of beans' squadron leader who had come to take charge of us—a complete contrast to the station commander we had left behind. Douggie and Jake were the only NCOs. I felt sorry for them as you missed out on so much out there unless you were an officer.

We had a pleasant night in the mess when we got to know each other. The next morning, the squadron leader gave us an idea of what we were going to do. Although the station came under 225 Group, we were doing this job for 222 Group whose headquarters were at Colombo, Ceylon. They wanted statistics on the minimum landing and take-off requirements of the Mozzie at various weights. He reckoned he had no idea why they required this information, and I think he was telling the truth. The drill was that as regards take-offs, we would carry a full load of fuel plus various weights of disposable ballast in the bomb bay (sometimes also with a weighted drop tank under the fuselage).

Observers on the ground would note the point at which the aircraft lifted off; that was what those lines painted on the runway were all about. Also, on take-off, the observer would call the airspeed out over the R/T. The ballast would be dropped before landing to bring the weight down to acceptable limits. After we had concluded the take-off trials, we would commence a series of landings. For these, we would only carry a minimal amount of fuel and no ballast. Here, the observers would call the airspeed over the R/T and a note would be made of the distance between point of touchdown and the optimum touchdown point, as would the point where the tail is finally down and the point of coming to rest. The idea was to arrive at the minimum landing run required. He showed us the forms that would be completed for each take-off or landing, which included temperature, wind speed, and direction as well as all the dope on airspeed, lift off, and touchdown points and the rest, such as weight. Someone queried the fact that no information was called for on rate of climb or clearance of obstacles after take-off. When not flying ourselves, we would be asked to help with the completion of the forms, either by being positioned along the runway edge or being in the watch office and taking down the airspeed over the R/T. We would have sessions of two hours in the morning and two hours in the late afternoon, but each crew would only do an hour at a time.

The take-off business was straightforward enough—run her up on the brakes to full power; give the Merlins a second or two to let the power build up; a chap on each side pulled the chocks away on the end of a long rope; another chap signalled that they were both clear. Then, let the brakes off; lift the tail; hold her straight; and pull her off as soon as possible, making sure she did not go into a roll. If the chap in front signalled 'down', you would have to throttle back and start all over again because it meant that one (or both) of the wheels had crept onto the chock and jammed it. It would have been fatal to have let the brakes off if one chock was still in place. After three or four days, the squadron leader, who was also taking part himself, seemed to be satisfied that we had gathered enough gen as regards take-offs, so we all had a day off.

I went for a walk with Douggie and Jake as I felt a bit guilty for not having seen much of Douggie in Bangalore. It was really rural Indian countryside around there. We watched folks ploughing with an ancient-looking wooden plough drawn by a mud-caked water buffalo; water buffalo wallowing in a muddy pond, only their noses and horns showing; two chaps digging together with one spade, one pushing it in and another pulling it out; and squirrels and brightly coloured birds in the trees. The folks were always interesting, and while the women stooped in the fields, the men folk would be sitting on their haunches in a little group in the shade of a tamarind tree, smoking those foul-smelling acrid cigarettes.

I found that if you smiled at them, said '*namaste*' and something in English, they would invariably respond. If then you sat on your haunches as well, they would be pleased to talk, especially if you offered them a cigarette. One little group told us, in jolly good English, that there were many sages round there who could perform miracles—one who constantly smoked cigarettes without ever blowing out the smoke; one who lived to be 150 years old and had not eaten for the last fifty years; one who could hold out his hand and let the gold from the gold mine flow from his fingers; and many who could bury themselves in the ground for days or weeks on end and then come up unharmed. They admitted that they had never seen any of these people themselves, although one man did say he did once see a man bury his head in the ground and stop breathing for many days. Nearing the end of our walk, we came to a little collection of mud huts with roofs made out of flattened tin cans, but the cooking utensils outside were all clean and beautifully polished. The women wore spotlessly clean kingfisher blue saris and a red flower in their hair.

It was now onto the landings. I was not very happy at all about these. We kept bringing the Mozzie in a bit slower each time. I would have been much happier with the Hercules engine, which gave you some instant power when you opened the throttles, but the Merlin seemed to need such a long time to think about it. If you were sinking a bit too fast and so shoved the throttle open, you went on sinking, then they would surge; if they did not surge together, you were rocketing about all over the place. Also, if you bumped her down too hard, this bouncy undercarriage with the rubber 'shock absorbers' put you back up in the air and you had to get the tail up quickly to prevent her flopping down again from a great height and spreading herself all over the runway. We had a great laugh watching each other do it, but after an hour of flying, you were damn nearly a physical wreck.

Much to our delight, the squadron leader decided that we should all have a couple of days off on our second Saturday and Sunday. He was going to fly to Madras for the weekend and agreed to Eric and I taking a 15-cwt truck to go to Bangalore. We took two of the other chaps with us. It was an easy drive on a reasonably good road, only very dusty, and on the odd occasions that we met another truck, we got covered in dust. It was just as well the traffic was mainly bullock carts and chaps on bikes. The monkeys greeted us as we neared Bangalore. The first stop was the hospital to let the girls know we were in town and not to be late in getting to the club. Maureen would be on duty, but the others would be free and would be bringing a new one along. Then, we went to the club. They had no rooms left but could fix the four of us up in a bell tent on the lawn at the back, so that was that. We went for a quick wash, a bite to eat, then a stroll to the town for another casual chat with the carpet *wallah*—not much progress this time.

Our two pals, Eddie and Martin, were very taken with Bangalore, especially the club and the Botanical Gardens. Rested and bathed, with a change of clothes and having eaten, we were ready for the evening. We met some of the lads from Yelahanka, who wanted to know what we were doing, then the girls arrived; we had already bagged our favourite table by the doors onto the patio. The lads wanted to know about the dogs; we had left them in the charge of David. A jolly good night it must have been because I walked slap into the pole up the middle of the bell tent when we eventually turned in; I did not feel much at the time, but the next morning, my nose and face were covered in blood and the lads wanted to know what 'that little Sue' had been doing to me.

The break did us all good. The squadron leader had had a bit of a do with his Mosquito at Madras. When he was ready to set off back on the Sunday afternoon, the temperature was about 103 degrees. His engines overheated before he got to the end of the runway, so he had to cut them and wait for them to cool. They showed little sign of doing so, and the temperature in the cockpit was like an oven. Eventually, when they had cooled sufficiently, he got towed to the runway, started them up, and took straight off without running them up; otherwise, they would have overheated again. We ex-radial engine types laughed about this, saying how silly it was to bring in-line engines to the tropics; he agreed with us and we said we hoped he would include this in his reports.

For the rest of the week, we continued at slightly different weights. One of the lads had got his approach speed down to about 80, putting her down in a three-pointer and stopping in something under 260 yards; surely, we thought, no one could expect better than that. However, the squadron leader wanted him to keep on to see whether he could do it consistently, and he wanted us all to match it. We found it meant being virtually stalled with damn nearly full power on, so you were just about hanging up by the props, the tail hanging low; consequently, the nose was up and spoiling the view. You were almost falling vertically and had to keep that last a bit of power in reserve, to put on at the end, so that you did not hit the ground too hard and bounce up again. I did not like it at all. With these engines not being quick to respond, we found that you had to get her into this sort of sinking, nearly stalled position, fairly high up so you got everything under control and then put the last bit of power on a bit before you would expect to do—to catch her before she touched. There were several strained undercarriages that needed seeing to, but fortunately, no one left a pile of smashed wood on the runway. It was a real tummy-sinking feeling to be dropping with your nose pointing up and bags of throttle on, especially, when you were not exactly enamoured with the performance of your engines. However, we all survived, but we were all getting more curious as to what this was all about.

In the mess, we would talk about our day's experiences and speculate what it was all in aid of. Someone suggested that it was to find out the minimum size of field necessary to land or take-off in a Mozzie; someone else suggested it could be to do with flying in agents or guerrillas. Another chap suggested we had a close look at one of those forms to see if there was a clue to be found somewhere; the only thing that struck us was that they did not seem interested in our rate of climb or descent. Then, one bright chap suggested that we should take note of all the jobs we had all done so far to see whether there was anything common to all of us that could give us a clue as to why they had got us together. This revealed that at some time or other, each one of us had been on torpedo dropping.

'That's it', exclaimed Martin, 'torpedo dropping and those bloody runway markings are supposed to be a Carrier'. 'Can't be', said somebody, 'they wouldn't carry out tests at somewhere near 3,000 feet above sea level for that'. The squadron leader shortly came in the mess and we asked him, 'Have you ever been on Torpedo aircraft?' Without hesitation, he replied, 'Yes, Torbeaus at Leuchars'. We reckoned that that clinched it and told him what we had worked out. Either he genuinely did not know what this was all about or he was a jolly good actor as he reckoned that he thought we were wrong as flying from Carriers was the Navy's job.

Anyway, it was agreed all round that we were not going to try and better our results, otherwise someone was going to get hurt. The last lot of forms were sent off to group, and for a couple of days, we all hung around, wondering what to do now. Then the squadron leader came into the mess and announced that we could all go back to where we came from. He had received a signal from group thanking us for the results and that the temporary unit could now be disbanded. So we never did know what it was all about, although it did look, on the face of it, as if someone had in mind putting us on a Carrier.

27

The Wedding Season

Back at Yelahanka, we were greeted by the news that our station commander had gone. The lads reckoned that they had driven him around the bend and that he was probably now at Deolali. We were not surprised; the sun soon caught up with him. The new chap seemed a great guy, so the station was its happy self again.

A small new course had just arrived, so we were able to take just one pupil each and have fun giving dual on the Oxford and some demonstrations on the Mozzie—not the silly sort of Mozzie flying we had been doing at Kolar, although I did feel that I could really handle a Mozzie after that.

The little dogs were growing up and now had their shaggy adult coat. Fortunately, David seemed quite fond of them, which was a good job, as one day, when he decided to re-wind his *pugri*, I saw David wrapping a seemingly endless length of white cloth round his head, and little Ginny tugging on the loose end as if it was a game.

Saturday nights at the club were resumed, followed by Sunday afternoon walks in the Botanical Gardens and the 'casual' calls at the carpet shop for a little more negotiation. The end of the war in Europe did not seem to be having any effect out here.

Our unit commander, a hell of a nice squadron leader called 'Stew', announced that he was to be married to an Anglo-Indian girl. He had known her about six months. Her parents and grandparents were all Anglo-Indians. Without any of us having to say anything, we all knew the problems he would have to face both here in India and back home in the UK. He fully appreciated these himself, saying that after the war, they would probably settle down in Malaya. We all liked Stew and wanted to help him as much as possible. At a mess meeting, we agreed to hold an open night so we could invite Stew's bride-to-be, her parents, and any of their friends. We laid on a 'help yourself' buffet and all the drinks we could lay our hands on, sorted out the best records for the gramophone, and got the servants to collect flowers for decorations. It turned out to be a real good night.

The girl was a real stunner—beautiful dusky complexion, long black curly hair, graceful features and fascinating hands with very long fingers, wearing a long straight green and gold dress with a long slit up one side. She was intelligent too, spoke beautifully, and was not short of conversation. The family and friends were all so polite, but natural and were obviously very pleased to be with us. Our lads were never slow in getting a party going, so there were no awkward moments, and very soon, everyone was chattering or dancing with everybody else. Towards the end of the evening, the station commander, who had been enjoying himself along with everybody else, managed to get a bit of silence and then announced that although he had not yet been able to put it to the mess committee, but in confident anticipation that that they would agree, he wished to invite the bride and groom-to-be to hold the wedding reception there in the mess and he hoped that they would accept. Stew looked pleased and his girlfriend threw her arms around him, absolutely delighted. We knew this meant a lot to them as the BUS Club would not allow them there, even though they were obviously a good class and an educated family and there was possibly nowhere else they could go.

The wedding was arranged two weeks later, and the mess committee formally agreed to the reception. We invited the bride's parents to come up one evening to sort out the arrangements as we wanted them to 'feel in on it'. As many of us as possible went to the service at the Anglican Church in Bangalore and back in convoy for the reception, the monkeys in the trees forming a guard of honour. The catering committee and the mess servants did a marvellous job, putting the extra mess fees we had agreed to chip in to very good use. David was delighted to be asked to serve at the meal, getting dressed in his best mess uniform; he outshone the major-domo. I just had to keep telling him to look after the guests instead of fussing too much around me. The meal over, a speech of sorts came from the best man, followed by toasts and responses, more toasts and more responses, a big iced cake, and a short break to clear up and shift the tables; then, it was on with the party. Everybody seemed so happy; we were not outwardly a sentimental lot, but I am sure everyone was determined to give the couple, and the bride's parents, a real good do because we knew the prejudice they would have to face and wanted them to know that they had some friends who did not care a bugger about the colour of their skin. It seemed so wrong that two grand people like these should have to consider leaving the countries where they were born in order to find somewhere where they would be socially accepted.

No sooner had we recovered from this wedding when some of us were invited to another. The observer chap we had got to know at the club was to marry his QA. The service was to be at the same Anglican Church with the reception at the BUS Club. This was a real boozy do. By the time the meal was over, the best man—a W/op/AG, who had been on the same crew as the bridegroom—was three parts cut. He kept putting his arm around the groom for support, and after getting him plonked on a seat in the garden for the official photograph, we had to carry him away to sleep it off. The hospital matron was there, along with a couple of the MOs, some chaps from group, and all the girls from our Saturday night crowd, plus a few more. The band had been booked for the evening—not the Saturday big band, but the smaller one that played on Wednesdays; it looked like being a long night. Those of us from Yelahanka had booked rooms for the night, so we were able to get a rest and a bath before the evening started; the girls went back to the hospital to change.

Some of the evening events remain rather hazy. I remember the heavy scent of the frangipanis in the garden—a sort of crimson jasmine with an almost overpowering perfume that hung around in the still night air. I remember trying to explain to someone why the crescent moon was right at the bottom; if you think of the crescent as being the bow of a bow and arrow, the arrow was pointing to where the sun is now, so that in latitudes like that, where the sun was dead overhead at midday, it must be dead underneath at midnight. It seemed logical to me. The sun was whizzing around in the plane almost at right angles to the one in which it moved around Iceland.

Now back from his short honeymoon, Stew got word that the unit would probably soon be closed down as with the end of the war in Europe, we would be getting crews from Europe and the Middle East, who were already experienced on Mozzies. This was just as we were mulling over the result of the election back home—the Labour Party had received an overwhelming victory. Since 1931, there had been a coalition government with a big Conservative majority. The result took us by surprise. We felt that the country had let us down by chucking out 'the old firm', who had seen us through the war in Europe, while the war out here was still to be won. It looked to us as if the people at home were not concerned about pursuing this war with the same effect that they had put into Europe, just leaving those of us who were already out here to get on with it. There was not any sign yet of us getting any help. What would the new Government's attitude be to the Far East?

It was duly confirmed that we were to be broken up. Stew obtained from group a list of postings that were available. I tried to get on the group communications flight, but there were no flying jobs going. I did not fancy Bombay, especially knowing that it would be raining like hell there for the next two and a half months; I had no desire to see anymore of Calcutta; and I certainly did not want to go to that awful place, Karachi, on the edge of the desert. I would have quite liked Madras, but there was nothing doing there, or in Bangalore. There were, however, two flight lieutenant posts coming up at Poona, so Eric and I plumped for these. We were interviewed at group, where we learnt that they were for a movements and a postings officer at the Aircrew Reception Centre, which had either just moved (or was in the process of moving) to the airfield there, now that it was no longer being used for Beaufighters refresher courses. They gave us the jobs and let us choose which one we each had; Eric opted for movements and I for postings. Neither of us had had any administration experience, so we embarked upon a two-week course at group to teach us the jobs. It was agreed that both Douggie and Jake could come with us and work in the signals and cipher section. We made the point that when we got back on to flying duties, we would like them to stay with us.

For two weeks, we were kept hard at it, but it was very interesting seeing what went on behind the scenes and how the system was supposed to work. During this fortnight, we 'boarded out' at the club. The club allowed David to come, too, to look after us. He looked after the dogs during the day. When I told him that I would be moving to Poona shortly, he immediately asked if he could come with me; he said he knew Poona, having looked after several Army *sahibs* there. I was jolly glad he wanted to come as I would have been lost without my David. Most nights, I played snooker. The last two Saturday night dances came and went. The carpet *wallah* had come down to around £12, so I bought the rug. It was 'goodbye' to the 'Town of Boiled Beans' (a literal translation of 'Bangalore') and to 'Les Girls'.

28

I Send Peter to the Cocos, Then the War is Over

It was agreed that two of the lads still at Yelahanka would fly us up to Poona in Oxfords as they had nothing else to do. What a lot of gear we seemed to have collected. It needed two Oxfords—one for Douggie and me, plus Ginny, our four tin trunks, rug, bedrolls, and loose bits and pieces; Eric, Jake, Tonic, and all their belongings filled the other. David went ahead by train the previous day; Eric reckoned that I would not see him again having given him the rail fare, but I knew David better than that. It took us just on four hours to do the 475 miles to Poona; as we converged with the Ghats, we saw the big build-up of cloud from the monsoon. It was almost exactly twelve months since we were there before. It did not look to have changed, except there were no Beaufighters there anymore. Looking at the monsoon clouds, which would be over the whole length of the western coast, I thought for a moment of the fantastic weather I had seen at Cannanore; it was hard to imagine that it would be flooded out by torrential rain.

I wondered how I would get along on my first 'ground' job and what the chaps we would be working with would be like. I need not have worried. They were a good friendly lot and made us very welcome. The unit CO was a squadron leader who let it be known that we could call him 'Steve' when we were on our own or in the mess. He seemed pleased to have two ex-Coastal Command chaps joining the unit, and fortunately, he liked dogs.

I was introduced to my little 'empire' comprising a *basha* with a room for me plus two rooms for 'Smithy', my NCO, and two clerks. For the last ten days or so, Smithy had been running the posting section himself, under the eye of Steve. He proudly showed me a big wall chart he had made on which he hung coloured tags on little nails. The idea was so that at a glance, we ought to be able to tell who we had in the 'pool', showing aircrew category, type of aircraft, and suchlike. It seemed a good idea, and I complimented him on it. Then he showed me a second board, also using coloured tags, which showed squadron requirements. Smithy suggested that although the first board could be on the wall in my office, where those I was interviewing could see it, he strongly suggested that the other one should remain in his room, where it would be out of sight; otherwise, he had found from experience that some unsuitable crews may look at it and start trying to pressurise us into sending them there. I took his advice. I inquired about the telephone on my table. He said it was OK for calls around the station and could be used for external calls, but if the call was other than local, it could take days to get through (if you ever did), unless you could get the operator to accept one of the higher priorities that only the CO could authorise, so it was usual to use the signals section using the W/T.

Douggie and Jake seemed quite happy with the signals set-up. The signals section was quite a long way from the other unit offices and they worked in shifts throughout the twenty-four hours. Douggie and Jake were each put in charge of a shift.

By now, David had turned up. The letter I gave him to show to the guardroom, along with his official bearer's identity card, got him in OK. He soon had my room sorted out and had the other servants running around.

Steve, the CO, showed Eric and me a typical day's pile of signals and explained the set-up; he said he would expect us to slip in to see him each day to keep him in the picture and talk over any problems and that roughly once a week, he would hold a unit conference at which we could get together and have a general discussion. He was a bit concerned about the 'input' we would expect now that the war in Europe was over. Were we to get boatloads of aircrew arriving at Bombay from Europe, the Middle East, and maybe even newly trained chaps from Rhodesia and South Africa? If so, how much warning would we get? He suggested that he, Eric, and I should pop down to Bombay for the day on *The Deccan Queen* to see the folks at Worli, to see what they knew and work out some routine so that we would not be taken by surprise and find we did not have enough accommodation or food.

The next morning, we were taking breakfast in the Victorian luxury of *The Deccan Queen* as she glided through the Ghats, through all the tunnels, over the viaducts, and under the waterfalls that cascaded down the sheer mountain sides. Bombay was hot, sticky, and wet. Shoving our way through the mass of bodies and beggars, we took a taxi through the packed and noisy streets to Worli. They did not seem to have any idea who to expect either. They knew when a ship was on its way and how many RAF people were on board, but they did not know how many were aircrew. Anyhow, we agreed a system whereby they could give us a provisional figure as soon as they could, then send a signal giving more details before they sent them along. We got to know each other and how the other side worked, so the trip was not wasted. Eric spent his time with his opposite number at Worli and also with the RTO getting gen on the best routing to various places (particularly to Calcutta and Colombo in Ceylon) as it seemed that for most of our chaps, these would be the first legs *en route* to their squadrons. It was soon time to rejoin *The Deccan Queen* for a leisurely dinner and a few drinks as we climbed back up the Ghats, rattled through the tunnels, got showered by the waterfalls, leaving Bombay behind for the temperate climate of Poona.

Any thoughts that this was going to be an easy job were soon dispelled after several days wading through signals with Smithy, trying to find chaps to fit in with squadron requirements. More seemed to be drifting in than we could get away. Some suitable ones were away almost immediately, as soon as all the documentation was completed, but like Steve had said, some looked as if they would be with us forever. Some chaps, keen to get away, were constantly calling at the office to see if there was any news. There was a bit of light relief when Mark, the messenger, came around to deliver signals or collect signals to be taken to the signals section. Poor Mark, I felt very sorry for him. He rode round the station all day on his push bike, collecting and delivering messages; he was the only person who wore his issue pith helmet although there was no earthly need for it here. What with his pith helmet, long shorts, boots, and a leather pouch over his shoulder, he looked to be straight out of a cartoon. He would come in, salute, nearly knocking his helmet off, and give me my signals. I would sign his receipt book, then he would salute again, tried to do a smart 'about turn' without falling over his boots, straighten up his helmet, and walk out. These were long days, with hardly any time for a break—much more tiring than flying.

After about a week of this, there was a knock on the door. I called, 'Come in,' and was conscious of a whole crowd of folks coming in. I finished what I was writing then as I looked up, I saw a blue uniform—that was odd for a start out here—with squadron leader rings on the sleeve. I quickly thought, 'Oh. Not another bomber crew'. As my eyes rose, I saw a DFC followed by familiar campaign ribbons—a VR badge on each lapel. Lo and behold, it was Peter Stembridge, who was best man at my wedding. They had just flown in with a Lib. We ribbed each other a bit, about me getting a commission at last and about it taking him a long time to get on a Lib. Smithy took down details of the crew (eight of them altogether) as we had no idea they were coming. They had flown out from England and were fully operational, Peter being halfway through his third tour when the war in Europe ended. Both Smithy and I knew there would be no difficulty in posting this crew—just what we wanted. Peter told his crew he would see them later in the mess; then, when we were on our own, he pointed to his middle ring, telling me that he was only an acting squadron leader and was there any chance of finding a squadron who had a squadron leader vacancy. I thought there was.

Smithy turned up the appropriate signal and sure enough, a Lib squadron on a little coral atoll way down in the Indian Ocean had just such a vacancy as one of their flight commanders was due for a rest. I showed him the Cocos Island on the map, and he was so delighted that I think he would have taken off again there and then. I got Smithy to originate a signal about their posting to make sure that no one from somewhere else got in first, but as neither Peter or any of his crew had tropical kit, I suggested that they should get some in Poona the following day and leave the day after that as there were no shops in the Cocos; also, they would have to get clearance from the MO before they could go. I warned Peter that I had heard that the station commander at Cocos was a bit of a character who wore his revolver in the mess and had someone cut out pigeons in celluloid, which he stuck up in odd spots in the mess roof. Then during the evening, he would suddenly draw his revolver and take shots at the celluloid pigeons and challenge anyone to a contest. Peter still seemed a very quiet lad to me—a very proper Liberator skipper—and I thought this may come to him as a bit of a shock.

We chewed the fat in the mess, discussing what we had both been doing and where we had been. After his first tour on Wellingtons in the Bay of Biscay, he converted to Libs at Nassau, then another tour of Libs in the Bay, a rest instructing in Nassau, then another tour on Libs that was curtailed when the war ended. He would not let on about his DFC; he merely said his name came out of the monthly draw. We talked about chaps we knew in Canada, about Harry Guest and his call on us in Assam; in fact, we just talked and talked. I asked him if I could have a look around his Lib to see how it differed from the old Mark Is and IIIAs, which I flew. I suggested that he ought to do an air test before leaving as I would like to go up with him, but he would not bite, not like Harry Guest. Anyhow, I did get a look over it; how I wished that we had had the latest ASV and gyrocompasses, not to mention the radio altimeter, like he had. It was quite nostalgic, and although I was glad I did not stay in Libs all the time, I would not have minded being back on them.

Peter got his tropical kit and his clearance papers, then headed off to Ratmalana near Columbo where he would pick up charts and get briefed for the flight to Cocos.

All the talk was about the atom bomb, which the Yanks had dropped on Hiroshima. For years, we had heard stories that if anyone succeeded in 'splitting the atom', it would be the end of the world as it would set up a chain reaction and everything would fall apart. It did not seem as if this had happened; nevertheless, it was something we did not understand and I think we were all a bit apprehensive. It might bring about the end of the war; on the other hand, the Germans had put up with cities being devastated. Had the Yanks got any more? Would they dare have dropped it if the Japanese had got one to drop on them? We sensed that we were into something new.

Three days later, we heard that another atom bomb had been dropped, this time on Nagasaki. We speculated that they must be coming from Super Fortresses flying from China, which was why the Yanks were so keen to get a way through to China. Was this one going to make them pack in? We knew they were a fanatical lot.

Signals were coming in thick and fast, amending some of the squadrons' requirements and locations. In the middle of these was a confidential one for the CO giving him notification that we were to make plans for the unit to move to Bhopal in about two weeks' time. Bhopal was roughly 400 miles to the north-east, equidistant from Bombay and Delhi. Steve flew up with Eric to see what the place was like. When they returned, they seemed very pleased, saying it was a good station with better accommodation than we had and more of it. Responsible for the travel arrangement, Eric was happy that the rail gauge was the same all the way to Bhopal so there would be no problem in fixing up a troop train.

On 14 August, we heard that the Japanese had surrendered, just five days after the Nagasaki bomb. There was no confirmation of this on the BBC, just that the Russians, who had declared war on Japan two days after the first atom bomb, were continuing their advance into Manchuria. This seemed very ominous. Why should they, at this late stage, declare war on Japan when it was clear that the end was only days away? Could it be that they wanted to share in the spoils that would indicate that they wanted a share of Europe too? At least that was how Michael (our intellectual admin. Officer) saw it.

Sure enough, Japan's surrender was confirmed. On the 16th, the BBC announced V-J Day. This left us all a bit bewildered—a mixture of elation and relief on one hand, yet a funny feeling of how we were going to make out in this unknown future. I flopped on my charpoy before getting ready for dinner. Ginny ran in and jumped up beside me. I told him the war was over and he put his head on one side as if he understood. I gazed up at the roof where a little lizard was waiting motionless, ready to pounce on an unsuspecting fly, while a kaleidoscope of thoughts went through my head.

For six years, I had never really thought about the war coming to an end. We had only thought of one day, or maybe a week, at a time. At times, we seemed to be in such a predicament that only our arrogance kept us going; we were the only country not overrun, and America stood back waiting to see what was going to happen before the Japanese gave them no alternative but to come in. Thank God there was no more fighting and I would be able to go home to Peggy and go to bed with her every night soon; I hoped I could be a good husband.

Yet this may mean I would never fly again. I would be chucked out of the Air Force; they chucked Churchill out, so they can certainly chuck me out. Maybe I will never again get that thrill of bringing an aircraft into life—that puff of smoke as the engines start and the instruments start flickering; the feel of easing her off the deck; of watching a little shadow race along snow white clouds surrounded by a complete rainbow, the colours of the sunrise and sunset; the satisfaction of making a good landfall; the vivid blue of the Arctic and the dazzling white of Greenland; taking off for new places; looking down at the Holy Land; the great blokes I had met; and the things you shared with your crew. Gosh, I did not want to give up flying, working 9 to 5 every day with no thought that tomorrow you may push off to somewhere new and see new things. It would be great to be back with Peg, but there must be some way I could keep flying as well. That St Elmo's Fire was really quite pretty around the props and those balls floating around the flight deck were strange, but I certainly did not want to get in a cu-nim again and icing was not much fun either, but it was great to descend through thick cloud and see the strip lights right in front of you.

I could not really believe that I had seen the end of the war; I thought maybe I was dreaming as according to all the odds, I should not have. I must have been damn lucky; there was Cyril, St John, the Wingco, Little Titch, Les, Pete, Dick and the other lads on the Torbeaus, the keen lad who never made Rabat, then the lads up in Assam (seems as if I could go on and on), Cousin Henry only a mere youth, and my dear old Dad. I was glad I never had to do any bombing on civilians; the Germans were in their evil U-boats, but it was not the blokes we were after, just a shame that they had to be in those diabolical U-boats and those on the ships we torpedoed may have got off. The Japanese were another matter, though; I did not feel the same about them and they were all soldiers anyway, not civilians.

There was a knock at the door, David walked in and I hardly noticed him till he said, 'Oh, *sahib*. Is *sahib* not feeling well? Has *sahib* had too much *Puggle-pani*? Other *sahibs* all in mess making great jollification'.

'No, David,' I replied, 'I have just been dreaming. Dreaming about the war being over and how I came to India. Your India, David, I like your India'.

'Oh *sahib*, may you have many more beautiful dreams. I will tell *bhisti* to fill your bath—time you were getting changed for dinner'.

29
Getting the Folks Home

Signals were pouring in. Some squadrons were to be deleted from the 'requirements' list; others were moving location, some to places we had never heard of before, so we had to find out where they were. There were also urgent requirements for PR crews to locate prison camps in the jungles, crews for Libs, Halifaxes, and any transport aircraft to bring back prisoners and internees. It was our job to find the crews; thank goodness, other units had to find the aircraft. We picked up signals to maintenance units and between groups, instructing them to modify aircraft to carry passengers and convert others to carry stretcher cases. We had to cannibalise some crews to make up one suitable crew for the job in hand, maybe taking an experienced observer who had been on Bostons or Marauders, putting in a Lancaster pilot as co-pilot, and perhaps a wireless operator off something else and making them into a Lib crew. We were sending wireless operators off to make up the transport crews and so on, trying to keep abreast of the type of aircraft available, which kept being amended from day to day. It certainly kept us busy.

On top of this, the unit's move to Bhopal was still on, so Eric had to work on the transport arrangements, although we did not know how many chaps we would have in the pool during the first week of September, which was when we were supposed to go. Tom and Michael had extra work to do because they had to calculate a 'Release Group' number for everyone who passed through, which had to be shown on their documents. It seemed that this release group system had been worked out as soon as the war in Europe ended; it worked on age and length of service, and some of the very early groups had already been released as the strength was being reduced, although so far, it had not affected us out here. My release group worked out to be '32'. We were now not supposed to post anybody under a certain group as they were due for early release, but it was only academic as far as we were concerned as they were chaps too old for aircrew. One of the points that came up at one of the CO conferences was that whoever went with the advanced party to Bhopal should try to fix a small private anteroom in the mess for permanent staff where we could have a quiet drink after dinner without being constantly interrupted by chaps trying to find out where they were going to be posted.

Just to give us a bit more to do, the station commander decided that we were to provide as big a turnout as possible for a parade through Poona to mark the victory over Japan and the official end of the Second World War. This was not up our street at all; nevertheless, Steve said we had no option. Copey, Derek, and Ray could stay behind to run the ship, but Tom, Michael, Eric, and I should each lead a squad, with Steve himself at the head of our unit contribution. The chaps were detailed as to which squad they were to join and then the fun started. We practised marching; starting and halting; coming to attention and standing at ease; saluting and eyes right or left; and some wheeling for an hour and a half until sundown—much to the amusement of the watching servants. The next day, we did it again, this time wearing our proper gear and with Steve in charge. We practised our spacing and taking up the right positions by our squads; actually, we were not too bad after I got the timing of the command 'Halt' buttoned up.

Then the big day came. We formed up at the army barracks, led out by an army band. We were well back behind the Army chaps so could not hear the band too well. We marched around the cantonments, touched a bit of the town, ignoring the 'Quit India' graffiti on the walls (Congress were a bit stronger around here and in Bombay), back into the Cantonment and into Empress Gardens, where the Army chap with a civilian at his side (presumably a government fellow) took the salute.

Little Mark, the messenger, was overjoyed about the war being over. I usually tried to have a little talk with him when he came around in his pith helmet and big boots because he looked such a lonely soul and it was no life for an AC2 in India. He would ask if he could stroke Ginny, and sometimes, he would get quite 'carried away'. He told me he was a violinist but not as good a violinist as his brother Max, who was a pilot and trained in South Africa. His brother played in some of the big hotels in London. Sometimes, Max would let him join the orchestra for dances; he spoke of the beautiful ballrooms and the ladies in their beautiful gowns, and it sounded as if Max ran his own orchestra. He showed me a photo of his wife and his 'two little darlings'. He was ever so anxious to know how soon he would get home now the war was over, and I promised to let him know when I heard how the release groups were going. I thought how different Mark must be from his brother Max; I could never imagine Mark running his own orchestra or being a pilot, but maybe he became transformed when he had a violin tucked under his chin. I asked Smithy if he knew Mark's surname; he said, 'Yes, Jaffa'.

It was time to move. David was, of course, coming with us, although some of the servants did not want to move. Eric's arrangements went without a hitch. We had a whole train. It took a long time—almost thirty-six hours—as we kept getting shoved into sidings, but that did not matter as we were ready for the rest and the meals were well organised. It was a fairly long train as Eric had arranged first-class suites for all the officers and NCOs, a couple of wagons for the equipment and stores, plus a third-class wagon for the servants. The servants cooked their grub at the trackside and showed no mercy in fighting off the boarders who tried to hitch a free ride. Our two *chai wallahs* were in business every time the train stopped.

30
Our Time at Bhopal

I liked the look of Bhopal, the smart *coolies* on the station wearing crimson turbans and matching shirts and the women all seemed to be dressed in bright colours (bright green, scarlet pink, or bright yellow); some did not wear anything above the waist, which seemed an anomaly for a state with a Muslim ruler, although there were a few burkas floating around, which presumably had a woman underneath. It looked like an interesting town to explore.

Within twenty-four hours, we were all settled and back in business with a huge backlog of signals to wade through. Michael's first job was to organise some talks to the lads in the pool to gen them up on the religions of India, explaining to them that we were not now in British India but we were guests in a princely state ruled by a Muslim: His Highness the Nawab Mohammad Khan, Nawab of Bhopal. It was essential, therefore, that they understood something of the Muslim religion and that they did not get up to anything that may be overlooked in British India but would be frowned upon in a friendly princely state.

We had managed to fix up our private anteroom, which we shared with the other permanent staff officers on the station—they were very nice too, with a nice little bar. The billets were good too—a suite of three rooms for each of us with nice wide verandas front and back, and brick up to about 3 feet with wattle above. We took up two blocks, which we roped off with white rope, mainly to stop the chaps in the pool, who did not know any better, from wandering around and trying to give our servants orders.

Eric and I had the joint use of a smashing little Austin Tilley truck—about 8 or 9 hp; cabin at the front just like a car; spare wheel kept on the roof of the cabin; an open back that could seat three on each side facing inwards; drop-down tail-board; and a tailored canvas cover that when fitted over three metal hoops, completely enclosed the back. If ever we could not find Ginny and Tonic, we knew where to look as they would be sitting in it, but we never did figure out how they managed to jump in as they only had little legs. As they had grown their longer hair, it was almost impossible to tell them apart as the white marks on their faces were no longer so distinct. Many a chap thought he was having hallucinations when he walked out of my office to go into Eric's only to see the same dog sitting under Eric's table.

The station commander took Steve to be officially introduced to the Nawab. He reported that the Nawab seemed very pleased to have us here; he was an extremely polite, well educated, westernised gentleman, who, in spite of being Muslim, had offered them some very fine genuine malt Scotch and cigars. He had also extended an invitation for us to shoot in certain areas—some jungle hills where there were a few tigers and very many wild boars, and an open area where there were hundreds of Black Buck. Muslims do not touch pig, which they consider unclean, but apparently, it did not matter to him if we shot them and ate them; however, as Steve pointed out, we should not be seen to be bringing them openly through the town on the back of a truck. Steve said he would arrange for us to draw rifles from the guardroom if we felt like taking up the offer. It was funny what the Indians refer to as jungle as any land that is not cultivated seems to be either a desert or a jungle. They do not always mean a rainforest like those in Burma, with thick, almost impenetrable undergrowth; it may be just a few scattered trees or something like an English wood.

Tata Airline's Lockheed Loadstars kept dropping in. They had their buildings on the opposite side of the airfield. They seemed quite a smart outfit with their red-lettered aircraft. In fact, the whole airfield was smart, with good concrete runways and a nice hangar. Seeing these aircraft, however, made me wish I could get back on flying duties. I wondered whether I would ever fly again. This ground job was interesting and certainly gave me an insight into the admin. side of things. I appreciated the multiplicity of things that went on behind the scenes just to keep aircraft in the air—the supplies of things from aircraft and fuel down to office desks; the staffing and movement of personnel; the communications; medical requirements; the maintenance units; records and pay and goodness knows what—things we just took for granted when you only had to think of flying. I got a good idea of the setup from Air Command, through the groups and down to little units like ours, but I did not want to be stuck on the ground for the rest of my time in the Air Force. I sounded Steve out about the chances of being able to stay in the Air Force; he did not think there would be much chance but promised to let group know that I was interested. After a couple of weeks, we seemed to have got on top of things; the influx of signals had calmed down, so we were able to get more time off to explore and take up the offer of a shoot.

We got hold of a couple of mess servants, who were not Muslims, who reckoned that they were good at hunting and could gut a pig. So, armed with two rifles and our revolvers, we boarded the Tilley, with Ginny and Tonic in the front seat, the two servants (who had each brought a sharp kitchen knife) in the back, some lengths of rope, and a bucket (though I was not sure what that was for). We rattled on for about an hour on a reasonable but dusty road until we entered a wooded area, then turned off down a rough track into the trees. We had decided that we did not want to get too far away from the truck in case we needed it for shelter. The servants thought we had got to a good area, so we loaded up and then drove a bit further, Eric in the open back with the servants. Then we all sat in the back, with our rifles handy and waited. We could see quite a distance all around as the trees were not very thick, although in places, the undergrowth was tall enough to conceal a boar. We broke into some of the grub that we had with us. After some time, the servants reckoned that if we made a fire, that would attract something; we agreed to try it, but I hoped it would not attract one of the tigers.

The servants were sure we were in a good place. When they got a fire going, they started wandering around; we called them back but one indicated that if a boar came, he would climb up a tree and then we could shoot it when it stopped at the bottom. He was a damn sight more confident in our shooting ability than we were. We kept looking at where we thought funny noises kept coming from, but it turned out to be a monkey or a bird; there were all sorts of funny noises and queer calls and screeches. Eric and I did not wander far from the truck and always made sure we were looking in different directions. We avoided any undergrowth as one of the servants had spotted a couple of snakes.

I was beginning to think that we may as well pack it up as a bad job, especially as Ginny and Tonic wanted to run off into the grass and I was afraid that they would get bitten by a snake.

Then, one of the servants pointed to some spot quite a long way away, telling us there was something moving there. I picked up Ginny and Tonic, threw them in the cab and shut the door, and we jumped on the back of the truck. We were all eyes on the place the servant was pointing out, and sure enough, a big, ugly-looking boar walked into the open. Eric let go with his rifle; it let out a great grunt and turned straight towards us. Eric let it have another. This made it grunt even more and it started to run. As it came nearer, I let go. It was bloody wild now all right, coming straight at us, dragging one leg but going even faster. Only a head-on target to aim at now, I let another three rounds off and Eric was firing, too. Some if not all of our rounds were hitting it. I shouted to the servants to get another clip, but when it was within about 10 yards of us, it collapsed, still grunting.

It was a hot day but by God, we were both in a bloody great sweat by now. The servants were as excited as schoolboys. They jumped off the truck, chattering and shouting. One plunged his knife into the side of its neck, and we all had a fag, still keeping a lookout in all directions in case there was another bugger about. It seemed to have bullet holes all over it, and I now knew why they call them 'wild'. It had great sharp tusks and was a hell of a size. The servants were excitedly chattering between themselves; one indicated that we ought to cut its throat, so the other gashed its throat from side to side while the other tied a rope around its back legs. Blood was pouring from its throat. We started to drag it towards the truck. It was a hell of a weight. Eventually, the four of us managed to haul it into the back of the truck, but it was too long to go on; its front end was overhanging the tail board and its head hanging down and still pouring blood.

After a breather, we decided to go back up the rough track to the road. It was a good job that the Tilley had good springs as it was riding very low at the back. When we arrived at the road, we stopped for a conference as we could not drive down the road with the thing hanging out the back, dripping blood. The servants told us that it should be gutted because of the heat. We looked around for two suitable strong branches, drove the truck into position beneath them, and then tried to haul it up by the ropes tied to its back legs and slung it over the branches. The servants seemed to have the knack of tying the ropes.

Having got the thing hauled up to an angle of about 45 degrees, we drove the truck away and left it hanging with its snout just touching the ground. While Eric and I stood well to one side, one of the lads started cutting down its belly. Its intestines started falling out, and then he must have cut a bit too deep as he punctured its stomach; it was like puncturing a tyre as stuff blew out and there was a hell of a stink. After a while, he had all the guts and stomach out. They were in a pile on the ground, and some vultures were watching from up in the trees. I hated the sight of these damn things. It must have been a couple of hours since we had shot the thing. The bleeding seemed to have stopped, but how were we going to get it on the truck so it did not hang out the back? We backed up the truck, pulled on its front legs so it was now resting on the truck still with its back legs suspended. We put up the tail board to keep its head in, then lowered the back legs and by shoving it crossways, we got its rear legs down to the heights of the front metal hoop, to which we tied its legs. We replaced the other hoops, erected the cover, and all was out of sight. The vultures still had their eyes on the guts, which were now under the truck, and as soon as we moved off, they swooped down; those things made me shiver.

We had to drive back very slowly with all the weight in the back as the rear wheels kept bumping. It was getting dark as we reached Bhopal, so we had to be careful not to run into any unlit bullock carts. We were glad to get through the town and passed the mosques; if the damn thing had come loose and slipped out as we were passing a mosque, it would have started a riot. We handed the rifles in as we passed the guardroom, then drove round to the back of the mess. We nipped in to tell the lads that we had brought them the week's meat ration, so they had better see about getting it unloaded. We gave the two servants a couple of rupees each and asked the major-domo to keep us a late dinner and went for a very necessary bath. We had pork every night for a week, but we told the other lads that next time, they could go and get it and make sure to take a bigger truck.

We were honoured by a visit from the Groupie, along with another couple of officers from group on a call to see how we were getting on. He was a nice chap who spent a bit of time with each of us as he looked around the unit. He seemed to be well briefed; he asked how I was liking the admin job. I told him it was interesting but that I hoped I would get back on flying duties soon and I tackled him about chances of staying in. He did not seem very optimistic but said he would see what he could do. The party stayed overnight, but we did not see the Groupie and the station commander in the mess. Steve said that they were on a 'good relations' job with the Nawab. They had flown in, in an Expeditor of the communications flight; I did not see them come in as I was not involved in the reception party. I talked to their pilot quite a lot; he was a squadron leader who had a small release group number and expected to be going home soon. He told me the Expeditor was a lovely little aircraft to fly—two Pratt and Whitney 450-hp Wasp Juniors, could do 230 mph, had eight seats, and was capable of a range of 900 miles. I made a point of watching them take-off; it looked great and the undercarriage flashed up in no time at all as it was electric-driven.

We seemed to have got a particularly restless lot of lads in the pool. Some were nagging about having been sent out here, reckoning that 'their' war in Europe was over, even if they had not done anything towards it, and as this one was over too, they ought to go straight home; others, particularly the ex-bomber types, could not see why they could not be on the job of bringing prisoners back. I could understand how some of them felt, but the fact was that they were not suitable for vacancies that cropped up and the pity was that most of them had no interest in India whatsoever; they never even bothered to look at the town. Everywhere I went, I wanted to see as much as I could.

Steve called us all to a conference one morning to announce that the station commander had passed on an invitation from the Nawab for the officers on the permanent staff to be present at the palace one day the following week at 6 p.m., to take dinner with the Nawab and members of his court. Our names had been submitted to the palace by the station commander. Steve asked Michael to give us another rundown on the points we should bear in mind about the Nawab, his family, and the state in general. It was decided that we would wear blue, which none of us had had out of our trunks for a long time. Steve ran over a few points of etiquette. I realised that I had not yet had my flight lieutenant rings or my ribbons put on my best blue. Anyhow, David soon got that job seen to and my uniform pressed. He got a special job done on a blue shirt and collar and found a black tie. I had to scrounge around for some collar studs and buy some black socks. My shoes were OK when the mildew was rubbed off.

31
Dinner with the Nawab

When the great day came, David came up trumps. He had all my gear smartly laid out on the charpoy. I asked him, 'Why two handkerchiefs, David?' He replied, 'One is for up sleeve, *sahib*'. He smiled when he handed me my cuff-links as I had entirely forgotten about them; he did well to find them. As I glanced in the mirror, I thought that I did not look bad at all in my best blue; David seemed satisfied too as, hands together and head nodding, he remarked, '*sahib* looks very good; very British. I look well after Ginny'.

We arranged for cars to take us to the palace. Heading for the two tall slender minarets, we passed a few shanty huts—mud and dung or beaten-out tins, but there were not many in Bhopal—beyond the narrow crowded alleys leading to the bazaar, onto the wide streets, passing the fine buildings of the hospital, the Legislative Assembly and the Courts of Justice, and so to the gates of the big white palace. A guard in his smart crimson uniform ordered a subordinate to let us in and we drove through a lawn garden to the palace steps, where liveried servants opened the doors and others ushered inside and we were greeted by an imposing gentleman, who instructed someone else to take us somewhere.

The first port of call was a big room with a huge Persian carpet, leather armchairs and sofas, writing tables and chairs, tables piled with English magazines (*Illustrated London News*, *Tatler*, and *Punch*), and open boxes of cigars. However, this was only the 'anteroom' for the toilets. Off here was another room, divided into smaller ones, each containing the full range of toilet facilities, including a bath with gold fittings and a very decorative loo. Servants seemed to be everywhere. When they seemed to consider we had had long enough to wash, we were escorted to a big room; some of the other guests were already there—other chaps from the airfield, a few Army, and some civilians. A few brightly dressed chappies, presumably a reception party, greeted us with many smiles and beckoned the waiters to bring us drinks. There were silver trays with glasses of dry and sweet sherry or pink gin. I got talking to a fellow who was on the Resident's staff. He suggested that we should stroll outside, onto the terrace overlooking the lake, as it was approaching sundown, and the court chappies would not be joining us for another half hour; he had been here before. We chatted and time passed. 'Well, the sun's gone. We'd better join the others'.

Others were arriving now; in fact, the room was getting quite full. I kept being introduced to very polite, well-spoken gentleman, but I could not understand who they all were—various titles, some I presumed were government ministers. Most wore turbans, some with a cone or frills sticking out the top, whom I assumed to be Muslims; some with tails dangling down the back whom I assumed to be Hindus. Turbans of all colours, some to match the colour, or design of their long tunics buttoned up to the neck, showing only little of their tight white trousers. A few wore no headdress, their jet-black hair plastered down; most of these wore well-cut black or white suits, and long bow ties. One wore something like a fez. There were half a dozen or so English people—two wearing a cream-coloured military uniform with starched shirts, wing collars, and black bow ties; the others in white or black dinner jackets. The servants were still walking around with trays of drinks, but I decided to switch to '*neera*' (the juice of the coconut, a bit sweet but refreshing) as I did not want to get too piddled.

An announcement was made, and the servants in their long red tunics (with wide sashes around the waist, gold trimmings and badges of rank, white trousers, turbans, and gloves) took up their positions flanking the doorway. Then, the Nawab appeared, with the Resident on one side and a splendidly attired gentleman on the other. Everyone bowed towards the Nawab, so we did likewise. He was a very good-looking, tall, slim man, in an immaculate long white jacket, diagonal blue sash, a big shining Star of India and insignia of the Royal Victorian Order but, most eye-catching of all, a big brooch of glittering diamonds in his pale blue silk turban. He slowly moved among us, having a few words with everyone. He seemed a jolly friendly chap, smiling and putting everyone at their ease, obviously making a joke here and there. He commented on my wings, asking what I had flown and where; he even recognised the ribbon of the 'Atlantic Star'. From the way he talked, I gathered that he flew his own plane sometimes and that his eldest daughter also flew. I remembered to call him 'Your Highness', so that part went off OK. Eric remarked we ought to try to get a job flying for this bloke, especially as his eldest daughter (who was the heir) had recently divorced her husband. Trust Eric, I thought he was going a bit short in Bhopal.

More drinks were offered but I stuck to the *neera*. After a brief trip to the loo, it was time to be ushered into the dining hall. The organisation was so quietly efficient, and we were shown to seats so that all the way round the great long mahogany table; it was a guest and member or official of the court seated alternately. Two elegant gentlemen between whom I was seated smiled as they introduced themselves; they were both something Khan. I did not know what their positions were, but they seemed quite important. All the way down the middle of this long table were silver candelabras, alternating with silver bowls of roses. Places were set with silver cutlery, crested China side plates and cut-glass stemmed wine glasses. No sooner had the Nawab taken his seat and we had sat down to unfold starched Irish linen napkins, when a whole army of servants appeared and, almost simultaneously, the whole forty or fifty of us were served with a gamey-tasting soup. The servants took up station behind us; there seemed to be a servant each. Then, with a nod of the head and a quick gesture from the major-domo's white gloved hand, every soup plate simultaneously disappeared.

Conversation was no problem. I only had to ask a question and one or other of my companions would eagerly respond in a flow of delightful, colourful oratory for the next few minutes. These chaps had a wonderful command of the English language and rhetoric; they made a simple reply sound like a poem and were never stumped for words—big words, too, which I would be afraid to use myself.

The main course was a vegetable curry, with all sorts of vegetables. The chap on my right was anxious to explain all the extra bits and pieces: 'These are the chillies, the little green ones are very hot; do you like ginger? Those are cardamoms, strong and sweet; do you like coriander seeds? There's the mango chutney'. Several *abdars* were attending to our drinks, but to be on the safe side (as I had no idea how long the night might be), I had *nimbu pani* (lemonade), which seemed to please my companions, especially when I asked for it in their language; they liked that. It was fascinating to watch the masterful control that the major-domo had of the servants. A tall imposing figure in his red jacket carrying four gold stripes on the sleeve, he had eyes everywhere; however, he hardly ever moved, just a nod of the head or a quick movement of the hand and the servants knew just what to do.

The dessert was rice pudding with a difference—sprinkled with almonds, raisins, and other fruits, surmounted with silver leaves, which my companions ate, as did I, but they did not seem to taste of anything.

By then, we were all very relaxed. Big bowls were placed in front of us holding pomegranates, pears, and mangoes. We leisurely picked up the pomegranates with little silver forks and got our hands sticky with the pears and mangoes, all the time in intent conversation. There was a toast to the King Emperor followed by a toast by the resident to His Highness Sikander Sanlat Iftikharul-Mulk, Nawab Mohammad Hamidulla Khan Bahadur, companion of the Order of the Star of India and commander of the Royal Victorian Order. Cigars were then handed around, or rather we were offered a selection from three different boxes and servants stood by to light them.

However, the meal was not yet at an end. The major-domo, having decided that we had all finished picking at the fruit, gave the signal for the tables to be cleared. Silver finger bowls miraculously appeared, soon to be whipped away and replaced by something wrapped up in a leaf. I learned that this was 'pan', a betel leaf with lime paste, stuffed with grated nuts, aniseed, and cardamom. It certainly cleared your mouth out, and after this, I decided that I would accept a Scotch whisky; it tasted like the finest malt. One of my companions apologised for there not being any champagne as the Nawab's supply was sadly depleted because he could not get it from France because of the war. The following was pointed out to me:

> There was no 'India' until the British came. When our Queen Elizabeth (the First) approved of the East India Company starting to trade out here it was only called East India to distinguish it from the West Indies. It was a subcontinent, partly ruled by a declining Mogul Emperor; two stable states in the south and the rest were a lot of feuding rulers all fighting each other. It was the British that brought the subcontinent under the one head and called it India. English became the great unifying language. The pity is that, in those areas

where you could not make Treaties with the local rulers you were obliged to defeat them, for the good of the country as a whole. I do not think you always sent your best men. You shut yourselves away in cantonments, set up your exclusive clubs and did not mix with the local people. The British have brought us good administration, guided us in government, built roads, railways and irrigation schemes, but only a few have wanted to make India their home. They have made good money and returned to England. We would have liked more of you to settle here. This has created the climate, in British India, for the rise of the Congress Party who want early independence.

Continuing our conversation in the splendid drawing room with its walls draped in pale blue silk, we got on to lighter subjects. We talked about the products of the state—rice, wheat, sugar cane, and poppies—and of the teak forests yielding fine timber. I remarked that these palace buildings did not look very old, not as old as many an English country house. I learned that nearly all the prince's palaces were built after the proclamation in 1877 because prior to that, the position of the princes was not secure; they had to spend large sums on maintaining armies, but when Queen Victoria guaranteed them security, they now no longer needed armies except for ceremonial purposes, as the British would defend their treaty rights, so they set about building themselves fine palaces.

The Nawab, who had been mixing and talking to various people, had now departed. The servants were still offering drinks and little sweetmeats. A youngish fellow, whom it would seem had only recently joined the administration here, remarked how wonderful it was when we could meet and talk together like we had been doing that night. We were of different religions, from different races, and from different backgrounds, but we were all British and with our different cultures and skills, we could do so much together. Nowhere in British India (those states taken over by and administered by the British and not run by local princes under treaty agreements) would we be able to do that. He had given up a good position in Delhi to come there, partly because of the 'over' government there and the red tape, but mainly because of prejudice that prevented him becoming friendly with those from England. 'Here it is so refreshing as we all work happily together and we get things done'.

It was a little after midnight when we left. David arose from his mat outside my door as he heard us coming; he lit the Tilley lamp, put my clothes away as I got into the mosquito net, put out the lamp, and went back to his mat on the veranda. India sure is a country of contrasts.

The pace of life had now slowed down compared with when I first joined the unit, when we were all working harder than prize bulls in the mating season. Derrick (the doctor) seemed to be busier than the rest of us as he had to see everyone on the station for a pre-release medical, presumably so that the Air Ministry would have details if anyone claimed that they had suffered some disability while in the service. Indications were that Group 32 would come up for release around about March 1946, so it looked as if I only had about four months left, unless they let me stop in. It was nice there, but I hoped I would be able to get back to flying somehow, although there did not seem much chance of that now.

Then little Mark came into the office with his signals. He inquired, as usual, if I had any news about how the release groups were going, and I assured him that he would be going home soon. As I went through the signals, I spotted: 'PILOT. MIN 2000 HRS TWIN OR MULTI. 2ND CLASS NAV. WARRANT. ADMIN EXPERIENCE. SLDR OR FLT. FOR OC COM FLIGHT BEGUMPET. REFER GROUP BEFORE ACTION'. I read through this signal two or three times, grabbed my cap, and nipped out to see Steve, with little Ginny hard on my heels.

Handing him the signal, I inquired, 'Have you seen this, Sir?' He read it a couple of times and handing it back remarked, 'We haven't anybody to fit that, have we?' 'Yes, sir, we have one chap', I replied. 'Have we. Who is it?' 'It's me. Will you put me in for it, sir?'

He promised that he would, saying that as an ex-pilot himself, he appreciated how I would like to get back on flying and that it looked as if this admin. job might have been a good thing after all. He thought that this unit might be closing down soon anyway and with the reduction in work, Eric could run the postings job along with movements. I would feel a bit sorry to be leaving Eric as we had done a lot together, both on the squadrons and since we had been back in India. Without Eric's company, there were a lot of things I would not have done and seen, especially in Bangalore, but he was due for release before me anyway and he might be off within a couple of months. Anyhow, I had not got the job yet.

In about a week, Steve told me that someone from group would be dropping in the next day for a few hours on their way south and they wanted to see me. I heard the Expeditor arrive, and shortly afterwards,

Steve ushered a Groupie and a squadron leader into my office. The squadron leader was the chap I spoke to in the mess on his previous visit. I did not know quite what to do when a Groupie called on me; I stood up, of course, but should I put my cap on? Anyway, he took his off so I figured that I did not need mine. We chatted very informally about the job with Ferry Command and on the Libs. He inquired why on earth I elected to go on Torbeaus after Libs but did not seem bothered about what I had done since coming out here. Then the Groupie left with Steve and the squadron leader suggested that as they would not be leaving for an hour, I may as well see what I thought of the Expeditor. I reckoned that this was not to see what I thought of the Expeditor but to see what he thought of me.

We got in—it was a posh little affair—he pointed out the controls, told me some speeds, and said, 'How about having a go?' It was dual control; he sat on the right and gave me a few tips, especially as regards speeds on the approach. I did a couple of circuits without bending anything. On the way back in the Tilley, he remarked that he hoped I got the job and then he would be away on release. 'If you do get it you will be made up to acting squadron leader'. They had a spot of tiffin then pushed off.

For several days, I heard no more. Then Steve sent a message for me to go and see him. 'You've got the job. Congratulations. Posted to Begumpet, as from the 5th—that's five days' time—as acting squadron leader, O.C. Group Communications Flight Detachment. That will cost you a few drinks tonight, acting squadron leader'.

It cost me a few drinks for a few nights. I told David I was moving. At first, his face dropped. Then I told him that I wanted him to come with me. 'Yes, *sahib*. Very good, *sahib*. Thank you, *sahib*. Where do we go? When do we move out?' He was a great one for 'moving out'.

'We go to Secunderabad, David. That's the cantonment part of Hyderabad—they call the airfield Begumpet. I'm being promoted to squadron leader to be in charge of a small unit. I'll be flying again as well'.

'Oh *sahib*, that is indeed very good news—now you are *bara sahib*. Do we take Ginny?' 'Yes, David. He will miss his brother, but Tonic's *sahib* will probably be moving soon—going back to England, but he will not be able to take Tonic to England'. 'Oh. That is very sad. Shall we take Tonic too?'

I gave Eric the job of fixing up our train arrangements. It was quite a long way—400 miles in a straight line, almost due south, more than half the way back towards Bangalore—but quite a bit further by train on Great Indian Peninsular Railway on a roundabout route through Nagpur to Chanda, then the Nizam's State Railway to Secunderabad. It was about a two-day job including waits and changes.

I obtained some squadron leader epaulettes to swap over on my way to the station. Eric took us down. David attended to all my gear in his usual efficient manner so that I had nothing to bother about except to look after Ginny; I had found him a collar and lead as I could not risk him getting under the train when we got out at the numerous stops. I felt rather sad saying goodbye to Eric as we had shared many experiences together; we had taken good care of each other. Yet, as the train drew away and I waved to him from the window, I realised how little I really knew about him, other than he had been a damn good pal and he liked the women.

32

Flying Again

Our arrival at Begumpet must have been a funny sight. A Jeep had been sent to pick us up at the station. We drove through the wide, tree-lined streets of Secunderabad on a pleasantly hot, sunny afternoon, with Ginny sat on my knee, paws up on the front to see where we were going; looking around, I caught sight of David. There he was, in his best mess attire, sitting on top of my two tin trunks, erect and arms folded, as if he had been making a triumphant entry after a battle. On arrival at the guardroom, he leapt down and presented his identity papers, saluting the LAC on duty. I saw some Tiger Moths flying around and hoped that they had nothing to do with me.

There were very nice quarters and, as usual, David had unpacked and got me organised in no time. He had the other servants sorted out, too. He was jabbering to them in a most authoritative manner with lots of gesticulations and head nodding; they seemed to take the hint that he meant business. A sweeper was soon rushing around the floor in a crouching position, flicking away with his bunch of twigs; another one had charged the thunderbox. The *bhisti* had filled my *chatti* and another one was given the Tilley lamp to get it filled. David asked where I would like *memsahib's* photo and at which side of the charpoy would I like the Tabriz rug. I decided that David deserved a rise. How these fellows existed on so little I never knew. They seemed to be able to live on just a few annas a week, and I knew that David was perfectly honest—at least as far as I was concerned. Early on, I had purposely left a few annas lying around and he had told me off about it, saying it was a temptation to the sweepers. I was getting a rise, so I did not see why he should not benefit, too. He seemed embarrassed when I told him that I was going to give him another rupee a week. I told him it was 'an order', so he smiled, put his hands together, and nodded.

The departing squadron leader, who I knew as Frank, introduced me around the mess. Then, blow me, I spotted Dave, now a flight lieutenant. Making my way over to him, he spotted me; we were then shaking hands and saying something corny like, 'Blow me, how did you get here?' Frank came up, 'You two know each other then?' 'We sure do, but only for a few hours—Dave here came to fish me out of Burma in his little Stinson'.

Frank introduced me to some others in the unit. There was Roger, a tall flying officer pilot; Chester, our middle-aged engineering officer; Arthur, our adjutant-cum-administrative officer; Ken, a flying officer pilot wearing the DFC; Don, a flight lieutenant observer with the Atlantic Star, so I knew he must be alright; and Vic, a flight lieutenant pilot. We all had a pleasant evening in the mess, where I expected they were weighing me up and wondering how their new OC would make out, so I played it softly but told them on leaving the mess that I was looking forward very much to working with them. I meant it. They seemed a jolly good bunch.

The next morning, Frank explained we were now called SHQ Comm. Flight (Southern Headquarters). There were other communications flights based in Delhi, Calcutta, and Karachi. Our 'area' was the whole of India south of 24 degrees north (as far east as 84 degrees east) and Ceylon—an area getting on for 400,000 square miles, over three times the area of the whole of the British Isles. He pointed out the main airfields to which I would find myself going and roughly how long each would take in the Expeditor, cruising at about 180 mph—Bombay, 380 miles (two hours and ten minutes); Poona, 320 miles (one hour and fifty minutes); Bhopal, 400 miles (two hours and fifteen minutes); Madras, 325 miles (one hour and fifty minutes); Kolar, 300 miles (one hour and forty minutes); Yelahanka, 300 miles; and Columbo, 725 miles (four hours). There may be the odd trip to Delhi, 775 miles (four hours and twenty minutes); or Calcutta, 725 miles (four hours).

> At present we have one Expeditor, two Daks, an Oxford, and a Proctor. Although we can carry a passenger in the Proctor, we usually only use it for taking documents and suchlike—your pal Dave is the Proctor specialist. Roger, Ken, and Vic fly the Daks and sometimes Dave goes as co-pilot. There is also a flight sergeant Dak pilot—

Kevin. I try to work it so they all get an even share, but if one of them fancies a particular trip, I try to oblige, although you'll find they all want a trip to Columbo. Anyone can fly the Oxford, except Dave, as he is not qualified for passengers on twins. We keep the Expeditor for Senior Officers and VIPs. HQ will expect you to do those trips yourself so, the Expeditor is virtually your aircraft and it's up to you who you take along as co-pilot but check up on the passengers first, as Groupie P. and one of the Wingcos at HQ like to be in the co-pilot seat themselves. When I'm away, I leave Vic to sort things out here; he knows the ropes. If Vic is away as well, Arthur takes over. I'll show you how the Flight Requests and other stuff comes in from HQ and how I plan things. Luckily, we are near enough to HQ to have a reasonable phone line which saves a lot of time. We've just time to pop over and see the NCOs and others before tiffin. This afternoon, we'll have a look at Chester and his maintenance setup—they are a good, reliable lot of lads. Then I'll run through the bumph which I have in the office and show you what I do about it. After that, if there is time, I'll get Arthur to show you his Admin setup.

It had been quite a day. I asked a lot of questions, some of which I hoped did not sound stupid.

After dinner, Frank suggested that he introduced me to the club. He invited Dave to join us. On the way, he remarked that I should take charge of the Jeep when he left; it was for my personal use. Although it was dark, Secunderabad seemed a nice, clean place, with wide roads, plenty of trees and gardens, and big white houses; also, it was pleasantly cool. Frank pointed out that although we were in a princely state, Secunderabad was a cantonment, built and planned by the British; the town of Hyderabad was about 5 miles away, at the other side of the river—a big, busy, and interesting town with lots to see.

The Secunderabad Club was a sprawling white building, in large grounds of lawns, flower beds and trees. First impressions were favourable. It seemed to have a much better atmosphere than the Poona Club, but I doubted whether it could match the Bangalore one. Membership was soon arranged, and I was introduced to some chaps from HQ. There seemed to be a lot of 'top brass' around, both Air Force and Army.

The photograph of the Nizam prompted me to inquire whether there was anything in particular I ought to know about him, adding that I knew he was regarded as the first among the princes; number one of the big five; a twenty-one gunner; a Muslim; ruler of the largest of the princely states; a staunch supporter of the British; very wealthy; and a miser but was supposed to have a very big harem.

'That's right', said Frank, 'Hyderabad is nearly as big as the whole of Britain, certainly bigger than England and Scotland together. The revenue is about £7 million. They say he has gold and stones worth more than £50 million tucked away in his vaults. He's a bit of a miser who doesn't go in for ostentation or entertaining. He's never been to Europe but is a great supporter of the British—he has to be when, as a Muslim, 90 per cent of his subjects are Hindu—he gave us enough cash for a Squadron of Hurricanes—110 "City of Hyderabad" Squadron—they are now on Mozzies'.

I had another day with Frank. Our first job was to arrange to send Roger, Arthur, and a flight sergeant wireless operator to Minneriya, Ceylon, in one of the Daks. They were to take some Naval chaps who were on their way down from Delhi and came in the previous night, together with some equipment. HQ had a couple of RAF fellows who wanted to go to Ceylon, too, so Frank arranged for them to get down there straightaway, so that they could go on the same aircraft. Then we visited the station commander and his various officers; after tiffin, we went across the airfield to see the folks who were flying the Tiger Moths. I had mentioned to Frank that I did not like the idea of these Tiger Moths buzzing around when we were taking off or landing as none of them would have had radios. He explained that they belonged to an Indian Air Force EFTS and that 'it was each of our pilots' responsibility, to phone both the CO of the School and the Control Tower well before take-off, telling them the approximate time we would be leaving, then they would ensure that their aircraft were all on the ground. Similarly, on returning, call control at least half an hour beforehand, giving the ETA and they would see they were all on the deck; nevertheless, keep your eyes peeled'. The Indian CO was ever so fussy to see us and show us his set up. He even wanted me to 'have a go' in one of his Tiger Moths, but I declined as I was not going to make a fool of myself in front of the pupils. Most of them seemed to be Sikhs; at least, they were wearing dark blue turbans. Back at the office, there was a request to bring four chaps from Madras. The most economical thing to do was to get Roger to call at Madras on his way back the following day; they would still be in the air so we got signals section at HQ to contact them on W/T, instructing them to return via St Thomas's Mount. We also sent a signal to Minneriya just to make sure there was no slip up. Frank said they would probably return with half a dozen other chaps; there were always guys wanting a lift. Roger would not want to stay long at Madras as it was their monsoon time and would be hot, wet, and sticky.

I was beginning to get the hang of things. Frank thought it would be a good idea if we ran down to SHQ, so that I could meet the folks there, know what they looked like, and what they did, which would make it easier when dealing with them and it would be all the better if they knew me. On the way, I asked him who I actually came under now. He advised me 'as regards local station matters, the station commander but, for "operational matters" you come directly under SHQ'. They seemed a pleasant lot; everyone I saw, from a Groupie down, was helpful and made me feel at home. I was particularly interested in the signals and the W/T set up—how I could contact them when away, either in the air or on the ground and how I could get hold of the lads when they were away. I got on with the chap in charge in this section like a 'house on fire', particularly when he knew I had been on a wireless course myself and could cope with Morse up to a reasonable speed. In the meantime, Frank had been seeing someone about his release and told me he would be leaving for Bombay in three days' time.

So far, about the only thing I had not done was bother about the aircraft, so the next day, after we had dealt with the usual bumph, we decided we would devote the rest of the day to the Expeditor. I liked it. It was nicely laid out at the front with plenty of elbow room and fully fitted for dual control. There did not seem to be many knobs, buttons, or instruments because there was no need for gun, rocket, or bomb releases, gun sights, and all the other operational paraphernalia. There was a nice view out the front and it was nice to see two reliable looking radial engines again, even though they were only 450 hp each. With a wingspan of 47 feet 8 inches and twin fins at the tail, she looked as if she would be nice and stable. She looked a bit clumsy on the ground as the fuselage was at quite a steep angle. There were eight very nice seats in the cabin and a door so that the cabin could be shut off. Frank said the first ones were built in 1936 by the Yanks as a 'Feederliner'; this was a Mark II. He reminded me of the levers, switches, and the like, which he had shown me at Bhopal and also how the autopilot worked. He pointed out where the maps were kept; he had a complete set on board.

When I came across a box full of pendants, I inquired what they were for. There were different pendants for all ranks from group captain upwards. 'When arriving at an airfield, as you are taxiing in, open the side window and stick the appropriate pendants in that little tube on that bracket. Leave it there until the Groupie, or whatever, gets out. Do the same before taxiing out for take-off, but don't forget to bring it in before you start the take-off'. He suggested that I should keep a spare set of toilet gear and a change of kit in the plane; 'it's useful if you have an unexpected overnight stop'. Having checked with control that there were no Tiger Moths airborne, we started up, took off, and did a couple of circuits so I could get the feel of my new steed: the Beechcraft Expeditor Mark II. I liked it and it was great to be flying again.

I suggested to Frank that I ought to try a few single-engined approaches so that I did not find myself having to do one for the first time with some 'big bug' sitting next to me. He thought it was a good idea, so we did several approaches with one or other of the engines cut. Then we flew around so that I could get a general impression of the surroundings, some of the time with one engine cut so that I could see what affect it had on the other. I was very happy with the way she performed; that big tail plane and twin fins seemed to make her easy to trim. I saw the sprawling town of Hyderabad on the banks of a river and a lake between there and Secunderabad; both places looked to be all white in brilliant sunshine. Yet 40 miles to the north, we saw a huge lake; it must have been at least 20 miles long, with a wide river running in one end and out the other. The countryside was a bit odd-looking—mostly a flat bare plain with huge boulders sticking up here and there as if they had been dropped at random. As well as the lakes, there were numerous little rivers, so the area seemed OK for water in spite of only getting about 30 inches of rain during the year.

On our way back, Frank suggested that we should drop in at Hakimpet, which was only a few miles north of Begumpet. 'It's a maintenance unit and they do our major inspections there, so it's as well if you get to know them'. It was a surprise to see a place like this—big concrete runways and large hangars—almost like an RAF peacetime station. There were all sorts of aircraft here from unserviceable Stirlings down to Tiger Moths. It seemed to be a sort of receiving depot for aircraft arriving in the country and for carrying out modifications, repairs, and servicing. The chaps we saw in control and at the hangar seemed a matey lot until I remarked about the Stirlings: 'Wish we'd never seen the goddamned things with their stupid controls—can't get the spares, so the things will just stay here and rot'. A nice little fifteen-minute trip saw us back to Begumpet. Nothing much had happened while we had been away, so there was time for an hour on the charpoy before having my bath. The temperature here was just nice—about 80 degrees at midday pleasantly cool in the evening although I was told it was very hot in the summer, averaging about 115 and often reaching 120 degrees, which sounded jolly hot. At 1,776 feet, we were fairly well up but not as high as Bangalore.

The following day, Frank left me to get on with it. I signed the first 'Unit Routine Order', which, among a few other things, gave notice that I was taking over the unit. We had a good night in the mess to see Frank on his way. I would have liked to have flown him over to Bombay as he had been most helpful to me over the handover, but I had to take a Groupie and two Wingcos to Madras and would probably stop overnight.

33
The Best Job in the RAF

You did not get a weather forecast for each trip out here like you did in Europe, where the weather is changing every five minutes. It only changes here four times year. Until the end of February, I knew we would be getting steady north-easterlies; until the end of December, these would be bringing the 'winter monsoon' to the east coast around Madras. The winter monsoon was not supposed to be anything like as bad as the summer monsoon, which hits the west coast, but I decided to check with St Thomas's Mount to make sure there was not a cyclone hanging about over the Bay of Bengal. They said it was OK—raining with some pools on the runway but the cloud base was 1,000 feet. I made sure that the Groupie, who was sitting up front with me, knew that I had checked on the weather and also that Don (who I had brought with me) was OK on the W/T, just in case we needed any W/T assistance.

As we crossed the Kistna River, climbing over the Eastern Ghats, there was a hell of a build-up of cloud and it got rather bumpy. I did not fancy bouncing about in this all the way to Madras, so I turned east towards the coast. When sure we were over the Ghats, I lost a little height and could soon see the ground and the coastline, which we followed south to Madras. As we approached Madras, it was raining cats and dogs, but at least the visibility was OK. We were warned about surface water on the runway. It came lashing up as soon as our wheels touched; I immediately whipped up the flaps to avoid damage. I got my arm soaked while sticking up the Groupie's pendant as we taxied in. They thanked me for the trip—they were all nice chaps—and provisionally arranged that we would return about midday the next day and suggested that we should stay in the Connemara Hotel, which was where they would be, so if there was any change of plans, they would let me know that evening. After seeing control and arranging for the aircraft to be taken care of and refuelled, Don and I set off by taxi for the Connemara.

Several hundred yards before we arrived at the hotel, the taxi could go no further. There was deep water right across the road. We were not going to get out and stand in the rain. Lots of folks had gathered around, all shouting and pointing. We eventually discovered that a river, which had a bend in it here and then snaked round behind the hotel, had burst its banks. After a while, two young lads appeared with rickshaws and said they would take us through. So we paid off the taxi driver and each got on a rickshaw. The lads set off, racing each other, the water nearly coming up to their waists; we lifted our legs up to keep them dry and we got through. We did not do any sightseeing; in fact, we did not leave the hotel until it was time to go to the airfield. It was a much better morning, but I had decided to fly back another way. We headed inland, almost to Bangalore, on the high plateau, and then turned north for home; we got out of the bad weather much quicker that way.

Almost immediately, another trip came up, this time to Bombay. There was no problem with the weather here—a blue cloudless sky but stinking hot, around about 90 degrees. What I did not like, however, was the bloody shitehawks. Turning in over Juhu Beach and heading for the runway, you passed by a packed shanty town; hovering overhead, there seemed to be hundreds of these black devils that went flashing past in all sorts of attitudes as we were on the approach. I never liked these things when I first arrived in India and I liked them even less now since that one (or something similar) hit us over Burma. Santa Cruz airfield at Bombay was certainly not one of my favourites.

Things seemed to be going OK. I made a point of being equally friendly with all the chaps on the flight so that no one could accuse me of favouritism; usually, they were able to pick their own trips. The ground lads did a good job without being told, as the aircraft were well-serviced and kept very clean. When I went to the club, I used to ask who wanted to join me rather than anyone in particular. Everyone seemed happy, and above all, I was getting on average about two trips a week. The flying was most pleasant. I was getting to know some of my 'regulars' quite well; the higher the rank, the more relaxed and amiable they seemed to be. One Groupie and one Wingco in particular loved to get in the co-pilot's seat and be in the air again; I could understand how they felt as it seemed to be such a pleasure for them to be away from the desk job for an hour or two. The atmosphere on the plane was great. As soon as they stepped aboard, it was taken for granted that I was 'the boss'; rank made no difference now and we all were all pals together. Conversely, as soon as we left the aeroplane, I was just squadron leader (acting). However, I got damn well looked after when we were away. At a station, some junior officer—a pilot officer or flying officer—was usually detailed to see I was taken to the mess or shown to a room and the maintenance chaps would fuss about the aircraft. Now and again, someone would ask if 'so-and-so' ever lets any gen slip out on some subject or other. To this, I replied, 'No, I'm only the taxi driver'. It was, however, handy knowing these chaps from SHQ, as a flight sergeant observer was about to leave us on release and I asked Groupie P. if there was any chance of Douggie (my old observer) joining us. He said he saw no reason why not and he would look into it. I had felt a bit bad about leaving Douggie in Bhopal as although I could not do much with him socially due to the British 'caste' system, he had, after all, hitched his way from Iraq to India to rejoin me and we had been through a few things together.

So to my second Christmas in India. Headquarters assured me that we would not be called upon for two or three days, so we were able to have some late nights in the mess and one at the club, but somehow, I felt lonely. I could not really be one of the lads and could have no 'special buddy' like I had always had before. I had to treat them all the same, although I did have a slight leaning towards Dave, perhaps because we had first met 'in our scruff' while on the job, not always on our best behaviour and properly dressed, like we were here. I reckoned that I had the best job in the RAF—running my own little airline, my own transport, free access to SHQ and all the rest of it, but what I would give if Peggy and I could be living in one of those bungalows in Secunderabad. On the other hand, if we did, we might turn into a pair of those rather boring 'cantonments types'. We served the Christmas lunch to the airmen on Christmas Day, after watching a soccer match between our lads and the Indian Air Force boys in the morning. They beat us in spite of most of them playing in their bare feet, and it was not even their Christmas.

Into January, the Groupie told me that Douggie was coming to join us and that he was now a warrant officer, not a flight sergeant. I thanked him and mentioned again the possibility of my staying in the RAF when I got back to the UK. He did not think there was much chance of this; the only thing I could do would be to write to the Air Ministry in London, inquiring the position as regards permanent commissions. He did, however, give me the gen on who to write to regarding civil jobs and said he would have no objection to giving his name for reference purposes, so I dashed off four letters, giving them my home address and telling them I expected to be released in March or April.

Douggie duly arrived and seemed delighted to think that he was going to get in the air again. About this time, I had done an assessment of the aircraft usage and came to the conclusion that we did not need the two Dakotas—one would be enough. By a bit of forward planning and routing and diverting aircraft that were away on a trip, we did not need both Daks in the air at the same time. There seemed no need for Chester and his men to be servicing two aircraft when one would do; he agreed, so we arranged for the one that was shortly due for a major inspection to go to Hakimpet from where it could be re-allocated to someone who needed it. Shortly after this, Vic left us to go up to Delhi and take over their Comm. Flight for which he was promoted to acting squadron leader, so that gave rise to a good farewell party.

Ceylon must be the most beautiful place in the world. How I would have liked to have spent more time there. In January, a job arose to take some 'high-up' Naval chaps, who had been flown down to us from Delhi, down to the Naval base at Trincomalee and to bring back a mixed party from Southeast Asia Command HQ at Kandy. As we approached the island, it looked to be the greenest place I had seen for years; we saw beautiful beaches, rolling surf, lush vegetation, coconut palms, and all sorts of trees. There were rivers and lakes, making it look like paradise. We landed at Minneriya about 50 miles south-south-west of Trinco. There were Liberators here. I spoke to some of the chaps to see whether any of them had come across Peter, but they had not. I wondered whether he was still down on one of the islands. I would have liked to have seen him and shown that I had caught him up in rank, even though he had had over two years' start.

Dave was with me. After dropping the passengers, we decided to get around to Ratmalana, just south of Colombo on the other side of the island, in the hope that we would have time to look around a little before the return flight in the morning. We did not fly direct but decided to fly round by the south, south of the high ground rising to nearly 8,000 feet, then have a look at the coast on the way up to Ratmalana. The whole island was covered in green, except for the numerous rivers; there did not seem to be a bare spot. There were tea plantations on the slopes, Buddhist shrines dotted about, paddy fields, then trees, trees, and more trees, which we later learned could be banana or rubber; some were masses of colour and there were fields of crops that we could not identify. As we approached the coast at the south-west tip, we saw huge, white rollers along the shore. I did not think anywhere like this really existed. We went up this exotic coast to Ratmalana, about 10 miles south of Colombo, but I almost felt like doing another trip around the island.

We booked in, saw to the aircraft being refuelled and the usual daily service, and contacted the folks at Kandy to let them know we were there. We were asked to be ready to leave at 10 a.m. the following day, so we were not going to have time to see much as it would be dark in a couple of hours. By the time we got to the hotel at Mount Lavinia and got booked in, there was not much time left. Mount Lavinia was not up in the high ground like you might expect; it was right on the coast, not far from the airfield. It got dark very quickly, so after a wash, we just managed to get out in time to watch the big red sun quickly disappear below the horizon—what a romantic spot, the old-fashioned, elegant hotel right by the beach and surrounded by gently swaying coconut palms. At times like that, I missed Peggy. That was about all we had time to see of Ceylon. Yet no wonder Lord Louis decided to locate his Supreme Command Headquarters here at Kandy. Someone in the hotel told us that Kandy was the most beautiful and pleasant spot in the whole of Ceylon, set by a lake, up in the hills with a perfect climate; there were lots of Wrens there too.

We had to fish out a full air marshal's pendant for the return flight and what a nice fellow he was, our air officer commanding. Shortly after take-off, Dave nipped back and asked him if he would like to sit up front. He accepted the invitation and thanked me for asking him. He seemed interested in the airplane, so I offered him the controls and he hand flew for the best part of an hour. He seemed to enjoy it. We dropped into Yelahanka to drop off a couple of the party. We did not stay long, just time for the passengers to be taken over to the mess for a drink and a snack, while I took on a bit more fuel and had a cup of char. It was nice to see Bangalore again, if only from the air, but the only person I saw who I knew was one airman. Just a gentle one hour and forty minutes and we were back in Begumpet. Some chaps from SHQ whipped the passengers away for the night. The next morning, someone from the Delhi flight was to pick them up to take them up to Delhi. It turned out to be Vic, who came in just before sundown and spent the night with us. He was anxious to know what the AOC was like.

We had our funny episodes, too. Once, shortly after we had landed and the passengers had disembarked, I was looking out of the window as I took the pendant in and noticed that our distinguished passenger, who was talking to the reception committee, had no 'scrambled egg' on the peak of his cap. Looking around the flight deck, I saw his cap; he had picked up mine. Now I could not very well walk out wearing a cap bearing scrambled egg, so I had to go to the door, wave an arm around, and beckon someone to come to me. I gave them the hat and told them to smuggle it to the rightful owner. Shortly after, my hat was returned and our distinguished passenger gave me a wave as the party moved off, all correctly dressed.

Then there was the time I was taking a party, headed by my favourite Groupie, Groupie P., (who never would let on whether the AOC was his brother) around several stations on a four-day tour—Yelahanka, Kolar, Ulundurpet, St Thomas's Mount, and Sholavaram; the latter was a most attractive little airfield, just north of Madras, with all the buildings and *bashas* set in tall palm trees, the *bashas* very ornamental and a smashing little mess. One of the jobs this party had to carry out was to sit at a court martial, so there was a judge advocate (or some such thing) with them—a real miserable little squadron leader with a cap that looked as if it had a gramophone record stuck in it to keep it flat. He had nothing to do most of the time, so I kept bumping into him and he was a pain in the neck; he was the sort of bloke who always looked for trouble. He asked me if I flew in shorts and my sleeves rolled up because it was against Air Ministry orders. I told him, 'Maybe I do, sometimes'. Yet, what I did not tell him was that in the front of the plane, I kept my old jungle suit, which, having been bashed against the rock so many times by the *dhobi wallahs*, was nice and soft, thus making a very useful 'overall'. I slipped it over my clean clothes when I got in the plane and took it off before getting out, so that I arrived looking reasonably smart; also, I had maps and things stuffed in the pockets. Well, when we were ready to leave one place, this chap was already in his seat as I went forward. He caught my arm; I could see him looking down at my bare knees and he was just about to say something. I told him I could not stop now, but he could come up to see me after we got airborne. I closed the door to the flight deck behind me and put on the jungle suit as the other passengers took their seats. Groupie P. came to sit beside me and we were on our way. Ten minutes or so after take-off, the cabin door opened and in came this miserable little chap. I turned around and saw he was about to go back, but I called him and shouted in his ear, 'What did you want that was so important?' He replied, 'Nothing', but I held his arm and insisted that it must have been something, had he lost his memory? He did not know what to say, so I suggested he wanted to know whether I flew in shorts; I did, did he want to see them? Afterwards, the Groupie wanted to know what that was all about. I told him and he had a good laugh. He said that chap never did have a sense of humour.

At the end of February, I heard that I would be finishing in another week or so, to come home for release. A chap from the Calcutta Comm. Flight would be coming down to take over, so that would make handing over easy with him already knowing the job. I was a bit bothered about what to do with little Ginny, as he had been such a good little fellow, following me about everywhere and seeming so pleased to see me when I returned from a trip. Two or three of the lads said they liked him and would have him, but I knew that this would only be temporary as they too would be going home before long. Then, when I was at SHQ, one of the Wingcos asked what I would be doing with him. He had his wife out here and he said she would love him so I agreed to that as it seemed that they would be here for quite some time and I wanted the little chap to be well looked after. I took him down one night after dinner and had a few drinks with them. They seemed a nice couple, but I did miss the little fella.

However, leaving David was even more difficult. We had been together for quite a long time and although we were strictly *sahib* and bearer, we did have some interesting chats together and, by Jove, David had made life so easy for me with looking after me so well. He wanted to come to England with me. He said he would look after me and *memsahib* very well. I told him that this was impossible, and that in England, *sahibs* do not live in palaces but just in little houses and did not have bearers. He said he did not want a big wage, just some food and somewhere to sleep and that he would do any work I wanted. I had to try to get him to understand that it was just impossible. I tried to make him see that even if he could come, he would not like it as it would be cold and wet in winter, sometimes with snow, and he would get ill. He kept on about being British and he did not want the British to leave India as Indian *sahibs* would not treat him fairly like the British did; they would beat him. It was all very traumatic, but he was faithful to the last. He packed my trunks and had a lingering look at Peggy's photo before packing it away and was grateful that I had arranged that he could take over as bearer for my replacement.

Some of the chaps from SHQ arranged to take me to dinner at the club, which I thought very nice of them, especially when Groupie P. and a couple of the Wingcos turned up. Actually, we had quite a jolly night and the Wingco who had taken Ginny said his wife was absolutely delighted with him and was spoiling him to death. I remarked that he would miss his bit of flying as he had been up quite a few times. Then it dawned upon me that I may not be flying again either.

The very last night was quite a party in the mess. The new chap seemed OK; Roger was in good form and kept us entertained with his blue stories, though some were very blue. They were all good lads. I promised to keep in touch with Dave, who lived at Wath upon Dearne, 'Meet you in The Fox, at Brotherton'. I was getting a lift to Bombay in the morning in the Oxford, as Ken was going there to pick up some goods that had to be taken down to Bangalore. So, the next morning, it was 'goodbye' to Douggie for the last time. I gave David some rupees, which, roughly speaking, would be worth about £5—an absolute fortune to him but he deserved it. He put on his best mess kit to see me off. I told him to look well after 'new *sahib*' and put my hands together this time as I said 'Goodbye', but I left the head nodding to him; he could do it better than I could.

Then it was into the Oxford with the two trunks, two rugs, bedroll, and bags full of odds and ends; I was beginning my journey home. I swapped my shoulder badges over—back to flight lieutenant and gave the squadron leader ones to Ken, telling him he may find them useful one day. I hoped we did not hit one of those bloody shitehawks coming in to land at Santa Cruz.

The drive into Bombay was sheer pandemonium; we seemed to get into the middle of a riot. There were Indian police hitting out at folks with their *lathis*, with lots of shouting and arm-waving. The Sikh taxi driver added to the noise by keeping his fingers on the horn button, saying that it was nothing to bother about, probably sparked off by a Muslim kicking a cow or Hindu dumping a dead pig on the steps of a mosque.

With no David to look after me now, I had to sort out some *coolies* out myself and keep a close eye on them until I found where I wanted to be as I did not want one of them skipping off with part of my luggage. I found that I was to be 'repatriated' by air, which meant I could only take a little kit with me; the rest would follow by boat. This meant a little repacking, getting fancy lines and marks painted on the trunks and the rugs done up in canvas. There was some flying kit to hand in; the rings on my blue uniform to be altered back to flight lieutenant and the Cox and Kings man to see to clear my financial affairs, then the roundabout train journey to Karachi.

On the journey, I was thinking, 'How can I describe India to the folks at home?' Wealthy, university-educated princes or illiterate, fly-encrusted, crippled beggars in filthy rags; fabulous palaces, temples, and mosques or primitive huts made from cow dung or flattened tins; the luxury of the wealthy or those who sleep on railway platforms under a white sheet; boiling dry heat or the sticky humidity of the monsoon; parched dusty soil crawling with ants or termites or the thick undergrowth of the rainforests; the bedlam and smells of the bazaar or the snooty opulence of Ooty; scrubby jungles with animals in the wild or the beautiful scented gardens, ablaze with colour; middle-class women in silk and gold saris and covered in jewels or the women who spend their lives bent double in the fields with a baby on their back? The different people, the unenviable Anglos, the servants—how David was proud to be British and loved to dress up in his mess attire. I wondered what would happen to the likes of David. There was so much more of India I would have liked to see. I had never seen Delhi, Agra, Benares, Kashmir, or the Himalayas, and I would certainly have liked to see more of Ceylon. I had learned a little about India, but the more you learned, the more complicated and contradictory it seemed. I reckoned you would need to spend a lifetime there to get anywhere near understanding it.

It sounded as if we would be away from Karachi in a Lib within a couple of days. I hoped it would be more comfortable than the ones they had on the North Atlantic Return Ferry Service.

34

I Come Home, Twice

An Avro 'York' arrived and took off again after a couple of hours. We did not see the passengers but were told that it was on the 'Stork Run', taking pregnant WRNS or ATS back home. Most of us agreed that we had not seen any WRNS or ATS out here, but it appeared that there were plenty at the headquarters in Kandy and Delhi—'comforts for the top brass' as one chap put it.

On day two, our aircraft had been on the tarmac all day but there was no sign of anything happening. Then word got around that we would be delayed as one of the crew was sick; we later heard that it was the co-pilot. One of the chaps with whom I had shared a compartment on the train was a flying officer; we had talked quite a lot on the journey and he knew that I had been on Libs. He came to me in the mess, saying that he had been over to the office to tell them that I was a qualified Lib skipper and that they wanted to see me. I met the skipper, an old Czechoslovakian chap, who reminded me very much of Zig. I told him what I had done on Libs, where, and how long ago. He said that we would nip off and do a couple of circuits to refresh my memory, and all being well, we would get away that night. So, I did a couple of circuits, sitting in the co-pilot's seat; we seemed to work OK together. It was a later version than the ones that I had flown, but it was basically the same; on returning to the office, he told them that take-off would be in an hour and a half. I was pleased to see that this Lib had a reasonable seating arrangement in the back—there was no wooden floor so high up that you could only crawl about, like I had had to do on those transatlantic runs—it was not luxurious, but at least there was room to stand. This was not going to be a bother me now anyway as I had a seat at the front.

The crew were, as usual, a grand lot of chaps; they all looked pretty experienced and only one was below flight lieutenant. We were away an hour before sundown. The rugged coast of Baluchistan looked very wild and forbidding as darkness fell. It was great to be in a Lib again with those two purring engines at each side and bags of room to move round. We had the ASV on—the sort we could have done with years ago; it showed a perfect pattern of the coastline as the scanner went around and around. It had a Gyro compass too, which was as steady as a rock. Come to think of it, I do not know how we managed in the Arctic with an ordinary magnetic compass. We had not taken full tanks so that we could take as many passengers as possible, so we were to make a refuelling stop in the Persian Gulf at a place I had never heard of. It did not exist when I flew out, but it was not far from Sharjah. All I could see of it was the flarepath but you could tell we were in the gulf as it was so warm and humid.

We were soon off again, this time on a longer hop to Lydda in Palestine. The skipper said he preferred to do this part of the trip at night. Navigation was no problem. The ASV picked up the coastline of the Persian Gulf just like a map; there were lights and flashing beacons here and there, and plenty of places from which to get D/F bearings. After we had tucked into the grub and drunk the coffee, the skipper decided to have a nap. Alec, the navigator, was working on the flight deck as the nose was full of luggage and the wireless operator was busy watching the ASV and tapping out the position report every half hour. It was a lovely, calm flight, probably much smoother than it would have been in the heat of the day. All I had to do was to reset the turbos every hour, ensure that we maintained the correct height, and stick to the airspeed and course that Alec had given me.

When the skipper woke up (I never could pick up his name, but the others just called him 'Skip' so I did likewise), I told him I was popping to the loo and went back to let the passengers know the estimated time of arrival. From my experience years before, in the back of a Lib going back to Canada, I knew what it felt like to be cooped up not knowing where you were and how much longer you would be just listening to the drone of the engines and not being able to talk properly. Everyone seemed to appreciate this, except one Army major who had looked a grumpy sort of chap ever since I first saw him in Bombay.

After some nine hours, we were at Lydda. It looked a big place with lots of lights. It was in the middle of the night but with something like two hours' difference in the time, it looked as if we had not been as long as we really had. The skipper announced that we would spend a whole day there, leaving about noon on the following day, to give everybody chance to catch up on sleep and get acclimatised.

It must have been nearly noon before we stirred; it seemed funny to wake up and find you were not under a mosquito net. I did not know where the passengers were as we were in a separate mess. After lunch, the crew decided we would go down to the town on the coast and then have dinner at a place they knew where they could get some 'smashing' kebabs. We were warned on the way out to avoid certain parts of the town as there had been a few bombings and to get back before dark. Skip said there was a lot of this going on around there and that not long ago, an aircraft was blown up on the airfield. Talk about the sunny Mediterranean—there was a howling gale blowing waves over the sea front and cold, making it like the seafront at an English resort in winter. I was dashed glad that I had changed into my 'blue'. The meal was jolly good, although we had it rather early so that we could get back before dark—there was evidence of buildings having been blown up all over the place, something to do with Arabs and Jews; we had curbed Jewish immigration into Palestine as so many of them had tried to get away from Germany and both of them seemed to be upset with us.

After our day's rest, it was a nice gentle afternoon trip of about five hours to Castel Benito, near Tripoli, over the sea all the way, except for a short time when we touched the bump that sticks up from Cyrenaica. Castel Benito had not changed since I came through the other way in 'Snakecharmer'; there was still the big green hangar doors riddled with bullet holes. We were to spend the night there before setting off on the last leg to England in the morning.

I went along to briefing with the rest of the crew. The weather over England seemed a bit doubtful; we were returning to the latitudes of high- and low-pressure areas, warm fronts and cold fronts, clouds, wind, and rain. We filed a flight plan for the squadron's base at Waterbeach (just north of Cambridge) with Lyneham as an alternative, but our clearance was subject to obtaining onward clearance from the Military Air Control Centre at Istres, in the south of France, not far from Marseille. It could be that they would instruct us to land there. I went out onto the tarmac first, to see the passengers aboard. Three Naval ratings were in good fettle at the thought of going home, one of whom was limping as he had slipped while trying to climb a date palm but he did not seem to mind. The major was as grumpy as ever. He strolled around the nose of the aircraft (this one still had a Perspex nose); peering inside, he noticed a rolled-up carpet and started demanding to know who it belonged to as the passengers were only allowed one item of hand baggage. It actually belonged to one of the crew. Then he demanded to know where we would land in England and at what time. In view of his sarcastic tone, I replied 'Maybe Waterbeach, maybe Lyneham, maybe even the south of France'. To this, he went on about this sounding highly inefficient if I was supposed to be one of the people flying this thing and I did not know where we were going, and he may have to do something about it. I suggested that he did whatever he liked, but if he was coming with us, he had better get in.

Istres gave us the OK to proceed. As we reached northern France, the cloud was waiting for us. We were still in cloud over the Channel as we called the RAF Air Traffic people at Uxbridge. They gave us a height to fly and a routing into Waterbeach. We were at about 700 feet on the SBA approach before we came out of cloud. The runway lights were on; it was a miserable, cold, wet, March afternoon. Spring seemed a little late this year.

I left on the crew truck. Customs let us through quickly, then we went to the mess for a meal. The skipper shortly arrived to join us and announced that 'they' wanted him to do another trip the next day, after which they would get seven days' leave. Turning to me, he said, 'You don't mind another trip do you? We should have two co-pilots on the way back. Bert's tummy should be OK by then'. I never thought twice about it, just said, 'OK fine'. I thought of ringing Peggy but decided it would be better not to. To tell her I was in Cambridge but going back to India in the morning might have upset her. It would wait till after this trip as it would only be a few days.

At 10 a.m. the following day (Wednesday), we were on our way. It was only going to be two stops in this direction. With only a dozen or so sacks of mail in the back, we were lighter than on the homeward run, so we could take more fuel. These Libs did not have the long-range bomb bay tanks that we had in the VLR Liberators, so the maximum capacity was 2,334 gallons, which would not leave a safe margin to do Lydda in one hop. The first leg was a short one of just over four and a half hours to Istres. Here we filled right up and were away within the hour, at 3.30 p.m. GMT, heading for Lydda. This was a fair stretch of about 2,000 miles, which, at 150 knots, the best cruising speed for maximum range, would be about thirteen hours. Out over the blue clear Mediterranean, in a couple of hours, we were passing over Sardinia, which looked mountainous and deserted but with some nice beaches, heading for our turning point, over Malta. It was beginning to get dark as we picked up the coast of Sicily on the ASV, out on the port side. Soon, we were chattering to Malta and using their radio beacon, then we saw the lights, masses of them and their red flashing beacon, over which we altered course for the second leg—a hell of a long leg, all over sea, 1,200 miles to Lydda. Shortly after this, the skipper decided to go to the back and have a kip among the mailbags. The rest of us set about the food we had picked up at Istres.

It was a very quiet, peaceful flight, with nothing to do but to exercise the turbos, keep dropping the revs if the airspeed built up, knock out the autopilot, re-trim, and put it back in again. Alex took a few star shots but spent most of the time sitting in the skipper's seat. I kept looking at the stars, trying to refresh myself on their various names (they had all been such good friends to me) and the wireless operator passed me a few signals, but none of them concerned us. After maybe four hours, Skip reappeared and suggested that I may as well go to the back and stretch out. It was quite comfortable among those mailbags. I must have gone out like a light as the next thing I remember was noticing that it was daylight, so I thought I had better get back upfront. We were about half an hour out from Lydda and landed at 5 a.m. GMT, but it was 7 a.m. local time. The skipper said we would sleep all day and push off about 8 p.m. local time (6 p.m. GMT).

We ate, slept well, had a nice dinner and were off again as planned, at 8 p.m. local time on the Thursday, just after dark. This was to be the longest leg—about 2,125 miles, overflying Kuwait and Oman on the way to Karachi. We estimated fourteen hours. He was a good skipper; we took it in turns to have a couple of hours or so on the mailbags. It was some five hours before we arrived at the head of the Persian Gulf, where, for the first time, there was something to see—lots of groups of flames, where they were burning off oil from the oil fields. Even at 4,000 feet, you could feel it getting warm and humid. As we flew down the 600 odd miles of the gulf, it very quickly got light; there was almost a straight line dividing darkness from the light, which incredibly rushed across the water below, from east to west. We still had some seven hours to go but thought it was time to see what we had packed for breakfast that Friday morning. It seemed a long drag along the grim-looking coast of Baluchistan. At 8.25 a.m. GMT (1.25 p.m. local time), we were taxiing by that ugly airship hangar, back in Karachi.

The skipper said we would leave at midnight local time. The co-pilot had recovered and rejoined the crew so we were a bit cramped on the flight deck on the way home. We shared the co-pilot's jobs, but there was nowhere to go for a kip; it meant making yourself as comfortable as possible on the floor. The route was the same as on the previous homeward trip. We were back in Waterbeach on Tuesday afternoon. This time, the sun was shining. I patted the fuselage as we left the aircraft, saying, 'Goodbye, old girl'. I wondered whether my flying days were over. If so, I was glad my last trip was in a Liberator.

I phoned Peg to let her know I was home, this time for good. I cannot remember what else we said.

Epilogue

I chose to finish Jack's story with him patting the Liberator and phoning home because it was the end of what in hindsight must have been the most exciting and fulfilling period of his life.

Back in the UK, he found the cities drab and run-down; people queued for everything and seemed resentful and unappreciative. His pre-war job at the Yorkshire Insurance Company had been taken permanently by a conscientious objector who had gained a march on him by being able to study for the insurance exams. No one had replied to his letters seeking flying jobs so he sent them reminders.

Although getting home in March, accrued leave meant he was to be paid up until 6 July. However, he started work back at the Yorkshire on 1 July but resigned three days later when he received a firm offer from British European Airways to be a pilot based at Heathrow. Jack and Peggy packed their bags and 'moved out' immediately to London.

From 1946 to 1953, Jack flew with BEA, living at Norwood Green near Heathrow. Just over nine months after getting home, Peter (my brother) was born, and I came along two years later. We were both born in York as Jack wanted us to be Yorkshire folk. Lay-offs in 1953 forced Jack back to insurance in North Yorkshire where we lived in Scarborough, while Dad worked out of Bridlington.

I now realise that it so happened that at the same age as Dad had been in India, I too travelled the Indian Railways, so can identify with the crowds, sights, and smells, if not the splendour of first-class travel as it was. Signs for tiffin were prominent in station restaurants and restrooms.

However, at the time, this aspect of his life was unknown to me until revealed in these pages.

Perhaps one regret about the book is that he did not use surnames, so it is not easy to trace his comrades and learn about their subsequent lives and families. However, perhaps this is a good thing. The times, places, and experiences were unique to them and perhaps best left as happy, sad, and sometimes amusing memories. I am glad they gave him so much pleasure at the time and when writing about them. Thanks, Dad, for your memories of Douggie, Eric, David, and Ginny; by the way, the Tabriz carpet is in my study. I close with Jack's original last paragraph of his memoir, reminiscing seven years on from the end of the war, just before leaving BEA.

> Peggy will be just returning from meeting Peter at school. He is 6 now—7 in January, Richard hasn't started school, he's only 4.5. I hope they get to see a bit of the world when they grow up. I've got tomorrow off and I won't be 'working' at night for another four days. Poor Peg, gets left on her own with the boys all night once or twice a week but she never grumbles. She's a grand one is my Peg.

APPENDIX I

Henry Everest Colman

Not all the Colmans during the war were as lucky as Jack. His cousin Henry, aged seventeen, had been evacuated to Canada with his younger sister (Bubbles) at the start of the war to stay with his mother's family in Toronto. Jack briefly saw them when he was learning to fly. Henry wanted to take after Jack and joined the Royal Canadian Air Force to become a pilot. Aged nineteen, he was sent to the UK as a Dakota pilot and his first operation was Market Garden, the Arnhem drop, and subsequent flights to resupply the ground troops. In the book *The Arnhem Battle*, Martin Middlebrook describes how the resupply flights became increasingly dangerous because of the need for a low-level approach over heavily defended areas and were eventually abandoned. While reading the book, I was moved to discover, by chance, the following story told by Flight Sergeant Dereck Gleave, flying in a Dakota of 48 Squadron flown by Pilot Officer Ralph Pring:

> There were flames in the cockpit and I was burnt on the hands and face. The pilot was absolutely marvellous. He saw this field and said, 'I'm going to land there'. He must have been burnt as well. I was struggling to open the escape hatch, which was right above me. I got it open all right but that caused a further rush of air through the cockpit area, although we were nearly on the ground by then. That's where it became very vague in my mind, but Ralph must have made a very smooth landing.
>
> I was first out, and the wireless operator and the second pilot followed me. As far as I know, the pilot never got out; he may have

been wounded by the flack. The three of us moved away from the aircraft because it was burning fiercely, but some Germans opened fire on us. All three of us were hit. Springsteel, the wireless operator, was killed at once; I was shot by two bullets in the abdomen, and COLMAN was hit several times. He told me to wave something white but I only had a blue RAF handkerchief.

Some German medic eventually came up. The other Germans were still firing at someone; the medics got annoyed with them and shouted at them to stop. Colman and I were taken by ambulance to St Elizabeth Hospital. Colman was still quite coherent, despite all his bullet wounds. A German surgeon operated on me and removed the bullets, and I was put in the basement with the airborne casualties. There were some terrible cases there—men shouting that they wanted to die, etc.—it was terrible. I asked about Colman but Father Egan, a Catholic padre, told me he was dead.

Henry Everest Colman, pilot officer aged nineteen, is buried in the war graves at Oosterbeek. My first visit there was when I was forty. In subsequent years, I took my Dad (Jack) and have taken most of my children to Oosterbeek to stand at the grave. I hope they will take theirs.

APPENDIX II

List of Significant Events

1943

Late October	To East Fortune for four months of Beaufighter training during six months 'rest'; made warrant officer.

1944

January	To Melton Mowbray to deliver two Beaus to Morocco.
15 February	One-month torpedo course starts.
March	Commissioned pilot officer.
April–May	Operational tour Torbeaus 254 Squadron, North Coates.
May	Cousin Henry gets his wings.
22 June	Sets off for the Far East.
1 July	Douggie gets sick.
8 July	Reaches Karachi, seventeen days after leaving UK. Re-united with Douggie.
July–August	Poona (four weeks) orientation and rocket training.
Late August	Sets off for KG (Khumbirgram near Silchar in Assam) Operational Unit.
September	Training and Action over Burma—Beaufighters.
October	Promotion to flying officer; has the fright of his life.

November	Moonlight night raids. Reunion with Harry Guest.
December	Op 24. Hits fuel re-supply barge. Beaus bow out for Jack after Op 25.
December–January	Training for Mozzies, Ranchi.

1945

January–February	Back in Assam; crash lands in the Chindwin.
Early March	Tour ends; sent to Yelahanka for a 'rest'; Mozzie conversion training.
Late March	Holiday Ooty and Cannanore with David.
6 May	Made flight lieutenant.
8 May	VE Day.
June	Postings officer, admin job, Poona.
14 August	Learns of Japanese surrender.
September	Unit moves to Bhopal.
November	Made OC SHQ Comm. Flight (Southern Headquarters), Begumpet; made acting squadron leader.
December	Second Christmas in India.

1946

January	Re-united with Douggie in Begumpet.
March	Steps in as co-pilot of a Liberator. Flies home twice.
6 July	Release date (pay stops); starts as pilot for BEA.